INTELLECTUAL
LIFE
IN AMERICA

Intellectual Life in America

A HISTORY

LEWIS PERRY

FRANKLIN WATTS
New York / London
Toronto / Sydney

FRANKLIN WATTS
387 PARK AVENUE SOUTH
NEW YORK, NEW YORK 10016

Library of Congress Cataloging in Publication Data

Perry, Lewis, 1938–
Intellectual life in America.

Includes bibliographical references and index.
1. United States—Intellectual life.   I. Title.
E169.1.P446   1984   306'.0973   83-23544
ISBN 0-531-09826-5
ISBN 0-531-05649-X (pbk.)

FOR
MY VETERAN TEACHERS
MAURICE F. NEUFELD
AND
GEORGE W. BROOKS

CONTENTS

CHAPTER III
AWAKENING AND ENLIGHTENMENT
95

CHAPTER IV
THE REORGANIZATION OF
INTELLECTUAL LIFE
159

CHAPTER V
EMOTIONS AND IDEALS IN
REORGANIZED AMERICA
205

CHAPTER VI
THE CULTIVATED CLASS IN THE
LATE NINETEENTH CENTURY
261

Contents

INTELLECTUAL LIFE IN AMERICA

PREFACE

Like all authors, I hope that my book will appeal to a
diverse readership. It is an introduction to American history from the perspective of the changing position of intellectuals in society. Readers might proceed from this book
to further study in such fields as religion, literature, psychology, and philosophy as well as history. I have kept the
book reasonably short so that other kinds of reading might
be carried out at the same time. And I have tried to keep
in mind the needs of nonstudent readers and the curiosities of all those, perhaps in other nations, who are approaching the study of American culture for the first time.

Yet a particular audience has been foremost in my
concerns: students who are preparing for professional careers in America. My assumption is that students, even
those who anticipate highly specialized careers, will benefit from knowing the general patterns of intellectual life
in previous generations. It is natural for Americans to think
of careers as ventures into an ever changing future. But
if we have no corresponding sense of the ways in which
others before us have thought about their lives, we are
likely to be disoriented and confused.

For most of American history up to now, it was possible to inspire the student with a story of unfolding intellectual purpose. The Puritan minister's intellectual perspective was grounded, as we shall see, in the Protestant Reformation and the ensuing obligation to advance a particular view of church and society. The young professional of the Jacksonian era might have read George Bancroft's multivolume *History of the United States,* with its hallowed references to the Pilgrim fathers and to the Revolution through which Americans were consecrated to the advancement of freedom. Bancroft inspired his readers to think of their accomplishments as signs of the progress of a democratic people. Later in the nineteenth century, teachers and writers praised the expansion of "culture" throughout more and more of the population. The glory of America was, not economic advance, but the spread of refinement and idealism. Early in this century, scholars who rejected that view of "culture" called nevertheless for the application of "intelligence" to solving social problems. In each of these instances, as in others that we shall discuss, there was a vision of the intellectual growth of America that gave purpose and direction to individual vocations. The history of intellectual endeavor was central to the history of the people.

I hope that this book will help a new generation of professionals to forge links with the American past. Certainly the problem of defining the responsibilities of educated men and women in a democratic society has not lost its relevance. But there are two reasons why the problem can no longer be addressed with the confidence in the role of intellect that we find in Bancroft's work or even in histories written a few decades ago. First, in our time the very notion of "intellectual life" has been treated with suspicion by those who have championed a "nonelitist" history. During recent decades historians have carried out brilliant research on groups of Americans—including blacks, Indians, Catholic immigrants, and women—who had remained off stage in previous accounts of history. This research has made it impossible to regard the intellectuals' history as central to everyone else's. Meanwhile, changes in American society created antagonism toward the thoughts and words, no matter how democratic, of the relatively narrow educated stratum. In an age of "open admissions," "affirmative action," and "innovation," anything elitist or traditional was in jeopardy.

The second reason is the fragmentation of intellectual life in our times. In some ways university education has become coordinated, more closely than ever before, with problem-solving in public agencies and training for employment in the private sector. Intellectuals, therefore, ought to be less vulnerable to the charge that they are elitists who live in an ivory tower remote from the people's culture. But so much specialization has emerged within disciplines and such chasms have opened up between different approaches to knowledge that there is no longer a ruling consensus about the nature of intellectual life. Students and teachers lack the agreement that prevailed in previous generations concerning the values that should characterize an educated person. There is no prevailing political ideology, religious faith, or psychological theory to link intellectual activities in varied fields to a common view of human nature or the future of society.

The themes of this book arise from these modern quandaries. We shall be interested, like our forebears, in the place of intellectuals* in a democratic culture. This

---

*The word *intellectual* was seldom used to describe a particular sort of human being before the start of this century. One of our themes will be the diversity of persons involved in intellectual activities in previous centuries. Another theme will be the narrowing definition of intellectual life in recent times.

means that we shall ask about the inclusiveness and social functions of intellectual activity in different eras. What degree of importance was ascribed to classes of people who may be described as intellectuals? We shall also be interested in the ways in which intellectuals perceived themselves as Americans. Did they see themselves as bearers of special responsibilities, for example, or did they distance themselves from other Americans? I believe that we can bring the contemporary concern about elitism into a historical perspective that will make it less destructive of intellectual confidence.

Similarly, we can understand the disorientation of intellectual life, and control its more threatening dimensions, by taking a long historical view. The very definition of intellectual life has depended on beliefs about the place of emotional and physical forces in a well-regulated life. We shall trace the great reversal by which the emotions, once regarded as subversive of orderly thinking, achieved respectability and even dominance in the most common views of morality. There emerged an American orthodoxy that accorded "the heart" precedence over "the head." But there were limits to this orthodoxy, problems it could not solve, and fears that it could not totally allay. Ours is not the first age in which students have discovered that some difficult questions about human behavior were unasked or unanswerable.

The themes of this book, then, are the position of intellectuals and conceptions of the intellect in American society. They are addressed in eight chronologically arranged chapters. Since each chapter covers a long period of time, and most chapters consider scattered groups of intellectuals, the focus is on broad patterns rather than minor variations. Nevertheless, I have not hesitated to discuss individual men and women who struck their contemporaries, or who impress me, as particularly incisive analysts of problems of intellectual life in their times.

Since this book emphasizes the dependence of all intellectuals on shared communities of discourse, it should be obvious that a book like this one has benefited on every page from my awareness of the thoughts and writings of others. Each chapter concludes with suggestions for further reading in works that go much more deeply into topics that I have sketched in general terms. These suggestions only begin to show the dimensions of a vast and rewarding literature. In writing this book I have been inspired every day by the guidance that other writers, some in years long past, many others who are my contemporaries, have furnished for understanding intellectual life in America.

I

OPENING UP
THE INTELLECTUAL
GLOBE

IMPOSITIONS

At first thought, the discovery and early settling of America do not appear to have been events with much bearing on intellectual life. There is no record of the ideas of fishermen and sailors who wandered into the Western Hemisphere before Columbus. The story thereafter more often depended on luck and cunning than on intellectual enterprise. It was the story, retold into the present, of tough-minded navigators and wretched transoceanic migrants pitted against pirates, aborigines, and nature's blasts. There is little of the life of the mind in Captain John Smith's well-known account of "gallants," their soft hands blistered by ax handles, swearing loudly in the woods; still less, in the disease and famine that destroyed entire populations or in the harsh regimentation through which others sulked along the way to precarious survival. Those few events remembered as brave acts of mind—the composition of the Mayflower Compact, for example—were more than offset by mutinies, massacres, shipwrecks, bondage, epidemics, and other brutal realities. Reports emanating from the New World might well apologize for being as "unpolished and rude," as direct and unadorned, as the outposts where they were scratched out.

This first thought is not wrong. If we look for intellectual life as a separate strain of history, as the record of a distinctive intelligentsia, we will find little enough of it in the beginnings of society in the West. We may wish to say that a sea captain who spoke of an "unpolished and rude" style showed signs of literary self-consciousness and, further, of thinking about the effects of the New World on the mind. But even he had more important chores than writing, and in any event he tells us almost nothing about those who worked and perished without occasion to contrive a literary voice.

The Christian religion provided so many of the ideas that Europeans carried to the New World that some historians have called it the main ingredient in the motives of early colonizers. The propaganda of most English colonial projects—tracts soliciting political or financial support, sermons bidding voyagers godspeed, optimistic narratives of adventures across the seas—stressed the Creator's providence more than human exploits. This stress suited the self-interested purposes of investors and promoters; it may also show that seventeenth-century Englishmen liked to justify their actions in terms of an elaborate religious cosmology. Nevertheless, the minds of early colonists, even those few whose writings survive for us to read, seem too complex for us to speak of one main motive. Captain John Smith was a boastful soldier and a tireless promoter of empire as well as a man of faith who trembled, at times, for his own salvation. Others may have been less colorful, but their goals were equally tangled.

Yet if we cannot prove that religious beliefs were the prime incentives to human action, there is no doubt that a view of providence runs through the writings of the shapers of the colonial enterprise. Though all men sinned with Adam, they retained the gift of reason entitling them to exploit the animal, plant, and mineral kingdoms. Through selfish actions they carried out a divine plan leading to ultimate reconciliation. Thus God, according to English writers, had delayed the colonization of the New World until after the Protestant Reformation so that America would not fall uncontested into papal darkness. And as men searched for gold, raised tobacco, and perished without seeing the consequences of their acts, they would also convert the heathen Indians and bring the world to unity under the divinely sanctioned, English, Protestant world order.

Discoverers and settlers had to conceive of the New World in terms familiar in Europe. They perceived, reported, and embellished new facts in language readers and listeners could understand. Though not primarily the work of intellectuals—we will return to the question who *was* an intellectual—events in the New World were fitted into the available systems of thought, which usually were barely articulated but were indeed capable of elaborate formulation. Among the strongest of these systems was the Christian view of man as a sinner in quest of redemption and of human history as winding, however circuitously, toward a destined era of renewal and harmony.

At first contact with Western isles and continents, there was no perception that a New World existed to be explained. Even as the realization of novelty dawned in European consciousness and readers thirsted for descriptions of what adventurers had seen, some writers were daunted by the task of relating the new in comprehensible language. Numerous reports stopped short with admissions like Cortés's account of Montezuma's palace: "I shall not attempt to describe it at all, save to say that in

Spain there is nothing to compare it with." One device was to assert that Western islands and cultures belonged to long-told myths and romances, both pagan and Christian, of lost places and peoples now regained in European acquaintance. The Atlantis discussed by Plato, the Antillia that sheltered ancient Christians, and many other wondrous spots had supposedly resurfaced from the fogs of the Western sea. There inhabitants, by many reports, lived in freedom from the warfare, exploitation, and harsh government that afflicted civilized sinners. In the struggle to come to grips with fact and rumor, the Christian world view enjoyed one great superiority: it predicted that the unforeseen would come to pass, that discovery was really recovery, that lost paradise would be found again.

Anyone wishing to understand what the New World portended would do well to ponder a letter written to Ferdinand and Isabella by Columbus on his third voyage in 1498. At the mouth of the river we call the Orinoco, he sought to decipher the meaning of his experiences. The earth was "not round" as men believed (and as generations of schoolchildren since then have memorized). The earth instead took "the form of a pear . . . upon one point of which is a prominence like a woman's nipple. . . . I believe it is impossible to ascend thither, because I am convinced that it is the spot of the terrestrial paradise, whither no one can go but by God's permission." The sweet water, the mild climate, the river's depth—all led to the conclusion that here was one of the four streams flowing from the tree of life. Perhaps God's permission was forthcoming; perhaps a good mariner could ascend farther if he returned with three seaworthy ships. Columbus never followed up this plan, but it revealed glimmerings of hope that adventurous men of faith stood in a new light in the providential scheme.

Nowhere was the imposition of European intellectual

systems plainer than in encounters with the native inhabitants of the Western lands. There was no way for explorers to know these peoples' origins, which are still disputed by scholars, and settlers were more likely to acquire practical information about particular native societies than to discern the intricate political networks covering wide areas of the New World. The facts that native leaders could sometimes speak European languages and were always ready to use Europeans to their own ends strengthened the likelihood of misperception. In European writings the American natives assumed mythological forms, as lost tribes from the Bible or distant survivors of a golden age. They were specimens perhaps of innocence, perhaps of the barbarity of life where society had not reached an advanced stage: there were contrasting experiences of which sense had to be made. The process was one, in any case, of European interpretation.

Even the most learned Europeans resorted to classifications worked out when Christianity spread across Eurasia. Thus the peoples of the New World, regardless of the variations among them, were all "infidels," "savages," or, in the erroneous term that became an enduring misnomer, "Indians." Their institutions of governance, religion, and family life were grouped according to resemblances to customs observed elsewhere at the margins of Europe. Occasionally, a wit or philosopher might contend that the "Indians" surpassed the supposedly civilized Europeans in some virtue, or he might compare the superstitions of his countrymen with those of men in the wild; but the thrust of the irony was still directed at European manners and expressed in European terms.

In the imagination of the Old World, the natives' societies sometimes figured as peaceable anarchies, without greed, strife, or repression. Every European frontier, however, posed the threat of a different kind of anarchy, an anarchy of sin where white men lied, plundered, killed, divided into rival factions, or rebelled against their leaders. To control white settlers was also inevitably to transfer European conceptions to a new space. Rulers who survived, as the historian Howard Mumford Jones has pointed out, mirrored the strategies of domination proposed in Niccolò Machiavelli's *The Prince* (1513), strategies designed to consolidate power over disloyal, conniving men in fragmented southern Europe. Jones does not describe direct intellectual influence: Machiavelli was frequently discussed in the Old World, but New World leaders did not need to read anything to learn "that founders of states must assume that all men are bad and will always, when they have a free field, give a loose rein to their evil inclinations, or that the wise founder of a commonwealth must endeavor to acquire an absolute and undivided authority." New World leaders learned on their own to act as ruthlessly as the lion and as guilefully as the fox in order to extend their sway and maintain at least a semblance of order. Those English leaders who endured, for better or worse, applied lessons learned in the conquest of Scotland and Ireland, in armies sent against the Turks, or in dealings with rough sailors and buccaneers. Measures of martial discipline nearly always echoed in the precepts of early New World government.

Ample theoretical justification existed for whatever measures had to be taken. Even pagan philosophers acknowledged the necessity of social order, and except for a few heretics, usually rooted out mercilessly, Christian political thinkers began from the premises that man was a disobedient sinner and that the Almighty detested the stench of anarchy. To the belief that government was generally ordained by God, the English Christian might simply add that the specific form of government required unequal degrees of power. Ideally, everyone gained from the security of a system in which each "order" depended on those above and watched over those below, but even when the benefits were ambiguous there should be no relaxation of control. Just as man retained after the Fall enough reason to repress the chaotic urgings of the passions, so men were to dominate women and children, noblemen to oversee their inferiors, and the king to reign unchallenged over all—with the proviso, of course, that God was the mightiest of potentates.

Ruthless expedients were unavoidable in the New World. But the English were not content to think of rulers as a necessary evil: they approved the man who consolidated power; the usurper or upstart they condemned. With a new consciousness of how institutions come into being and change, there was widespread sentiment that government ought to meet standards of human approval. The implications of this sentiment were not thoroughly explored; few literate Englishmen advocated even the vaguest notion of democracy. They assumed instead that rulers ought to have standing in an appropriate rank of society. English colonists repeatedly endeavored, not to invent new forms of government, but to reinstitute familiar hierarchies in perfected form. Thus Virginia leaders petitioned in 1621 for the appointment of a nobleman as governor, a man to whom "by nature every subordinate is ready to yield a willing submission without contempt or repining"; few would be willing to obey an ordinary man, "one no better than selected out of their own rank."

The belief in appropriate gradations of power could have a paradoxically utopian tinge. Colonial promoters claimed that England fell short of the ideals of dependency and privilege: a drifting surplus population was not snugly placed under the watch of overlords, and the costs were tallied in crime and misery. The New World's social order might conceivably reach closer to perfection. England would be rid of anomalies, and the "vast and empty chaos" of America (as one propagandist, forgetting the Indians, called it) would be filled out with the ranks that God loved to observe. One fantastic instance of such utopian projections, the Fundamental Constitutions of Carolina (1669), written in large part by the philosopher John Locke, provided for three levels of nobility—absentee proprietors, landgraves, and caciques—with increasingly larger ranks of freeholders, serfs, and slaves below them at the lowest level of society. Carolina in reality became the most glaring instance of the inequalities of a slave society, with few persons in the middling orders that were supposed to give society its harmonious proportions. That the vision went unfulfilled tells us something about the unpredictability of New World experience. The elaborate detail in which it was conceived tells much about the enduring links in European thought between social order and hierarchy.

The meaning of the New World in European imaginations sometimes went beyond the imposition of old schemes and images. If brave mariners had expanded Europeans' knowledge of geography, were there other fields of knowledge that had been kept in darkness by traditional authorities, fields that now invited patient, fearless exploration? Columbus's bravery might prefigure a new style of intellectual inquiry concerned with accurate observation of the nature of the created universe. By the nineteenth century this rendition of Columbus had made its way into popular poems and orations: the lonely, forward-looking adventurer ignoring the warnings of unrealistic schoolmen and his superstitious crew. It is less well known that a similar meaning was drawn from his journeys almost from the start.

Francis Bacon was a prominent advocate of the "new

philosophy" challenging the adequacy of medieval depictions of nature. We still use the term "Baconian science" as shorthand for themes that he articulated: the existence of an orderly universe concealed by ages of credulity; the advantages of empirical observation over deductions from a priori systems; the necessity of instruments and experiments to correct the fallibility of these observations; the desirability of a publicly supported scientific establishment; and the utility to society in general of enhanced control over nature. The frontispiece of his *New Organon* (1620), a critique of the science derived from Aristotle and the ancients, depicted a ship passing through the Pillars of Hercules, with a favorite motto from the prophet Daniel: "many shall go to and fro on the earth, and knowledge shall be increased." In the same work Bacon compared the prospects awaiting science to the "wonderful voyage" of Columbus, whose conviction of the existence of new continents was "made good by experience." Bacon's *New Atlantis* (1627) pretended to report on a scientifically advanced enclave in the South Seas, a society of Christians prospering in isolation from the Catholic Dark Ages. The rulers of Atlantis secretly kept track of the new spirit of inquiry dawning to the east, and they erected a statue of Columbus among those of important inventors. How pitiful it would be, Bacon wrote on several occasions, if the "material globe" opened up while the "intellectual globe" remained shut. Yet Bacon was lord chancellor of England, a fervent patriot, and also a Bible-reading Christian who believed that new knowledge unfolded according to the intentions of providence. Was it not "ordained by God" that the boldest geographical discoveries and the deepest penetrations into the secrets of nature should be accomplished in the same age?

Two questions emerge from this perspective on discovery and early settlement. In the transfer of European ideas to the New World there was a tension between culture and experience—between values embedded in the language people acquire from childhood and the conflicting events through which they pass—a tension of central importance in understanding historical change. How would old conceptions be modified by the experience of migrants living at the edges of European society? The second question arises from Bacon's use of the discoveries to further a program of intellectual transformation, urging men to turn their backs on fixed beliefs and to adopt a less well charted route to knowledge. The culture of seventeenth-century England was not a tidy system to be embraced without strain; it was itself an arena of challenge and dispute. Would those who actually journeyed westward hasten the program of intellectual adventure, or would they be more inclined to hold fast to secure moorings of tradition?

CIVILITY AND VIRTUOSITY

Let us define more precisely what intellectual life meant in the colonial period. Francis Bacon, whose program for the *Advancement of Learning* (1605) included plans for more accurate and comprehensive history, complained of most chronicles of past eras that they represented "the magnitude of actions, and public faces and deportments of persons," but passed over in silence "the smaller passages and motions of men and matters." Since it was frequently "the workmanship of God" to "hang the greatest weight upon the smallest wires," such histories "rather set forth the pomp of business than the true and inward resorts thereof." Bacon was not really interested in the "nonelitist" history, focused on dispossessed groups and underclasses, that has attracted historians in recent decades; nor was he calling for "psychohistory" in the modern fashion that digs the causes of individual actions out of repressed desires and memories. His own historical writings assumed the importance of the spread of Protestantism over ignorant superstition and of the widening hegemony of the English monarch. But his new history might have treated the populace in the study of "the arts"—the skills and systems of information that put the materials of nature to human use. It would have comprehended trades and technology, the effects of heat and cold on foods and metals, the devices by which smiths and sailors carried out their tasks. In this history the craftsman would have been linked to the philosopher, each trained to use confidently the instruments that furnish *homo sapiens* some degree of mastery and comfort.

In our day a tourist may visit a "living museum" like Plimoth Plantation, a reconstruction of the Pilgrim settlement in Plymouth, Massachusetts, where the guides enact the roles of settlers in 1626. They will not respond to questions framed in post-seventeenth-century terms: they know nothing of airplanes or microbes, electricity or alarm clocks. The visitor discovers that many of the men are artisans hoping to earn a living from making objects like barrels or gloves once the population thickens and commerce thrives. In the meantime, almost against their will, they work as farmers and fishermen eking out an existence, wishing they knew more of the skills needed in these temporarily accepted callings.

A look at the promotional literature from other colonies makes it clear that artisans like Plimoth's were eagerly recruited. Thomas Harriot's *Brief and True Report of the New Found Land of Virginia* (1588), for example, furnished an early list of men who would be useful: bowstave preparers, gluemakers, makers of spades and shovels, basket makers, "grubbers and rooters up" of trees, millwrights, sawyers, carpenters, joiners, blacksmiths, coopers, chandlers, "mineral men," brickmakers, and sinkers of wells, among others. In England, according to some seventeenth-century reports, such artisans might have found nothing to do but beg alms. America invited them to take their place in a system of graded privilege. Passenger lists show that when chandlers, salters, and weavers sailed, they brought with them "servants"; and in the New World they served as masters to young men assigned to learn their arts. They may not have fit nicely into semi-feudal schemes like the Fundamental Constitutions of Carolina, but they nevertheless occupied stations below "gentlemen" and above the great majority of simple farmers. Yet not infrequently, especially in the earliest years, they too might have blistered their hands with hoes and oars.

They were not intellectuals. But they were more than fixtures in a social hierarchy: they were rungs on a ladder leading upward to advanced civilization and science. That is, they required training—though more of the hands than of the intellect, more in *how to* than in *why*—and they participated in the extension of trade that was the means by which the Christian world progressed.

Some vocations, called in England the professions, ordinarily required a college education: law, medicine, and the clergy.* That the first two of these were not always recruited eagerly in America may be inferred from remarks by William Penn: "Of lawyers and physicians I shall say nothing because this country [Pennsylvania] is very peaceable and healthy; long may it so continue and never

---

*Bacon complained that, since all colleges served the professions, none were "left free to arts and sciences at large." In his view, which may sound familiar to modern readers, this was shortsighted, for those who thought "philosophy and universality to be idle studies" failed to appreciate that the professions applied general knowledge.

have occasion for the tongue of one, nor the pen of the other, both equally destructive of men's estates and lives; besides, forsooth, they, hangman like, have a license to murder and make mischief." And one Virginian saw this advantage in the shortage of trained lawyers: cases were settled without "impertinences of form and nicety" and without "the trickery and foppery of the Law." According to the same source, the climate was so healthful and cures for the few diseases were so widely known "that there is not mystery enough to make a trade of physic there as the learned do in other countries, to the great oppression of mankind." Even those colonists who were less suspicious of professional intellect may well have felt that, where choices had to be made, artisans were more indispensable. Yet in England lawyers and doctors were sometimes leading participants in political and scientific discourse; thus, a society lacking in these professions was to some extent uncultivated. As for the third profession, educated ministers were an import that only a few anticlerical colonists sought to do without. An English local minister was a man of quality, second in prestige only to the lord of the manor, and without him Protestant civilization made little sense.

Not all the English uses of education were so vocational as the training of artisans and professionals. Wealthy families already followed a more decorative custom of giving young men some exposure to refined learning, a custom that set them off as a more leisurely, less harried class. Their attainments were not necessarily useless; their knowledge might serve them well in business dealings, legal responsibilities, or political affairs. Some became practitioners of the "new philosophy," though it was not essential to be wealthy to be a scientist. Throughout the colonial period, sons of wealthy North American families traveled to England to gain this kind of polish. One Virginia father urged his son to work hard at acquiring the ability to converse with learned, prosperous men, since this "will preserve you in the same class and rank among mankind."

Intellectual history is not simply an account of the goals of education, particularly when those goals conformed so closely to social stations. In seventeenth-century America, furthermore, society fell short of English models. The training of artisans was seldom connected to scientific inquiry; few colleges existed to provide the basis for learned professions; and the discourse of gentlemen was not always elegant and polished. Progress in these directions may have seemed more promising during the first generation, when leaders had been born and brought up in England, than for some time thereafter. The circumstances of intellectual life in the New World were limited. But two ideals, quite separate but not necessarily in conflict, underlay colonial hopes for intellectual improvement. One was the ideal of Christian civility; the other, of scientific virtuosity.

The first ideal referred to the virtues of English civilization emerging from the struggles of centuries. England was a nation of military valor, good laws, and stable government—or so one hoped—confidently extending its empire over barbaric outlanders. In the same view—never mind the talk of foul cities and unemployed workmen—it was a nation of commerce and hard work where man's God-given mastery over lower orders of nature was gloriously being achieved. As history unfolded, men and women stepped forward out of sloth and superstition and realized, for all their backsliding, such preeminent civic virtues as chastity in marriage, honesty in business, and moderation in all pleasures. One token of civility was literacy. Let us make no mistake: no visionary imagined that the ability to read and write would ever be universal, reaching every peasant and underling. But one sign of order, approved by God in the new age, was the extension of civil discourse among increasing numbers of Englishmen, not just nobles and gentlefolk but even worthy tradesmen. What gave all these signs their meaning was England's leading role in Protestantism. Regardless of the reasons for which Henry VIII and Elizabeth I had removed the land from Rome's clutches, England had become a nation where those who mattered could read, or at least recite, the Bible and knew the forms of worship appropriate to God's sovereignty. An illiterate person might learn to be a cooper or a tailor, but a worthier one could quote Scripture and understand a sermon.

A virtuoso was more precisely intellectual than the merely civil, literate man. He could quote the works of the ancients and other writers besides the Bible. But what chiefly characterized the virtuoso was his curiosity: his inveterate collecting of coins, shells, and fossils; his travels and far-flung correspondence; his interest in drawing and painting; his passion for new means of studying nature. The house where he spent his leisure gave proud evidence of his taste for knowledge: his cabinets of relics; his library, garden, and gallery; his microscopes and telescope. Country gentlemen so eagerly displayed their virtuosity that their style of living was satirized in popular plays and in Jonathan Swift's *Gulliver's Travels* (1726). But in his own mind the virtuoso was anything but foolish. He eschewed the cynicism of a wit and the vanity of a fop; a work by the chemist Robert Boyle idealized *The Christian Virtuoso* (1690). There was some agreement that virtuosos erred in paying too little attention to the uses of knowledge, that they strayed too far from "the arts." Bacon criticized gentlemen who were exclusively concerned with knowledge as ornament and entertainment. And in a more refined usage, the term was reserved for true scientists, "natural philosophers" like Boyle and the great Isaac Newton, who were not idle dilettantes but serious investigators of nature.*

The virtuosos lived out a sense of historical change. In the medieval view, from which they diverged, the shape and movements of the universe conformed to divine commands. All the regularities of nature proceeded from the actions of the *primum mobile* at the outermost sphere of the firmament, the sphere inhabited by seraphs and closest to God. Each category of things had its own soul or "essence" that explained its character and purpose. Within each category existed a divinely ordained scale of priority (sometimes called a "great chain of being"). Although this traditional view allowed for flux and imperfection, it taught that everything tended to revert to its appropriate sphere. Thus it gave meaning to events such as the rise of flames and vapors as well as the restoration of the monarch at the end of a Shakespearean tragedy. The virtuosos were not rebels; at first, they were mainly proud gentlemen displaying their possessions. In the seventeenth century, however, their activities converged into a Baconian program to learn as much as possible about visible nature without reference to unseen agencies and essences. It was unclear just how far this program would go in altering religious conceptions. While criticizing the old view for unwarranted certainty about the mysterious intentions of the Creator, virtuosos were content to observe in their experiments evidence of the workmanship of God. At the same time, they celebrated historical progress toward new confidence in human ability to take the measure of the immediate universe.

---

*The term has nothing to do with the modern virtuoso who is a musician of technical brilliance. That usage came later.

If civility was the ideal of a progressive, nonbarbaric society, virtuosity was for the English folk who came to the New World the closest approximation to the modern notion of an intellectual as an individual defined by habits of mind. We must note, however, that the virtuoso was defined by the range of his attainments rather than by any specialized mastery. He was a social type within a civil commonwealth. Like all good Christians, he knew that wealth could be a snare as well as a means to edification; and though he was frequently a wealthy man, his travels and dealings were not solely tied to commerce and gain. In fact, in the more restricted scientific use of the term, he might even be a minister or follow one of the other professions. Seen in seventeenth-century eyes, then, the intellectual progress of America would be measured not only in the spread of civility, which was binding together a well-mannered nation, but also in the rise to eminence of virtuosos, with their ostentatious curiosity about the wide universe.

These two ideals should not mislead us into exaggerating the intellectual uniformity of seventeenth-century England. To contemporaries it was an age of confusion and strife as well as historical advance. There was no shortage of polemics against newfangled science, and religious antagonisms led to the horrors of war and regicide. Galileo's discoveries challenged familiar conceptions of the cosmos; the Crown's hegemony in distant quarters of Britain was always shaky; Protestantism's prospects rose and fell mercurially with the fortunes of war on the Continent; London, teeming and cosmopolitan, went down in flames; transatlantic migrations and the uncertainties of trade heightened a feeling that the world was in danger of falling apart at the edges. " 'Tis all in pieces," wrote the poet John Donne; "all coherence gone!"

How much more perilous such dangers looked in the New World. All English settlements could view themselves as insecure centers (where there was a village or town open to such pretension) with margins crumbling around them. They were conscious of savages and alien empires to the north, south, and west. Migrations of Dutch, Germans, Scots, and Scotch-Irish diminished prospects for an ordered, homogeneous society; and not all English colonists were sturdy yeomen, tradesmen, or proper gentlemen. Worst of all, on the frontier men could follow inclinations that were supposedly impermissible and take off in directions that authorities could hardly foreclose. Colonists came from strife and confusion to circumstances that threatened to intensify the strains and uncertainties of the century. As we view the contours of intellectual life, we may keep in mind the central ideals, but we should not ignore the threat of disintegration.

THE SOUTH

Intellectual life in the colonies did not diverge irreversibly from English norms. To be sure, the possibility was open for North Americans to parade their distinctive roughness. "I am an Indian and don't pretend to be exact in my language," Robert Beverley postured in his *History and Present State of Virginia* (1705). English readers should not be critical of his "plainness" of style, he wrote, but should credit him with "honesty, which is what I pretend to." Yet historians have remarked that in some ways colonial culture became more self-consciously patterned on English models as time passed and wealth accumulated. The issue is a complex one: even in the twentieth century tempers sometimes boil over the question of the derivativeness of American culture. No doubt the outcomes looked different from one colonial society to the next, depending on ethnic diversity, class structure, and other factors. There were many Americas. We may begin to understand the process, however, by examining the fortunes of civility and virtuosity in the southern colonies, especially Virginia.

There English society received its first definition in a campaign against the customs of the "idle, improvident, scattered people" who already lived in the forests, a campaign to make them, in John Smith's words, "tractable, civil, and industrious." What supposedly uplifted the program of the Virginia Company from a nakedly commercial enterprise were the good works toward the Indian. What could be "more praiseworthy and charitable," asked Ralph Hamor in *A True Discourse of the Present State of Virginia* (1615), "than to bring a *savage* people from barbarism to civility?" Civilizing the Indians would offer military and economic benefits to the settlers. But no contradiction was seen in these side effects, any more than when Columbus encountered the Taino people and wrote in his diary, "How easy it would be to convert these people—and make them work for us."

The campaign depended on a sentiment of distant kinship with the savages, who lingered in primitive conditions once prevalent in England and still lamentably familiar in the wilds of Scotland and Ireland. "Wild as they are . . . so were we," wrote a Virginia poet. "To make them civil, will our honour be." It was simply taken for granted that the civilizing process would entail, as it had in Britain, conversion to Christianity. The sermons and tracts surrounding the colonists' departures praised the work of giving the heathen good manners, industrious habits, and humane politics, along with the Protestant religion. "For what more pleasant sacrifice can we offer in this life, unto our God," asked one Englishman, "than to labor in all that we may, to bring the barbarous to civility,

the rude to knowledge, the superstitious to the true & lively
worship of His name, to win them from vanity to verity,
from death unto life?"

The campaign was ardently conceived, and it was given
more than lip service. Jamestown's settlers were urged, and
even ordered, to bring Powhatan children into their homes,
though usually this meant as captives, since the "savages"
were reluctant to part with sons and daughters. At the
king's direction, bishops collected funds in England, and
land was set aside for a college for the Indians. It was more
difficult to think of ways to change the manners of adults,
who were not generally welcome within white com-
pounds. But an English-style house was built for the
chieftain Opechancanough. In the best known episode, the
princess Pocahontas, who showed favorable interest in
English ways, was taken from her Powhatan family (including a husband), evangelized by an English minister,
then courted and wed by John Rolfe. For Rolfe the match
threatened to undermine his own civility; so he fought off
feelings of "unbridled desire" until he fixed his own purpose as that of converting a savage to Christian life. Pocahontas eventually went to England as the grand exhibit
of Virginia's success: she had been taught to speak comprehensible English, was "well instructed in Christianity,
and was become very formal and civil after our English
manner."

Despite this interracial idyll, no one has ever claimed
that the campaign as a whole was successful. The college
was never established, and the native people showed little
interest in rejecting their life ways. The doctrine of civility, always double-edged, permitted instances of great
cruelty toward the "barbaric" Powhatans. In 1622, desperate over repeated affronts from the settlers and moved
by a religious cult spreading among Indians, Opechancanough lulled the English into letting down their defen-

ses by pretending to accept "civilization." He then led an uprising that killed 330 whites. (Had the plot not been revealed by one of the few Christian converts, the death toll would have been even higher.) All of the distant and theoretical sentiments of kinship disappeared. The Indians were nothing more than brutes or disciples of the devil; "Uniformity and Order," in the words of one contemporary ballad, threatened to give way to "Chaos." Though officials back in England urged leniency, Virginia's leaders explained that the code of "civil" war could not be extended to brutes. Even in England, some drew the lesson: "Civility is not the way to win savages." White soldiers hunted Indians down with mastiffs, burned their towns and fields, enticed them to regroup in villages, and then slaughtered more of them. In ensuing years they pushed the surviving Indians farther west and finally erected a string of military blockhouses to separate them from white civility. Not until this solution was secure could any Virginian have tried Beverley's conceit of calling himself an Indian.

In miniature this story captures the rhythm of pious intention, violent misunderstanding, and hostile separation that frustrated the progress of civility in Indian-white contacts almost everywhere. Indians became a political issue in the West, where families demanded harsher repression; they remained objects of charity principally where it was safe to behold them in remote fascination. Historians who wish to put a happier face on the story point out that the ideology of conversion did not vanish. Bequests were made from time to time, and appeals issued throughout the South, in behalf of educating and Christianizing the savages. Further evidence of the staying power of the ideal may be gleaned from occasional criticisms of colonial governors for neglecting Indian education, though these emanated from England far more frequently than from America. By the nineteenth century some southern Indian nations had gained the reputation of being civilized, and they lived in contact with whites—until the Andrew Jackson administration drove them westward. But it would surely be impossible to speak of Indian-white relations in terms of the triumph of good manners and humane polity. It is more accurate to admit that the ideal of civility from the start signified the virtues that Englishmen hoped to advance in their own societies and to ask how successful they were in this endeavor.

As historians have often pointed out, freehold tenure—that is, personal land ownership—was much more common in the New World, after a century or so, than in the old; furthermore, some economic historians assert that the standard of living of "the great bulk of the population" reached a remarkably high level. These divergences from English life would have enhanced the expectation of widespread civility. No statistical measure will give precise indices of all the sober habits clustered among the meanings of civility. Customs undoubtedly changed. Such signs of civility as dining implements and private sleeping quarters, for example, were more common in the early eighteenth century than they had been before. Of the industrious work habits of many small farmers there can be little doubt: in the eighteenth century they participated in a world market with great success. Population in the South was too dispersed to support a system of education, but many sorts of schools afforded at least a smattering of education, keyed more to practical subjects than to English-style classical learning. The family also provided basic instruction to children and apprentices, so that white male literacy rates on the eastern seaboard compared favorably with those in the better parts of England. And in frontier areas, especially those settled by Scottish Presbyterians and some Continental immigrants, matters were not always worse. Since education was always regarded as crucial to the spread of Christianity, we may add that even at the edge of the wilderness, despite the recurrent nightmares of easterners, the essential Christian loyalty of settlers does not seem to have abated. Southern writers complained that the absence of towns impeded education, Christianity, and prosperity. But everywhere some yeoman farmers were reading, however haltingly, Bibles, prayer books, and devotional works like *The Whole Duty of Man, Laid Down in a Plain and Familiar Way, for the Use of All, but Especially the Meanest Reader* (1684).

Behind these generalizations, which must remain rather imprecise, we may imagine an impressive transmission of civility. In the long run, by the nineteenth century certainly, that English idea was transformed into a comprehensive view of life holding out the hope of respectability to all free white citizens in an earnest and industrious society. Well might a backcountry missionary praise the Lord in 1770 that "a desert and forest, overrun with wild beasts, and men more savage than they," had in "a short space of time" been brought under English law and liberty. Yet it is a central fact of southern colonial culture that, from an early point, the environment was thought to encourage a distinctively un-English return to barbarism. To the underlying conviction of man's sinfulness was added a newly fashionable belief that "tropical" surroundings would influence English folk to lose their national characteristics and acquire less worthy traits. The prospect already lurked in early discoverers' accounts of blessed isles whose inhabitants lived with the innocence of children. It became more menacing in John Smith's tales of tender-skinned gallants and hopeless victims of the "starving time," giving up the will to work and descending even into cannibalism. It recurs throughout the histories and descriptions of life in southern climes.

In Hugh Jones's *The Present State of Virginia* (1724), for example, praise for the colony as "the happy retreat of true Britons and true churchmen" who were spared the ethnic diversity and religious impurity of other colonies, was balanced by criticism that Virginians were "climate-struck." They were hospitable and generous, to be sure, but in what became an enduring stereotype of southern life, they were also lazy. Robert Beverley extolled the gentleness of the climate, which he took to be parallel to "the Land of Promise" and other "gardens of the world." At the same time, he admitted that it led to intemperate eating and drinking: "the extraordinary pleasantness of the weather and the goodness of the fruit lead people into many new temptations." Clear sky, warm sun, and shady groves lulled the spirits, and "all their senses are entertained with an endless succession of native pleasures."

> Their eyes are ravished with the beauties of naked nature. Their ears are serenaded with the perpetual murmur of brooks. . . . Their taste is regaled with the most delicious fruits which without art they have in great variety and perfection. And then their smell is refreshed with an external fragrancy of flowers and sweets with which nature perfumes and adorns the woods almost the whole year round.

The consequence of this "liberality of nature," Beverley said in ending his report, was "slothful indolence": men sponged up pleasure and begrudged the pains of working.

A similar picture emerges from the most caustic southern report, William Byrd II's *History of the Dividing Line betwixt Virginia and North Carolina* (1728). Across the border from Virginia, Byrd found the land of "Lubbers," stragglers and ne'er-do-wells from nearby colonies who had degenerated in a land of fertile soil and mild climate. By his satiric account, partly intended to boost land sales in civilized Virginia, they snored, smoked, and yawned away most of the sunlight hours. They hovered indoors when the weather was slightly cool: "When the weather is mild, they stand leaning with both their arms upon the corn-field fence, and gravely consider whether they had best go and take a small heat at the hoe: but generally find reasons to put it off till another time. Thus they loiter away their lives, like Solomon's sluggard." It was a "thorough aversion to labor" that brought men to this land "where plenty and a warm sun confirm them in their disposition to laziness for their whole lives." Although we may discount these aspersions on backcountry folk, the fact remains that in the most imposing effort to demonstrate the vitality of intellectual life in the colonial South, the historian Richard Beale Davis concluded: "Hedonism was a quality of character common to all southern classes, . . . objectionable or sinful only if it induced obviously harmful laziness or indolence."

One alleged virtue of civility was its contribution to "humane polity"—a condition notable for political stability, respectful public manners, and a common feeling of advantage in good order. How extensively southerners achieved this state of affairs was a matter of dispute; in the burgeoning scholarship on colonial politics disagreement still prevails. Some regions, remote from eastern courts, were reputed to be infested with bandits and ungovernable by central authority. It is clear that officials faced indignities that contemporaries would have viewed as barbaric. That turmoil was not restricted to the earliest stages of settlement may be suggested by a 1725 episode in which a former governor of North Carolina, accompanied by ruffians, roused his successor from bed and shouted, "You are a Sancho Panza, and I'll take care of you, numbskull head." A different kind of face-to-face encounter was the drunken revelry of Virginia's monthly court days, when justices complained of hooligans running into their chambers and shouting epithets. By the eighteenth century, election days saw elaborate rituals of public voting for nabobs who, in return, supplied ample means of intoxication. Yet to emphasize these incivilities is to neglect historians' estimates of the emergence of a class of gentlemen who imposed at least a semblance of English common law on the former wilderness and dominated the creation of a stable rural society. Although this society varied in key respects from Old World models—it had no noblemen and many African slaves—it did not generally strike travelers as barbaric.

Though Virginia used the terms of English hierarchy, it lacked the intricate upward gradations of privilege and responsibility that English folk could count on. Instead, there evolved several broad social categories called vaguely by English names. At the bottom were black slaves, about half of the population; above them, indentured servants, tenants, and landless folk. Then came a large class of "simple" people or yeomen, who might range in wealth from humble farm families to owners of considerable properties including some slaves. These were no "Lubbers." They were practical, conservative people whose dwellings conformed to English models and fairly boasted of the tools and paint that stripped off bark and bested nature. This large middling class struck English observers as a "strange mixture," hard to define. Yet the class lines were guarded jealously, as when a tailor was fined in 1674 for entering his horse in "a sport for gentlemen only." And William Byrd II commented at the marriage of a planter's daughter to her uncle's overseer: "to stoop to a dirty plebeian . . . is the lowest form of prostitution." Dominating over all were the "gentle" folk and their families, an aristocracy of wealth, seeking to distinguish their lineage by further acquisition of profits from tobacco and land and by achieving a cultivated life-style. The emergence of this class, not always from "gentle" origins in England, and its quiet maintenance of a system of deference was one of the remarkable developments of colonial history. Clergymen, doctors, lawyers, and merchants, in a society with no great cities, welcomed association with this patrician order.

To identify the hierarchy is to raise the question whether virtuosos arose to ornament it. Scholars normally make some negative observations. For one thing, there were not many powerful gentlemen, perhaps no more than a hundred families, despite the romantic lore of a later Virginia about its cavalier past. Then there is the anthropologist Henry Glassie's reservation: "the gentleman was as close to being a peasant (in the anthropological sense of being a participant in a conservative, insular, basically self-sufficient, agrarian community) as he was to being an aristocrat." Though he controlled slaves and dominated politics, his buildings and life-style were usually more like those of "a lonely farmer" in Britain than of a lord of the manor. Further, hard work and financial worries occupied his time and dampened his aspirations to leisured gentility. Tension and conflict characterize accounts of Virginia gentry life. While efforts were made to perform the minuet, company turned more easily to "vulgar capers" and jigs danced to "some Negro tune." Sallies at refined conversation gave way to talk of tobacco prices and racehorses. Underlying the decorum was brutal competitiveness.

Yet southern settlements were never out of touch with the world of English virtuosity. There were learned men among the sponsors of the Virginia Company, and they saw to it that the earliest expeditions included physicians and educated gentlemen. While serving as treasurer in Virginia, George Sandys finished much of his beautiful verse translation of Ovid's *Metamorphoses* (1626). Throughout the seventeenth century, some colonists served as clerks and agents of "curious gentlemen," back in England, who wanted seeds for their gardens and relics for their cabinets. Thus the private collection that eventually became the Ashmolean Museum at Oxford exhibited "Powhatan's robe" along with other specimens of nature from America. Drawings and paintings from the South embellished the halls of English country houses. In addition, the southern colonies furnished material for quite a long series of volumes, from Thomas Harriot's *True Report,* with drawings by John White, to Mark Catesby's magnificent *Natural History of Carolina, Florida, and the Bahama Islands* (1770), with illustrations of the flora and fauna of the strange New World.

Reports from the South appeared from the first issue of the *Philosophical Transactions* of the Royal Society of London, chartered in 1662 in realization of Bacon's dream of collaborative scientific inquiry. In 1669 the Royal Society trusted to Edward Digges, a Virginia planter, a program of twenty-four queries, which prompted a number of subsequent communications in the *Philosophical Transactions.* Writings addressed to English popular readership took for granted abundant curiosity about the rattlesnakes, opossums, mosquitoes, alligators, buffalo, and other peculiarities as well as the air and weather that affected the lives and character of human inhabitants of the South. Often these writings proceeded in the form of lists, thus reflecting the collecting habits that typified English curiosity: John Lawson's *A New Voyage to Carolina* (1709) has been termed a "verbal pictorial." In the eighteenth century southerners took part in the labor of classifying all living things according to the system proposed by the

Swedish naturalist Linnaeus. This system well suited the habit of mind that worked from lists and queries rather than from logical disputation or experiment. The persistence of these habits will be clear to any reader of the principal book of the most brilliant southern colonist, *Notes on the State of Virginia* (1787) by Thomas Jefferson, which for all its often-quoted discursive passages remained an omnium-gatherum structured in response to queries from a French diplomat.

Mention of Powhatan's robe and other curios should not give the impression that idle curiosity was the leading motive of southern discourse across the Atlantic. Southern information was expected to be practical. Southerners did little in mathematics or the more philosophical realms of science. Their reports were concerned with what could be eaten, grown, or mined; how climate affected health and herbs effected cures; or how improvements might be made in the arts and agriculture. Colonial inquiry may have been the work of amateurs, but it was seldom dilettantish.

Similarly, the libraries assembled in the South were adapted to the practical needs of physicians, ministers, and planters. From wills, advertisements, and catalogs scholars have shown there were throughout the South hundreds of book collections, most of them private, a few of them lending to members of earnest clubs. The trunks of some of Jamestown's leaders contained books, and in 1633 a lawsuit disclosed one collection of five hundred volumes. In the eighteenth century, as book reading became a more important means of communication throughout the Western world, some southern libraries were quite extensive and up to date. Books were not easily obtained; some were ordered from London business contacts in lists that also included seeds, herrings, cheeses, and hats. Nevertheless a few men acquired enviable reputations as biblio-

philes: Richard Bland became known as the "Virginia
Antiquary" (his cousin Jefferson eagerly acquired what he
could at Bland's death); and William Byrd II, a member
of the Royal Society, enjoyed a sizable collector's library,
along with gardens, portraits, and other hallmarks of the
virtuoso. For the most part, however, southern gentry had
practical libraries, with a Bible and several devotional
works, a manual or two on the attributes of a gentleman,
some aids for legal and judicial practice, and advice on
herbs, agriculture, and medicine. Gentlemen occasionally
owned histories, philosophical treatises, or novels, but the
surviving evidence shows that their reading, when they had
time and inclination for it, usually served particular useful purposes. On the whole, like the yeomanry, they were
more at home in an oral culture than among their books.

A few were remarkably accomplished intellectuals. The
Byrd family epitomized the ideal course of southern society toward the attainment of virtuosity; thus, their story
has been retold dozens of times in works of regional
chauvinism. William Byrd I was the son of a London
goldsmith, yet in Virginia he became a prominent gentleman. His fortune began with inheritance of land and goods
in Virginia from his mother's father (a merchant and sea
captain) and his wife's father (a royalist who had fled England during the civil wars). He improved his position
through trade with the Indians, through tobacco and slaves,
and through appointment to lucrative official posts. He
consolidated his status as a new-style gentleman by building a wooden "mansion" at Westover, starting a garden of
flowers and shrubs, and acquiring books. Though he was
on the building committee for William and Mary College,
he sent his own children to schools in England. As he sent
minerals and fossils to England for identification, he
showed the widely recognized connection between wealth,
status, and inquiry.

William Byrd II trained for the law at the Middle Temple and was admitted to the bar in London. His circle of acquaintances included both dramatists and scientists. On the one hand, he was among the wittiest satirists in colonial America, and during one of several cherished return visits to England he may even have co-authored a Restoration play called *The Careless Husband*. On the other hand, he was one of the few planters who fulfilled a daily program of reading, often in ancient languages; his gardens at Westover were world-famous; he acquired a telescope and thermometers and contributed articles on the skin of Negroes, among other topics, to the Royal Society's *Transactions*. Like his father, he patronized useful work by naturalists in America. He replaced the wooden house that he inherited with a more fashionable brick mansion, and in his dealings with the lower orders he maintained an icy reserve appropriate to the hardening of class lines. He liked to think of himself, not just as a gentleman, but as the Virginia equivalent of a nobleman, a patriarch self-sufficient among his bondsmen, basking in "a kind of independence of everyone but Providence," stretching out his life with ginseng in "this silent country."

If there was a virtuoso in the South, it was surely William Byrd II. Yet to friends' imprecations for him to write more, this urbane gentleman replied that he was too preoccupied with projects "to improve our infant colony." Beyond question, he held time-consuming political positions that went with his station in society; but he was also so saddled with debt that his cares extended beyond the usual ones of managing a slave work force and corresponding with financial agents. Many of his writings either recount business enterprises—*A Progress to the Mines* (1732)—or seek to lure settlers to lands he owned for speculation. An astute literary critic finds in his writings an "ordered wit," a mocking recognition of the pretensions to which other men must adhere if his ventures were to succeed. In this vein, he called his overseer his "prime minister," located sites for manor houses, and mapped the future locations of great markets. "Thus we did not build castles only, but also cities in the air." Though this remarkable man deserves praise for his many talents, he lacked the time for sustained work in natural history or any other science.

His son William Byrd III went bankrupt, futilely opposed the coming of the Revolution, and killed himself. The great Byrd library was carted to Philadelphia and sold off piecemeal. While this sad outcome underscores the insecurities of gentle life in Virginia, the attainments of the first two Byrds point out the importance of the English ideal of virtuosity in consolidating a system of status and privilege in the colonies. If few contemporaries were as cultivated as William Byrd II, he embodied an ideal that could be shown, in less perfect form, in the pursuits of other patriarchs.

This ideal defined the intellectual as a man* of wide curiosity about nature—particularly about how it could be classified and put to use—and with the financial means to give this curiosity visible shape. To the modern reader, it may appear that there was a contradiction between practicality and class privilege, but as far as Byrd was concerned, the only conflict was that a man of wit was obliged

---

*I use the masculine gender here and elsewhere in this chapter because virtuosity was a masculine ideal. A few southern women—for example, Eliza Lucas Pinckney of South Carolina—were quite accomplished intellectuals, but they were exceptions to the pattern. Most women were illiterate and even well-to-do women were schooled in the "graces" rather than trained to participate in public discourse. Even Pinckney is known through her letters rather than through more "masculine" public writings (see page 39).

to expend so much energy on financial schemes. There was a practical streak, a concern with political responsibility and economic development, in Byrd's awareness of himself as an American virtuoso. Yet if he sought the general improvement of life in Virginia, he also personified the strong identification of intellectual life with the interests of a ruling elite. He studied Greek and Latin and respected physicians and clerks who, with the patronage of his class, could dig up and apply useful information. But his contempt for backcountry yokels was equaled by that for tradesmen who tried to dress stylishly and imitate the luxuries of the aristocracy. What is absent from his writings, as from the colonial world in general, is any notion of intellectuals signified only by the power of their minds or their delight in knowledge, regardless of class. From the ruck of whites the best to be hoped for was mere civility, and even that was hard won in America.

REASON AND PASSION

For agrarian societies with scattered populations far from the cultural metropolis of London, the southern colonies in the seventeenth and early eighteenth centuries showed abundant signs of intellectual life. There were, to be sure, expressions of frustration in reaching cherished standards in "infant" civilizations. William Byrd I sent his children across the ocean to spare them a poor education in hinterlands where they would be surrounded mostly by black slaves. Others complained of too few churches and too many second-rate ministers. Families developed the custom of making prolonged visits to compensate for the loneliness that afflicted those who lived on small farms and plantations. Yet in maintaining schools and churches, building homes, carrying on correspondence, collecting books, writing poems, and many other activities, southern colonists persisted courageously in transplanting English standards of civilization.

There may have been characteristically American notes in this tenacity: the emphasis on practicality, for example, and perhaps a strain of hedonism. When southern colonists ventured into print, their topics often were the curiosities of nature in the New World or the effects of an exotic environment on the people's temperament. For a summary of these developments, we could hardly improve on Jones's *Present State of Virginia,* the very title of which reiterated the familiar topic. According to Jones, the climate fostered a fluent, bright upper class, whose manners and clothes resembled those in London. But their business preoccupations limited their inclination for "profound study, and prying into the depths of things." Their knowledge was sufficient but superficial, and when their children attended English schools, they resisted the "roundabout" system that kept them "drudging on in what is of least use to them, in pedantick methods, too tedious for their volatile genius." They were likely to cause dissension among their school fellows if they felt "imprisoned and enslaved to what they hate, and think useless." Thus Jones recommended giving them "civil treatment with some liberty" and, in particular, teaching them "all the arts, sciences, and learned accomplishments of the ancients and moderns" in English, without fatiguing them with foreign languages.

Although the emerging social order left its imprint on the meanings of intellectual activity, if we turn to the ideas discussed in the South we find little that went beyond the task of keeping up with English fashions in a practical way. The most diligent historian of intellectual life in the southern colonies, Richard Beale Davis, filled volumes with fascinating and otherwise neglected information, but he found no unifying framework of beliefs or ideas. In science and philosophy, even the most eager suppliers of information were seldom reflective enough to enter into great arguments of their era. In religion, Davis noted the absence of any "all-absorbing" world view such as the one that gives coherent focus to studies of New England Puritanism. Similarly, we can acknowledge the spread of civility across a broad segment of the population and aspirations to virtuosity in a self-conscious elite class, but we must refrain from seeking a distinctive "southern mind."

Nevertheless, southern colonists took part, often avidly, in intellectual activity as conceived in the English-speaking world. Their quiet acceptance of long-standing assumptions about human nature may have been more decisive for the subsequent history of American intellectual life than any distinctive shadings in the numerous accounts of the "present state" of Virginia. In the orthodox view, which they scarcely questioned, man was a divided creature, struggling to restrain carnal impulses and hold on to glimmerings of divine truth. One grand statement of this view was the *Phaedrus* of the ancient Greek philosopher Plato, with its image of the soul as a charioteer reining two horses, one obedient, the other impetuous and lusty. Here was depicted the enduring struggle to achieve moderation and temperance, to master the animal impulse by developing superior faculties. Retention of the view did not depend on reading Plato. It permeated medieval and Elizabethan accounts of man as an intermediate creature, bereft of the intuitive understanding of the angels, resorting to reason to sort out the animalistic proddings of the senses. And it flourished in Protestant doctrine. Both Luther and Calvin had adopted from Saint Augustine the image of man's will as a beast of burden.

If God rode, it went where he directed; if Satan rode, it went the other way. Luther added ominously: "Nor may it choose to which rider it will run, nor which it will seek." Though Protestant divines took a grim look at the probable outcome of skirmishing for rational control of the will and subjection of the passions, they taught that the contest was still of utmost significance for the individual's salvation.

Wherever English colonists turned for guidance, in the books they read and the sermons they heard, this view of the conflict-ridden human soul lay in waiting. While it primarily addressed moral behavior, it had the power to invade thinking about any other mental activity. The scientist and belletrist relied on the same faculties of reason and imagination in which unremitting battle raged. Many illustrations could be enumerated, but it may suffice to recall that this view was implicit in depictions of colonists beguiled by their senses and to add that one attribute of a gentleman was adherence to the classical ideal of moderation in all things. William Byrd II believed that "female passions," in particular, had to be managed carefully "to confine them in bounds and keep them like a high-mettled horse, from running away with their owner." But women were only the extreme case of the general human predicament. Even if we glance ahead to the second half of the eighteenth century, when some southerners began to champion scientific reason over Christian superstition, the obligation to temper the passions remained foremost.

While this orthodoxy prevailed everywhere, the extant writings from the colonies do not indicate that southerners confronted it with much urgency. Perhaps that generalization would have to be qualified if there were more documentation from the earliest settlements. According to the literary historian E. M. W. Tillyard, "The battle between Reason and Passion, the commonplace of every age," was "peculiarly vehement" in the sixteenth and early seventeenth centuries. But in the South the issue appears to have been subdued. Planters blandly accepted the tamest resolutions, when they pondered the issue at all, settling for a reasonable urbanity. In fact, sometimes appeals to moderation came closer to justifying a certain degree of pleasure than to checking passion. Consider a 1742 letter in which Eliza Lucas Pinckney of Charleston opined that there was no "real hurt" in card playing and dancing: " 'tis the use we make of them. The danger arises from the too frequent indulging our selves in them which tends to effeminate the mind. . . . For when these airy pleasures have taken entire possession of the mind the rational faculties are more and more inactive . . . and will degenerate into downright dullness so that 'tis not playing a game at cards or going to a ball now and then to relax the mind—but the immoderate love of them is sinful."

Pinckney's interest in relaxing her mind brings us back to the "general southern hedonistic philosophy" that some observers detect in the colonial period, a philosophy epitomized for Richard Beale Davis in a sermon entitled "Innocent Mirth Not Inconsistent with Religion," preached by Thomas Cradock in Maryland in 1747. Listeners were told that "the morose surly uncheerful man can never answer the end of his creation." The good things of earth existed for use—not for excessive indulgence, of course, but for merry enjoyment. Davis thought this sermon "unlike any other known existing religious writing from the colonial period"; thus, even for the South it would have to be taken as an extreme, if telling, example. Its significance diminishes, however, when we note that in 1707 Benjamin Colman, minister to a prosperous congregation in Boston in Massachusetts Bay, had preached in favor of mirth—not the low-life uproariousness of the alehouse but the cheerful pleasures to be enjoyed in good society. He, too, doubted that a dour, "drooping" man could be an exemplary Christian. Comparable examples could be drawn from sermons composed for polite eighteenth-century audiences in England. What they delineate is not so much the hedonistic consequences of climate or environment as a genteel interest in tempering puritanical estimates of human nature. Moderation was still the watchword, but the balance in the gentry's minds shifted in favor of a good measure of gaiety as well as piety.

To explain this adjustment further would hurl us into the subjects of later chapters. But we may conclude by noticing in Pinckney's letter and Cradock's sermon the comfortable stability of a patrician viewpoint closely identified with cultural life in southern colonies. Where the battle between reason and passion slackened, we may be sure that the virtuosos' privileges were unchallenged. Because these men and women cared more about the necessities of the plantation and the adornments of their status than about "prying into the depths of things," they avoided the early stages of London's philosophical disputes over the powers and limits of reason. New England never skirted the fray, as we shall see, and in the long run neither did the South.

FOR FURTHER READING

Perry Miller's *Errand into the Wilderness* (1956) is a collection of essays by the most influential historian of intellectual life in the colonial period. Two excellent interpretations of the literature of discovery are Howard Mumford Jones, *O Strange New World: American Culture, The Formative Years* (1964), and Wayne Franklin, *Discoverers, Explorers, Settlers: The Diligent Writers of Early America* (1979). For an extremely useful collection of the discovery literature, see David B. Quinn, ed., *New American World* (5 vols., 1979).

Walter E. Houghton, Jr.'s "The English Virtuoso in the Seventeenth Century," *Journal of the History of Ideas* (1942), is the essential introduction to its subject. For the more specialized scientific ideal of virtuosity, see Richard S. Westfall, *Science and Religion in Seventeenth-Century England* (1958). Guides to the English intellectual background include Basil Willey, *The Seventeenth-Century Background* (1934), and E. M. W. Tillyard, *The Elizabethan World Picture* (1948).

On civility and the Virginia Indians, see Bernard W. Sheehan, *Savagism and Civility: Indians and Englishmen in Colonial Virginia* (1980), and J. Frederick Fausz's essay on Opechancanough in David G. Sweet and Gary B. Nash, eds., *Struggle and Survival in Colonial America* (1981). For a brilliant introduction to the place of the Indian in white cultural systems, see Robert F. Berkhofer, Jr., *The White Man's Indian* (1978). The standard account of the accomplishments of the Virginia gentry is Louis B. Wright, *The First Gentlemen of Virginia: Intellectual Qualities of the Early Colonial Ruling Class* (1940). More critical assessments may be found in Carl Bridenbaugh, *Myths and Realities: Societies of the Colonial South* (1952), and Daniel J. Boorstin, *The Americans: The Colonial Experience* (1958). The evidence of material culture is considered in Henry Glassie, *Folk Housing in Middle Virginia* (1975), and the perspective of family history is explained in Daniel Blake Smith, *Inside the Great House: Planter Family Life in Eighteenth-Century Chesapeake Society* (1980).

Richard Beale Davis's *Intellectual Life in the Colonial South, 1585–1763* (3 vols., 1978), is a compendious treatment of its subject. Philip J. Wiener, ed., *Dictionary of the History of Ideas* (5 vols., 1973), serves all students of intellectual history.

II

THE INTELLECT
AND THE
HEART IN
NEW ENGLAND

CIVILIZATION

The most thoroughly studied intellectuals in the history of the New World are the ministers and political leaders of seventeenth-century New England. According to the standard history of American philosophy, nowhere else in colonial America was "so much importance attached to intellectual pursuits." According to many other books and articles, New England's leaders established the basic themes and preoccupations of an unfolding, dominant Puritan tradition in American intellectual life. To take this approach to the New Englanders normally means to start with the Puritans' theological innovations and their distinctive ideas about the church—important subjects that we may not neglect. But in keeping with our examination of southern intellectual life, we may consider the original Puritans as carriers of European culture, adjusting to New World circumstances. The New England colonies were the scenes of important episodes in the pursuit of widely understood ideals of civility and virtuosity.

The early settlers of Massachusetts Bay included men of impressive education and influence in England. Besides the ninety or so learned ministers who came to Massachusetts churches in the decade after 1629, there were political leaders like John Winthrop, an educated gentleman, lord of the manor, lawyer, and official of the Crown before he journeyed to Boston. These men wrote and published extensively, reaching both New World and Old World audiences, and giving New England an aura of intellectual earnestness. Samuel Willard, for example, devised a *Compleat Body of Divinity* in 250 sermons delivered on Tuesdays between 1687 and 1707. Not long after finishing the last one on the Lord's Prayer, he took to his bed and died.

We should not forget, however, that most New Englanders were less well educated. While few artisans or farmers, let alone dependents and servants, left literary compositions to be analyzed, it is obvious that their views were less fully intellectualized. Their thinking often had a traditional superstitious quality. A tailor named John Dane, who emigrated in the late 1630s, left an account of his reasons for leaving England that is filled with signs and portents. Sexual confusion, economic frustrations, and religious hope—all came together in a decisive moment when he opened the Bible, told his father that the first line he saw would settle his fate, and read the magical words: "Come out from among them, touch no unclean thing, and I will be your God and you shall be my people." One wonders what Dane thought of the careful sermons expounding Scripture that he heard in Puritan churches. Many settlers had slighter religious commitments than Dane's, as one clergyman learned in confronting folk along the coast who jeered that they had not come to the New World for religion. "Our main end was to catch fish."

Like all English colonial ventures, New England proposed to lead the Indians out of sloth and satanism. "Come over and help us," begged the Indian depicted on the seal of the company in charge of Massachusetts Bay Colony. A few ministers heeded this appeal, most notably John Eliot of Roxbury who conducted services and translated the Bible into the Algonquian language. Some Indians were drawn away from their tribes and resettled in English-style villages with a meetinghouse, house lots, and "civil" manners. By the last quarter of the seventeenth century there were fourteen such "praying towns" in the Bay Colony, and nearly a quarter of New England's Indians were in some stage of conversion. By that time, however, bloody wars had commenced that brought a merciless halt to this experiment in conversion.

In any event, the congregational organization of the churches afforded town ministers little time for missionary work, and the complex theology of the Puritans impeded conversion. It is surprising that the experiment was as successful as it was in view of the settlers' prejudices against a people they regarded as alien, lewd, and menacing. New Englanders were inclined to view their surroundings as a wilderness awaiting orderly civilization, and the Indians were dramatic reminders of the gap between Old World life-styles and New World experience. In October 1631 the lordly Winthrop recounted the events of an awkward night that summed up this incongruity. After supper he took a walk, with gun in hand in case he met a wolf. As it grew dark he lost his way and strayed near the empty home of an Indian sagamore. There he stayed, gathering wood for a fire, pacing to and fro, and singing Psalms, until it began to rain. He managed, with some exertion, to get into the house, where he took shelter until morning, when a squaw arrived. "Perceiving her before she opened the door, he barred her out; yet she stayed there a great while essaying to get in, and at last she went away." He then hurried home, where his servants had been searching for him, hallooing and firing gunshots all night. John Dane recounted a similar adventure: as he traveled up to Ipswich on an Indian trail, trusting to God to show him the way, he met a procession of Indians who laughed and imitated his cries of "what cheer, what cheer." Both stories recapture what in English eyes was an uncomfortable, even ludicrous, alienation to be overcome in the conquest of the forest.

In New England civility emerged more easily than elsewhere because of the colonists' determination to establish orderly towns. In Virginia the docks along the rivers that cut into the coastline never attracted populous settlement, and the practical requirements of tobacco culture led to dispersion and isolation, punctuated by moments of raucous hospitality. New England settlement was more thickly clustered, and manners were more solemn: No one complained that the climate fostered laziness or hedonism.

A preoccupation with order was evident from the start. The Mayflower Compact (1620), devised on board ship before the founders of Plymouth Colony set foot on land, is often presented to schoolchildren as a charter of liberty. In fact, it was a response to "discontented and mutinous speeches" by some irreligious passengers. It starkly asserted the need for "a civil body politick," subservient to the king and dedicated to the "advancement of the Christian faith." In "A Model of Christian Charity" (1630), a lay sermon preached on board the *Arbella* by John Winthrop, migrants to Massachusetts Bay Colony were warned of the unending need for hierarchy: "God Almighty in his most holy and wise providence hath so disposed of the condition of mankind, as in all times some must be rich, some poor, some high and eminent in power and dignity, others mean and in subjection." This condition, which was in "conformity to the rest of his works," was nothing to grumble at; it meant that "every man might have need of other, and from hence they might be all knit together in the bond of brotherly affection." The powerful must exhibit justice and mercy, and the lowly must be contented with their service. By achieving such a civil order, under the influence of Christianity, they would build "a city on the hill" that others would strive to imitate. If they failed, they would set back God's cause, and their ruin would be ignominious.

After a few years of trial and error, New England developed a land system of townships regulated by the authorities of the colony. The system differed from English precedent in that virtually all families owned some land; thus, every peasant was a potential yeoman. The procedures of land allotment also differed from those that resulted in huge, scattered holdings in Virginia; instead, the procedures enforced the necessity of close living and hierarchical degree. When Sudbury was settled in 1639, for example, the town received a large tract of well-surveyed land, with its title cleared of Indian claims. A committee of three then "ordered" the town by screening fifty heads of households and ranking them: the minister came first, and others followed according to their wealth, distinction, and usefulness. These rankings fixed the size of the meadow lots and upland lots they received in addition to village sites for their houses. To place the town in order was to institute a system of ranks, with the understanding that richer men would shoulder heavier monetary burdens in protecting the town's weak and promoting the town's welfare.

The term *gentleman* was maintained as watchfully as in the South, though New Englanders tended to think in terms of only two social orders (the other being "the people"). The legislatures of both Massachusetts and Connecticut passed laws against upstarts wearing fine apparel. The Massachusetts government expressed "our utter

detestation and dislike that men or women of mean condition, educations, and callings should take upon them the
garb of gentlemen, by the wearing of gold or silver lace,
or buttons, or points at their knees, or to walk in great
boots, or women of the same rank to wear silk or tiffany
hoods or scarfs, which though allowable to persons of
greater estates, or more liberal education, yet we cannot
but judge it intolerable in persons of such like condition."
Yet gentlemanly distinction carried no implication, as it did
in Virginia, of aloof privilege or of patriarchal domination over a large company of dependents and slaves.
Though wealth conveyed social distinctions, a large percentage of males were entitled to participate in the political process. Despite English protests, there was no Massachusetts equivalent to the House of Lords. There was
some recognition, based on early political disappointments, that gentlemen were not always the fittest political
leaders. Conversely, it was recognized, sometimes unhappily, that those men who gave much time to political service were apt to accumulate less wealth than merchants and
traders could amass. Some governors in the North died
poor.

To describe the perfection sought in New England
towns, the historian Kenneth Lockridge has offered the
label, "Christian Utopian Closed Corporate Communities." The civility of these outposts was extraordinary: it
was not the outcome of centuries of historical process but
a planned imposition on the wilderness. The towns upheld some traditional signs of good order such as public
respect for older males and the subjection of dutiful
women. The towns developed institutions to inculcate religious uniformity and obedience to law. From the 1640s
on, towns were required to offer public education so that
all children would share the "ability to read and under-

stand the principles of religion and the capital laws of this country." Literacy levels were unsurpassed in the English-speaking world. In addition, the towns centered around churches where God's word was expounded and where attendance was compulsory. Though state-financed religion was a matter of dispute among English Puritans, New England towns had little hesitation in compelling people to pay the ministers' salaries and maintain the buildings. A system of courts settled disputes among neighbors, kept watch over public morals, and kept out strangers and heretics. There were no ecclesiastical courts—another source of contention among English Puritans—but church members were in double jeopardy, punished for their crimes by the civil government and disciplined for their sins by actions of the other church members. These towns were never theocracies, for the ministers held no political positions, but they were remarkably effective embodiments of an ideal Christian order.*

Were they also centers of virtuosity? Idle refinement enjoyed less favor here than in England or the South. To be sure, the link between wealth and curiosity was a familiar notion, but there was less literary interest in the fauna and flora of the North. One of the few works on natural history to parallel the lavish southern pictorials was *New England's Rarities Discovered: In Birds, Beasts, Fishes, Serpents, and Plants of that Country* (1672) by John Josselyn, son of a royal official of Maine and a critic of the Puritans. The vast outpouring of literature from southern New

---

*Though historians have discarded the term *theocracy* because the ministers held no civil office, the Puritans themselves used it. In their view a theocracy was not inconsistent with a separation of church and state. Religion, though shielded from political encroachments, would have an elevating influence on society.

England was much more likely to address religious topics. The two universities that dominated intellectual life,* Harvard (founded in 1636) and Yale (1701), were centrally concerned with the training of ministers, and their libraries were heavily theological. The same observation applies to the books owned by ministers and secular leaders, though by the eighteenth century a thriving popular book trade had emerged in Boston.

Furthermore, ostentatious separation and leisurely elegance were despised in the ethic of New England plain living. Thus to some extent civility was at odds with virtuosity. New England towns did not boast of the gardens and portraits owned by privileged classes but rather sought to venerate the rich as responsible stewards of the Lord's bounty. John Winthrop, for example, was revered for teaching the people "frugality" by giving up "a thousand comfortable things which he had allowed himself elsewhere. His habit was not the 'soft raiment' which would have been disagreeable to a wilderness; his table was not covered with the superfluities that would have invited unto sensualities." He was a paragon less of virtuosity than of generous charity. The great preacher-leader of Connecticut, Thomas Hooker, explained to English readers that one of his books wore "a homely dress and coarse habit" because "it comes out of the wilderness where curiosity is not studied."

Yet New England's leaders believed that scientific knowledge enhanced appreciation of God's works, and they strove for a record of improvement in "curious" attainments. Subsequent generations of Winthrops marked a progress fully comparable to that of Virginia's Byrds. John

*As a sign of the leaders' belief in the importance of hierarchy, class rank in the universities was awarded during much of the eighteenth century on the basis of wealth and status.

Winthrop, Jr., attended Trinity College, Dublin, and studied law in London, though he did not finish either course and became instead a self-made philosopher. Before the Puritans left England, he spent a long tour on a merchant ship through Mediterranean cities, where he conversed with learned men and cultivated scientific interests. He took time out from a long career of public service in Massachusetts Bay and Connecticut—he was governor of the latter colony from 1662 to 1676—to revisit Europe and meet with inventors and scientists. His enterprises included lead mining and iron making, and he was also a reputable physician who formulated a secret remedy for New World ailments. The first man in New England to own telescopes, he donated one to Harvard in an effort to attract more students to natural philosophy. He was also the first American member of the Royal Society and its chief correspondent in the West. He sent rocks, plants, crustaceans, beer, a bow and arrow, and other specimens, even a copy of Eliot's Indian Bible, to the learned gentlemen in London, and his publications in the *Philosophical Transactions* touched on such subjects as the making of tar and pitch and the uses of maize. He encouraged a circle of a half-dozen other New Englanders who laid the basis for more sustained scientific investigations in the late seventeenth century. One of his descendants, also named John Winthrop, was appointed in 1739 to a Harvard professorship in mathematics and natural philosophy and for forty years trained students in the new mode of exact observation and experiment. In the 1770s a poet paid this Winthrop the high compliment of comparing him to "Godlike Newton."

A comparable progression distinguished the Mather family. Richard Mather ranked among the most beloved early ministers of Massachusetts Bay. Of yeoman descent, he was a schoolteacher who received only a brief education at Oxford before receiving the call to preach. He lacked great scientific accomplishment, but first in Lancashire and then in Massachusetts, he personified the Puritan ideal of the minister as a gifted instructor, chosen by his congregation and blessed by Christ. His style was a simple one, "aiming to shoot his arrows not over his people's heads, but into their hearts and consciences." He was one of the authors of the *Bay Psalm Book* (1640), which translated the Hebrew psalms into English meter to be sung in church. As a moderating influence on other ministers, he was chosen to write the Cambridge Platform, which codified New England doctrine in 1648. It was not virtuosity, but closeness to the people and the ability to command their obedience, that made him an effective first-generation leader.

Several of Richard Mather's children moved back to Britain. Increase Mather followed his Harvard B.A. with an M.A. from Trinity College, Dublin, and then took up a promising career as a preacher in England. The restoration of the monarchy once again ruined the prospects of a Puritan minister, however, and he was driven to follow his father's flight to New England. He furnished decades of stalwart leadership as minister of North Church, Boston, and for sixteen years (1685–1701) as president of Harvard. In the 1690s he returned to England to negotiate a new charter for the colony—only one instance of his prominent involvement in worldly controversies. Increase Mather's conception of ministerial duty was far more scholarly than his father's. He spent days each week in his study, and his sermons were learned discourses. In the spirit of improving New England's intellectual life, he founded a Boston Philosophical Society on the model of the Royal Society. He also wrote a number of works on natural science, especially *Kometographia* (1683), which recounted the history of all comets since the Creation and described his observations through the Harvard telescope of the appearance of Halley's comet in 1682. Despite his exact calculations of the comet's course, he scoffed at the notion that future occurrences were predictable. His reflections on nature emphasized the wonder and mystery of God, too easily neglected in busy Boston. Though acknowledging that foolish superstitions obscured natural phenomena, *Kometographia* warned that the comets might well portend calamitous changes in human affairs.

His son Cotton Mather, who joined him in the North Church pulpit (though never in the presidency of Harvard), was probably the most learned man in colonial America, certainly the most conversant with the work of Europe's new scientists. Though he never journeyed far from Boston, he conducted a vast international correspondence. Owner of a huge library—a visitor compared it to the Bodleian at Oxford and called it "the Glory of New England"—and author of over four hundred published works as well as a gigantic manuscript on biblical scholarship, he was both a strenuous participant in colonial controversies and an avid champion of the new philosophy. He sent to the Royal Society annual reports on the "curiosities" of America, ranging from practical observations on medicine (he had early prepared for this calling and was a courageous advocate of inoculation against smallpox) to credulous accounts of two-headed snakes and other monstrosities. On the one hand, he discovered through microscopes that "every part of matter is peopled"—leaves with parasites, the skins of animals with smaller animals, cells with crowds of "imperceptible inmates." On the other hand, he gazed through telescopes at a universe of "so many worlds" that the earth looked "but as a pin's point" and his ability even to conjecture explanations was overwhelmed. Sometimes he appeared to anticipate twentieth-century anxiety over science and the human predicament, over the perils of fixing meaning in an infinite universe. Actually the teeming worlds that he witnessed impelled him to the same conclusion as did the hurly-burly of Boston: imperfect human beings need to humble themselves before God's majesty.

When Cotton Mather learned in 1713 that he was going to be elected to the Royal Society, he recorded satisfaction at this "marvelous favour of Heaven," which he hoped would fortify his good influence among his townsmen. What did he owe God in return? "I entertain these things, prostrate in the dust before the Lord, with all humble self-abhorrence, and cry from thence unto Him, that He would enable me to make a due improvement of the things in which He smiles upon me, and hereby quicken my diligence in His holy service." Similar humility informed his erudite compilation of the findings of science, *The Christian Philosopher* (1721), which was patterned on Robert Boyle's work (in fact, the first title was "Christian Virtuoso"). It argued that science furnished "an incentive" rather than opposition to the Christian purpose of glorifying God. The philosopher discharged "the office of a priest" deepening reverence for the work of "the Almighty Architect." In his respect for science as an international community, Mather's stance was dramatically at variance from the country gentlemen's pride in collecting curiosities. He hoped that his incessant quoting of scientists would not be mistaken for the "impertinent vanity" of those who liked to show off their learning. After all, if it had required so much collective "wisdom and penetration" to uncover parts of the "wonderful order and design in the structure of the world," the crucial point was that one sovereign intelligence had invented the whole. He commended French savants whose language provided the impersonal pronoun *on* so that they did not use the word *I* to denote the source of scientific discovery. Collaborative scientific inquiry suppressed self-importance, just as "Christian piety will annihilate our I and ME, and human civility will suppress it."

Mather hoped that "virtuosos" throughout the world would approve his delineation of "the true Philosophical Religion." His example shows that there was no fundamental antipathy in Puritanism to the accumulating discoveries of science, though there may have been some apprehension about science straying off on its own course. In histories of science, Mather stands as a transitional figure between old theological accounts of nature and later habits of narrowly scientific investigation. For our present purposes, Mather may stand as an example of intense Puritan commitment to the ideal of virtuosity. He, like John Winthrop, Jr., dabbled in so many fields that his achievements in any one of them were limited. But in no case was Puritan virtuosity to be compared with the dilettantism or ostentation of an aloof ruling class. Puritan virtuosity was bounded by requirements of honoring God and humbly doing good in civil society. To understand these requirements, which differentiated the New England intellectual class from the Virginia elite, we must turn to the religious system of the Puritans.

SIN AND GRACE

New England's leaders commented repeatedly on the obligations of civil life. Going beyond the conventional contrast between barbarians and well-behaved Englishmen, they bore down on the distinction between animals and humankind. Wild animals had the liberty to plunge in whatever direction their sensual appetites led them; man before the Fall had been able to pursue an intuitive grasp of right behavior. For Adam's sinful descendants, however, unbridled action meant the rankest and most destructive anarchy. It meant to forsake a higher nature and descend into brutality. Society consisted of arrangements to institute systems of authority. Men and women had some freedom in choosing the forms of authority (within limits clarified in the Bible), but once the arrangements had taken hold, unless the authorities were flagrantly sinful, they imposed duties of undeviating obedience. When men in one Massachusetts town complained that Governor Winthrop had violated their "liberty," he dismissed their notion as a vulgar "natural" liberty, which "makes men grow more evil, and in time to be worse than brute beasts." In contrast, "civil" liberty enabled men to conform to God's law. This higher liberty induced men to submit cheerfully to well-intentioned magistrates, just as a "true wife" after choosing her husband "accounts her subjection her honor and freedom."

This was not an easy doctrine to accept in newly established towns. Winthrop remarked that there was "a great mistake" in popular conceptions of liberty, and other leaders' reiterations of the obligations sustaining civil life suggest that disorder was an ever-present threat. Here we confront a paradox that goes to the heart of the complexity of Puritan thought. Despite the New England Puritans' resolution to impose order on the wilderness, their theology often seemed to disparage the ultimate value of civility. Despite the New Englanders' remarkable success in fashioning orderly towns, the sermons of their ministers regularly criticized human efforts to live virtuously.

The historian Edmund S. Morgan discovered in New England sermons "a type of man whom the Puritans never tired of denouncing":

He was a good citizen, a man who obeyed the laws, carried out his social obligations, never injured others. The Puritans called him a "civil man," and admitted that he was "outwardly just, temperate, chaste, carefull to follow his worldly businesse, will not hurt so much as his neighbors dog, payes every man his owne, and lives of his own; no drunkard, adulterer, or quareller; loves to live peaceably and quietly among his neighbours." This man, this paragon of social virtue, was on his way to Hell, and their preachers continually reminded him of it.

Morgan finds good illustration of this theme in a sermon by Thomas Shepard attacking the "proud conceits" of men who thought they deserved God's mercy because of their education, their clean habits, or their "smooth, honest, civil life." They remained "full of rottenness, of sin, . . . for God looks to the heart; guilty thou art of heart whoredom, heart sodomy, heart blasphemy, heart drunkenness, heart buggery, heart oppression, heart idolatry; and these are sins that terribly provoke the wrath of Almighty God against thee."

If the paradox had a resolution, it followed from the fact that not all men stirred up God's eternal anger. Some he elected to save, and it was crucial to know how, if at all, they could be told apart. Certainly there was nothing they could do to earn salvation. Education, church attendance, morality—none of these qualities tempered their inward sinfulness. As heirs of the Protestant Reformation, Puritans knew that it was Roman Catholic error to think that good works and penances could erase the brand of sin. The purpose of religion was to glorify a majestic God, whose commandments were not so easily fulfilled. Grace came only through faith. In their desperation to be saved, many dissembled at being faithful, but to no avail. The Puritans believed that salvation was gratuitous, unearned, a gift from the Almighty. Only those whom God chose to "justify" could be truly faithful. These folk, the "elect," were God's saints, and they would live in the civil way that he loves, not in the vain effort to curry favor, but as the irresistible outcome of their justified souls. Something deeper than an awareness of sin's outward costs motivated them to shun ungodly ways. Once they were justified, their hearts were redirected so that glorification of the Creator became their abiding purpose.

Their lives were as civil as the rotten lives that Shepard denounced. Cotton Mather reported of his father: "they who do good works because they are already justified will not come short of those who do good works that they may be justified; and . . . they who renounce all pretence to merit by their good works will more abound in good works than the greatest merit-mongers in the world."* Here we glimpse the sources of the self-effacement that mitigated Puritan virtuosity. While striving for the good order and high achievements that dignified English society, the Puritans sought them on different terms. Their goals were sincerity and cohesiveness instead of the pride and competitiveness that came from forgetting man's essential imperfection. They appealed to the moral standards of the "primitive" church, buried beneath centuries of ecclesiastical tyranny, rather than to the historical progress of civility. The result might be similar—they were inevitably

---

*But Richard Mather's own Dorchester congregation was criticized because "most of them . . . had builded their comfort on unsound grounds." Some relied upon "the reformation of their lives; others upon duties and performances. . . . They had not come to hate sin, because it was filthy, but only left it, because it was hurtful. . . . They expected to believe by some power of their own, and not only and wholly from Christ." This belief—that good deeds per se were worthless unless preceded by a faith in Christ that human beings were powerless to reach on their own—was a sharp sword that could cut in many directions.

men of their time—but the motivation was supposed to be purer.

The Puritans clung to the tradition of the Protestant Reformation, particularly the Calvinist or "Reformed" side of that tradition, which mourned man's almost irreconcilable distance from God. It was in Calvinist Geneva, for example, that exiled Puritan scholars had turned out the Geneva Bible (1576), their great translation of Scripture into English with elaborate notes on the links between Old and New Testaments and future redemption. (This work roiled up so much controversy that the Puritans' antagonists produced the authorized King James Version, which retained much of the translation but eliminated all notes and other incentives to dispute.) In the Reformed tradition, Puritans stressed the deformity of human nature in the wake of original sin, a condition of disobedience to divine law that could not be set right by any pretense of individual human merit. At the same time, they believed in the fundamental beauty and ingenuity of God's creation. For simple folk there was comfort in the Calvinist view of wretched existence in a majestic universe; it underlay the wonder that a man like John Dane experienced amid the temptations and losses of civil life. Should anyone doubt the view's accuracy, the ministers were ready to beat down such resistance in learned explanations of biblical texts.

The American Puritans acted their historical roles a century after John Calvin had propounded the Reformed view of the cosmos. Their leaders inherited a complex theology that went well beyond the stark contradiction of man's baseness and God's sovereignty. In part, this theology responded to theoretical questions about how a perfect sovereign could consign subjects to uncomprehending, doomed lives. In part, it answered practical questions about the necessity of human striving against foreordained fates and about the possibility of the elect gaining some confidence of salvation. The elaborate and not always consistent intellectual system, which scholars call the covenant theology, taught that Adam had violated man's original contract with God, that new terms had been tendered to Abraham's progeny, and that since Christ these terms had been extended to all believers. Ultimately, at the end of history, Christ would restore the world to a condition of orderly glorification of God similar to that which Adam had forsaken. In the meantime, all was not lost. Though Satan's guiles showed up everywhere, individuals who experienced regeneration—the assurance of justification that amounted to a new birth—would achieve a reasonable degree of reconciliation. They would become faithful haters of sin.

In addition, the covenant with Abraham opened the way for bands of Christians to please God collectively by enforcing his law and pledging their energies to his service. Although grace was not earned by good lineage or civil manners, the Almighty had not left post-Adamic humanity bereft of knowledge of his law. Both the Bible and the created universe revealed to human reason the doctrines of religion and the rules of proper behavior that God approved. There was no ambiguity concerning what was right. Individuals were obliged to struggle for the capacity to behave in a sanctified way, notwithstanding that the struggle was hopeless without God's aid. And in communities convenanted to exact obedience to God's law, as expounded by his ministers, the struggle would be less frustrating. God would see to it that grace conformed to the expectations of enlightened human reason: those who were justified, however fervently they reiterated their unworthiness, would discover an abundant capacity to do good works. Civil and charitable deeds were outward indications of an inward grace. No man could point to them to wriggle out of condemnation of his rottenness, but persistent civility might give welcome evidence that an undeserved salvation had been bestowed.

The Puritan ministers' exhortations did not depict human beings as hapless victims of predestination. Christians must be prepared to recognize the spark of faith, communicated by the Holy Spirit, and once it was experienced, they were obliged to do everything possible, within the devotional context of the church, to bring it to flame. As the ability to behave civilly emerged from the disorders of childhood, the adult had to search for signs that this ability stemmed from justification. Taken out of context, the ministers' exhortations seemed to curtail God's independent power: "when thou art on a sure ground, take no denial, though the Lord may defer long, yet he will do it [justify the sinner], he cannot choose; it is a part of his covenant." Many historians see in Puritan beliefs an elaborate pattern of deception, one that hemmed in God's sovereign power and ennobled human strivings. Yet these uses of the covenant should not be misread as attributing salvation to human free will. The constant denunciation of the civil man reminds us otherwise, and Increase Mather's incessant disparagement of his own merit is close to the heart of Puritanism. What the covenant theology offered was a system in which the ministrations of the church made a difference and one in which orderly behavior was subject to biting examinations of motive. It never diverted Puritan intentions from overriding recognition of God's glory and mankind's inveterate failings.

The word *Puritan* originated as a term of reproach. As late as Dr. Samuel Johnson's eighteenth-century *Dictionary of the English Language,* it denoted "a sectary pretending to eminent purity of religion." A sectary was someone who cut himself off from the national church and disrupted unity in Christ. The pretense to superiority extended to public behavior as well as churchly organization: the Puritan was stereotyped as giving or listening to long sermons while other folk attended plays, danced, or reveled. Ever since Henry VIII in the 1530s severed ties between the Church of England and Rome, there had been zealous advocates of reforms to push English religion and behavior to higher planes of purity. Never a tightly organized movement, they were generally agreed in assailing the ceremonialism embedded in the Book of Common Prayer and enforced by the church hierarchy. Thus Richard Mather, before migrating to New England, was stripped of his parish for refusing to wear priestly vestments. Some reformers wished to get rid of the bishops and other worldly powers who seemed to deprive congregations of their learned ministers while showing abominable tolerance of immoral and ignorant clergymen. There was some consensus that churches should expel from communion those laymen with incurable propensities to drink, fornicate, or dance on the Lord's day. The term *Puritan* fit these elements well enough, though it was never the name by which these reformers preferred to identify themselves.

There were deep cleavages among foes of the established Church of England. To replace the bishops, some would have established associations, or presbyteries, of church leaders with disciplinary authority over even the best-intended congregations. Others, more influential among the migrants to New England, cherished the bond between an independent congregation and its spiritual leader. Both presbyterians and congregationalists believed in a single national church despite their detestation of its current organization and rituals. They joined in denouncing as "sectaries" various groups of zealots who believed that the very notion of a national church was sacrilegious, who envisioned the faithful as inevitably a tiny remnant in an epoch of prevailing sin. Sometimes these groups called themselves "pilgrims" out of their conception of the lonely Christian's journey through the trials and woes of life. Another name for them was "separatists," people who severed connections with earthbound ecclesiastical institutions. Some of these groups touched off feelings of frustration and disaffection among the lower orders of society; all were accused of undermining the Crown.

In the 1590s, faced with laws that threatened dissenters with jail and exile, a group of separatists who had wealthy and influential friends made an abortive effort to settle on the Magdalen Islands in the Gulf of St. Lawrence. Thereby they might have assisted England's economic empire, signified their temporal loyalty to the Crown, and avoided the contamination of the state church. The same vision of the New World as a refuge for pilgrims inspired the separatists who in 1620 sailed on the *Mayflower* and settled Plymouth Colony. Since they had to take along irreligious "strangers," their success in realizing holy separation was always perilous. But their understanding of the church was quite different from that which dominated the larger Puritan migration to Massachusetts Bay. The latter colony, which eventually absorbed Plymouth, would not give the slightest countenance to separatism or any trace of insubordination.

The historian Perry Miller found it useful to call the Massachusetts Puritans "nonseparating congregationalists." The term is admittedly awkward, reminding us of the bewildering complexity of religious factionalism in England. The bishops and monarch considered themselves champions of a prudent middle way between papistry and discordant zealotry. The Puritans in turn defined their own middle way between the unholy compromises of the establishment and the unworldly withdrawal of pilgrims and other fanatics. Such distinctions may have mattered little to a man like Dane who trekked credulously in search of inspiration and guidance. Even that pillar of New England orthodoxy, Thomas Shepard, had in his youth in England "felt all manner of temptations to all kinds of religions, not knowing which I should choose," and had nearly succumbed to a separatist fragment that promised complete escape from the sphere of sin. But in Massachusetts Shepard, Winthrop, and the other leaders profited from their knowledge of mistakes that, in their view, had wrecked previous critics of the church's corruptions. Those tainted with sectarian views either confessed their errors or left the colony, as two famous rebels of the 1630s, Anne Hutchinson and Roger Williams, abruptly discovered. Other heretics were whipped and denounced. The New England church was to be an uncontested orthodoxy in its own right, a model for reorganizing the Church of England on congregationalist principles, with the godly in control and with no trace of the babbling disintegration that enemies of congregationalism thought inevitable.

Nonseparating congregationalism embodied a dilemma: to seek after purity without shrinking from the impure world. The institution that embodied this dilemma most clearly was the church. The church was central to the New England town, not shielded from the snares of the temporal world. Puritans thought of their churches as separate from the state: the king was not their head, and the ministers were not curates who owed their livings to anyone beyond the membership. Nevertheless, the state punished heresy as a crime, and it prosecuted those who profaned the Sabbath or failed to contribute to the minister's support. The church, for its part, identified and guided a membership worthy to dominate secular affairs. Some New England colonies attempted to restrict the franchise to church members; even though these measures were of limited effect, there was no questioning the civil preeminence of the saints.

Volumes have been written about the theory and practice of determining church membership as they evolved and flourished in the so-called New England Way. Like most Protestants and Catholics, the Puritans distinguished two churches: one pure and invisible, comprising all those from every age whom God destined to be saved; the other visible but not entirely pure, doing its best to minister to the faithful within the limits of earthly time. Dissatisfied with English practice and convinced that a new era of divine providence was at hand, Massachusetts ministers, under the leadership of Boston's John Cotton, developed a system in which membership included only those who gave evidence of being saints. We may think of this system as a merging of the old catholic notions of the church with the radical tenets of sectarian exclusiveness. Attendance at services was good for everyone, but only members took communion and only their children were baptized. Puritans acknowledged that some hypocrites would always slip into membership and some saints would stay outside, but they nonetheless staked a great deal on the presumption that election to church membership could mirror God's fateful determination of his elect.

The system of inducting members became so routine that the procedures needed only terse summary in a minister's notebook: "Sarah Fiske upon satisfaction given to the church touching her knowledge of the principles of faith and the work of grace upon her soul, upon testimony given by [three members], was received into full communion and covenant with this church." In other words, the applicant met three requirements: she knew the doctrines that Puritans believed to be sacred; she narrated—or in this case, because she was a woman, had her narration read by the minister—the experiences in which grace became known to her; and her good behavior was established. She might have been questioned by the members on several points. Did she understand that only "closure with Christ," not human deeds, gave assurance of salvation? Had any biblical text, as expounded perhaps in a sermon, figured in her regenerative experience? Was it true that she had misbehaved toward one of the members on some occasion? In such questions we see the practical consequences of the covenant theology. The saints had personal experience leading to righteous behavior within a discipline that assigned key influence to the Bible and the ministers.

It was not easy to promote the New England Way. Churches were supposed to be the voluntary creations of bands of people who joined hands together; they did not belong to any external agency. Thus little could be done about a few churches that rejected the advice of neighbors to go along this path. Furthermore, from the beginning some men bristled at being denied political privileges because they were not church members. Some critics worried that one-half or more of the adult population was excluded from the sacraments; instead of bringing the heathen Indians inside Christianity they were casting English folk into the condition of heathens. The system might have seemed even more troublesome had it not been for the infectious zeal of the migrants of the 1630s. In a few months after Cotton arrived to preach in Boston, for example, sixty-three persons were able to narrate their regenerative experiences satisfactorily. In later centuries this would have been called a revival. Clearly, history was progressing, grace was abounding, and the requirement of a "relation" (as the narratives were called) served good effects.

In time, however, the system ceased to work so har-
moniously. Local church records show thorny problems
arising when church members moved from one town to
another. Either they retained membership elsewhere or
they went through a new examination to join a new fellowship—and the results in either instance could be embarrassing. Worse still, the numbers willing to make a relation diminished. The second and third generations were
less susceptible to the fire of Cotton's first converts. Ministers were uncomfortable before congregations with a
dwindling percentage under the discipline of membership, and the laity saw disconcerting evidence of ebbing
sanctity at the center of the social order. Too many children who had been baptized never took the second step
expected of them as adults: they never experienced grace
and never offered a relation. When they had children,
should they be baptized? This seemingly minor question
provoked the ministers to convene in association and to
codify their practices in a manner that smacked of presbyterian church government. Some New Englanders found
themselves in a kind of semimembership somewhere between the elect and the damned, a puzzling reminder of
the ambiguities of change across generations.

Ultimately, in the latter half of the seventeenth century, many churches dispensed with the relation as a proof
of grace—a change greeted more favorably by ministers,
who wished to have substantial memberships, than by laymen, even those who failed to meet traditional requirements but still believed in their scriptural authority. To
alter those requirements, some felt, was to repudiate standards that had been dear to the generation of Cotton and
Winthrop; it was to prove false to the fathers. In the 1630s
the issue of church membership emboldened New Englanders to face up to the dilemma of nonseparating con-

gregationalism. After midcentury it became a smoldering issue suggesting the holy commonwealth was in decline.

CHANGE

The earliest New England writings furnished stirring images of the future. Winthrop's evocation of a "city on a hill" is only the best remembered of numerous depictions of the colossal implications of the Puritan enterprise. Many ministers spoke of the "last things," signs that a long, gloomy stage of human history was drawing to a close and that glorious conflicts revealed in biblical prophecies were nigh. It is never easy for human beings to sustain such feverish anticipation for very long. Even the most enthusiastic sects either disappear or consolidate into calmer organizations, perhaps awaiting future reawakening. New England was no exception. Historians of that tightly knit civilization have to take account of the fact that much of its literature formed a lament on diminished zeal and lost opportunity.

The belief that society was changing was not merely fanciful. Kenneth Lockridge concludes that the closed utopian institutions suffered so much erosion that subsequent generations' "famous laments over the decline of the spirit of the founders were fully justified by events." In the 1630s, when about twenty thousand English folk joined in "the Great Migration" to Massachusetts, it was possible to view town and church as harmonious creations of a direct laying on of hands by a covenanted people. This solidarity was reinforced by clear recollections of oppressive English circumstances that they wished to avoid. Before long, however, the town's business became the charge of aging officials who were regularly reelected. Families found ways to consolidate their private landholdings; some moved out of the villages, and others put up fences. Wealthy men managed to seal themselves off in large estates and to hire substitutes rather than join in the town's work. Court records show incessant quarrels over matters of pride and honor. In the church, fewer members rose to prominence by offering gripping narrations. After the 1660s groups of non-Puritans—Baptists, Scottish Presbyterians, Quakers, Anglicans—took an anomalous place within towns whose fundamental premises should have excluded them. As the senior worthies died off, it was possible to wonder whether God had turned his back on those who survived.

The civil wars in England (1642–1660) perplexed the Puritan enterprise in the New World. The wars altered the potential importance of events in Massachusetts and ended any promise of reforming the English church by good example. Some men hastened back to the main scene of conflict; those who stayed had to face the implications of colonial inconsequence. When the English Puritan army was forced to extend toleration to fighting men of radical sects, Massachusetts was pressured to abate its notorious intolerance. New World men had no say about the actions that led to the execution of the king and to Oliver Cromwell's dictatorship, but when monarchy was restored, the Puritans in New England were convenient symbols of a puritanical narrowness to be wiped out. They could no longer get away with expelling or whipping religious outsiders; nonseparating congregationalism became a thing of the past.

In the most resented turn of events, Massachusetts and other colonies in the 1680s lost their charters and were merged into a Dominion of New England ruled by a royal appointee. Even when new charters were secured, royal supervision remained a fact of life. While intellectual leaders made the best of their reverses, suppressed memories found their way into folklore. Tales of the atrocities of the royal governors became legendary, and stories spread of people in little towns hiding the judges who had condemned the king to death and who were hunted in New England after the Restoration. One of these fugitives, "the angel of Hadley," reportedly arose in ancient uniform to rally people in the West against Indian attacks that were further proof of Satan's machinations against the good society. These chimney-corner stories took their place alongside reports of witches and wondrous events; they kept alive the sense of New England's special attachment to providence. But in their own way they also expressed discomfort with an altered political order.

In some locations the ideal of the Puritan town—the ideal that had controlled the founding of the original towns—became almost unrecognizable. Certain port cities grew rapidly. Boston reached twelve thousand in 1720 and seventeen thousand in 1740—well beyond the several score of families once deemed ideal. In the cities some merchants became extremely wealthy, and much of the urban population had only a tenuous connection to Puritanism. The careers of Increase and Cotton Mather at North Church, Boston, must be understood in this context. On the one hand, they bickered with merchants who disliked the Calvinistic portrait of human nature and the restrictive system of church membership; they thought it undecorous to make a relation in church. By the 1670s some merchants were attracted to Anglicanism, sometimes intermarrying with wealthy English families. But Boston's growth, the congregational polity, and the Crown's insistence on toleration all prevented the Mathers from blocking the merchants' development of their own religious way. When wealthy men set up the new Brattle Street Church in 1698—with the minister Benjamin Colman who preached in favor of mirth and with liberalized requirements for the admission to the sacraments (all that was needed was "visible sanctity")—the Mathers could do nothing but seethe. When men of substance looking for handsomer pews seceded from Old North in 1713, the Mathers had to admit their church was overcrowded.

Keenly aware that the religious and social orders were diverging, the Mathers also directed their attention to sailors and the urban lower classes. Cotton Mather's *Bonifacius* or *Essays to Do Good* (1710) prescribed a concerted program of voluntary societies to succor the needy and restrain the vicious. The Mathers actually led about twenty such societies, bringing relief to those in distress, urging the magistrates to punish the wicked, and spreading "nets of salvation" to catch both the prosperous who gave alms and the paupers who received them. They made lists of men who frequented brothels and sent them letters of admonition. They also succeeded in organizing a society of free Negroes. Turning to an old theme, *Bonifacius* called for renewed efforts to Christianize the surviving Indians, "to keep a watchful inspection on their manners, and to make what progress we can in Anglicizing of them."

The subsequent influence of *Bonifacius* was enormous. Reprinted time and again, it has been called the prototype of middle-class Protestant moralism. But in its own time it bore witness to the irreversible fragmentation of Puritan control. When Cotton Mather summoned Christians to use "the intervals of our business" to ponder God's majesty, he admitted how much time was monopolized by other reckonings. The tactics of *Bonifacius* recognized that the magistrates needed prodding to enforce virtue. In pointing out that reform societies could unite men of different sects, it admitted the fact of religious diversity. And in warning do-gooders that they were likely to be ridiculed, it suggested that urban manners had retrogressed:"your civility may prove your disadvantage." One irreverent young artisan took the pen name "Silence DoGood" to poke fun at verbose busybodies. Years later, Benjamin Franklin confessed that the voluntary societies had furnished a useful model for his own projects, but his initial irreverence was symptomatic of what to the Puritans was a debilitated, faithless society.

Western settlements were also incongruous with the town ideal. While no one complained of any "lubber-land" in New England, the evolving social order of western towns scarcely resembled the perfections dreamed of in the Great Migration. When young people moved west, perhaps because the older towns had no more land to allot them, family controls broke down. New towns often had to go without churches; towns that were more fortunate were sometimes accused of underpaying their spiritual leaders. Those preachers who succeeded in overseeing large frontier areas—Solomon Stoddard of Northampton was the exemplar—worried that many families went their way outside the watch and care of the church. The Mathers stoutly attacked Stoddard for loosening the restrictions on communion and for publishing the *Doctrine of Instituted Churches* (1700), which seemed to dismiss the notion of congregational autonomy in favor of a more presbyterian form of organization. But it was questionable whether the old-style Puritan church, the voluntary creation of the regenerate, could be requickened in the West. Worse than the meanderings of simple folk outside the system of civility and piety was the rise to power in the West of wealthy men who lived in a sort of baronial autonomy—or so it seemed to orthodox minds in Boston. In the Connecticut River Valley, such men were called "river gods." Though none of them equaled William Byrd's splendid habits or prodigious learning, they were by no means men of humility. Their power implied a disintegration of towns living in a spirit of harmonious interdependence.

Population was never as scattered in New England as it was in the South, and even in the port cities Puritan ministers retained great authority. The sense of divergence between religious and secular life was hardly illusory, but it was disconcerting only because of memories of the intense initial commitment to a holy commonwealth. To bewail the divergence was, in effect, to reassert the importance of that early commitment and thus to shore up the intellectual dominance of Puritanism and its ministers.

Although the dispersion of the population and the widening social distance between rich and poor could be presented as signs of a failed mission, Puritanism became an expansive force in its own right, spreading the cultural assumptions of eastern Massachusetts across outlying areas. The much hated Dominion of New England ironically bolstered this force in the southern and western regions, wherever settlers contrasted the atrocities of royal government to the cherished purity of the Great Migration. In what the historian Charles E. Clark terms "the Puritan conquest," the congregational system, though with less severe membership requirements, moved northward into lands settled by fishermen and woodsmen, while whole communities made their incursions into agricultural areas and Puritan merchants took control of political centers and promising harbors. Since many Indians were half-Christianized by Canadian Jesuits, racial and religious warfare consolidated the allegiances of white outlanders with the New England Protestant heritage. Despite the dispersion, there was sufficient shared ideology that New England ministers, unlike European intellectuals, never complained that there were corners of the land with different ways of speaking and thinking.

To the modern eye, the effective way in which the New England ideology reached out over new areas is more impressive than any appearance of decline. Eventually New England–style towns would be carried across the continent to Oregon, and New England scholars would infuse their history into a general understanding of the unfolding American destiny. The premises of this history looked back in awe to the founders' intention to build a society that would glorify the Almighty. In Winthrop's lay sermon on the *Arbella* and in dozens of other early invocations, the founders had voiced the belief that in New England sacred and secular history flowed together. The rewards for success would be cosmic, but if the colonists dealt falsely with God, if their daily lives were impure—Winthrop and the others had warned—they would deserve unmitigated scorn and merciless punishment. From the earliest years the founders used public occasions—military musters, election days, fasts, and thanksgivings—to tote up the transgressions that endangered the special contract between the Puritan tribe and God. For these purposes they adapted a style of sermon, conventional enough in Europe, that condemned earthly vices: greed, pride, lust, insubordination, and other digressions from God's way. Speeches in this style have come to be known as jeremiads because of their resemblance to the cries of Old Testament prophets. New Englanders adapted the style with this difference: they did not simply contrast the vices to biblical moral standards; they regarded them as specific violations of the fathers' vision. Recording the disturbing tendencies of the day, from dancing to Sabbath-breaking and from price-gouging to political restiveness, while revering the holy purposes of the first generation, became the dominant form of literary expression in New England.

In trying to interpret such speeches, historians have enjoyed quarrels of their own over whether conditions could accurately be described as in decline. Probably the sanest judgments are those that treat the jeremiads as ritualistic reaffirmations of God's concern, as well as Satan's interference, with affairs in the New World. The jeremiads allowed the changing society to maintain a connection with the past and to emphasize the significance of present endeavors. The light of gospel judgment still burned fiercely over the land; there was still need for soul-searching; the future still was promising. The closest student of the jeremiads, Sacvan Bercovitch, sees "no threnody over a lost cause" but "unshakable optimism" about the eventual fulfillment of sacred purpose.

No one used the mode of the jeremiad more persistently than Cotton Mather, whose name recalled two devout grandfathers, John Cotton and Richard Mather. His *Magnalia Christi Americana* (1702), a history of the great deeds of Christ in America, proceeded for the most part through biographical sketches of departed worthies. In his skirmishes against the pretentious rich and degraded poor, he might well have forsaken the founders' confidence in New England's place in providential design. The "malicious and calumnious and abusive world" in which he preached might have appeared more like the Old World they left behind than the New World they sought to build. Yet the logic of the jeremiad emboldened Cotton Mather to believe that the conflicts and disappointments of his era heralded a climax of history, the millennium—that is, the thousand-year kingdom of Christ on earth that would precede the final judgment. In Cotton Mather we can see most clearly how the veneration of the fathers and inspection of contemporary sin served to disconnect "America"—a word he used triumphantly—from European history. In his account of John Eliot, for example, he wrote that the Atlantic, "like a River of Lethe," had caused forgetfulness of Europe. The work of saintly men had graced these shores, and perhaps the wonders and trials of the present age pointed toward Boston as the New Jerusalem.

One of Mather's contemporaries, Samuel Sewall, no less given to jeremiads but a much more graceful writer, left an image of the abiding faith of New England amid the passing duties of man and the changing seasons of nature. After speaking of church members in one coastal town, he wrote:

As long as Plum Island shall faithfully keep the commanded post, notwithstanding all the hectoring words and hard blows of the proud and boisterous ocean; as long as any salmon or sturgeon shall swim in the streams of the Merrimack; or any perch, or pickerel, in Crane Pond; as long as the sea-fowl shall know the time of their coming, and not neglect seasonably to visit the places of their acquaintance; as long as any cattle shall be fed with the grass growing in the meadows, which do humbly bow down themselves before Turkey Hill; as long as any sheep shall walk upon Old Town Hills, and shall from thence pleasantly look down upon the River Parker, and the fruitful marshes lying beneath; as long as any free and harmless doves shall find a white oak or other tree within the township, to perch, or feed, or build a careless nest upon, and shall voluntarily present themselves to perform the office of gleaners after barley-harvest; as long as Nature shall not grow old and dote, but shall constantly remember to give the rows of Indian corn their education, by pairs; so long shall Christians be born there, and being first made meet, shall from thence be translated, to be made partakers of the inheritance of the saints in light.

How different this account of the environment is from Robert Beverley's description of nature lulling Virginians into sloth. How eloquently it conveys the faith that the covenant continued to bless New England even in times of trial.

THE DIVIDED SOUL

Among the many paradoxes of Puritanism was its equal emphasis on the goodness of the created universe and the evil that dogged the path of human creatures. "O rational, immortal, Heaven-born SOUL, are thy wondrous faculties capable of no greater improvements, no better employments? Why should a soul of such high capacities, a soul that might arrive to be clothed in the bright scarlet of angels, yet embrace a dunghill?" This was Cotton Mather's critique of the time and energy men spent for "secular advantage" in their daily callings. In a broader view of nature, salvation would take place as surely as the doves gleaned the barley harvest. But when the Puritans looked at human nature, they saw ailments requiring the remedies of meditation and ruthless self-examination.

As Puritan ministers detailed the stages of conversion, they inevitably defined a psychological process. As would-be church members wrestled to distinguish authentic from counterfeit regeneration, as they plumbed the motives of such civility as they could muster, they fleshed out the same psychology. The utterances of both clergy and laity, moreover, focused on links between reason and religiosity that were becoming crucial issues for philosophy. For as Mather's remarks indicate, it was reason that ennobled the soul; yet a humiliating emotional introspection kept the true Christian from deadening pride. The relative merit of intellect and the emotions was a subject for earnest examination by Puritan thinkers.

The starting point was the faculty psychology lingering from the Middle Ages. Man was an intermediate creature, tugged toward vice by his base nature, lifted toward angelic purity by the higher elements of his soul. In this virtually unquestioned view, the soul was not biologically reproduced; it was separately transmitted by God, and it was immortal. The details of mental process were so intricate that modern students may have difficulty in believing that anyone ever gave them credence.* Yet they made sense of commonly perceived drives and conflicts, and Puritans simply alluded to them as familiar to all thinking people. Briefly put, the brain had many chambers in which different faculties were lodged, among them the imagination, the common sense, and the memory. The imagination formed an image of an object presenting itself to the senses; the common sense sorted out this image from others; and the memory kept the image to be dredged up for further comparison. As the reason, or understanding, sat in judgment over this process, it took counsel from the conscience, which related God's opinion of a proposed action. The reason could then send directions for an appropriate response—or an inappropriate one, if the process worked faultily—to the will, which resided in the heart. Although the reason was associated with angelic or pre-Adamic purity, there was always the danger of its judgment being clouded by the passions or appetites. It was one thing for the will, in control of the passions, to mobilize the muscles for correct action; it was quite another

*Perhaps it is easier to understand "faculties" if we remember that in our century psychologists use similar terminology to speak of ego, id, and superego or even of left-hemisphere and right-hemisphere functions in the brain. But the heart has not for a long time had much psychological function except in popular songs.

for the passions, like stormy winds, to blow the sinner off course.

For our purposes, it is essential to note, not the elaborate structure of different faculties, but the divided and potentially rebellious state of human nature that this view depicted. Prior to the Fall, Adam and Eve had a clarity of perception similar to that of the angels. The English Puritan poet John Milton illuminated the aftermath of the Fall in a memorable passage of *Paradise Lost* (1674). In their shame, looking for leaves to cover their nakedness, Adam and Eve experienced the change in mental function that infected their posterity:

> *They sat them down to weep, nor only Tears*
> *Rain'd at their eyes, but high Winds worse within*
> *Began to rise, high Passions, Anger, Hate,*
> *Mistrust, Suspicion, Discord, and shook sore*
> *Their inward State of Mind, calm Region once*
> *And full of Peace, now toss't and turbulent:*
> *For Understanding rul'd not, and the Will*
> *Heard not her lore, both in subjection now*
> *To sensual Appetite, who from beneath*
> *Usurping over sovran Reason claimed*
> *Superior sway.*

It was not entirely clear how the regenerate experienced the grace that justified them and restored them to some semblance of angelic clarity. No doubt the Holy Ghost implanted the impression of grace, but what faculty initially received it? Since reason was the highest faculty and God had covenanted to act reasonably, some thought of grace as predominantly intellectual. Solomon Stoddard, for example, subscribed to the traditional formula that "the will always follows the last dictates of the understanding."

Thus it was "a spiritual sight of the glory of God" presented to the reason that brought men and women to obedience to God. But other Puritans followed a different tradition built on the recognition that many sinners understood perfectly well what was right, but still acted in an evil manner. In this view, grace must affect the will in what may be called a more emotional process. The influential minister Samuel Willard explained: "All true obedience is rooted in the heart, which firstly points to the will in man, which is in him the supreme faculty, and unless that be devoted to the service of God, all else that he doth, though it carry never so fair a show with it, cannot properly be called obedience." Both positions were intellectually respectable. In the actual practice of the ministry there might be little difference between men who referred to sovereign reason and those who viewed the will as supreme.

The truth is that clear reason and emotional will both figured in the seventeenth-century Puritan approach to religious conviction. The Bible kept the search on an orderly, intellectual plane. Sermons tirelessly laid out the doctrines found in scriptural passages, the reasons for them, and the uses to be made of them, always with the assumption that the unregenerate would find much to disagree with. The rebellion against truth and law was central to the preconversion groping for assurance, and saints reported how the Lord finally "met" them in a particular verse of the Bible. Church members would question closely any applicant who had avoided this stage of intellectual alienation and conviction. If an applicant failed to tell "what scripture or word he minds to have stood by him" in moments of doubt, there were grounds for suspecting this person of hypocrisy. In Puritanism superstitious uses of the Bible (like Dane's finger pointing to a magical passage) were subsumed within a rational drama of dissenting from and then coming to understand a doctrine.

Stoddard's grandson, Jonathan Edwards, born in 1703, left moving accounts of this internal drama. He reported that "from my childhood up" his mind had objected to the doctrine of God's sovereignty "in choosing whom He would to eternal life, and rejecting whom He pleased." That God should leave the rejects to everlasting torment appeared to be "a horrible doctrine." But the time came when "I seemed to be convinced, and fully satisfied, as to this sovereignty of God, and His justice in thus eternally disposing of men." Edwards was unable to explain at first why his mind changed, for he did not apprehend that "an extraordinary influence of God's spirit" had been received. It was an intellectual transformation for which he could not give an explanation: "my reason apprehended the justice and reasonableness" of the doctrine; "my mind rested in it; and it put an end to all those cavils and objections." Eventually the change in reasoning had an effect in how he felt about the doctrine. "I have often since had not only a conviction, but a delightful conviction. The doctrine has very often appeared exceedingly pleasant, bright and sweet. Absolute sovereignty is what I love to ascribe to God. But my first conviction was not so." Edwards's reason, aided by the Holy Ghost, had redirected his will and brought his emotional life into new harmony.

The drama of objection followed by assurance could center on a particular passage of the Bible. The youthful Edwards regarded as "insipid" the text that says "one generation passeth away and another cometh, but the earth abideth forever." The death of older people was, as we have seen, a key subject in New England's historical consciousness, but what purpose did it serve to recall that the earth endured? The moment came, however, when his understanding of this passage changed, and this time the process went beyond strictly intellectual illumination:

> Upon an occasion, I was more than ordinarily affected with the passing of one generation after another; how all those, who made such a noise and bluster now, and were so much concerned about their life, would be clean gone off from the face of the earth in sixty or seventy years time, and that the world would be left desolate with respect to them, and that another generation would come on, that would be very little concerned about them, and so one after another: it was particularly affecting to me to think that the earth still remained the same through all these changes upon the surface: the same spots of ground, the same mountains and valleys where those things were done, remaining just as they were, though the actors ceased, and the actors just gone. And then this text came into my mind.

These reflections reverse the images of human change and natural continuity in Sewall's hymn to Plum Island, and in this instance the immediate concern is not the collective destiny of the Puritans but the internal drama of consciousness. The struggle seems less purely intellectual than in Edwards's encounters with the doctrine of divine sovereignty. The emotions affecting him, rather than any clearing away of cavils and objections, moved him to assent.

As we shall see, Edwards eventually became a predominant figure in an era when the role of the emotions became the critical issue in religious controversy. But even in the New England of his forebears, it was understood that no one could reason his way to grace. The passions could do mighty harm, but they were natural elements in human psychology, not to be deadened and suppressed. While the ministers addressed logical sermons to the intellect, they also labored to break down the formalities and rationalizations by which the sinner ducked his hopelessness. They worked to create an emotional state that prepared the individual for grace. This state was not one of emotional abandon; the individual sought a "serious heart." While the relations offered by church members mentioned intellectual consent to scriptural passages, they also detailed intense moods of fear and despair that preceded an almost mystical rapture when the Holy Spirit ravished the defenseless heart.

Was New England Puritanism more heavily weighted toward intellectual or emotional life? The question might seem contrived, were it not for the Puritans' fascination with the division of the soul. On the side of intellectual life, we may note the importance attached to a learned ministry preaching from well-organized notes to explicate the meanings and uses of Scripture. In keeping with such instruction, much of the population strove for clear mental functioning and intellectual acceptance of the Bible as signs of regeneration. Yet on the side of emotional life, we may recall that it was purification of the heart that the much denounced civil man had not attained. A relentlessly probing introspection, with a passionate rhythm of depression and exaltation, of doubt and hope, was requisite to assurance of salvation. Though the austerity of membership requirements imposed some restraints, there is no overlooking the ecstatic transports that the regenerate could recount after their closure with Christ. After John Winthrop had "grown familiar with the Lord Jesus Christ," he was constantly soothed with love. "He lay down with me, and usually I did awake with him: and so sweet was his love to me, as I desired nothing but him in heaven or earth."

The sermons usually stressed the intellectual aspects of faith, but the laity could not avoid a more complex self-examination. In a great sermon, "Meditation," preached in Connecticut in the 1650s, Thomas Hooker dissected the process. It began with the "serious intention of mind" to keep in view its utter sinfulness. It proceeded to a battering of the heart that would leave ordinary sinners in a melancholy condition. But for the regenerate this humiliation was "as the setting open of the floodgates, which carries the soul with a kind of force and violence, to the performance of what he so bestows his mind upon, as a mighty stream lets out a mill." The outcome was "like raising a tempest in the heart, that carries out all the actions of the man by an uncontrolled command." The Puritans have been called the "self-suppressed" because of the force with which one set of feelings overcame another. Reason had dominion over the will, to be sure, but the passion of the total experience is unmistakable. In the quest for salvation that shaped character and singled out the elect in New England, powerfully emotional impulses could not be checked.

In their view of the functioning of the soul, Hooker and the first-generation New England Puritans differed little from Cotton Mather and his contemporaries a half-century later. Both the illuminated reason and burning passions characterized the truly regenerate person. The faculty psychology served to express a dynamic appreciation of how the mind operated, and the same human nature was found in a Cambridge- or Harvard-educated man and in a semiliterate man in the fields. The New England poet Edward Taylor recorded beautiful images of the first sensations of grace, which left his heart an inflammable tinder box. He asked God to turn his laws into a garment of heavenly color,

> *Then clothe therewith mine Understanding, Will,*
> *   Affections, Judgment, Conscience, Memory;*
> *My Words and Actions, that their shine may fill*
> *My ways with glory and thee glorify.*

Views of human nature ordinarily resist rapid changes in fashion. There were by Mather's time subtle variations in the emphasis that spokesmen for different social groups put forward. Ministers like Benjamin Colman, some college professors, and other leaders who were attentive to the sensitivities of wealthy third- and fourth-generation New Englanders tended to dissociate the intellect from earlier images of coordinated mental activity. Though mirth was innocent enough, passionate outbursts looked vulgar, ungenteel. Meanwhile the Mathers and others who sought to renew piety in a disintegrating society sometimes found themselves concentrating entirely on the heart. Men of the first persuasion wrote paeans to the reason. One Harvard professor noted that "I have hardly at all allowed myself to address the passions. . . . I have studied to preserve a due moderation and temper, which the laws of civility and Christianity oblige to." Conversely, the Mather coterie became in curious ways anti-intellectual, fearful that the apotheosis of reason was leading people away from the Bible. According to one of the Mathers' followers, "your hearts are the principal and most peculiar things which God regards." Now *reason* was emerging as the key word in a new taste for upper-class respectability; *the heart* was the key phrase in countervailing movements for popular piety.

We should take care not to exaggerate this split. No one was likely to state that his view of psychology was a new one or that it differed substantially from that of his opponents. Instead they bantered with one another from within the old view of the soul's coordination. Yet it was becoming evident that men of reason could be distinguished from people of the heart in partisan definitions of human psychology—a split that would alter intellectual life later in the eighteenth century. As the distinctions hardened, old conceptions of civility and virtuosity within a covenant that restrained human pride and consecrated the entire society to God's service were lost. A more stratified understanding of human nature took their place, one in which contrasting modes of feeling and thinking pertained to different social classes. We shall pursue these themes in the next chapter. First, however, it will be useful to take a summary look at intellectual life in early New England.

In the preceding chapter we noticed that "the battle between Reason and Passion" was subdued in southern colonies where an aristocratic class achieved an impressive hegemony. Virginia lacked a distinct intellectual class to worry about such questions publicly: the powerful landowners adapted the model of English virtuosity to make their cultural possessions—their gardens and libraries—the signs of legitimate rule. Everyone acknowledged the variations among the habits of different classes, regions, and ethnic groups. If anyone invented categories to point out common terms of existence, those categories had more to do with how the environment altered English norms than with how providence treated shared aspirations. Aristocrats pictured themselves as men of moderation within a rawly competitive society, but they did not batter their souls too persistently with threats of perdition. Ministers were scarce and, by some accounts, uninspiring; in any event, they lacked the security required to uphold doctrines of human nature or social obligation inconsistent with the gentlemen's world view.

In New England's intellectual life, entirely different issues stood foremost. There was an intellectual class, the clergy, whose members were well educated, dispersed throughout the region, in frequent communication with one another, and secure in their incomes. This class regularly analyzed the directions of the intellect and promptings of the passions, and it did so within a seldom challenged ideology of collective holy purpose. Their writings show much concern for improving the patterns of English town living so that they would meet biblical standards of justice; they gave little countenance to the pretensions of would-be aristocrats. None of them championed social equality: if "the people" dressed like "gentlemen" or behaved in surly manner, and if the wealthy were greedy or insolent, these were terrible invitations to God's wrath. While social distinctions were inevitable, the ministers viewed cultural diversity with utter intolerance. They sought to Anglicize Indians and to exclude religious and ethnic groups who in New England would have been deviants. Their success, imperfect at best, was frustrated by the politics of the charter, but there is no mistaking the extension of the New England Way over the fishermen and western farmers. Just how many New Englanders were indifferent to their preaching will never be known, but for several generations the ministers spoke confidently as teachers and pastors to everybody.

The ministers existed within the social structure of the towns. They were not a celibate priesthood lifted above other men. They had no supernatural powers, though their preaching was the ordinary means by which God communicated with the temporal world. Distinguished by their learning, these emissaries of Christ in the first generation constituted a highly respected intelligentsia, consulted on earthly problems as well as sacred matters. In later years, Harvard-trained ministers sometimes felt remote from Europe's intellectual centers. "I have so long conversed with oaks and Indians," wrote a Connecticut minister to an esteemed English Puritan in 1669, "that I find myself very much disenabled to manage any due and humble intercourse with those that are so much exalted in the more ocular and curious societies of men." Such ministers cultivated qualities of meekness quite different from the imperious manners of many first-generation ministers. Yet they remained a special class of gentlemen, often connected by their own marriages and their children's to wealthy mercantile families. They wore fine clothes and (despite some protests) periwigs. In their own way, they may be said to have conferred the prestige of learning on the wealthy class, though it was not their chief function and the fashion was very different from the self-embellishment of the Virginia aristocracy.

Yet there proved to be something ephemeral—in retrospect it looks contradictory—about an intellectual class with a firmly implanted location in a scheme of power and subjection. The ministers' attention to preaching and publishing differentiated them from men who amassed wealth in other ways. Their roles as meek spiritual guides to the generality of people jeopardized their eminence in a society that was never frozen within the lines of traditional hierarchy. The duty to upbraid the rich, seldom overlooked in jeremiads, could also fray connections with the gentlemanly class.

It is not hard to understand why some men of substance, even when they remained Puritans, eventually enlisted a less austere ministry, thus introducing distinctions within the ranks of the intellectual class. Nor is it hard to see why the Mathers found themselves in a middle position between temporizing merchants and the godless population of the docks. As the cleavage between reason and the heart widened, some ministers went on to voice popular resentment of wealth; others became wealth's servants. Still others would redefine themselves as a new category of humble spiritual men, outside the class structure. Eventually it would be possible for some men to re-conceptualize intellectual life so totally that they made no reference at all to the ministerial profession. Though for centuries some Americans would look back to the Puritan fathers to moor their destiny, their organization of intellectual life was left behind forever.

FOR FURTHER READING

The best introduction to American philosophy, beginning with the Puritans and relevant to many topics in subsequent chapters of this book, is Murray G. Murphey and Elizabeth Flower, *A History of Philosophy in America* (1973). Helpful comments on Puritanism and popular culture are found in David D. Hall's essay in another wide-ranging book: John Higham and Paul K. Conkin, eds., *New Directions in American Intellectual History* (1979).

The magisterial historian of the New England Puritans is Perry Miller. For his major works on Puritanism, see *Orthodoxy in Massachusetts, 1630–1650* (1933); *The New England Mind: The Seventeenth Century* (1939); and *The New England Mind: From Colony to Province* (1953). Some useful corrections of Miller's interpretations are found in David D. Hall, *The Faithful Shepherd: A History of the New England Ministry in the Seventeenth Century* (1972). A recent survey, intended for students, is Francis J. Bremer, *The Puritan Experiment* (1976).

Edmund S. Morgan is another master of Puritan studies. His highly readable works include a life of John Winthrop, *The Puritan Dilemma* (1958); a study of social relations, *The Puritan Family* (1966); an illuminating essay on church membership, *Visible Saints* (1963); and a study of a Puritan rebel, *Roger Williams* (1967). A narrative of the troubles with Anne Hutchinson is Emery Battis, *Saints and Sectaries* (1962).

The best approach to civil life is through the studies of towns and cities, for example, Sumner Chilton Powell, *Puritan Village* (1963), and Darrett B. Rutman, *Winthrop's Boston* (1965). Kenneth Lockridge's *A New England Town* (1970) stresses the peasant outlook of ordinary New Englanders. A valuable study of Puritan social philosophy is Stephen Foster, *Their Solitary Way* (1971). For an analysis of an eighteenth-century Puritan, using some of the methods of modern anthropology, see David D. Hall, "The Mental World of Samuel Sewall," *Proceedings of the Massachusetts Historical Society* (1980).

On virtuosity among the Puritans (and other colonials), see Raymond Phineas Stearns, *Science in the British Colonies of America* (1970). There are two excellent modern studies of the Mathers: Robert Middlekauff, *The Mathers* (1971); and David Levin, *Cotton Mather* (1978).

On the extension of the New England ideology to outlying areas, see Charles E. Clark, *The Eastern Frontier: The Settlement of Northern New England* (1970), and Paul R. Lucas, *Valley of Discord: Church and Society along the Connecticut River* (1976). Sacvan Bercovitch has offered two provocative essays on the persisting influence of Puritan ideology: *The Puritan Origins of the American Self* (1975); and *The American Jeremiad* (1978).

For a brief introduction to Puritan ideas about psychology, see J. Rodney Fulcher, "Puritans and Passions: The Faculty Psychology in American Puritanism," *Journal of the History of the Behavioral Sciences* (1973). The most authoritative discussion of these ideas appears in a difficult but penetrating reexamination of Puritanism: Norman Fiering's *Moral Philosophy at Seventeenth-Century Harvard* (1981). Interesting broad generalizations about personality may be encountered in Philip Greven, *The Protestant Temperament* (1977).

Those who wish to read the Puritans' own writings should begin with Perry Miller and Thomas H. Johnson, eds., *The Puritans* (2 vols, 1963). The dry bones of church membership and discipline come to life in Robert G. Pope, ed., *The Notebook of the Reverend John Fiske* (1974). The anguish of a Puritan merchant is evident in Bernard Bailyn, ed., *The Apologia of Robert Keayne* (1965).

AWAKENING AND ENLIGHTENMENT

THE SURPRISING
WORK OF GOD

Fire and light were potent images for early settlers in the New World. Theirs was a colder and darker world than ours. They rose and went to bed earlier than we do. Farming people never lost sight of the cycles of darkness and light, the shorter and longer days that determined how their hours were spent. They had good reason to believe that the Son of God came to life in the season when the sun begins to emerge from the blackness of winter. Town dwellers were ever conscious of the daily routines of lighting fires. When preacher or poet compared grace to a spark in a tinder box, he referred to the common awareness of how light broke into the shadows that covered everybody.

In a world of frame houses fire was not always beneficial. Like many other settlers, John Dane in 1661 watched his house burn down. He consoled himself by remembering special "providences" that followed the loss of shelter and provisions: his health improved, his swine grew fat from eating burned corn, and he was able to feed the good friends who helped him rebuild his home. In Boston ru-

[97]

mors of fire sent men and women into panic. When bells
and gunshots announced the birth of a male child to King
James II, people rushed into the streets in fear that the
sounds brought warnings of flames. Even prayers in church
stopped short at a cry of "fire." Sometimes house fires were
started by unfaithful servants and slaves. To commemo-
rate the defeat of the wicked Catholic incendiary Guy
Fawkes, the lower classes lit bonfires and burned effigies
of the pope and the devil. Satan entertained his converts
around fires.

These associations with fire and light remind us of the
folklore of agricultural life that blended into Christian
theology. Spooky tales told in chimney corners, the ashes
of burned-down houses, torchlit holidays, the warmth of
the sun, the bonfires of hell, and the light of Christ—all
had their places in the New World experience. These associations were not restricted to simple folk. Urbane Samuel Sewall noted in his diary that the children fled into his
room after an earthquake, lit a fire, and huddled together all night. When a new town hall was built, he prayed
that the light flowing through a "large, transparent, costly
glass" would help place the deliberations of men in a truly
God-given light.

In the eighteenth century a perception became popular that human affairs were somehow changing. Much
of life still obeyed the traditional rhythms of darkness and
light, but more was to be expected than endless ignorance
and disobedience brightened by occasional sparks of faith.
New expectations went beyond small communities with
special links to God. The almost inevitable metaphor was
of "further light"—more than in Abraham's time, more
even than in the days of the founders—spreading across
America and the globe. In the eyes of some colonists, the
change was a morning or springtime of faith, a great

"awakening" in which the truth of religion reached the hearts of more of the people. Hosts of converts, called "new lights," were beginning the work that would lead to God's promised harvest. But not everyone believed that these hopes would bear good fruit. Some viewed the new lights as benighted folk playing recklessly with fire. True social progress would come through extension of the light of reason, and opponents of the awakening preferred the term "enlightenment" to describe hopeful tendencies in the world around them.

The clash between two perceptions of the spreading light embittered localities; at the same time, it raised persistent questions about intellectual life throughout the North American colonies. Should the heat of passion or the clarity of reason predominate in human affairs? The issue engaged speakers and writers in southern and middle colonies as well as in New England. How deep and how permanent were the transformations in feeling and thought? Was this one more rotation in the cycles of experience, or had a brightness come to illuminate all the dark corners of America?

The religious awakening hit towns in western New England that for decades had been scenes of bickering over church membership. Ministers, following the leadership of Solomon Stoddard, tried to reform the churches by using the sacrament of the Lord's Supper and other ceremonies to draw new converts into fellowship. Sometimes, after an earthquake, Indian attack, epidemic, or other calamity, this tactic succeeded in moving scores of men and women to a lively concern for their piety. But in many towns nonmembers were pursuing a "reformation" of their own, with greater emphasis on moral behavior and good character. It was not uncommon for nonmembers to use the town meetings, since they had no vote in church, to get rid of the wielders of sacraments and to reinstitute the churches under lay control. In 1714 a council of ministers, led by Stoddard, tried to dissuade the people of Enfield, Massachusetts (now Connecticut), from driving out their minister. Their failure marked a low point in ministerial morale.

Stoddard was famous for years of combating other ministers, particularly the Mathers, over the forms of church government. In a 1718 pamphlet he confessed that the ministers had been reasonably flexible, but the ignorance and hostility of the laity, who had great power in the congregational system, were ruining the churches. In a series of other publications up to his death in 1729, Stoddard denounced the worldliness that had seeped into the New England Way. Too many ministers had meekly submitted to the laymen's concern for their comfort. The only remedy was a hard-hitting style of preaching that Stoddard immodestly felt explained his own success in Northampton. In a sermon called "The Defects of Preachers" (1723) he warned that "learning and morality" did not provide an adequate foundation for effective sermons. A minister must be inspired by his personal experience of grace. He should speak without notes and avoid any trace of dullness as he drove home the fear of damnation, the worthlessness of reasonable civil lives, and the inescapable necessity for a particular moment of "intuition" when grace came to the sinner. Too many sermons allowed the flock to nod off into assurance that if their lives were moral and if they concurred intellectually with Christian doctrines, they had grounds for hope.

Many western ministers did their best to repair morale by taking Stoddard's advice. They looked for evidence that "powerful preaching" would evangelize the people, restore ministerial control, and stifle the contentiousness of churches and towns. From the 1720s on, there were heartening reports of mass conversions in great "outpourings of the Spirit." Stoddard's grandson Jonathan Edwards, who joined him in the Northampton pulpit in 1727 and stayed on after his death, saw the ministerial labors—or those of the Holy Spirit—reach fruition in the mid-1730s. In *A Faithful Narrative of the Surprising Work of God* (1736), the first of many works that made him world-famous, he reported "general awakenings" on an unprecedented scale. In his parish the wildest young people had been terror-stricken and brought around to thoughts of religion. Older people and even children experienced similar conversions, and almost every household became a haven of intense joy. He provided stunning descriptions of the transformations of two females—one a young invalid who died in bliss, the other a four-year-old with deep feelings for the poor. Strangers came to scoff at Northampton's distempers and went away amazed at the nearly indescribable exaltation of the town. Edwards detailed the differences in individual conversions: after humiliating terror some persons were brought suddenly into "glorious brightness"; others felt first a little light, "like the dawning of the day," which gradually grew brighter; still others were uncertain when the light first came; and a few had experiences that were undoubtedly delusions. It was clear that the intense public discussion of conversions and the spectacle of scores of converts had an inspiring effect on those who had formerly been Christless. And news of similar events in other towns, as well as in the middle colonies, propelled the work to further heights. Edwards depicted his own role, not as that of a revivalist drumming up conversions, but as that of a guide, helping individuals to sort out genuine light from vain imaginings.

Edwards was obliged to conclude that the awakening had been stalled or, as he put it, the Holy Spirit had withdrawn from the work. In the midst of all this emotional intensity, a merchant gentleman, Edwards's uncle by marriage, had become deeply depressed and cut his throat. Then "multitudes" had had to "fight with all their might" to resist suicidal impulses. In the aftermath conversions were rare, though Edwards reported that good effects remained. Rough men had been "remarkably softened and sweetened," and many were still filled with light and love. Within a few years, moreover, the Holy Spirit returned, and mass conversions began again. In the second wave of awakenings Edwards preached the well-known sermon, "Sinners in the Hands of an Angry God" (1741), with its elaborate simile of a wrathful hand dangling a human soul like a spider over the flames. He delivered it as a visitor to Enfield, where the once contentious laymen shrieked and moaned uncontrollably. As in the first wave, terror preceded the bliss of regeneration.

While Edwards occasionally asserted that the new conversions resembled those witnessed by his grandfather, that was mainly a response to critics of a novel and threatening emotionalism. Page after page of the narrative made it clear that the laity had behaved astonishingly. The events had a momentum that had to be narrated faithfully, with attention to different ranks, ages, and sexes, before the comprehensive work of the Spirit could be appreciated. Edwards at this stage discounted rumors that "the world was near to an end." But he also observed that those who knew the most about religion—and Northampton was a town "where there has always been a great deal of talk of conversion and spiritual experiences"—were most "confounded" by the extraordinary experience. Readers 250 years later naturally make comparisons to types of revivals that have become routine in American Protestantism, but Edwards was struggling to give an accurate account of events that had an exhilarating, if sometimes, deadly spontaneity.

One cherished quality of the Northampton awakening was that everyone listened seriously to the minister, though with more cries and tears than ever before. On the whole, however, the events that followed did not reunite the laity or refurbish ministerial authority. In many ways the campaign initiated by Stoddard and his colleagues backfired, undermining their own supremacy and encouraging a spirit of deeper rebelliousness. The ministers had accepted a certain amount of itinerancy to go along with "powerful preaching." Thus Edwards visited Enfield and other towns, and a few ministers lived as traveling evangelicals. By the 1740s, however, the experiment was in danger of getting out of control. Some men who had no training or standing as ministers gathered followings. From outside New England came marvelously effective speakers who drew great throngs. But when they hammered at the theme that unconverted ministers harmed their congregations, their listeners were tempted to despise rather than respect local pastors. Not only did the itinerants speak without notes, but sometimes their ranting and crying struck critical observers—respectable ministers and political leaders—as more appropriate to the theater than to the meetinghouse. Supposed converts swooned, writhed, or laughed uncontrollably, and some exhorters encouraged the belief that these were true signs of grace. In some cities converts burned books and denounced local authorities. Even where crowd behavior was less extravagant, there was a tendency for small bands of holy men and women to wander off on the old path of separatism. They dismissed the old churches as unsanctified and demanded religious liberty for themselves.

Edwards and other ministers of the mid-eighteenth century were caught in the middle of a storm. They wished to preserve the "wondrous" effects of the Holy Spirit and, at the same time, to keep the awakening within established institutions. Yet they could not suppress movements teaching common people that God had shed new light on America: "Be entreated no longer to take things by tradition." Ultimately these movements were more damaging than Quakers, Anglicans, and other sects that had previously been accorded a grudging toleration. The new sects, loosely federated as the Separate Baptists, had broken off from Puritanism itself in the name of greater purity. After the late 1750s the call to remove state support of the churches never died out. The call came from pious men and women, some of whom went to jail for their insubordination. After the Revolution it was inevitable that New England congregationalism would be disestablished.

The awakenings had another consequence. They emboldened a liberal, rationalistic element to enter intellectual discourse more actively than before. Previously in the thickly settled eastern areas there was a covert tendency among many ministers to preach only a moderate Calvinism. The Mathers occasionally fulminated against this tendency; others complained that young Harvard students overestimated the worth of human free will and virtuous works. It was undoubtedly true that wealth and education weakened attachments to the most miserable views of human ability to withstand the scrutiny of the Almighty Sovereign. But the covenant theology had permitted many variations of orthodoxy, and the nondogmatic "free and catholic" temper of almost all English theolo-

gians after the Restoration influenced literate colonials.*
There were shadings of opinion among the eastern ministers, and a few actually took ordination as Anglicans; but
there were no great fissures in the clergy.

Some Boston ministers were initially delighted at events
in Northampton. Edwards's *Narrative* actually took the form
of a letter to Benjamin Colman, and the ministers invited
the great English evangelist George Whitefield to venture
onward from the South to preach in New England
meetinghouses and in the open air of Boston Common and
Harvard Yard. As the pattern of events became more disturbing, however, some of the moderates found themselves reformulating their views. The most notable was
Charles Chauncy, who reportedly traveled three hundred
miles, consulting with scores of ministers and town leaders, to gather evidence of the excesses of the awakenings.
It took eighteen pages to list all the sponsors of his blast-
ing critique, *Seasonable Thoughts on the State of Religion in
New England* (1743). Chauncy's reportage was even more
detailed than Edwards's, and its governing assumption was

---

*The word *catholic*, with a lower-case *c*, did not refer to Roman Catholicism. It referred instead to a spirit of nondogmatic inclusiveness intended to restore the Church of England as a national entity after the
hostilities of the civil wars. The word *liberal* is used in this chapter to
refer, not to political doctrines, but to anti-Calvinistic tendencies in
eighteenth-century religion, including greater respect for human nature and less emphasis on divine judgment. Men of catholic temperament might well hold liberal views, as they tried to interpret religious
issues with as much "latitude" as possible, thus blurring sectarian distinctions with regard to sin and grace. They were likely to preach that
this was the best of all possible worlds in which human reason and
feelings provided a secure basis for moral behavior. Where they emphasized reason or the feelings I have used the terms *rationalist* and
sentimental, respectively, though both these terms have more precise,
technical meanings in philosophy.

that here was a history, not of God's "surprising" work, but of human delusion. Chauncy scolded ministers who neglected their parishes to preach elsewhere: if everyone did this, there would be "no such thing as *Church Order* in the land." He ridiculed uneducated laymen who presumed to preach: this was as foolish a disruption of the natural order of society as for ministers to pretend to be mechanics. He denounced the anti-intellectualism of the awakenings (Whitefield had said, "As for the universities, . . . their light is become darkness") and the lack of Christian meekness in assaults on the unconverted. He criticized the unscriptural solicitude that allowed women to speak and permitted people to praise "womanly" feelings in men. He had only contempt for the shriekings and swoonings. The pathetic intimations of the millennium led only to wrangling about matters beyond human ken. Chauncy had no patience with Edwards's efforts to sort out divine from erroneous aspects of the extraordinary events. If all the disorderly, uneducated, and deluded manifestations were subtracted, nothing would be left to make current religious practice "different from what it used to be."

Chauncy took the stance of a defender of Puritan orthodoxy. During the early 1740s he and other "opposers" wrote tracts and sermons citing John Winthrop, Thomas Shepard, and other old worthies and reasserting the time-honored views of the ways in which the Holy Spirit operated. The awakening stood condemned by its own novelty. The opposers were not content, however, to compare new heresies with old extravagances or to contrast modern rabble rousers to the traditional local pastor. As they proceeded in more secular terms to define the awakenings as an unfortunate episode in mass psychology, they centered their attack on misguided invitations to the passions. The evidence of insanity, on the part of both laymen and itinerant ministers, was dreadful enough. But the entire drift of the awakenings was to rely on emotionalism where reason ought to lead. To describe this drift, Chauncy used the smear word of the time, "enthusiasm," which implied a disregard for biblical revelation in favor of imaginary visitations of the Spirit. "The human passions" were, to be sure, "capable of serving many valuable purposes in religion"; they might "to good advantage be excited and warmed" so long as they were "kept under the restraints of reason. . . . Light and heat should always go together." There was no mistaking which was more valuable. "The plain truth is, an enlightened mind, and not the rais'd affections, ought always to be the guide of those who call themselves men." Chauncy identified a character type in whom this guide prevailed: "There is such a thing as real religion . . . and 'tis, in its nature, a sober, calm, reasonable thing" to be observed in "the conduct of men of sound judgment."

Chauncy at times spoke the language of the old faculty psychology, reminding his readers of the corruptions of original sin and the struggle for control of the will. There was nothing new in linking the passions to lower-class or feminine insolence and the reason to worthy leaders of society. In criticizing the tumult of the awakenings, however, Chauncy went a step further toward freeing the reason than the Puritans had dared to go in earlier treatises on meditation. Sedate behavior looked more meritorious than it had in old Puritan dissections of religious motivation. In the growing opposition to evangelicalism, furthermore, Chauncy's revised positions earned the respect of many colleagues. His was not a lonely fight. In the long run he led others to articulate an increasingly liberal theology that questioned the fundamental doctrine of human depravity—a doctrine that had long been the bedrock of Calvinism, but one that now seemed responsible for popular convulsions. Chauncy is usually considered a forerunner of Unitarianism, which several decades later won over many eastern, once Puritan churches.

Among the consequences of this opposition to the awakenings was a style of intellectual life and disputation that called for intensive study of biblical languages in order to reexamine traditional doctrines. Chauncy, for example, devoted seven years after the awakenings to linguistic study of the Bible in a "free, impartial, and diligent manner." Eventually religious controversy required a scholarly, analytical stance that had not previously been prominent in the ministry or any other profession. Furthermore, as the liberal-minded opposers fortified the claims of reason over religious emotionalism, they lowered the barriers around the ministry as the specific intellectual class. They saw themselves in alliance with educated merchants, physicians, and lawyers, men of "sound judgment" with whom they soon joined in high-minded urban clubs. Bitterness among ministerial factions may also have made other professions more attractive. The young John Adams saw so much wrangling between his liberal minister and the people of his congregation and such a vehement pamphlet warfare over the points of Calvinism that he decided he was not "made for a pulpit in such times" and "began to think of other professions." In the law he enjoyed political discussions with men of "urbanity, candor, and politeness," and he steered clear of theological controversies over matters beyond human understanding.

Inland, Jonathan Edwards tried valiantly to expose the fraudulence of unwelcome deviations to the left and right, to steer Christians away from false hopes in the excessive emotions unleashed by the wilder preachers and at the same time to destroy the rational pretensions of seaboard liberals. Inevitably, his writings turned to psychology. In two great works, *The Distinguishing Marks of a Work of the Spirit of God* (1741) and *A Treatise concerning Religious Affections* (1746), he laid the basis for a distinctively American theology based on revivalism. It has sometimes been claimed that in these works he was the first American thinker to accord major importance to the emotions. That is false: no Puritan had denied that both sin and grace had emotional dimensions. On many occasions Edwards reiterated the formulation that there must be both "light and heat." But from his western perspective as a defender of the awakenings, he started from an unquestioning belief that God was acting in unprecedented ways and on a glorious scale. Eventually he dared to believe that the millennium, "the most glorious renovation of the world," had originated in America. Therefore, while he agreed with Chauncy that there was too much madness and delusion, he did not move toward enhanced celebration of reason but instead sought to distinguish what was genuine in all the clamor. This obliged him to study human emotions in their own right, rather than to apply theological formulas to them—a study that separated him from his predecessors. In doing so, he was impelled not only by events in Northampton and the opposers' critique. He also placed himself, however awkwardly, in a new current of European philosophy. In Norman Fiering's words, "The guiding assumption behind almost all the new work [in philosophy] was the belief that God's intentions for man, His expectations of human beings as moral creatures, could be discovered independently of the traditional sources of religious authority, through a close investigation of human nature."

Although the drift of Edwards's work probably did give validity to a kind of emotional behavior previously uncommon in New England, he certainly did not absolve human nature of its innate depravity or praise all emo-

tions indiscriminately. None of his contemporaries surpassed him in suspicion of the ruses by which human souls
counted themselves blessed. But signs of deceit and folly
did not prove that the awakenings as a whole lacked divine inspiration. Other great moments in providential
history had shown the same blemishes, so much so that
the apostles had warned against false prophets and leaders of the Reformation had fought their own overzealous
followers. But there were true marks of salvation that could
not flow from man's carnal impulses or Satan's misguid-
ance, among them, a deep-stricken awareness of man's
miserable nature, earnest respect for the Bible, and overriding benevolence toward other creatures. Two emotional states, in Edwards's view, resulted from God's influence: (1) "humility and self-diffidence," and (2) "a sincerely
benevolent propensity of the soul." Neither of them con-
noted a free-flowing emotional expression of the natural
self. Both were at odds with the selfishness and comfort
of a bustling commercial economy; they collided with the
boisterousness and hardheartedness of society. While many
of the "common people" may have behaved too enthusi-
astically in public, especially in the initial stages of the
awakenings, one telling quality of the holiness of these
events was their softening, sweetening effect on daily conversation. Blessed towns went beyond civility to display a
severely chastened and loving climate.

Like his Puritan predecessors, Edwards set one category of emotions at war with another. Like them, he noted
that counterfeit grace was likely to be bolder, more confidently put forward, than true; a pretender could be
proud of his humility. The elect were more likely to be
"spiritual persons," not self-seeking or self-assertive. Their
character was very different from Chauncy's sedate and
rational leaders of society. It was no accident that beautiful instances of grace appeared in women and young chil-

dren (though Edwards did not make the connection), since their lives were shielded from displays of public importance. He made it clear that "the desires of the saints, however earnest, are humble desires: their hope is a humble hope; and their joy, even when it is unspeakable, and full of glory, is a humble, broken-hearted joy, and leaves the Christian more poor in spirit, and more like a little child, and more disposed to an universal lowliness of behavior." This characterization of the elect suggested a shift away from old-style emphases on the haughty prerogatives of rank. Though Edwards was himself a man of aristocratic bearing, his ideal convert was as meek and loving, as forgiving of enemies, as Christ.

While leading a popular religious movement, Edwards remained a man of intellect. Though warning that reason—"merely speculative or notional" understanding of grace—was inadequate without spiritual rebirth, Edwards regretted the anti-intellectualism of the awakenings. Those who disparaged the educated ministry and preferred ignorant exhorters "leave the guidance of the pole star and follow a Jack-with-a-lanthorn." Edwards was himself a man of wide reading and penetrating logic, who by his own example shows us not to take too lightly the intellectual milieu of the New England frontier. His works, ranging from youthful descriptions of natural phenomena in the style of a virtuoso to such lengthy tomes as *Freedom of the Will* (1754) and *Original Sin* (1758), have engaged the attention of one generation after another of European and American scholars. He has remained a key figure in successive efforts at self-definition by American intellectuals. He was the fountainhead of "Edwardsean" movements in nineteenth-century seminaries, and twentieth-century "neo-Calvinist" intellectuals have applauded his stubborn, intricate restatements of old doctrines in a time of secular change.

For a long time, Americans celebrated Edwards as an isolated genius, ecstatically reading John Locke's *Essay Concerning Human Understanding* (1690) as a "backwoods adolescent" and rushing to conclusions of startling originality. In this treatment, he took his place beside other self-made men and frontier oracles. Locke, who eventually became the most prominent critic of the faculty psychology, claimed that a child was born with a *tabula rasa*, a blank slate, and that thought processes derived from sense experiences and reflections on those experiences. Edwards used terminology similar to Locke's. Although he also referred to faculties, he complained that commonly used terms were artificial and imperfect. What distinguished each person, for better or worse, was how he or she felt about what was perceived and thought. Instead of distinguishing thought and feeling in the Puritan style, Edwards preferred to merge them in accounting for individual inclinations. What moved the saints was a "sense of the heart" tending toward self-forgetfulness and love. According to some influential studies of Edwards, this "sense" was the rustic young American's imaginative extension of the doctrine that all knowledge, even that of grace, must be received through the senses.

Scholars today are skeptical of intellectual creativity occurring outside systems of support and communities of discourse. They are not inclined to romanticize the frontier. They suggest that Edwards's significant reading of Locke took place either when he was a postgraduate student at Yale or after he became a settled minister, by which time he was deeply immersed in conversations on philosophical topics and quite well read in both Continental and British philosophers who had anticipated Locke's concerns. In addition to books, he had access to magazines and encyclopedias that digested a wide range of philosophical and scientific explanation. He actually rejected most of what he had heard about or read in Locke: the "sense of the heart" was explicitly spiritual; it was superior to the impressions made through the senses on the brain. What is remarkable about Edwards is his creation of a highly original religious psychology responding to both the novelties of the awakenings in his immediate context and to the latest currents of change in European and American secular thought.

Edwards is a key example to show that eighteenth-century New England ministers participated in an international "republic of letters." He and Locke tackled similar issues and used similar terms, though to different conclusions, because it was difficult to read, think, and write in the context of their times without doing so. Some of Edwards's most philosophical treatises, like *The Nature of True Virtue* (1765), dispensed with the biblical citations that once peppered every minister's arguments. That does not mean that he was less religious than his ancestors; it simply means that he participated in a new era devoted to explaining the highest goods of human life through close investigation of human nature. It also means that *minister* was only one aspect of his identity since he wrote for an international audience of "men of learning." He insisted, nevertheless, that the worldly virtues celebrated by learned contemporaries were inferior to the transforming effects of grace. And while he dispensed with citations in some writings, he never questioned the authority of the Bible. He is the first of several examples we shall see of tension between the international discourse of intellectuals and the habitual attitudes of a particular profession or class.

Edwards joined other participants in the "republic of letters" in scrutinizing the ethical abilities of ordinary people. The subject drove him into conflict with his congregation. " 'Tis a hard thing to be a hearty zealous friend of what has been good and glorious, in the late extraordinary appearances, and to rejoice much in it; and at the same time, to see the evil and pernicious tendency of what has been bad, and earnestly to oppose that." Edwards was aware of his incongruous role in the awakenings, and he pursued his course with great courage. For the most part, men of learning did not think well of "enthusiasm," and there is awkwardness in many passages of his writings where he tried to make emotional outbursts less frightening.

Meanwhile, his own ministry ended unhappily. Unlike Chauncy, he lost the support of nearby ministers. In his determination to sort out authentic from bogus conversions, he reintroduced the requirement, long since outmoded in the Connecticut Valley, of a "relation" for church membership. He thereby alienated many parishioners with newly kindled dreams of sainthood. His visions of the reformed community did not please the rich and powerful, particularly after he rebuked the behavior of some of their children. Led by the son of the gentleman who had committed suicide, an anti-Edwards faction managed to get him dismissed.

For a while this proud, periwigged man served as missionary in charge of a small boardinghouse for Indian boys in westernmost Massachusetts, a post that gave him time for extensive writing. His originality threatened to be equaled by his obscurity, but his influence slowly expanded. Despite his personal defeat, he retained the affection of a group of "New Divinity" ministers who regarded his works as authoritative versions of religious truth. On all sides, doctrinal issues took on new importance in defining church membership and ministerial credentials. As Edwards's international fame grew, he was called to the presidency of Princeton, a new college founded by evangelical Presbyterians in the middle colonies. He arrived in February 1758 in the midst of a smallpox epidemic, was inoculated, and a month later died. Through Princeton and other seminaries his influence was consolidated after his death. He became the intellectual hero of ministers who held on to some guiding control over religious experience by interpreting it within terms now favored in international intellectual discourse. We shall return to this influence when discussing the Didactic Enlightenment in Chapter IV.

THE MORAL SENSE
IN VIRGINIA

One exciting aspect of the surprising events in Northampton was to see them as part of a worldwide campaign to rouse religious feelings among common people. There was news of similar events in New York and New Jersey. Itinerants like Whitefield came from farther south. Much of the early revivalistic impulse, though this was less clear in New England than elsewhere, arrived with immigrants from Britain and the Continent, where related movements called Wesleyanism and Pietism were under way. Students of Judaism recognize a similar tendency in the eighteenth-century Hasidic movement. If the republic of letters encouraged a calm faith in humanity's benevolent nature, it did so amid widespread religious enthusiasm.

George Whitefield itinerated, ostensibly at least, to raise funds for an orphanage in Georgia, a worthy cause that no one could criticize. His first tour of North America in 1737 raised no great hullabaloo, but by the time he came again in 1739–1740 he had earned a reputation as a vehement assailant, within the Church of England, of the "free and catholic" spirit that dominated religion in the mother country. He had published charges that Archbishop John Tillotson, the suave theologian who was the most popular English religious writer among southern elites, knew no more of Christianity than Muhammad. Whitefield was also praised as one of the most powerful Christian orators since the apostles. The combination of his extemporaneous preaching, which moved audiences to tears, and his inflammatory charges against the English establishment attracted huge crowds. On his second visit he proclaimed two themes that went on to pervade a general awakening in many localities throughout the colonies. One was the Reformed notion of "irresistible grace": regardless of what clergymen claimed for their ministrations or for ethical living, only God could determine to save a human soul, and when he made his choice, the force was overwhelming. The second theme was the importance of a "new birth," an absolute transformation of human personality in the instant of grace. "The constant tenour of my preaching in America," he boasted, "has been Calvinistical." Though these were indeed old doctrines, the effect of their thrilling assertion before throngs of smitten converts was, not as of old to remind hearers of mankind's boundless misery, but instead to suggest the accessibility of salvation to unparalleled numbers of men and women. A new day appeared to be dawning; only the nasty opposition of a remnant of unholy ministers held it back.

Religious upheavals thrive on opposition. This foe of the British elite immediately gained a southern oppressor to lend plausibility to his charges against ministerial misrule. In South Carolina Alexander Garden, the bishop of London's representative, tried to invoke ecclesiastical authority to silence Whitefield. When that failed, he published his disagreements with the itinerant over the workings of grace. Whitefield, Garden said, was using a kind of emotional power that belonged in the theater in order to arouse men's and women's passions and confuse their minds. He was a conveyor of "enthusiasm," hurrying folk into "fits of religion, which must terminate either in Bedlam, or Deism, or Popery." His chief mischief lay in suggesting that grace was the "work of a moment" comparable to emergence from the womb. Outside New England, there was no compulsion to pay lip service to Calvinistic doctrines; therefore, Garden identified conversion with the moral law of the Gospel as reinforced by the sacraments of the church. It was a slow, steady process, not a disruptive fit. Whitefield's ranting was reminiscent of the intolerant bigotry of the English civil wars, and there was an implication that he was a tool or dupe of the pope, sowing discord in a Protestant kingdom. The warning was urgent: "Suffer not your passions to be moved, but as your minds are instructed."

Whitefield did not cause the awakenings singlehandedly. He was too restless an itinerant to claim such influence. His journeys did succeed, however, in calling attention to popular religious movements shattering the tidy hierarchical world that typified much of the South and in creating a sense of common cause with awakenings elsewhere. Gentlemen prided themselves on the prevailing tolerant attitudes in the land they dominated. They had no objection to the divergent religious allegiances of western Scotch-Irish or German communities. It was a different matter, however, when people in an eastern county, led by a bricklayer, began to meet in their own homes to read and discuss religious books. As the movement grew, they erected special "reading houses" and announced a loose affiliation with Luther's Reformation. Whitefield came to stir up the spirit of protest, making it plain that many Anglican authorities were unconverted men. Of more lasting consequence, "new side" evangelical Presbyterians came down from the middle colonies to gather the enthusiastic readers into churches. Some of these newcomers were powerful preachers and learned theologians; the best known, Samuel Davies, had a fine reputation as a hymn

writer and classical scholar and eventually succeeded Edwards as president of Princeton. They had little difficulty
in cementing the loyalties of newly organized congregations. As Davies reported, men and women, who had formerly been calumniated as "whimsical" and "hypocritical"
dissenters, enjoyed being in harmonious congregations with
settled ministers of their own choosing. In a second wave
of revivalism, Separate Baptists descended from Connecticut, and in the 1760s their recruits intensified religious
feelings in the Virginia countryside. In all these movements, the purity of Calvinism stood in opposition to a
slipshod social order, thus reversing the pretensions of the
gentlemen who associated their own leadership with the
perfection of society. Both Presbyterians and Baptists took
special pains to offer conversion to the slaves—with profound consequences for American Christianity.

In the eyes of some of the colony's great men, toleration was going too far. They issued severe warnings against
false doctrines afoot, and they took measures to suppress
itinerancy and refused preaching licenses to intruders from
other colonies. New lights were ridiculed and flogged. But
all these measures were futile, and religious controversy
gave a new tenor to public affairs in Virginia. Debate over
compulsory tithing to support the Anglican priesthood
became incessant. Proposals to establish a bishop in
America—supposedly to upgrade the priesthood and
forestall popular delusions—sparked unprecedented
complaints about unwelcome hierarchy and British tyranny. Not only did the unconverted populace hold fast to
new religious practices, but wealthy planters failed to agree
to schemes for reorganization and repression. Some
planters moved farther in the direction of liberalism or
even indifference to religion.

Both populace and aristocracy were experiencing
profound changes of world view. The Baptists were con-

sidered a "melancholy people" because of their solemn talk, their austere appearance, and their avoidance of horse races, cockfights, and alcoholic revelry. If antagonists found too much "seriousness" in their public deportment, they also called Baptist services too informal and passionate. Through intense convictions of sin and joy within the fellowship, disorderly character was reformed and reborn Christians distanced themselves from the world's imperfections. Whatever hedonism existed in society was renounced. The historian Rhys Isaac captures the ironic contrasts between new lights and old order in this formulation: "Where the liturgical services of the establishment had been short intervals of authoritative decorum in a rambunctious social world, the worship of the evangelicals was a tumultuous release from a social life upon which they sought to impose intense orderliness." The awakenings were seldom explicitly linked to economic or political protests,* but the fear that religious upheaval undermined old patterns of deference and submission was not imaginary. In religious terms the awakenings signified a profound sense that the world was in disarray. In social terms they separated the lower orders into institutions of their own making.

There was no exact southern equivalent to Chauncy and the New England liberals who moved toward Unitar-

---

*There were exceptions. One Carolina new light, Herman Husband, became a leader of the "regulator" movement of the 1760s and later participated in the "whiskey rebellion" in Pennsylvania. A South Carolina white took to the woods to live like a hermit; in 1742 he prophesied that God would use the slaves to destroy Charleston. Whether the slaves heard these prophesies, as was feared, is unknown, but there were instances of Christian slave rebels obeying direct revelations. The thrust of the new religion was to greater personal orderliness, but its opposers were understandably wary of the visions of vengeance and denunciations of luxury that it sometimes inspired.

ianism. The establishment was already anti-Calvinist, committed to the spirit of "latitude" and moderation that Tillotson exemplified; and extravagances among the common folk simply bolstered that commitment. The warning that reason must outweigh passion, repeated frequently after Garden's attack on Whitefield, required no modification of theology. The clergy, in any event, had never gained preeminence as an intellectual class in the South; they had an accessory status to the gentry. In the years up to the Revolution they watched helplessly as a majority of the population fixed allegiances in new sects. Jefferson's *Notes on the State of Virginia* estimated that "two-thirds of the people had become dissenters," outside the Anglican establishment. In the years of Revolution, the Virginia church lost its privileged status, and descriptions of empty churches in disrepair became commonplace.

Some old-style aristocrats maintained their loyalty to the Anglican order, at the same time blaming the clergy for its failures. In bitter proceedings in 1773, British ministers were rooted out of their stations at William and Mary because of their allegedly Unitarian views and their fashionable emphasis on human benevolence rather than on the old sacraments and mysteries. But there really was no chance of undoing the popular awakenings by reforming the established clergy. The older gentlemen were caught in the untenable position of despising the people's religion and disowning the liberal styles of intellect associated with England. Eventually they would either accept their positions in an unpopular Anglican denomination, redefined as an exclusive remnant in a transformed society, or find their way into the more respectable wings of new denominations. They might cling to images of a patrician ideal that had flourished in days of yore, somewhat like the northern jeremiads' images of the piety of the first generation of fathers. But visions of a unified society in the new southern age could not dismiss the religious aspirations of the yeomanry.

According to some reports, gentlemanly life after 1750 was less convivial and hospitable than it had been in the old order. The softening influence of the plantation lady is sometimes credited, or blamed, for the constricted importance of the home. Though great fortunes still depended on the management of slave work forces, the lives of individual planters became more private and, in some instances, contemplative. The traditional link between patrician status and intellectual virtuosity proved to be the key to profound redirections of life for the younger aristocracy.

In the seventeenth century, the signs of leisurely attainments, from the maintenance of gardens to the education of children in English schools, sufficed to demarcate a ruling class. In the eighteenth century, the ability to initiate conversation on advanced transatlantic themes acquired more significance. A tutor in one of the great Virginia houses recorded a good example of this use of the intellect. The master of the house directed all the "ceremonies at table," saying grace, proposing toasts, carving the meat, then starting "a conversation on philosophy, on eclipses, the manner of viewing them; thence to telescopes, & the information which they afforded us of the solar system; whether planets be actually inhabited etc." On another occasion the master began conversation with an observation about the delicacy of sentiments in songs and poetry. We can well believe reports that men and women of the subservient classes stammered and blushed in the presence of men of quality who could hold forth on such abstract themes.

After the awakenings, however, the commoners took increasing pride in their own religious culture and in the enhanced respectability of their own lives. Furthermore, the international "republic of letters," as evident in the manuals and encyclopedias by which gentlemen kept *au courant*, took increasing interest in the innate virtues of ordinary folk. (That was why Edwards, for example, worked so relentlessly to distinguish true grace from the much praised ordinary morality.) In Virginia, and to some extent elsewhere in the South, the younger aristocracy came to view themselves as an intellectual class rather separated from the evangelized lower classes. Anyone who has looked at the published correspondence of Jefferson and other young Virginians* will respect their earnest— sometimes even lonely and haunted—spirit of mutual inquiry into the principles of morals and politics. Theirs was not the elegant conversation of men who could take for granted aristocratic prerogatives. Few of them could find it in themselves to imitate William Byrd II's sneering attitude toward plebeians. They were concerned instead with the sources of individual merit and public morality. In its own way their correspondence mirrored the awareness of a disorderly society to be transformed through self-control that was evident in the Baptist revivals.

But the Baptist services furnished a highly emotional, communal context for the strivings of the yeomanry and lower orders. The gentlemen were aware, sometimes acutely, of their isolation even as they read and discussed European treatises on the social virtues. Though the

---

*These are available as a result of the massive publication projects sponsored in recent decades by the federal government. The first editor of *The Papers of Thomas Jefferson* (1950–), the greatest of these projects, was Julian K. Boyd. Other projects include the papers of Madison and Washington. There were occasions, it should be noted, when the milieu seemed to favor unphilosophical displays of wealth. Jefferson complained to one young friend that "the man who powders most, embroiders most, and talks most nonsense is most admired."

theologies of enthusiastic religious movements were distasteful to them, some gentlemen took the stance of admiring the transforming effect of religion on the character of ordinary people. They were men of reason praising, however faintly, popular movements from which it was their fate to be removed. They were separatists without much religion to sustain them or give them confidence in their superiority. A few left gloomy letters comparing themselves to the ancient stoics, enduring life and seeking to face death with dignity. One wrote, "in vain do I endeavor to explore the deep designs of Heaven, and to understand for what end man was created. . . . Sometimes I am impatient to know what compensation a future state of existence may make us for what we suffer here." On the whole, however, the student of post-1750 gentlemen is more impressed by their rising interest in political responsibility, by their shared understanding of republican institutions and loyalty to their homeland that came to the fore in conflicts with England.

The most articulate of these gentlemen was Thomas Jefferson. In some ways his position as an intellectual was as conflict-ridden as Edwards's. His name came to symbolize the political aspirations of the common people in a world where old, privileged institutions were thrown out; yet the personal loneliness of this man of reason was so poignant that subsequent generations have been fascinated by rumors of a liaison with a slave mistress. He disciplined himself to extraordinary programs of intellectual self-improvement and conducted a voluminous correspondence with philosophers and scientists in other colonies and in Europe. He had little in common with evangelical leaders of the people for whom he provided political leadership, and his own religious views remained something of a mystery, partly because he learned to conceal advanced and skeptical opinions that might be political liabilities. He wrote the law disestablishing the Virginia church, which can be regarded as a tactic to remove from politics the one issue that might have destroyed the political hegemony of the large landowners. Yet there is no doubt of his frequently reiterated respect for the morality of the evangelized small farmers, even though he was personally remote from their religion. In his case, approval of the lower orders seemed to intensify in proportion to social distance from them.

He went to great lengths to attribute the morality of the common people, not to the religious changes that they took so seriously, but to an innate moral sense that flourished amid free institutions. He was also a devastating critic of the morality of his own class, though here, too, he assigned responsibility not to the religion taught in the established churches, which had been weak institutions at best, but to the effects of slavery and unmitigated power. In *Notes on the State of Virginia,* he moved from condemnation of the state religion that stifled the aspirations of dissenters to analysis of the "boisterous passions" churned up by slaveholding: "The parent storms, the child looks on, catches the lineaments of wrath, puts on the same airs in the circle of smaller slaves; gives a loose to his worst of passions, and thus nursed, educated, and daily exercised in tyranny, cannot but be stamped by it with odious peculiarities." Instead of decorous hierarchy, Jefferson depicted a world of "unremitting despotism" and "degrading submission," a world in collision with the progress of benevolence, a world destructive of good manners.

Slavery was not abolished, though its justification became problematic to men who liked to investigate universal sources of virtue. Slavery unmistakably violated many principles elevated by the new interest in human psychology: it forced the slave to "lock up the faculties of his nature," with little chance for self-improvement and little likelihood of developing sentimental attachments to his country. The slave always presented an ominous threat of rebellion that required the use of uncivil force. Yet if enlightened men praised human freedom, an abstraction rooted in the rational and benevolent propensities of human nature, they also had great respect for earthly institutions and property. Jefferson and his class lived in a world in which bondage was the accepted basis for human wealth. It was not a trivial institution that could easily be engineered out of existence. They recognized it as a problem, and when pressed to devise solutions, they looked to a slow process of emancipation or improving conditions in the fields and quarters. They questioned whether blacks were intellectually or psychologically identical to other races or whether they could withstand the competition of whites in a free economy. While deferring this problem for consideration by future generations, they thought more seriously about the intellect and morals in the transformed society of whites.

In writing about white farmers, Jefferson focused on the "husbandmen" as an ideal type, calling them "the chosen people of God whose breasts he has made his peculiar deposit for substantial and genuine virtue." Farmers, in contrast to urban mobs and manufacturing populations, had an incorruptible love of freedom and an abiding loyalty to their land. In Jefferson's opinion, this was true in all times and places: "Corruption of morals in the mass of cultivators is a phenomenon of which no age nor nation has furnished an example." This opinion helped to differentiate the American Revolution from the terrors Jefferson saw and deplored in Paris. The persistence of such paeans to the agrarian population is a well-known theme of American democratic politics. Viewed in the context of the post-1750 South, however, one of its implications was to reorient the perspectives of gentlemen in power. Jefferson did not style himself a patriarch in a courtly hierarchy surrounded by indolent lubbers. So long as he focused on the "chosen people," he averted his eyes from the coercions of slavery as the source of wealth for his class. At the same time, he lavished praise, politically useful in a society where deference could no longer be taken for granted, on the great majority of whites without referring to the specific historical events that had altered interclass relations. It was the husbandman of all ages, not the reborn Presbyterian or Baptist wheat farmer, whom God had chosen. When he did see something distinctive in America, Jefferson liked to imagine that "ours are the only farmers who can read Homer."

It is interesting to contrast Jefferson to Jonathan Edwards, who was also aware of fashionable currents of belief in the psychologically intrinsic virtue of ordinary folk. While conceding that something like a "moral sense" was sufficiently prevalent in human affairs to make civil life tolerable, Edwards stubbornly distinguished it from the highest or "true virtue," which came only with supernatural aid. The virtue that philosophers rushed to praise actually was infected with traces of rationalization and selfish interest; what was commonly deemed benevolence was inferior to the blessed perceptions and actions of the saints. Edwards's fascination to modern thinkers is as a nay-sayer in an intellectual milieu that was increasingly optimistic about ordinary morals; using the new terminology, he held fast to the Puritan disparagement of the merely civil man. In Edwards's view of grace, aristocratic manners must be chastened and the souls even of blacks might be beatified. Jefferson, highly sensitive to the beliefs of intellectual leaders abroad, wrote some of the most memorable accounts of the morality of the ordinary farmer—and he did so with none of the references to sin and grace that were the evangelicals' stock in trade. For the most important philosophical treatments of the moral sense, one might turn to Francis Hutcheson's *Illustrations on the Moral Sense* (1728) and Adam Smith's *Theory of Moral Sentiments* (1759), British works of the sort that Edwards sought to refute. For the most memorable practical descriptions of the moral sense, one would turn to Jefferson.

"I think it is lost time to attend lectures on moral philosophy," Jefferson advised a nephew. Men had been uttering similar sentiments for at least a century (Cotton Mather, for example, had deplored the introduction of courses on ethics at Harvard). But Jefferson's argument was not the traditional one that held religion to be the proper arbiter of moral behavior. Courses in this subject were irrelevant because humankind, particularly farmers, knew right from wrong without instruction:

> He who made us would have been a pitiful bungler, if He had made the rules of our conduct a matter of science. For one man of science, there are thousands who are not. What would have become of them? Man was destined for society. His morality, therefore, was to be formed to this object. He was endowed with a sense of right or wrong, merely relative to this. This sense is as much a part of his nature, as the sense of hearing, seeing, feeling; it is the true foundation of morality. . . . The moral sense, or conscience, is as much a part of man as his leg or arm. . . . This sense is submitted, indeed, in some degree, to the guidance of reason; but it is a small stock which is required for this: even a less one than what we call common sense.

He concluded with a famous discounting of academic learning: "State a moral case to a ploughman and a professor. The former will decide it as well, and often better than the latter, because he has not been led astray by artificial rules."

This kind of statement was in vogue. Though scholars have argued over which British or Continental philosophers had the greatest influence on Jefferson, he could hardly have dipped into the "republic of letters" without discovering the idea that the Creator of this marvelous universe could not have botched his work. The Creator could not make man a social animal without planting "social dispositions" in his breast. Thus the philosophical role of the master of a great house brought with it anti-elitist interpretations of virtue. This was not to take seriously the religion and morality that the plowman himself prized. Jefferson's formulation avoids the sectarian zeal unleashed by revivalism; it avoids even the faint praise of saying it served the plowman well. Moreover, the terms Jefferson employed—"state a moral case"—were those of the classroom or refined conversation. Only the ability to act rightly was reserved to simple human nature. The ability to discuss morality remained a distinction of society's leaders, and Jefferson esteemed the "rational society" of educated men. While a "small stock" of reason sufficed for civil behavior, Jefferson is justly famous for his own commitment to the disciplined use of reason. In this letter, and some others like it, he discouraged the study of moral philosophy, but at other times he discoursed at length on the subject and advised acquaintances on which books of ethics to add to their libraries. On other subjects, such as architecture, music, science, or politics, he made no claim that the untutored intellect was adequate. Even in religion he was sure that God "must more approve of the homage of reason, than that of blindfolded fear."

Jefferson retained a psychology of faculties—of uneven endowments. Not only was the strength of the moral sense distributed unequally among human beings, "as force of members is given . . . in a greater or less degree," but it was probable that entire groups of people, like Africans, were weaker in reason than others. Jefferson speculated at length on the evidence that blacks, though equal to whites in memory and stronger in sexual passion, were deficient in reason and imagination. They had not "availed themselves of the conversation of their masters," had not contributed to science or philosophy, had excelled in religious feeling but in a manner that did "more honour to the heart than to the head." These deficiencies impeded emancipation, Jefferson contended, in the specific case of blacks. They indicate more generally that there were severe limits to the egalitarianism of the philosophy of the moral sense.

It may also be significant that it was the adult farmer, not the child, who earned Jefferson's encomiums. Jefferson's values had little room for primitivistic praise of the newborn or born-again creature, despite the extravagant contrast of plowman and professor. In his plan for education, in fact, he allowed for instilling "elements of morality," which needed training and exercise, along with a generally useful literacy. This plan took for granted the superior education of the wealthy but sought to have the "best geniuses" among the poor "raked up from the rubbish." The capacity for moral discrimination was universal; intellectual ability, however, was distributed unequally.

Not only did Jefferson have little good to say about the child, except to prescribe programs of educational improvement, but there are important strains of dominance in his remarks about women. One biographer concludes that "Jefferson liked women who were gentle, feminine, and yielding." He criticized the French king for subservience to an overreaching woman, and he advised his daughter at the time of her marriage to devote herself to pleasing her husband and, above all, not to disagree with him in public: "Modesty and diffidence are the greatest ornaments of a married woman. . . . Anger and violence and rage deform the female figure, and a turbulent woman disgraces the delicacy of her sex." He guided his daughters' education to make them suitable spouses for gentlemen of taste and intellect. He used the terms "Amazons" and "Angels" to contrast women who interfered in public affairs with those who found contentment in "the tender and tranquil amusements of domestic life." Psychobiographers have mined such evidence, which is bountiful, to show fear of women as a crucial element in Jefferson's personality. For our purposes, its importance is to suggest further boundaries implied by the philosophy of moral sense. Women called forth tender feelings of the heart, and at their best they personified an angelic, domestic style of life, but they were excluded from the highest plane of intellectual attainment.

The contrast between plowman and professor might confuse us into seeing more egalitarianism and anti-intellectualism than actually existed in Jefferson's philosophy. It is important to recall that he belonged to a planter class, with strong inclinations to see blacks as inferior, children as undisciplined, and women as needing the restraints of the home. He belonged to a class whose view of life delineated spheres of appropriate action for different groups. He certainly admired the professor's uses of reason, and he knew that reason was a hallmark of power in conversation in the great estates. But there was no doubt that the heart also signified refinement. Just as the seventeenth-century nabob was notable for his "liberality," his Jeffersonian counterpart displayed benevolence as well as reason. One of Jefferson's best-known writings was an elaborately contrived dialogue between "My Heart" and

"My Head"; here again we observe the continuing sense of divided faculties. It is important to understand this dialogue if we are to make sense of late-eighteenth-century ideals.

The dialogue appeared in a letter to an unhappily married English woman, a painter named Maria Cosway, with whom the widower Jefferson enjoyed a romantic involvement while representing the new American government in Paris. No one will ever know whether theirs was a sexual liaison, but the flirtation and infatuation were unmistakable. Jefferson had injured his right hand while leaping over a fence to amuse her; then after parting from her, he composed twelve artful pages with his left. The occasion of the letter, in short, concerned a conventional lover's dilemma: whether to see the lady again or break off the affair. In the conventional formula we might expect the head to speak for Jefferson's better nature, telling him to behave morally, and the heart to speak for lustful impetuosity. But lust was entirely offstage, just as the will had no place in this kind of dialogue. So what remained was an argument between the head, to which nature had assigned in the "divided empire" of his personality "the field of science," and the heart, which held sway over morals. The former, trying to preempt the latter's field, advocated selfish calculation and intellectual privacy; the heart voiced the claims of charity and sympathy. The specific topics of the debate had little connection with dalliance and pleasure. The heart summoned up regrettable episodes when the head had counseled against aiding a wounded soldier and an impoverished woman. The heart hoped that Maria Cosway might even move to America where there were so many picturesque scenes to paint.

The dialogue was contrived and duplicitous—throughout, Jefferson feigned interest in Mr. Cosway's

INTELLECTUAL LIFE IN AMERICA

company as well as hers—and perhaps it is unfortunate that it has become the best-known example of American philosophizing on the heart. Nevertheless, it shows how elaborately a learned man could think of his mental life as a divided arena. Impressed with the image of Jefferson as a man of reason, many scholars have seen the head as victorious. More recently, scholars have pointed out that the heart has the stronger arguments and the last word. The debate concerns morals, after all, and there is no doubt that Jefferson, like many contemporaries, considered the reason a poor guide to ethical decisions. The heart and passions were cleansed of their erotic, disorderly connotations in the faculty psychology of an earlier era. In the new sentimental view of morals, duty and virtue were believed to spring naturally from the heart. In the letter to Maria Cosway, moreover, it was not the virtue of common people that merited praise. Jefferson was recording the morally healthy side of his own nature and demonstrating his status as a man of feeling. Yet those scholars who saw the head as victorious in the dialogue were not entirely wrong. While a poor guide to morals, the head upheld values of great importance in other spheres of life, those which were less "womanly," those in which a man of intellect distinguished himself from commoners and slaves. The author of the dialogue agreed with the head when it treasured "the inestimable value of intellectual pleasures. . . . We ride, serene and sublime, above the concerns of this moral world, contemplating truth and nature, matter and motion, the laws which bind up their existence, and that eternal being who made and bound them up by those laws." (The head sounded a bit like the master of a manor introducing lofty conversation.) The elevation of the heart in the sphere of morals did not imply a displacement of reason in the fields of science and contemplation. Perhaps we may simply conclude by seeing Jefferson as a late-eighteenth-century virtuoso, true to the needs of his class, a man of intellect but also a man of feeling, and inclined to give enlarged respect to the evidence of common benevolence.

Popular evangelicalism had signaled a partial disintegration of the old patriarchal and hierarchical world, but Virginia's leaders adjusted to the threat. Some, like Patrick Henry, adapted the passionate preaching styles of the awakenings to their political orations. Henry was compared, in fact, with "that stupendous master of the human passions, George Whitefield"; it was often said that Henry's powerful addresses could not be written down because they depended on the "lightning" of his delivery and spontaneous use of homespun expressions. Others, like George Washington, epitomized a new style of moderate, enlightened leadership. Like his predecessors, he was renowned for his horsemanship and excellent conversation. But he was well read in the philosophy of an enlightened age, and his dignity was tempered by patience and respect for others. Of them all, Jefferson went the furthest in glorifying the morals and customs of American citizens. In the new milieu, no aristocrat was forthrightly hedonistic, and none complained that the ordinary wheat farmer was indolent.

Enormous chasms remained between the intellectual life of the top class and the religious strivings of the strata below them. Perhaps the chasm was wider than ever before, as the philosophic preoccupations of the top class identified them with European currents of thought and the lower orders looked increasingly to their own institutions for validations of self-worth. The aristocrats sometimes donned rustic clothes to act out their places in a Revolution, but the farmers could not presume to be lords of manors. Occasionally, in the privacy of their own circles, the elite might mock the emotionalism of folk religion; more frequently, like Jefferson, they ignored the subject and kept it out of politics. Southern intellectual life retained its association with the interests of large slave-owners, but it was altered by a new consensus on the virtues of the ordinary American farmer and by a deepening spirit of participation in an international, secular enlightenment.

THE MIDDLE COLONIES

The social structures and ideologies of the middle colonies, below the Hudson River and above the Chesapeake, cannot be described as neatly as can those of New England and the South. The origins of these colonies were diverse: New York was initially a Dutch enterprise; the mouth of the Delaware was for a time a New Sweden; and New Jersey's English proprietors turned it into a maze of unregulated fiefdoms. Pennsylvania belonged to English Quakers aspiring to a holy unity not unlike the visions of the Puritans. But Dutchmen, Swedes, and Finns were already there when the Quakers arrived, and the Quaker policy of encouraging immigration by persecuted religious groups magnified the ethnic diversity. Many thousands of Germans settled in Pennsylvania during the first half of the eighteenth century, and Presbyterian Ulstermen were also plentiful.* Besides their diverse origins and distinctive ethnic populations, the middle colonies had highly varied forms of government and social structures.

---

*The Scotch-Irish became the largest non-English ethnic group in the American colonies, which in general south of New England were preponderantly non-English. In the 1760s there was a significant flow of immigrants directly from Scotland. Touring the western islands of Scotland in 1773, Samuel Johnson reflected on the population losses: "a nation scattered in the boundless regions of America resembles rays

No single set of generalizations could take in all the gradations of wealth and poverty, trade and agriculture, urban and frontier existence, to be found in these colonies. Furthermore, travel even over shorter distances was laborious and hazardous. Nowhere else is the modern student so aware of the crazy-quilt complexity of life in the American provinces. It is not surprising that neither religious awakenings nor secular enlightenment seemed to give the same pattern to culture in the middle colonies as they did to the north and south.

Religious awakenings in the middle colonies depended on links between colonial ethnic groups and their kinsmen overseas. Theodore Frelinghuysen, the first notable revivalist, was sent over from the Netherlands in 1720. It was said that he thought he had agreed to go to Brabant or Flanders, but when he discovered his commission was to the New World he accepted the news as a divine command. Descended from a family that had recently converted to Calvinism, he brought a harshly exclusive concern about church membership to the Dutch Reformed community in New Jersey. While he did not have outstanding success in gathering new converts, the division of religious people into pro- and anti-Frelinghuysen factions foreshadowed subsequent conflicts and made him a hero in the eyes of other evangelists. William Tennent, an Ulsterman educated in Scotland, was a former Anglican clergyman who had converted to Presbyterianism and immigrated in 1716. First in New York and then in Pennsylvania, he and his sons were highly successful evange-

---

diverging from a focus. All the rays remain but the heat is gone. Their power consisted in their concentration: when they are dispersed, they have no effect." Some landlords were so concerned that there were proposals for Parliament to bar further British emigration.

lists who divided Presbyterianism into new light and old light factions. His son Gilbert Tennent preached the single most illuminating sermon of the awakenings, "The Danger of an Unconverted Ministry" (1741), arguing that it was better to have no minister at all than one of the genial, uncontentious sacramentalists whom so many communities were saddled with. Antagonism to religious authority was, predictably, reinforced by that great emissary from the Old World, George Whitefield, who attracted huge crowds in the middle colonies (and who hailed the Tennents as "the burning and shining lights of this part of America").

The awakenings in the middle colonies furnished a linchpin for events to the north and south. The Tennents struck out as itinerants in both directions, and they sent ministers to the disaffected yeomen of Virginia. Intellectual leaders like Jonathan Edwards and Samuel Davies ended their careers at the evangelical mecca at Princeton. In persuading a Scottish luminary, John Witherspoon, to accept the presidency of Princeton, a young Philadelphian explained that Davies had been "as it were the Bishop of all our American churches." Davies had modernized the Princeton curriculum by introducing more Newtonian science and mathematics to create a ministry fit for the new age. Witherspoon added works on the philosophy of the moral sense, no longer the anathema it had been to Edwards.

Despite their liking for conflict and their hostility to the unconverted ministry, the Tennents and other new lights did not advocate an uncontrolled folk enthusiasm. They repudiated uneducated exhorters who preached without preparation. Instead, they called for new seminaries to train zealous preachers who would have a sterling education in Greek, Latin, Hebrew, and other subjects pertinent to theology. At a little house in Neshaminy,

Pennsylvania, William Tennent set up such a school—
scornfully dubbed the "log college" by his critics—and his
followers instituted similar informal enterprises. In all these
new light establishments we can see the origins of subsequent effort to base a native American evangelicalism on
a soundly educated ministry. Learning without piety was
worthless, to be sure, but the cause of piety needed its own
learned men to drive out the liberal-minded pharisees who,
it was thought, were corrupting religion everywhere. The
awakenings in the middle colonies fostered a Bible-
oriented ideal of intellectual life that rejected antireligious tendencies in the transatlantic republic of letters but
absorbed its science and moral philosophy.

The "log college" identification, embraced by the new
lights, suggests the advantages of linking a new American
movement to the cause of ordinary men and women. A
term meant to disparage these ventures actually enhanced their attractiveness. The Tennents, for their part,
were only too willing to attack traditional elites, particularly the ministers, in the name of the still older authorities of the Reformation and the Bible, and the awakenings stirred up anti-English sentiments that came easily to
many ethnic and religious groups in the middle colonies.
Nevertheless, religious enthusiasm had less dramatic consequences for the social order than did the Presbyterian
and Baptist movements in Virginia, if only because there
was no broadly dispersed planter hierarchy to be threatened by popular fervor. Although there were critics who
voiced a concern for reason and order akin to Chauncy's
or Garden's, they could scarcely pretend to speak for a
well-established orthodoxy, Puritan or Anglican, and they
could not overlook the evangelicals' own strong interest
in the advancement of learning. We must also remember
that ethnic loyalties kept many groups separate from any
sense of common cause. Within old light Presbyterianism,

for example, there was an important faction of Ulstermen, with their own seminary at New Ark, Delaware, who
kept apart from both the Tennents and native new lights.
It was not upper-class conservatism, but an attachment to
local standards and customs, that motivated their resistance to innovations. Many colonists could not read or listen to English speakers like Whitefield or Edwards. Some
writers on the Great Awakening, a term coined a century
later, have depicted a universal emotionalism sweeping up
the common people all along the continent, but the awakenings in the middle colonies, though the linchpin of much
that occurred, remind us how segmented these societies
remained.

Some of the commoners, moreover, were fired up by
much more secular views of the world. We know too little
about the urban working classes anywhere in North
America, but in Philadelphia there were reports of
mounting secular radicalism. Whitefield's great successes
there are famous, if only because of the description in
Benjamin Franklin's *Autobiography* (1771) of one open-air
meeting when the evangelist's voice carried far enough to
reach thirty thousand people. Franklin, though a friend
of Whitefield's, had no personal use for evangelical religion. He did, however, concede in the intellectually fashionable style that it was useful for common folk to be believers. Rather than stirring up disorder, religious
excitement changed their manners and made them industrious and moral. In fact, it supported the same purposes found in Franklin's popular series, *Poor Richard's
Almanack* (1733 and thereafter), which encouraged thrift
and respectability. Philadelphia was taking its place as the
largest city in North America, with declining numbers of
slaves and white servants and increasing numbers of free
white families striving to become economically independent. Many of these whites despised "riotous livers" among

the wealthy and unprincipled degenerates at the bottom of society. They saw themselves as honest, sober people; and the awakenings, with their projections of a better world in the offing, reinforced their aspirations.

The emergence of mechanics and artisans in the political life of Philadelphia was an extraordinary development in prerevolutionary America. Eventually the Pennsylvania government, in which the Scotch-Irish supplanted the genteel Quakers and Anglicans, gained a reputation for democratic radicalism unequaled anywhere in the world before the French Revolution. To conservatives, it became a fearsome symbol of unwelcome challenges to the rule of the privileged few. The best-known voice to emanate from this milieu was that of the immigrant Thomas Paine, who had knocked around England long enough to be well versed in both working-class religious radicalism and in more secular forms of denouncing the party in power. Arriving in 1774 (on a ship filled with German immigrants), he fell in with a circle of remarkably articulate Philadelphia artisans, including Benjamin Rush, son of a farmer-gunsmith, an Anglican converted to Presbyterianism, educated at a log college and then at Princeton, and now a busy physician. A fervent hater of the English monarchy, Rush proudly traced his lineage to an ancestor in Cromwell's army, and he equated "a pope in religion and a king in power." It was Rush who urged Paine to write a pamphlet advocating independence and gave it the title *Common Sense* (1776), a pamphlet that was read so widely and discussed so furiously that it was probably the single most important literary event of the American Revolution. In ridiculing the very idea of monarchy and contrasting the simple virtues of America to the dissipation of the Old World, it evoked images of a new utopia in which all men would be free. *Common Sense* was important, not for its theoretical subtlety or consistency, but for bringing to public debate strains of antagonism and visions of liberation that were never extinguished thereafter. Even some of those who agreed with its immediate purposes worried that it introduced into political discourse the rudeness of street and tavern. Written for a mass audience, it seemed too abandoned in its invective against king and gentlefolk. Yet its successes earned Paine at least temporarily the comradeship of slaveowner revolutionaries like Washington and Jefferson.

Paine knew his evangelized audience well enough to infuse *Common Sense* with the language of the Bible and Protestant millennialism. He called monarchy, among other things, "the most prosperous invention the devil ever set on foot for the promotion of idolatry" and "the popery of government." Yet Paine himself privately felt contempt for the Bible and already had in mind the attacks on institutional Christianity that, when published years later, would blacken his reputation. Rather than regarding him simply as a spokesman for artisan viewpoints, there is reason to see him as a self-conscious and somewhat manipulative pamphleteer, ahead of his time in realizing the power to be wielded by mobilizing mass opinion. But his goal was not personal influence or economic self-aggrandizement; it was the promotion of truth in revising social arrangements. He stood out as a new kind of intellectual, different from the clergy and the planter class. As Eric Foner has suggested:

> Paine should perhaps be considered one of the first intellectuals [in this new sense], a social group which emerged into prominence in the second half of the eighteenth century. Then as now, intellectuals hailed from diverse social origins and . . . often thought of themselves as being above narrow personal, party or class loyalties. "Independence is my

happiness," Paine wrote in *The Rights of Man* [1791], "and I view things as they are, without regard to place or person; my country is the world, and my religion is to do good."

Intellectual classes had existed before, of course, but usually in a specific relation to the social hierarchy. They promoted God's word or showed the adornments of gentlemen. Cut loose by the revolutionary ferment in Philadelphia and by later revolutionary movements abroad, Paine came to view himself as having a free-floating connection to the "republic of letters." Given honorary citizenship in France as a hero of popular freedom, he wound up in prison as an independent, and unwelcome, critic of the radical revolutionaries known as Jacobins.

Philadelphia had other remarkable men with backgrounds in the artisan class who made a similar pilgrimage, though with less controversy, from political roles in a changing city to independent status in the international enlightenment. It is ironic that studies of Jefferson, in seeking to understand this Virginia gentleman as an American philosopher, usually focus on his communications with Franklin, Rush, David Rittenhouse, Charles Willson Peale, and other notable artisans of Philadelphia. Many of these men adopted liberal, rationalistic views, and they did so without any of the overtones of conflict that prevailed in Massachusetts or Virginia.

Franklin, a fugitive from the Mathers' Boston, never questioned that "the most acceptable service we render to [God] is doing good to his other children." After a youthful period as a freethinker, he became at least a nominal supporter of Presbyterianism, until he dissented from the awakening's infatuation with a new birth. "The Day begins in an insensible Dawn," he wrote; virtue emerged by degrees, and "men don't become very good or very bad in an instant." After that, he preferred the liberal anti-Calvinism of the Anglican church. In fact, no religion was really important to his lifelong experiments in studying and practicing "the art of virtue," which was more like a craft or discipline than a crisis of faith requiring supernatural aid. Similarly, Rush rejoined the Anglicans because they seemed more liberal and enlightened. Although the importance of religion never slackened for him—he compared the American Revolution to the birth of Christ and stressed the uses of the Bible in teaching morality to a republican electorate—his views became so liberal that he is today counted among the founders of Unitarianism and Universalism. Rittenhouse, a self-taught farmer who used the simple pen name "A Mechanic," was exorbitantly praised for his contributions to astronomy. According to Jefferson, "he has by imitation approached nearer its Maker than any man who has lived from creation to this day." Jefferson referred to Rittenhouse's famous orrery, an ingenious replica of the Newtonian universe in which all the planets moved with clocklike precision, to musical accompaniment, in keeping with their positions on any day of the past or future. Not surprisingly, the inventor of this machine had religious views tending toward deism, a movement that celebrated the regularity and sufficiency of the universe without its Creator's continuing intervention. So did the views of Peale, a saddle maker turned portrait painter, who established a museum of America's curiosities where visitors could deepen their knowledge of the New World and contemplate the wisdom of the Creator. So nonevangelical were these artisan intellectuals that Philadelphia provided an obvious haven for Joseph Priestley, a Unitarian, political radical, and chemist, who was driven from England by hostile mobs. It was Priestley who recorded Franklin's world-famous experiments with kites and electricity, experiments that virtually symbolized the Enlightenment's reduction of God's mysterious light to the level of human explanation.

Priestley disliked city life and chose to move out to the Pennsylvania "wilderness," much as Jefferson pursued his studies at Monticello. Other contemporaries turned to classical images depicting a life of frugal meditation and patriotic duty away from the distractions and corruptions of the city. John Adams wrote wistfully of returning to his "little hut and forty acres," living on potatoes and seaweed; and Washington's love for Mount Vernon epitomized an ideal of virtuous retreat. By and large, however, anti-urbanism has been an exaggerated theme in accounts of this period and of American culture in general. Revolutionary Philadelphia exemplified the values of the city as a matrix for intellectual life. Sustained contact with one another permitted Paine, Franklin, Rush, Rittenhouse, Peale, and other acquaintances to nurture a sense of themselves as independent minds in quest of self-improvement and truth beyond the requirements of any faction or geographical interest. They aspired to speak for virtue and truth from a disinterested viewpoint, not from the perspective of a particular group like the New England clergy or the Virginia slaveowners. The aspiration had its illusions: their lives were inextricably tied to the social history of the Revolution, which was not so kind to other intellectuals. Except for Paine, none of them earned his living as a thinker-writer; all had other trades. Nevertheless, their location permitted the delights of association that strengthened their emphasis on the measure of their time that was devoted to the intellect. Jefferson sometimes dreamed of luring better neighbors, including Priestley, to his part of Virginia because he missed such sustaining intercourse.

Jefferson was instrumental in moving the new nation's capital from Philadelphia because he associated some elements in the city with intrigue and corruption. But if we look at the Philadelphia intellectuals, we are not struck by any frivolity or dissipation. Moored in the artisan class, their collective endeavor aimed at virtuous improvement. Franklin's Junto, founded in 1727, is a familiar example of ambitious young men banding together for regular conversation about their latest reading. Their immediate purpose was to improve their conversation and manners—in other words, to advance themselves—but they also discussed the advantages to "the public" of new laws and methods of eliminating "ignorance and wickedness" from the populace. It is no wonder they were prepared to approve the effects of Whitefield's and the Tennents' work, even while conceiving themselves as somewhat detached observers.

A more important example is the philosophical society, modeled on the Royal Society in London, that Franklin first proposed in a circular letter in 1743. "The first drudgery of settling new colonies . . . is now pretty well over," he asserted; every colony boasted men "in circumstances that set them at ease, and afford leisure to cultivate the finer arts, and improve the common stock of knowledge." The time was propitious for bringing together "all philosophical experiments that let light into the nature of things, tend to increase the power of man over matter, and multiply the conveniences or pleasures of life." Not until 1769 did the old Junto give way to the American Philosophical Society, Held at Philadelphia, for Promoting Useful Knowledge. Franklin was the society's first president, and Rittenhouse the second, with Jefferson succeeding him in 1796. Both Franklin's original letter and Jefferson's eventual succession show the intention of linking together a far-flung intelligentsia, and the society's *Transactions* may justly be regarded as an organ of American cultural unity. If Princeton gave a common focus to evangelicalism throughout the American provinces, the American Philosophical Society had similar meanings for Americans of philosophical temperament. But in both instances local contexts remained crucial. While Jefferson, except for a few years in government, maintained his intellectual ties by correspondence, the Philadelphians enjoyed frequent contact.

There was shared excitement in events like Peale's exhumation of the skeleton of a mammoth or the transit of Venus across the sun. The latter event in 1769, not to be repeated for a century, promised to make possible significant new calculations in astronomy—and to demonstrate to skeptical Europeans the progress of America in science. An array of clocks and telescopes was set up outside Philadelphia, and sightseers watched the recording of crucial observations. The results clinched Rittenhouse's international fame, though the great mechanic had swooned at the difficulties of seeing the contacts exactly in the mists of Venus's atmosphere. The moment "excited," in Rush's words, "an emotion of delight so exquisite and powerful, as to induce fainting." Quite apart from its significance to eighteenth-century science, we may be impressed by the amiability of this scene of intense emotions. Well might these intellectuals be impressed by the moral sense God gave all persons to act well in society as well as by the extraordinary insights that a few achieved.

The give and take inside a small circle, within a growing and changing city, made Philadelphia exciting. Much as some intellectuals admired a Whitefield or Davies, there were sharp divergences of purpose and affiliation. Within Philadelphia, the political decline of the Quakers created openings for the advance of artisans and philosophers. Within the Quakers, in turn, extraordinary reconstructions of purpose produced great exemplars of piety and benevolence like the antislavery hero Anthony Benezet.

INTELLECTUAL LIFE IN AMERICA

Paine, Rush, and some other intellectuals had Quaker backgrounds. In various efforts to "do good" they were inevitably allied with men like Benezet. They could even join in international acclaim for the Quakers as a true-hearted sect distinct from the popish hypocrisy that too often infected religion. Yet Quaker exclusiveness had little appeal in the secular discourse of intellectuals.

The artisan circle also proved to have interests in conflict with efforts to shore up the Anglican church in the middle colonies. Both the New Englander Samuel Johnson, who in 1753 became the head of the new King's College (later Columbia) in New York, and William Smith, a Scot who in 1755 became provost of the College of Philadelphia, had visions of a liberal Anglican establishment solidifying a provincial elite. The vision was attractive, as the affiliations of Franklin, Rush, and others with Anglicanism for various lengths of time may indicate. Smith could brag that the Anglican church, "by soft and easy means, daily gains ground." Johnson was a learned man who continues to interest students of college curricula and early American philosophy, but he resigned the presidency of King's in 1763 without having achieved substantial success in his larger objectives. American Anglicanism did not give King's the preeminence that evangelicalism gave Princeton. Smith's career is more complex, for he was temporarily able to wield great influence in Pennsylvania. He launched a philosophical society that merged with Franklin's in the great 1769 venture, and he was deeply involved in the observations of the transit of Venus (even commandeering some equipment on its way to Harvard). Through his *American Magazine* and other enterprises, he introduced a widely admired *bon ton* into Philadelphia society. In the late 1760s, under his leadership, the cause of polite Christianity, as distinct from gloomy, severe Calvinism, had a promising foundation. Yet in a few years it was to crumble, in part because artisan radicals linked it to upper-class frivolity, in part because to evangelicals the Anglican cause smacked of English corruption. Accused of scheming to become an Anglican bishop, Smith was arrested as a Tory sympathizer and lived out the Revolution in discredited impotence.

In a 1773 address to the American Philosophical Society, Smith had hymned the westward progress of civilization: "the regions on this side of the Atlantic, as well as those on the other, shall enjoy their *Day* of Freedom, Light, and polished Life." As that faith, shorn of its elitist pretensions, deepened among some circles of American revolutionaries, Smith went to jail. The crash of his hopes for genteel enlightenment foreshadowed further divisive consequences of the Revolution, a subject of the next chapter. Already we may note that there were problems in the conception of intellectuals transcending narrow interests: in a revolution it made a difference which side one took. Despite confidence in the light spreading across America, there were also signs that for some groups the light could turn to ashes.

REVOLUTIONARY FAITH

The second half of the eighteenth century was a period of profound change in American attitudes and behavior. Social historians have detected such diverse indications of change as declining birth rates and altered housing styles. Economic historians point to the increasing prosperity of individual farmers working hard to supply grains to Europe. Immigration intensified; where there were cities, they grew larger. Many of the patterns remain unclear, but there was certainly less reason to think of the colonies as merely outposts of European civilization. We have noticed a number of speculations on the progress of America, as in Jonathan Edwards's musings on the onset of the millennium or Benjamin Franklin's appeals to men of intellect to join together. Yet both the major contemporary interpretations of cultural change in the New World—the faith in a Great Awakening and the vision of an Enlightenment—had European counterparts. Both could be regarded as broad movements in Western culture that gained particular importance in the provincial societies.

In fact, the effects of the awakenings varied greatly from one colony to another. America did not have a single metropolis, an Edinburgh, London, or Paris in which cultural change could take a single coherent shape. In New England, the awakenings were the occasion for the fission of the Puritan orthodoxy into at least three major fragments: the Baptists as a common people's religion; a seaboard intelligentsia with little use for the Calvinist outlook on human nature; and Edwardseans who sought to reassert old doctrines with new sophistication. In the South, the awakenings posed a clear threat to the power of the top class, as great numbers of converts removed themselves from institutions and patterns of behavior on which the hierarchy seemed to depend. While the Anglican church distintegrated, however, the slaveowning class survived, frequently by identifying itself with philosophical respect for the virtues of the commoners. In the middle colonies, the most heterogeneous of all, there were endeavors to consolidate an advanced, genteel culture, usually under the banner of Anglicanism. But the results were less impressive than the stability of Presbyterian evangelicalism under the leadership of Princeton and the achievements of less intensely religious circles, preeminently in the American Philosophical Society.

Historians have tried for years to link the Great Awakening to the Revolution. Some colonists had learned to think of America as a special place, to take pride in their own institutions, and even to denounce the corruptions of the Old World. The awakenings help to account for the cataclysmic rhetoric in which some colonists understood political provocations and crises. But it has proved impossible to show that any pro- or anti-awakening groups were preeminently responsible for the Revolution. In every region, revolutionary leaders came from both evangelical and liberal backgrounds (as well as from Edwardseans, Princetonians, and others who defended old doctrines in terms of new philosophies). The Revolution did not have religious causes, and its coming cannot be explained merely by looking at the important reorientations of intellectual life. In spite of the religious labors of a Whitefield or the circular letters of a Franklin, philosophical Americans still had more contact with Englishmen than with colonists in other regions. One of the subplots of the Continental Congresses and other efforts to rally concerted resistance to England was the way in which delegates from each province took stock of strangers from the others. In time, as we shall see, vastly different conceptions of the meanings of the Revolution competed for dominance in the new nation's cultural life and politics.

If the Great Awakening does not adequately explain the coming of Revolution, what of the Enlightenment? Some historians have indeed contended that the American Revolution "institutionalized" the Enlightenment: that is, it set up a nation without a king, hereditary aristocracy, or established church. But others have countered that this is too negative a definition of the Enlightenment: it merely focuses on what was lacking after a diversely motivated war for independence. There was no American equivalent to the erection of a statue of Reason atop the Cathedral of Notre Dame in Paris, no establishment of a secular religion to replace Christian superstition with its own values and ceremonies. If we equate the Enlightenment with the extreme anti-Christian manifestations of revolutionary France, in other words, America was out of step. But few European historians would accept such a narrow equation, if only because some enlightened *philosophes* of Europe were as skeptical about reason as they were about Christianity whereas others were religious men. We may conclude this chapter by taking a closer look at the vexatious term *Enlightenment*.

We have previously used the term in two senses. First, it signified the belief that human knowledge was spreading into new areas and reaching greater numbers of the population. In both Europe and America, there were many who felt that science had shown the way "to increase the power of man over matter" and even to make better social arrangements. Franklin's Junto was not the only group to discuss whether new laws might offer advantages to society. While it would be foolish to discount the power of vested interests or, more generally, the affection of many colonists for traditional institutions, political discourse on both sides of the Atlantic revealed a growing tendency to defend proposals in the name of social improvement and human freedom. Even the awakenings benefited from the weakening force of the argument that older ways were necessarily better ways. In this century, as more and more men and women supposedly were liberated from ignorance, slavery came under denunciation as an unjustifiable violation of human autonomy.

Second, we have referred to the international "republic of letters" as a network guiding intellectual life. The ideal went beyond the longstanding communication of theologians and philosophers in Latin; it superseded the notion of the country gentlemen as a virtuoso. Though there was still some assumption that ease and leisure were essential to intellectual life, a popularizing tendency in the manuals and digests—even in the newspapers—enabled ambitious men and women to keep abreast of new beliefs by reading about them in their native languages. Clergymen were participants in discourse over scientific and ethical issues, but the discourse itself extended well beyond the church. By midcentury the "republic" gladly included thoughtful mechanics and farmers; too much leisure might even seem antithetical to hard intellectual work. Much intellectual discussion centered on the capacities of ordinary people. Without the published guides to intellectual life and the ideology of common pursuit that underlay them, it would have been difficult for gifted American provincials to address their works to international audiences. In concentrating on men like Edwards, Jefferson, and Franklin, we should not overlook the strivings of others—college students, urban club members, prosperous planters—who turned to the same guides in order to improve their manners and conversation. College towns and urban environments were especially hospitable to those who enjoyed learned discourse, but the ideal of intellectual life was adaptable to many different local circumstances.

The Enlightenment might be thought of simply as a faith in mental progress that furnished a transatlantic identity to intellectual life. Many Americans shared this faith and sense of themselves. But European historians sometimes adopt a more programmatic definition of the Enlightenment, focusing on a small "party" of radical thinkers—among them, Voltaire, Rousseau, Diderot, Gibbon, Hume—who subjected the institutions of the old re-

gimes to devastating criticism. "The men of the Enlightenment," in the summary of Peter Gay, "united on a
vastly ambitious program, a program of secularism, humanity, cosmopolitanism, and freedom, above all, freedom in its many forms—freedom from arbitrary power,
freedom of speech, freedom of trade, freedom to realize
one's talents, freedom of aesthetic response, freedom, in
a word, of moral man to make his way in the world." Gay
was responding to more critical historians who have
stressed the overweening faith in science, "the superficial
rationalism, foolish optimism, and irresponsible Utopian-
ism" of the *philosophes;* and Gay conceded that these charges
were sometimes hurled by one against another. Without
attempting to resolve disputes about European intellectual history, the point seems clear that very few Americans shared in the most skeptical attacks of this kind of
Enlightenment. Jefferson kept his religious opinions to
himself, and Paine suffered a drastic loss of reputation
when he wrote his antireligious *Age of Reason* (1794–1795).
The typical American stance was to defend respectable
religion while denouncing papal tyranny and the worst
abuses of enthusiasm. There were few proponents of radical reconstruction of American institutions. Revolutionary rhetoric was more likely to assail the corruptions of
European aristocracy than to express displeasure at what
had evolved in the new.

In the midst of the Stamp Act crisis John Adams published his eclectic *Dissertation on the Feudal and Canon Law*
(1765), which attempted to summarize a common American outlook. It embraced a view of history that Gay has
shown to have been central to the European Enlightenment. It paid pious respect to "the great examples of
Greece and Rome," ages of simple republican government and wise accomplishments in philosophy, and de-

plored the Dark Ages of absolute monarchy and Christian bigotry. The "Romish clergy" had imprisoned human nature in a hateful ecclesiastical system, and feudal lords had perfected schemes of hierarchy that doomed "the common people" to "servile dependence." Since the Reformation, however, "knowledge gradually spread in Europe, . . . and in proportion as that increased and spread among the people, ecclesiastical and civil tyranny . . . lost their strength and weight." Adams wrote with special fervor on the strivings of the English people for liberation. He praised the spirit of Magna Carta and the love of liberty that had "severed the head" of Charles I. He asserted that "the spirit of liberty is as ardent as ever among the body of the [English] nation, though a few individuals may be corrupted." In short, to the general historical consciousness of the European Enlightenment was added a specific sense of traditional English liberties endangered by a conspiracy of corrupt men plotting a return to despotism. This sense was widely shared in English opposition politics—Paine also popularized it in America—and it was as fully consistent with evangelical zeal as with Adams's liberalism.

In Adams's view, the struggle between the tyranny of the Stuart kings and popular liberty had "peopled" America. By taking the Puritans to stand for all colonists and by regarding as their purpose the establishment of religious and political liberty, he was able to write with awe of the settlement of America as "the opening of a grand scene and design in Providence for the illumination of the ignorant, and the emancipation of the slavish part of mankind all over the earth." To eradicate ignorance and protect liberty, the founders had set up schools and colleges and encouraged the art of printing, with impressive consequences for the intellect:

A native of America who cannot read and write is as rare an appearance as a Jacobite [a partisan of old-style monarchy] or a Roman Catholic, that is, as rare as a comet or an earthquake. It has been observed, that we are all of us lawyers, divines, politicians, and philosophers. And . . . all candid foreigners who have passed through this country, and conversed freely with all sorts of people here, will allow, that they have never seen so much knowledge and civility among the common people in any part of the world.

The immediate point of this sketch of history was to denounce the Stamp Acts, which threatened to load "the press, the colleges, and even an almanack and a newspaper, with restraints and duties." Adams linked this threat to other signs, as he imagined, of schemes by "high churchmen and high statesmen" to establish a bishop and subjugate America. But it is interesting that he could take for granted an American intellectual establishment prepared to withstand the challenge:

Let the pulpit resound with the doctrine and sentiments of religious liberty. . . . Let the bar . . . inform the world of mighty struggles and numberless sacrifices made by our ancestors in defence of freedom. . . . Let the colleges join their harmony in the same delightful concert. . . . In a word, let every sluice of knowledge be opened and set a-flowing.

In the Old World the international Enlightenment sometimes stood in combat against the privileged orders, but Adams reveals a very different cast of mind, determined to preserve the legacy of the American past against external enemies.*

The American Enlightenment refrained from vehement criticism of religion. It observed only a few vestiges of antiquated privilege to be eradicated in America. If it had a prevailing faith, it rested in the moral sense of the ordinary man—the white man, at any rate—who already had a good measure of freedom. Its implications for white women were untested, though it was more likely to glorify motherhood than to promote female independence. Its aspirations for the general improvements of manners were clear enough, and there was a provincial longing for greater recognition of American achievements. Nevertheless, in a land that already boasted its Rittenhouses and Franklins, who were admired even in Europe as exemplars of a new and relatively open society, the intellectual classes were comfortable with their prospects. Enlightenment may not have caused revolution, but it helped to make it tolerable and competed with evangelicalism to give it definition. We should not neglect the dashed hopes of some polite moderates; no doubt many émigrés were men of enlightened sentiments. But there was widespread belief in America's good fortune, a belief expressed by Washington at the end of the war: "The foundation of our Empire was not laid in the gloomy age of ignorance and superstition, but at an epoch when the rights of mankind were better understood and more clearly defined, than at any former period." At this "auspicious period," when

---

*Readers of preceding chapters will notice that the specific points of this historical ideology were mostly false. But that does not diminish their significance in helping us comprehend Adams's and many contemporaries' view of the world. A similar sense of American history has remained influential to the present day.

"philosophers, sages, and legislators" had done so much to enlarge human knowledge, the United States came into existence; "and if their citizens should not be completely free and happy, the fault will be entirely their own."

FOR FURTHER READING

The most comprehensive study of conflicts in mid-eighteenth-century American culture is Alan Heimert's *Religion and the American Mind: From the Great Awakening to the Revolution* (1966). Its interpretations are supported in a valuable collection of documents: Alan Heimert and Perry Miller, eds., *The Great Awakening* (1967). For criticism of exaggerated interpretations of these events, see Jon Butler, "Enthusiasm Described and Decried: The Great Awakening as Interpretative Fiction," *Journal of American History* (1982).

Charles Chauncy and the New England opposers of the awakenings are analyzed in Conrad Wright, *The Beginnings of Unitarianism in America* (1955). For a brief biography of the leading Separate Baptist, see William G. McLoughlin, *Isaac Backus and the American Pietistic Tradition* (1967). An outstanding study of cultural change in one section of New England is Richard L. Bushman, *From Puritan to Yankee: Character and the Social Order in Connecticut, 1690–1765* (1967). For a more general survey, see Edwin Gaustad, *The Great Awakening in New England* (1957).

The literature on Edwards is vast. Perry Miller's *Jonathan Edwards* (1949) is brilliant, but many of its interpretations are now considered erroneous. A good introduction to Edwards's theology is Conrad Cherry, *The Theology of Jonathan Edwards* (1966). By far the most important study of Edwards's role in intellectual history is Norman Fiering, *Jonathan Edwards's Moral Thought and Its British Context* (1981). Modern editions of all Edwards's works, with scholarly introductions, are being published by Yale University Press.

On evangelicalism and social change in Virginia, an exciting work is Rhys Isaac, *The Transformation of Virginia, 1740–1790* (1982). On the conflict of religious viewpoints, as shown in the diary of an Anglican minister among the evangelicals, a good source is Richard J. Hooker, ed., *The Carolina Backcountry on the Eve of the Revolution* (1953).

The standard authority on Presbyterianism, especially in the middle colonies, is Leonard J. Trinterud, *The Forming of an American Tradition* (1949). It is modified by Elizabeth I. Nybakken, "New Light on the Old Side: Irish Influences on Colonial Presbyterianism," *Journal of American History* (1982). A lucid introduction to the artisan culture of Philadelphia is Eric Foner's *Tom Paine and Revolutionary America* (1976).

The most comprehensive and sensible account of American varieties of the Enlightenment is Henry F. May's *The Enlightenment in America* (1976). A combative reconstruction of "the lost language of the Enlightenment" is Garry Wills's *Inventing America: Jefferson's Declaration of Independence* (1978). The reader should note, however, that its dismissal of Locke as a major influence on the Declaration has been challenged by other scholars. See, for example, Ronald Hamowy, "Jefferson and the Scottish Enlightenment," *William and Mary Quarterly* (1979). A searching psychobiography of Jefferson, one that gives much attention to the Head-and-Heart dialogue, is Fawn Brodie's *Thomas Jefferson: An Intimate History* (1974). Daniel J. Boorstin's *The Lost World of Thomas Jefferson* (1948) links the great Virginian to the philosophical circle in Philadelphia.

For a helpful survey of the social backgrounds of intellectual life in this period, see Richard Hofstadter, *America at 1750* (1971). The most penetrating study of revolutionary rhetoric is Bernard Bailyn's *Ideological Origins of the American Revolution* (1967). On science and the "republic of letters," see Brooke Hindle, *The Pursuit of Science in Revolutionary America* (1956).

Peter Gay has offered a two-volume study of the European Enlightenment under the general title, *The Enlightenment: An Interpretation* (1967, 1969). Crucial developments in European and American intellectual history are brilliantly analyzed in David Brion Davis's works: *The Problem of Slavery in Western Culture* (1966) and *The Problem of Slavery in the Age of Revolution* (1975).

IV

THE REORGANIZATION OF INTELLECTUAL LIFE

VIRTUE

A significant gulf separated theory from belief in late-eighteenth-century America. In theory, many subscribed to optimistic views of human nature. Enlightened men celebrated the powers of reason to comprehend the created universe and the capacities of the moral sense for virtuous social behavior. Some of their writings suggest a virtual amnesia on the old topics of the lustful passions and the conflict-ridden will. Horrible events sometimes happened, of course, and people sometimes behaved wickedly, but there was no inclination to blame an evil human nature. As corrupting institutions (like slaveholding) disappeared and good institutions (like schools) trained the moral sense in habits of virtue, the unhappier forms of human behavior would recede from history.

The evangelicals had trumpeted their loyalty to Calvinism, and they spoke feelingly of corruption and depravity. Yet the notion of a Great Awakening, as distinct from the conversions of small remnants of believers in a universe of persistent sin, fostered an optimism not too different from that of the Enlightenment. However corrupt human nature might have been originally, the exciting facts were the spread of regeneration and the approach of the millennium. Improvements in the institutions of religion, replacing unconverted sacramentalists with a new light clergy, opened the way to the transformation of human nature. As Jonathan Edwards's most influential disciple, Samuel Hopkins, explained in *A Treatise on the Millennium* (1793), Christ's kingdom would no longer be "confined to very narrow bounds" but would instead subdue "all hearts to a willing subjection." The dawning era would bring "a great increase of light and knowledge to a degree vastly beyond what has been before," with "sufficient leisure" for all classes "to pursue and acquire learning of every kind, that will be beneficial to themselves and to society." Error would vanish, charity would govern human transactions, and peace would prevail. By the time of the Revolution the most successful evangelical movement, the Wesleyans or Methodists, ignored the Calvinistic doctrine of human inability to see clearly and behave rightly. In theory, all men and women were free to close with Christ, and many thousands accepted the invitation to step forward to redemption.

Regardless of these converging theories of sweetness and light, the habit of believing the worst of one's opponents was deeply ingrained. Revolutions generally raise contradictions between ideal schemes of human perfection and immediate fears of wide-scale corruption. American revolutionaries denounced British courtiers and American Tories in the traditional language of religious vituperation, and they feared that ordinary citizens were prone to advance selfish interests rather than the common good. The postrevolutionary years witnessed so many frenzied charges and countercharges that one historian summed up the era as an "Age of Passion." Republicans portrayed Alexander Hamilton and the Federalist party as men of satanic ambition. Federalists spoke of "a mental epidemic" overturning authority throughout the world. The republican physician Benjamin Rush coined the word *"anarchia"* to denote the new "form of insanity," which he described as "the excess of the passion for liberty," inflamed by war and unrestrained by reason. And if evangelicals saw glimmerings of the millennium, they also voiced recurrent fears that the world lay at the edge of destruction. Edwards's grandson Timothy Dwight, president of Yale, expressed the immoderate fear that if the Jeffersonians ever came to power "we may finally see our wives and daughters the victims of legal prostitution."

The inflated rhetoric and unbridled fears of the postrevolutionary decades did *not* reintroduce searching examinations of lust and passion in American intellectual life. Rush praised the restraints of reason; Dwight trembled that reason was about to be deified in the French style. But remarkable agreement actually united them and other partisans. They embraced similar visions of temperate behavior in simple republican settings; they agreed on the utility of religion and education in shaping a virtuous citizenry. Assessments of human nature became, if anything, even blander and more optimistic in subsequent decades, not to be reappraised until the terrifying death tolls of the Civil War and World War I, and most of all the Holocaust, brought humanity's destructive capacities inescapably back into view. Despite the exaggerated flights of denunciation and the genuine fears of subversion and misrule, the Revolution launched a long era, between Calvinism and depth psychology, when evil was unaccountable in prevailing theories of human nature.

A key word of the revolutionary years was *virtue*. The simple definition of that word in Dr. Johnson's *Dictionary* was "moral goodness," but everyone knew it had classical roots associating it with love of one's homeland, concern for its safety, and willingness to suppress selfish interests in order to benefit the public. The philosopher Montesquieu had described it as the characteristic attribute of a republic, just as fear was characteristic in despotisms and honor in monarchies. "Most of the ancients," he reported, "lived under governments that had virtue for their principle; and when this was in full vigor they performed actions unusual in our time, and at which our narrow minds are astonished." It was opposed to the "effeminacy" and vice that were supposedly undermining English liberty; it was the "manly" quality that John Adams was pleased to see at large as Americans defended their civilization. With a "suddenness" that Adams found "astonishing"—and that has puzzled historians ever since—leaders in every colony rushed to the conclusion in the 1770s that America must be governed by this republican principle. "Idolatry to monarchs and servility to aristocratical pride" were eradicated; in their place must arise dedication to "the public good."

Montesquieu associated virtue with "the love of equality," and theologians had broadened its meanings to include "benevolence" to all beings. It would be a mistake, however, to exaggerate the egalitarianism or libertarianism of most early revolutionary praise of republican virtue. In some ways it was reminiscent of John Winthrop's ideal of a moral hierarchy infused with a spirit of self-sacrifice and respect for law. According to John Adams in 1776: "There must be a decency, and respect, and veneration introduced for persons in authority, of every rank, or we are undone"; the people must obey republican rulers out of "love and not fear." After visiting Versailles in 1788 a young Philadelphia gentleman, Thomas Shippen, reflected on the blessings of his homeland. Hereditary distinctions fostered wretchedness among the poor and "ennui" among the privileged. "Happy above all countries is our country," which exhibited the *"degree of equality"* required for human contentment, "without destroying the necessary subordination." The revolutionary Samuel Adams fused the republican goals of selflessness and discipline in a single phrase: "the *Christian* Sparta."

As the historian Gordon Wood has shown, many revolutionary leaders expected to dominate American republican government as a gentlemanly elite class. Many shared John Adams's resentment that under royal governors offices and prestige had been grabbed by an undeserving clique "to the exclusion of much better men." Once ties to England were severed and the Tories had departed, prominence and authority would flow to the meritorious, "a natural aristocracy" who were best equipped to see the good of society as a whole. The natural leaders were not flattering toadies of the Crown, not a corrupt hereditary elite, but they took for granted a connection between social position and discernment. Planters, merchants, lawyers, college presidents, and ministers from every colony debated with one another at intercolonial assemblies and communicated through letters displaying classical learning and knowledge of the "science of politics." There was a steady outpouring of treatises that did not appeal to the populace as a whole (as did Thomas Paine's *Common Sense*) but addressed an American equivalent of what the British called the "political nation"—a constricted network of rational and decent men whose opinions inevitably guided their deferential countrymen. For the most part, they paid no disrespect to lesser men (though they referred occasionally to the "ignorant vulgar" or the "rubbish"). The republican ideal obliged them to care about the common good and to base the legitimacy of their governments on the general consent of "the people." In an America that now seemed blessed to have developed without the trappings of Old World nobility, social prominence seemed roughly equivalent to merit. All that was necessary was to keep opportunities open for the Rushes and Franklins who were able to improve their minds' and fortunes. (For example, Jefferson's educational plans provided, as we have seen, for a gifted few to be "raked up" from below.)

These leaders disagreed, sometimes vehemently, on numerous issues. It was naive to expect men to repress, in the name of a vaguely defined common good, class and regional motives that had evolved over years of separate colonial development. The revolutionary situation presented many novel problems, compressed in a short term of years, that cherished political traditions had barely anticipated. The importance of religion in America was bound to be a divisive problem. There was no consensus on how far commonwealths should go in shaping morals or promoting particular economic interests. Without rehearsing in these pages the history of political parties and constitution making in the early Republic, we can appreciate that there was a unique, brief interval in American history when the political leadership was taken to be both a social elite and a moral intelligentsia.

In the first of the changing fashions that have proved an enduring feature of republican culture, these men hungered to institutionalize classical virtue. Some of the manifestations are well remembered to this day: the names of new polises (their Athenses, favored for college towns, Ithacas, and Corydons); the name of the veterans' organization and land-speculation scheme (the Society of Cincinnati, after a Roman general who returned, like Washington, to his farm); the names of gentlemen's clubs (their

Atheneums and Aedian societies); the classical insignia (the motto and Roman numerals on the national currency) and monuments (from Monticello to Masonic temples); the terminology of government (the capitols and senators); the names of children who later came to prominence (Cassius Marcellus Clay in Kentucky and Solon Robinson in Indiana); more mockingly, the names of slaves (the Pompeys and Catos); and endless orations and lyrics on lofty themes. Timothy Dwight's *Greenfield Hill* (1794) depicted a village schoolmaster who

> *Inchanted hung o'er Virgil's honeyed lay,*
> *And smiled, to see desipient Horace play:*
> *Gleaned scraps of Greek; and, curious, traced afar,*
> *Through Pope's clear glass, the bright Maeonian star.*

Many spoke of a "new Athens." One revolutionary general confessed that he had longed to live in the third or fourth century of Rome until he matured to appreciate the glory of American institutions.

Classicism was a theme drawn from the eighteenth-century Enlightenment, which approached a heady climax in the early years of the new Republic. It was a highly stylized response to an unusual juncture in history. There were other rituals intended to signify how many American leaders were accomplished in science. So many Americans filled letters and diaries with observations on climate that, in Wood's wry comment, "temperature-taking became everyone's way of participating in the Enlightenment." After the invention of the telegraph, these amateur meteorologists were linked together in a national weather service.

A similar spirit prevailed in gentlemen's clubs. The ends of the American Academy of Arts and Sciences, incorporated in Boston in 1780, were "to promote and encourage the knowledge of the antiquities of *America* and of the natural history of the country, and to determine the uses to which the various natural productions of the country may be applied; to promote and encourage medical discoveries, mathematical disquisitions, philosophical inquiries and experiments; astronomical, meteorological, and geographical observations, and improvement in agriculture, arts, manufactures, and commerce; and, in fine, to cultivate every art and science which may tend to advance the interest, honor, dignity, and happiness of a free, independent, and virtuous people." The principal figure in the academy's seal was Minerva, with a field of Indian corn and agricultural tools on her right side and, on her left, a quadrant, telescope, and a ship sailing toward a town. Over the entire scene the sun was rising, and the motto appeared: *Sub Libertate Florent.* Lest we adopt too light an attitude toward these pretensions, it is well to note that the academy sponsored valuable scientific work, particularly in astronomy. Furthermore, in the spirit of the Enlightenment provisions were made to establish universities in the Northwest Territories, and initial steps were taken to abolish slavery. A convention of abolition societies in 1794 found in recent history heartening evidence of "the irresistible, though silent progress of the principles of true philosophy."* An energetic sense of purpose,

---

*The Enlightenment was not the sole intellectual influence in the development of antislavery commitments. Some evangelicals played a role, and the Quakers were crucially important. Arthur Zilversmit, in his account of the elimination of slavery from northern states, says, "Quaker abolitionists, whose plea [was] that slavery was incompatible with Christianity[,] prepared the way for the Whig-abolitionists' argument that it was irreconcilable with the Rights of Man."

as well as confidence in gradual improvement of human conditions, was implicit in the vision of a republic set free from the tyranny of the past.

Yet it is difficult to comprehend this era without thinking of it as "lost," to use the word many other historians have chosen. If the revolutionary leaders imagined a tidy republican system in which merit would be naturally recognized and the virtue of the people would steadily increase, their vision was falling apart almost as soon as it was conceived. Paine had shown the way to a powerful form of pamphleteering, belittling would-be authorities and moving an audience that was well outside the "political nation." Paine himself was drawn away to France, but the new style of discourse, which used coarse language and eschewed dainty displays of classical rhetoric, bedeviled meritorious gentlemen. Finally, in the Sedition Act of the 1790s John Adams and his party tried to silence malicious attacks from undistinguished riffraff. But by that time it had become all too plain to thoughtful men that intellectual distinction and social prominence might be liabilities in American politics. The wealthy and talented were popularly accused of subverting republicanism. "We have probably," wrote Washington in a moment of disillusionment, "had too good an opinion of human nature in forming our confederation." But no revised psychology was offered. The French minister to America reported a prevailing frustration: "there is a class of men denominated 'gentlemen,' who, by reason of their wealth, their talents, their education, their families, or the offices they hold, aspire to a preeminence which the people refuse to grant them."

In politics it was a great puzzle how to create legislatures of wise men while appealing to the popular vote. From the first moments of Revolution there were hopes of establishing dignified senates that would include learned and experienced men even if they lacked "popular qualities." Electioneering was distasteful to the enlightened; besides, it jarred with the treasured sense of a common good. James Madison had observed in prerevolutionary Virginia that a candidate who disdained to "treat" voters with liquor had a poor chance of winning election. Would republican virtue cleanse the process, or would popular hostility to aloof "aristocrats" worsen the situation? Madison in 1777 lost a race for election to the Virginia House of Delegates to a former tavern keeper because he avoided practices that, in his view, were inconsistent with classical purity. Everywhere in succeeding years there were alarming stories of "upstarts" unseating "excellent" men.

Conflict arose between "merit" and "popular qualities." Hugh Henry Brackenridge, the son of a Scottish immigrant farmer who made his way through Princeton, tried a career in literature, then turned to the law, and became a Pennsylvania legislator, epitomized the opportunities for a meritorious man to rise to the top. But the voters turned him out of office in favor of an ex-weaver who lacked Brackenridge's education and other attainments. In a bitter novel, *Modern Chivalry* (1792), Brackenridge expressed his disenchantment with the republicanism of the populace. In one scene a weaver is preferred by voters even though he is a "fish out of water," a "ridiculous" example of a man attempting "what is above his sphere." Infatuated by the event, an Irish servant named Teague—a "bog-trotter" with exalted faith in "a good day a-coming"—stands for election and wins, partly "owing . . . to there being several of his countrymen in the crowd; but more especially to the fluctuation of the popular mind, and a disposition to what is new and ignoble." He had never read a political treatise or a word of classical history, but the "common people" were inclined "to trust one of their own class" or jealously to "put down the high." Eventually Teague fell from favor, was tarred and feathered, and was sent as a scientific specimen to France, where the radical mob received him as a hero. Revolutionary politics threatened to destroy any dreams of a natural hierarchy in America.

The clash between classical and popular conceptions of republican equality made the 1780s and 1790s bitter enough, but there were other sources of conflict. For one thing, the revolutionary image of "a *Christian* Sparta," an abstemious society in shining contrast to the dissolute societies of Europe, led to a censorious examination of any trace of "luxury" in America. During the war it was possible to mobilize considerable support for prohibitions against fancy dress, theatergoing, dancing, gambling, and other costly extravagances. Almost inevitably, however, after the war some old revolutionaries began to see a deplorable resurgence of licentiousness sapping the virtuous simplicity of the Republic. Cultural life in almost every city was embittered by shrill denunciations of loose manners and by indignant counterattacks on demagogic invaders of liberty. Second, the meanings of the Enlightenment became newly controversial as revolution spread from France to other lands, including a great uprising of slaves in St. Domingue. American gentlemen might hold fast to the classical ideal of republicanism "with the necessary subordination" and yet deplore the modish "theorizing" they associated with Jefferson and popular radicalism. In an age of worldwide revolution, the Enlightenment ceased to provide a unifying ideology for the well-to-do, and *reason* itself came to have opposed meanings. To some, reason suggested the power to rearrange society; to others, a cautious respect for existing institutions.

Third, during the war evangelicals had cooperated

remarkably well with rationalistic and skeptical thinkers; together they undercut Anglicanism and other religious establishments. But in ensuing years the evangelicals issued mountingly desperate warnings against the dangers of "infidelity" and "atheism" that were courting God's wrath. The common opposition to England and superficially similar visions of the rising glory of America had only temporarily concealed gaping conflicts of viewpoint. To the evangelicals, Jefferson was the most horrible symbol of elitist indifference to true religion, but Adams's Federalists were not much better. The movement into Kentucky of tens of thousands of Virginians—including leaders proud of their enlightened rationalism and a populace depicted as brawling and irreligious—dramatized the evangelicals' most lurid fears. The devil appeared to be succeeding in a pincer movement that would use wild backwoodsmen and godless elites to destroy Protestant America. Throughout the 1790s ministers made frightening prophesies of impending doom; then in 1800 a new wave of revivals began to echo the tumult of sixty years before. This time, the outdoor occasions were institutionalized as extended "camp meetings," and reports of convulsive behavior, including "barking the devil up a tree" were more prominent than before. Yet to those who participated, the revivals were "one of the greatest wonders that ever the world beheld." As eastern ministers waited to see whether these were further signs of Satan's mischief or true sources of republican repentance, the revivals spread from the Carolinas to Kentucky, then into the Northwest, and from there back toward the East. Everywhere they left dignified visions of republican culture in shambles. This time, it was not chiefly the "unconverted" ministry that revivalists assailed; it was the intellectual aspiration of the entire Enlightenment.

There is no way of making the sides in these postrevolutionary conflicts congruent. The Federalist–Republican split in politics overlapped the conflicts of simplicity versus luxury, classicism versus theorizing, and revivalism versus Enlightenment. All that can be said with certainty is that in an era of confusing and unrelenting conflict the unique interval in which it seemed possible to link political leadership with intellectual eminence, and both with social position, came to a halt.

Gordon Wood detects a disingenuous strategy in some attempts to restore "high-toned" government. Speaking of the hopes that the Constitution would enlarge the influence of "men of intelligence and uprightness" by strengthening the executive and Senate and widening the electorate—hopes advanced in the name of government "by the people"—he concludes that men like Madison "helped to foreclose the development of an American intellectual tradition in which differing ideas of politics would be intimately and genuinely related to differing social interests." He continues that, in particular, they "hastened the destruction of whatever chance there was in America for the growth of an avowedly aristocratic conception of politics," and they helped to create "a hiatus in American politics between ideology and motives that was never closed again." By concealing their antidemocratic fears, they fostered a semblance of agreement on basic issues, including the wisdom of the people and the existence of a common good, where none may have existed. The results were not satisfactory to them all. John Adams actually contemplated the introduction of noble titles and courtly rituals in order somehow to empower a disinterested elite and to temper detestable popular insubordination. Though it is impossible to know whether anti-aristocratic sentiments would have advanced differently without the Constitution, we can say that the republic of order and virtue was not protected from the onslaught of equality. By the time that Andrew Jackson defeated John Quincy Adams in 1828, the idea that virtuous character was the criterion for officeholding was nearly as discredited as the idea of hereditary privilege. Distinction and talent would have to be expressed in other spheres.

We may broaden Wood's point by emphasizing not what vanished from politics—the preeminence of an intellectual elite and the forthright articulation of different interests—but what persisted in society. The word *virtue* came to be regarded as antiquated, but some of the qualities associated with the word—an intellectual reserve, a disciplined use of reason, an interest in finer things, control over the passions—continued to define a social type. A wealthy merchant, an attorney, a college professor—all might display these qualities, no longer as a prerequisite to governmental service, but rather as signs of social distinction in an increasingly stratified culture. As nineteenth-century cities, including new inland ones, showed increasing residential segregation, the gulf between "rational society" and popular institutions widened. We may not assume, however, that all intellectuals were wealthy or, even less, that rich men were all intellectuals. In fact, as some men accumulated great fortunes in nineteenth-century America, and as antagonism to "aristocracy" intensified in democratic politics, men of old-fashioned virtue struggled to distinguish themselves from crude parvenus. The goals of politeness and gentility, with their roots in Enlightenment ideals of reason and morality, took on new meanings in the nineteenth century. Initially, they promoted an inward-turning tendency within elites, but in time they would reveal the capacity to shape the aspirations of a widening segment of the population. In this chapter we shall see how these aspirations surfaced in visions of republican "respectability." We shall encounter them again when discussing the late-nineteenth-century ideal of "culture" in subsequent chapters.

EQUALITY AND RESPECTABILITY

It is unclear how much deference ordinary folk continued to accord those who once would have been called their betters. There is contradictory evidence in the impressions (1806) of Benjamin Henry Latrobe, a British-born *philosophe* whose mother came from a prominent Philadelphia family. As a talented architect and engineer (he designed the capitol in Washington) who traveled extensively, he was amused by the respectful language with which "decent" young artisans of Delaware addressed him and by differences between their "phraseology" and that of "the upper circles of society." On the one hand, he said, "Thus inequality . . . grows up in society" in spite of laws and regulations that "oppose every growing separation of our citizens into *orders* and *ranks*." On the other hand, Latrobe despised tenants and poor farmers in Virginia: "These dogs are independent of every human being, they are saucy, care not *a damn* for the best Gentleman in the land, own no controul, either of morals, manners, principles, or law, and have no Master but *Whiskey*." Many of the Founding Fathers had envisioned a new educational system to discipline the populace. Rush spoke of turning men into "republican machines" by teaching them that their lives belonged to the state. But freedom, in the view of many others, seemed instead to dissolve traditional social bonds. In *Home as Found* (1838), the novelist James Fenimore Cooper deplored the crudities of a land where all assumed the right to come and go as equals but where no one knew his proper place: "No country has so much altered for the worse in so short a time."

The notion of a society in which all white men were equals had a subversive effect on the very language of authority and submission. This effect was illustrated in a story told by the Duke of Saxe Weimar, who heard a coachman say, "Are you the *man* going to Portland? because if you are, I'm the *gentleman* that's a-going to drive you." The British actor Tyrone Power, who visited the United States in the early 1830s, did not believe that language could be so topsy-turvy until he heard it himself. Not only did he hear a coachman called a gentleman, but a drunken idler in a tavern took the same title (to the guffaws of his companions).* Power was not a European who berated Americans; he called them friendly and helpful once a visitor accepted their curious "reversal of conventional distinctions." But his story is similar to many others, sometimes exaggerated to emphasize the rapidity of democratic change in America, claiming that parents had less authority over their children, that husbands had looser command over their wives, and that there was generally less subordination than in the Old World.

Even if we discount for exaggeration, the weakening of traditional social distinctions raised once unthinkable questions about authority. Probably every subservient group was exposed to the idea that humankind had universal rights, that no condition of dependence was justifiable without consent. After the Revolution, for example, slave revolts throughout the Western Hemisphere based their legitimacy on the abstract rights of all people. When

---

*Forty years later, Mark Twain pointed out to the English: "Your words 'gentleman' and 'lady' have a very restricted meaning; with us they include the barmaid, butcher, burglar, harlot, and horse thief."

college students rioted, as they did with alarming fre-
quency in the first quarter of the century, trustees learned
that the "genius of the age" no longer allowed authorities
"to tell of whipping and to practice scolding. . . . The
understanding and the heart must be addressed by persuasion and reason, and the bayonet and the rod reserved for the last emergency." The women of the Republic were less willing to view themselves as subjects of
their husbands. Foreigners called American women the
most assertive in the world, and husbands were advised
that they, too, must exercise authority in a spirit of persuasion and reason. In the revivals that burned eastward
from Kentucky, some common folk proclaimed their liberation from dead structures of ecclesiastical hierarchy. All
men and women were saved and free, according to Universalists, Disciples of Christ, and others who proclaimed
Jesus Christ "the most *genuine* REPUBLICAN that ever
existed."

Obviously, the pursuit of equality was not immediately successful. Slavery was not abolished for decades, and
racial oppression never has ended. Colleges learned how
to keep students in check. Women's suffrage was slow in
following that of white or black males, and other rights
for women had few advocates. The older denominations
absorbed much of whatever threat the Universalists and
Disciples posed. It takes more than statements of universal principle to effect major changes in society. While
conceding the limits of revolutionary ideology, however,
we should recall that for early-nineteenth-century Americans these limits had scarcely been tested. The tune that
Cornwallis's army had played at Yorktown was "The World
Turned Upside Down," and both anxiety and exhilaration were understandable as Americans watched to see, and
Europeans came to observe, just how far the Revolution
would penetrate society.

Respectability was another word whose meaning underwent a kind of reversal. In eighteenth-century Virginia there had been defiance in the emotional meetings of Presbyterian and Baptist farmers and in their dissociation from the sports and pastimes of the gentry. They were repudiating the social authority of respectable folk. But in the nineteenth century the civilizing consequences of the revivals became important to the social order. According to one report, Kentuckians in 1802 were already "as distinguished for sobriety as they had formerly been for dissoluteness." A gentleman like Latrobe was bound to be rather patronizing in his comments on the "Bathos style," the "colloquial tone," and the quivering gestures of a Methodist revivalist whom he observed in 1809. He was unable to see the similarity between the blacksmith preacher's depiction of reformed character ("Temperance, Temperance, Temperance, I say. . . . There, there, stands an unconverted coxcomb, dress is his God and his delight, will it help him then, when he must face the fiery gulf") and his personal ideal of virtue ("The philosopher . . . sacrifices the pleasures of Bacchus and Venus, the enthusiasm of the gaming table and of the raceground, to the enjoyment of . . . temperate and never cloying gratifications"). In time, however, as evangelicals became persons of influence in their republican communities, *respectable* referred to the pious, moral behavior that derived from true religion, whatever the convert's social origins. A movement of defiance was transformed into a system of social propriety, one that could truly authorize commoners to think of themselves as respectable gentlemen or ladies.*

---

*Evangelical religion was highly appealing to women. Latrobe feared that his wife might be susceptible: "With the most rational, but very pious and sincere religious sentiments, she joins a warmth of imagi-

Genteel was another term of distinction that underwent reversal. Noah Webster's *American Dictionary* (1851) omitted familiar references to an economic class, referring instead to general qualities of politeness and refinement. In practice one would hardly expect a workingman or farmer to adopt the term, but certainly it was clear that these qualities were available to all who were well brought up and well educated, not just to the well born. The idle and extravagant rich were considered ungenteel just as surely as were the raucous poor. To the inward-turning temperament of the elite, then, we must add the uplifting sense of respectability and gentility to which men and women at the middle of society could aspire. By midcentury a prestigious magazine editor could report, as "the best phenomenon of American life, thus far, that the word 'gentleman,' which in England still designates a social order, is here more apt to refer to personal character. . . . This change alone is worth the transportation across the Atlantic. The use of the word 'lady' is yet more comprehensive, and therefore more honorable still; we sometimes see, in a shopkeeper's advertisement, 'Saleslady wanted.' " While this example may not strike us as so honorable, it is clear that the nineteenth-century ideal of *the lady,* in some ways so limiting to the gender, was part of a more general expansion of gentility. In fact, women became the most often praised exemplars of that selfless devotion to the public good which had formerly been associated with republican virtue.

It took decades for the signs to emerge that churches and schools could turn republican children into well-be-

---

nation, which might receive a shock, if not an impression from the *incantations* which form the business of their assemblies." It is not hard to understand the appeal of new constructions of *respectability* to a gender traditionally associated with lust and passion.

haved ladies and gentlemen. In the meantime, a swaggering tone came to be associated with some parts of folk culture. Everyone knew tales of frontier braggarts who could lick bears and tear men apart, and revivalists themselves gloated over the greatest deeds that men had ever seen. This boastfulness was prominent in the marketing of entertainment which was central to the influence of republican equality on culture. Genteel audiences might subscribe to tasteful presentations by singers and actors who faithfully imitated the highest standards of European society. Enlightened critics might hope for a theater of refined sentiment that "allures the people from an attendance upon barbarous and brutifying spectacles—from brawls, boxing-matches, and bull-baitings"—and "accustoms them . . . to intellectual enjoyments and recreations." But the people paid their money for different fare. In the popular theater, segregated in working-class neighborhoods of cities or taken on the road, extravagant claims of spectacles offered to the public became commonplace. Latrobe, who traveled with hard-drinking actors, said that they deliberately made a great commotion during scene changes because *"noise* seems to be universally considered as the evidence of mirth and hilarity." Heroes characterized by braggadocio, from firehouse boys to Davy Crocketts, were stock figures, whose irreverence toward upper-class authorities was equaled by that of regional types, especially Down East Yankees who spoke in dialect. Some theaters specialized in spoofs and burlesques of current fashions. It was P. T. Barnum, a Universalist, who exploited the new republican taste most successfully, with his extraordinary claims of wonders on exhibit and his irreverent attitude toward academic authorities invited to put these claims to the test of reason and observation. Charles Willson Peale had designed his "museum" to educate a virtuous citizenry; Barnum bought Peale's collections and assembled his shows in a "dime museum" with notably less lofty intentions.

To those who had imagined that independence would inaugurate a more stately period of republican art, this commercialized irreverence was more than a little disconcerting. The arts appeared to diverge in "high" and "low" directions, with the elevated course beset with frustrations and the popular course submerging all traces of balance and decorum. Scholars have written sympathetically—almost elegiacally—of the problems of artists during this period. One takes note of many careers terminating in unfinished masterworks and nervous debilities. Others tell us sadly of William Dunlap, who was a New York counterpart to the artisan intellectuals of Philadelphia. The son of a shopkeeper, a portrait artist who painted, and revered, George Washington, and a skillful amateur historian, Dunlap sought his fortune as a playwright and theater manager. He wrote dramas about the Revolution, in heroic verse, that are still anthologized, but the lesson he learned was that, without the patronage of the "wise and good" or support from the state, "the manager must please the vulgar or shut his theatre." Since the people wanted tearjerkers, the more heartrending the better, he translated such plays from the French and produced them by the score. Many historians have paused over the public rejection of Horatio Greenough's 1841 sculpture of Washington in a pose intended to suggest "the apotheosis of [self] abnegation": he sat in a Roman toga, his chest and shoulders bare, his left hand extending his sword in a scabbard, his right hand pointing to the heavens. The style had gone out of fashion: there were so many protests about the hero's semi-nudity and so many jeers (he looked as though he were basking in a Turkish bath, said one wag), that Congress, which had commissioned the work, soon removed it from sight.

Too much sympathy with artists who felt that republican culture had fallen into the doldrums may cause us to overlook an extraordinary expansion of opportunities. The dimensions of change are suggested, for example, by the increasing numbers of theaters, of which there had been only a handful in the colonial period (to the disappointment of polite gentlemen sensitive to the provincial shortcomings of America). Imposing new theaters were erected in every major city in the 1790s; and after a brief leveling off in the early decades of the new century, proliferation was even more rapid. Specialized theaters abounded in large cities: by the mid-1850s there were five halls for minstrel shows alone in San Francisco and ten in New York. Clever managers linked theaters in hundreds of towns all over the continent. As rapidly as Americans moved into new areas, theaters followed them. These were entertainment institutions, to be sure, but they offered employment to writers, painters, and musicians as well as actors. Many young men (and a few women) escaped old-fashioned lines of apprenticeship and authority by jumping off into this booming world. Adoniram Judson, for example, took a tour as an actor before becoming an illustrious Christian missionary.

The growth of newspapers was even more spectacular. In 1763 there had been 23 newspapers, with circulations much larger than their colonial forerunners; by 1800 there were over 230; and by 1810, over 370 selling more than 22 million copies annually. The trend escalated until the newspaper became the outstanding response to democratic literacy. An American traveler in Innsbruck in 1845 discovered a newspaper exhibited in a museum as a specimen of the peculiarities of his homeland. Magazine and book publishing mushroomed in much the same way, with some publications serving narrowly segmented portions of the population, but with others indicating that great fortunes might be earned from mass sales. Some 200 magazines were founded between 1790 and 1820, and many talented young men found their first employment as editors. The proceeds from books swelled to $2,500,000 by 1820 and $12,500,000 by 1850. Novel reading was widely disparaged as being unserious and immoral. But, starting with the fantastic success of Susannah Rowson's *Charlotte Temple* (1794), which went through a hundred nineteenth-century editions, the public devoured stories that presented tearful scenes of seductions and betrayals, always with plenty of earnest moralizing. This taste may not have been classical or refined, but it was a far cry from "anarchia."

It was difficult to determine how much these expanding markets had to do with any respectable definition of intellectual life. Journalists and novelists alike might be considered hacks or panderers to vulgar appetites, not at all like Paine, with his sense of himself as an independent critical mind, even less like Paine's opponents, who styled themselves men of leisure and discernment. Yet the literary marketplace undeniably opened up dreams of intellectual advancement. In 1830 the young John Greenleaf Whittier, a small-town Quaker who lived to become a wealthy and distinguished poet, expressed great excitement about the prospects that lay open, but he also felt there was something sordid in using his talents for commercial gain. Once a "friendless boy" who "vowed to triumph over the scorners of his boyish endeavors," he was now "haunted by an immedicable ambition, perhaps a very foolish desire of distinction, of applause, of fame, of what the world calls immortality."

The tensions are even more apparent in the life of Catharine Sedgwick, whose *A New England Tale* (1822), *Hope Leslie* (1827), and other novels foreshadowed the successes that would elevate a long list of female writers to fame in later decades. Descended from the "river gods" of the Connecticut River Valley and from a prominent Federalist family, she received a reasonably good education for which there was, as yet, no acceptable career. Obviously the expanding market for fiction provided an outlet for gifts that would otherwise have gone unfulfilled. She remained unmarried and childless; yet as fiction writer, like many women who followed her, she celebrated the contentment of marriage, "whence all the relations of life radiate, and the source of all political and social virtue." In some ways an eloquent believer that "woman has an independent power to shape her own course, and to force her own separate sovereign way," she was careful to utter these sentiments in a remarkably undefiant, even self-effacing, manner. And she generalized the need for humility in the midst of rising educational opportunities. While she wished to see "the humblest stimulated to the cultivation and enjoyment of their intellectual faculties," she wrote to a professor of her acquaintance in 1838, she also wished for even a female servant to "feel that a dutiful performance gives dignity to the lowest office."

If Barnum epitomized the showman reaping fantastic success from the irreverence and boastfulness of the culture of equality, Whittier and Sedgwick remind us of a lingering awareness of spheres that could not without a lapse in decorum be exceeded. Merit and equality seemed to be antagonistic principles in politics: would success in the booming intellectual marketplace provide a more secure measure of distinction? Could the meanings of *ambition* and *fame* be refashioned to convey a sense of public worth?

INSTITUTIONS
AND PROFESSIONS

As elites turned inward and popular culture offered expanded opportunities for success, the early nineteenth century was nothing less than an era of reorganization in intellectual endeavor. From common schools and academies to political parties and limited-liability corporations, there was extensive experimentation in new forms of organization-building. Some of these new organizations eroded the prestige of old elites; others defined the terms for new opportunities in America. New institutions brought educated people together in subcommunities of common discourse. One of the paradoxical consequences of popular democracy was the segmentation of culture into specialized groups that talked mainly to one another, yet often depended on public acceptance of their claims to expert knowledge.

The process is visible in the changing definition of science, which had come to this continent largely as the custom of men of leisure to collect curiosities and record observations of nature. In the postrevolutionary period, science existed as an avocation attracting different kinds of enthusiasts. The historian Harry J. Carman and the economist Rexford J. Tugwell recaptured the diversity of old-time scientists:

> There used to be a kind of man . . . who stood to a whole countryside as the representative there of learning. He might be a doctor or a lawyer; sometimes he was a craftsman; at any rate his ubiquitous interest in things of the mind made him notable. . . . For this kind of man had an interest in all the branches of knowledge: archeology, geology, astronomy—none of the sciences excluded him. Likely enough he had a chemical laboratory

in the woodshed; and it was not strange if his wife should catch him, on cold winter nights, gazing at the stars through a long brass telescope, he being meanwhile all too thinly protected from the weather. Perhaps his hobby was to discover the burial places of earlier inhabitants and to lay Indians' bones bare to the weather on some local hillside. He may have been the local atheist, his bent for learning taking a theological cast and he being by temperament contentious; or he may have been the schoolmaster interested to test for himself the conclusions which seemed too easily reached in books; then again he may have been the minister with interests other than those which were strictly legitimate to his profession. . . . It did not seem effrontery in earlier years to combine one's interests in this way.*

In an eastern city this sort of virtuoso might have been either an inquisitive mechanic or a well-to-do merchant. The example of Jefferson reminds us that such a man might have been a slaveowner. But the ideal was increasingly democratized. A civic-spirited Cincinnati physician, Daniel Drake, noted an old distinction between the mere observer of nature and the "philosopher" who penetrates its laws and, in 1840, announced: "Hitherto, the philosophers have formed a distinct caste from the people. . . .

---

*See Carman and Tugwell's introduction to Jared Eliot, *Essays upon Field Husbandry in New England and Other Papers, 1748–1762* (1934). The comment is placed in a broader interpretation of postrevolutionary American science in Walter Muir Whitehill's contribution to an important symposium on the reorganization of intellectual life: Alexandra Oleson and Sanford C. Brown, eds., *The Pursuit of Knowledge in the Early American Republic* (1976).

But this delusion should be dispelled, is indeed fast disappearing. Philosophers, like kings, are but men; and all men to a certain extent may become philosophers. Our faculties are the same and if exercised in the same manner we should at length differ only in degree."

Ubiquitous interests and equal attainments were important expressions of republican principles, but they were not realized in any lasting way. Science in actuality became more, not less, constricted. Drake's vision of a broad-based Western Academy of Natural Sciences foundered on the dissatisfactions of men who strove for a rigorously professional view of science and who complained that amateurs were ignorant of even elementary schemes of classification in fields like conchology and meteorology. What happened in Cincinnati was repeated elsewhere: general societies for scientific discussion found themselves in competition with more exclusive organizations of men of science. The sponsorship of the wealthy was still welcome; edifying lectures were still addressed to the curious public. But there was an emerging recognition that some men had the credentials to be considered scientists and others did not. Just what these credentials were remained a little uncertain; there were few successful efforts at licensing. "Science" included many physicians and college-educated lawyers as well as the several thousand men who by 1860 held specifically scientific posts in colleges and government. National organizations like the Association of American Geologists and Naturalists (founded in 1840) and the American Association for the Advancement of Science (founded in 1848) were designed to separate the interests of scientists from the pervasive amateurism, as the founders saw it, and diffuse eclecticism of local societies, including Philadelphia's American Philosophical Society and Boston's American Academy of Arts and Sciences.

Though the most important steps in the development of science as a major force in professional and intellectual life came later, by the time of the Civil War science was partly shorn of its associations both with the customs of genteel adornment and with the republican faith that all men could be philosophers. It was well on its way to redefinition as a network of professional subcommunities specializing in particular fields of inquiry. Men of science tended to be distinguished by college training, subscription to professional magazines, knowledge of methods, proven accomplishments, and certification by their peers— criteria that had little or nothing to do with public virtue or republican enthusiasm. A few men—like Yale's Benjamin Silliman, Harvard's Louis Agassiz, and the Smithsonian Institution's Joseph Henry—gained national fame, but for the most part, in a time of expanding commercial opportunities in literature and entertainment, the scientist could not expect great remuneration. In a time of uncertain links between merit and acclaim, science offered the advantage of verifying authority by referring to standards established by a restricted subcommunity.

Similar tendencies might be charted in medicine and law. In each instance there were endeavors, not fully realized, to establish common standards of professional competence and thereby to overcome the free-for-all implications of democratic society. These fields were being reshaped, neither as gentlemen's callings nor as wide-open opportunities for the people, but as internally certified sources of relevant knowledge. We may best outline the effects of professional reorganization on intellectual life in the first half of the nineteenth century by examining the group in which they were most clear-cut—the Protestant clergy.

In the colonial period, ministers were virtually born to their vocation. That is, they were frequently the sons of ministers or of well-to do families or of both. After a general education they learned their roles by residing with a veteran minister. Once settled in a parish, they tended to stay for long tenures, regardless of their own or their parishioners' dissatisfaction. They were addressed as "reverend sir" with the honor owed to godly gentlemen, and they enjoyed respect as learned luminaries in their particular localities. (That is why the attacks of a Whitefield or a Tennent seemed to threaten the social hierarchy.) By the 1830s, however, ministers were more likely to be recruited from poorer backgrounds and to receive a seminary education with help from scholarship funds. They were supported voluntarily and could not take deference for granted. Many of them sought to emphasize their professional training and intellectual standing, but to laymen these were less important than specific abilities in preaching and saving souls. Ministers gave up their connections to politics; in the new era, they were expected to stay out of partisan controversy. Through the seminaries and denominational organizations, they stayed in contact with one another as a far-flung professional entity. Because of their own ambitions and their flocks' disloyalty they moved rapidly from one post to another. Their local station, for all these reasons, was secondary to the goals of their individual careers in a national, or at least regional, profession.

It is possible to interpret this transformation as a defensive reaction to sweeping changes in American life. Without the traditional obedience to hierarchical authority, other ways of establishing merit were required. It is also possible to stress the response to opportunity that transient ministerial careers meant for some young men. They were trained, however, not in a spirit of professional response to secular change: that would have been unthinkably selfish. Seminaries were established and scholarships solicited with the goal, usually expressed in millennial terms, of Christianizing America and the world. The seminaries boasted, not of the good positions their graduates landed, but of hosts of evangelists sent forth to do good work among the heathens. One advantage of the clergy over other crystalizing professions was the belief in mission that gave their endeavors legitimacy. The sincerity with which this belief was upheld was apparent in the decisions of prominent clergymen to move to small seminaries launched to tame the West. The energetic Lyman Beecher left Boston, for example, to preside over the fledgling Lane Seminary in Cincinnati; and the greatest of pre–Civil War revivalists, Charles Grandison Finney, left New York to accept a professorship at tiny Oberlin in Ohio.

To speak of the ministry as a profession is not to deny the fragmentation of organized Protestantism. The cleavages opened in the eighteenth-century awakenings grew wider in postrevolutionary years. The persistent infighting between liberals and Calvinists in New England culminated in the first decade of the nineteenth century with the emergence of a new denomination, Unitarianism, that denied the divinity of Christ and the depravity of man. The social and intellectual leaders of Boston and other seaboard towns no longer subscribed, even nominally, to the faith of the Puritans. Harvard, where tuition swiftly doubled, became an institution for a Unitarian elite—a telling example of the segmentation of American culture during this period. Furthermore, after 1800 revivalism created new sects and aggravated rifts in old ones, so much so that Princeton, once the intellectual mecca of the awakenings, became the bastion of "Old School" antirevivalistic Presbyterianism. While older institutions like Harvard and Princeton accepted their identification with restricted constituencies, new sects and the schismatic wings of old ones established their own colleges and seminaries. After the loss of Harvard, for example, Presbyterian and Congregational evangelicals united to found Andover Seminary (1808), which took great pride in the number of missionaries, preachers, and educators among its alumni. The Disciples of Christ in Kentucky opened Bacon College, named after the great champion of modern science. Almost everywhere, the lingering "log college" tradition inspired the founding of countless sectarian institutions, some short-lived, others surviving well into the twentieth century.

In spite of this fragmentation and diffusion, the careers of ministers show that they sometimes moved across denominational boundaries in a fluid and mobile society. Moreover, in the era of reorganization these men often came together in nonsectarian cooperation. The revivals usually depended on interdenominational collaboration; in fact, that was one of their exhilarating meanings in an era when Christianity saw itself as endangered by secular change. To supplement the "spontaneous" responses to the words of individual preachers, some revivalists traveled in groups and issued their own newspapers, tracts, hymnals, and manuals. In addition, missionary and reform societies, organized on a national basis, marshaled so much cooperation that historians have called them the "evangelical united front" or an "empire of benevolence."

The roots of these organizations went back to Cotton Mather's *Essays to Do Good* and to women's service and reform societies sponsored by local churches to protest public immorality, raise funds for missionary education, and accomplish other worthy ends. Some denominations experimented with their own missionary and moral-reform projects. But from 1815 on, most attention went to national societies to coordinate missionary work in North

INTELLECTUAL LIFE IN AMERICA

America and overseas;* to bring the Bible and edifying tracts to Indians, seamen, and the urban poor; to establish Sunday Schools; to combat intemperate drinking; and to remove free Negroes from a white society in which they were hated and impoverished (and, incidentally, to use them as instruments to Christianize Africa). The business of publishing and disseminating literature offered a way of participating in the expanding literary marketplace that was not tinged with selfishness. Traveling agents were needed to give lectures and collect subscriptions, and of course most of the societies employed missionaries. Many ministers, disenchanted with local pastorates, became functionaries in professional reform, and they recognized their resemblance to performers and commercial travelers working in other businesses. The same reformer who uttered jeremiads against the godless chaos of modern times might celebrate the railroad that hurtled him on a great circuit from one station of influence to the next. The national societies met simultaneously during one "holy week" in New York City every year; their regional affiliates also held simultaneous meetings. When hundreds of reformers huddled together in one city, there was a re-

---

*To old men of the Enlightenment, this development was lamentable. "Would it not be better, to apply these pious subscriptions, to purify Christendom from the corruptions of Christianity, than to propagate these corruptions in Europe, Asia, Africa and America!" wrote John Adams to Thomas Jefferson in 1816. "What would they say were the Pope to send annually to this country colonies of Jesuit priests with cargoes of their Missal and translations of their Vulgate, to be put gratis into the hands of every one who would accept them?" replied Jefferson. But these were the complaints of men who feared, as Adams put it, that the nineteenth century would "extinguish all the lights of its predecessor." There were also a few diehard Calvinists who felt that the missionaries too zealously took God's work into human hands and who, in any case, resented all the eager fund-raising.

markable demonstration of both the internal consolidation of professional groups and the opportunities for expanding influence in a changing America.*

Not all the new organizations aimed at reforming outsiders. Some of the most important institutions of the new era offered edification to their own members. This was true of subscription libraries, for example, and even more so of the lecture series that became a prominent feature of urban cultural life. Some series were designed to "diffuse useful knowledge" to particular groups such as "young men," philosophical societies, or unions of skilled artisans. Some series appealed to audiences interested in a special subject such as health or slavery. By the 1840s, however, most towns of more than a thousand people had quasi-public groups sponsoring a general series of lectures, for a small fee, to a "miscellaneous" audience. Larger cities offered multiple series. It is estimated that 400,000 people attended lectures in the North and West every week in peak seasons during the 1850s. The lecturers at the town halls and lyceums were sometimes, especially in the early days, local ministers, doctors, professors, or lawyers, but more important were the traveling speakers, who earned sizable incomes. They included men and a few women from a variety of newly emerging intellectual careers:

---

*In later decades new reform societies took on more radical purposes, among them pacifism, women's rights, and the abolition of slavery. Many complained that these radical movements disrupted the concerted interdenominational work. Instead of bringing literacy and morality to groups outside the evangelical consensus, they attacked "sins" in the mainstream of American culture. Despite the conflict, these new movements met alongside the more conservative ones and imitated the publications and lecture circuits that gave employment to "agents" of reform organizations. Closer in spirit to the original benevolence societies were the "missions to the slaves" that were effective in promoting black Christianity after 1830.

journalists, reformers, fiction writers, and essayists. A few great stars—men like Henry Ward Beecher, Horace Greeley, and Bayard Taylor—attracted great crowds and became wealthy national figures. According to one observer, "the chief Lyceum lecturers are personally more widely known than any other class of men in this country"; thus they ranked "among the intellectual sovereigns of the land." Another called them "the intellectual leaders of an intelligent progress in this country."

In a penetrating analysis, Donald M. Scott relates the lyceum profession to a phenomenon that received much comment in the 1830s and 1840s: "a glut of young men trying . . . to establish legal, medical, and clerical careers, and . . . crowds of young men trying to figure out how to get a hold onto some kind of intellectual life." Many of them eventually followed careers that moved through "a series of institutions, places, and activities that had not existed when they started out and that they themselves often had to invent." Some old-timers felt that the country was overflowing with professional misfits: "There were more lawyers than could get a living honestly," wrote one critic. "There were doctors to be found in every street of our village, with their little saddlebags; and they must have a living out of the public. There were too many clergymen who, finding no place where they could be settled, went about the country begging for funds and getting up rag-bag and tag-rag societies." The young men, who were themselves nervous about the commercial side of their careers, spoke of "raising up a sort of literary men from among sons of middling classes to fill the public offices and to give a tone to public opinion."

In this unsettled moment for public intellectual life, the lecture system provided examples of dispensing knowledge in a beneficial way. It suggested the opportunity of forging careers that were not ostensibly sullied by cash motives, careers as intellectual middlemen interpreting science, history, and geography to the public. There was repeated testimony that meeting the test of the public, though ultimately measured in financial terms, was a sign of intellectual preeminence much nobler than that which came from sectarian and political preferment. Thus in a time of segmentation and professionalism, the lecture circuits struck one commentator as "a living shuttle, to weave together this new web of national civilization." Though the lyceum was often compared to the theater, few complained that it rewarded the meretricious or debased virtue. Here was one instance of remarkable agreement that success in the republican marketplace could elevate something like an aristocracy of merit. That was possible because the lecturers, unlike Barnum, were supposedly distinguished by their earnest wish to deliver knowledge in a broadly instructive fashion to a public eager for self-improvement. Themselves the products of an era of vast reorganization, they could sing the advantages of further, ceaseless change in a progressive and moral direction. Perhaps it was possible, after all, to identify America with an enlarging circle of enlightenment.

THE SURVIVING ENLIGHTENMENT

In many respects the Enlightenment seemed to have died with the eighteenth century. Despite a few flagrant deists, radical skepticism had never posed much of a threat in America, and in the nineteenth century responsible public figures kept silent about whatever doubts they had of the truth of Christianity. As we have seen in this chapter, some of the more moderate versions of Enlightened political views sank beneath the waves of social equalitarianism. Nevertheless, in a diluted, uncontroversial form, most of the main concerns of the Enlightenment worked their way into the world views of literate, educated Americans. The happy inevitability of Progress, the utility to society of Science, the importance of individual Morality—these concerns, rather than beliefs in unending human misery and divine wrath, typified a respectable American orthodoxy. They were concerns voiced as warmly by Unitarians as by Presbyterians, in the West and South as well as in the Northeast, among politicians and journalists as well as among doctors and lawyers; and they constituted the larger faith of orators on the lecture circuit. They did not indicate a program for state action (John Quincy Adams's proposals for a national university and scientific establishment were denounced by the Jacksonians), but they framed a widely upheld public faith in the general direction of the nineteenth century.

A similar comment applies to the most widely accepted views of human nature. The cautions imposed by the ancient picture of anarchic passions, surging to escape the reins of the driver reason, had been quietly laid aside. They might have been revived by the emotional torrents of the revivals, by the extravagant tears and yelps on the popular stage, or even by deepening fascination with novels about the frailty of passionate women. But once it was clear that the revivals enhanced personal morality and that public manners seemed to be improving, however one might deplore fashions in entertainment and literature, there was little inclination to reincriminate the depths of human nature. What prevailed instead was an almost unquestioned confidence in human feelings as the basis for civic morality.

What certainly expired, though it was not acknowledged everywhere, was Calvinism. Church historians call the period after 1815 "the Methodist Age," not simply because that denomination expanded most impressively, but also because other Protestants widely adopted the revivalistic message that holiness was available to all and that all had a duty to seek it. Even those theologians who cherished their ties to Edwards and Calvin soft-pedaled grim teachings that contradicted popular confidence in progress and morality. In the New Divinity every loophole in Edwards's thought was widened to give freer play to the human capacity to be virtuous. Men and women had "natural ability" to behave with "benevolence" as society progressed toward the millennium. There was much dispute over the character of God and his reasons for requiring Christ's sacrifice to atone for human sin. In the extremely attractive "governmental theory of the atonement," God no longer was an arbitrary potentate to be propitiated by sacrifice; he was a just moral governor. Christ had died to equalize Adam's sin and thus to symbolize God's righteousness in punishing all transgressions. Christ had not paid the sinner's debt; he had given notice of everyone's moral accountability. Human beings were, in this view, responsible for their own record, not Adam's long ago. The emotional burden of closing with Christ was subsidiary to the task of living a blameless life.

Eventually some theologians came to fear that they had gone too far in accommodating the concept of God to human standards of goodness. In the 1850s Edward Beecher,* a minister and college president, described

---

*Edward Beecher was the son of Lyman Beecher, one of the most influential early-nineteenth-century ministers. His distinguished siblings include Henry Ward Beecher, a minister and star of the lyceum circuit, Harriet Beecher Stowe, author of *Uncle Tom's Cabin,* and Catharine Beecher, a well-known writer on women's domestic and vocational life. Though the family had not been eminent in the colonial period, their prominence in many different spheres of nineteenth-century intellectual life was remarkable.

Christianity as a steamboat going around in circles as its sidewheels pushed in contrary directions: one wheel proclaimed God's sovereignty; the other, God's morality. In the early decades of the century, however, theologians congratulated themselves on successfully revising Calvinism. They still considered God a majestic governor, but they had made his attributes acceptable to a republican age. They made the seminaries and colleges important fixtures in a transdenominational orthodoxy that coexisted with revivalism in the hinterlands and the bustle of reorganized professions everywhere. The orthodox joined the Unitarians in learning biblical languages and reading Scripture symbolically in order to show that there was moral progress in the world.

If there was a system of ideas that shored up this orthodoxy, it was the theoretical approach to human knowledge that Henry May has called "the Didactic Enlightenment." Derived from Scottish philosophers, particularly Thomas Reid and Dugald Stewart, this approach dismissed vexing issues that had arisen concerning a human being's inability to prove the reality of the ideas formed of the external world. Some philosophers had taken this impasse in Locke's account of the human mind to show the logical necessity of God; others, notably David Hume, had taken a skeptical stance toward all metaphysical thinking. Reid and Stewart maintained, to the comfort of many American Protestants, that there was no reason to doubt the actual existence of the realities most people believed as a matter of "common sense." Only a reckless, useless philosophy could prove, or question, God's existence by doubting everyday direct experience. There was a tidy correspondence between human faculties of perception and the natural world. In many ways the argument paralleled proofs of the existence of a moral sense: God could not have bungled creation by leaving mankind devoid of the capacity to learn and understand. Armed with this convenient approach to knowledge, ministers, teachers, and lecturers were free to go about the business of inculcating morality and reporting on their observations without pausing to confront fundamental questions about the limits of reason.

The popularity of this approach owed much to its avoidance of abstract dogma. At the same time, it avoided the skepticism inherent in viewing mankind in utterly materialistic terms. That kind of materialism was sometimes an attractive corollary of enlightened efforts to view human affairs as a field of scientific inquiry. The *Philosophy of Human Nature* (1812) by one of the shining lights of the Kentucky Enlightenment, Joseph Buchanon, had argued that "the elements of matter possess active powers adequate to any celerity and subtleness of action in the human mind." In various *Lectures on the Mind* (1791–1812), Benjamin Rush invariably treated mental functioning as a physiological problem, though he worried over the implications of this treatment for the soul's immortality. In the 1820s Jefferson and John Adams corresponded about experiments that revealed changes in the feelings and behavior of animals when parts of the brain were dissected. Jefferson was content to believe that the power of thinking rested in material organs rather than in a divinely implanted soul, but Adams was unsure: "the Saint has as good a right to groan at the Philosopher for asserting that there is nothing but matter in the Universe, as the Philosopher has to laugh at the Saint for saying that there are both matter and spirit." With no independent perspective on the processes of material causation, Jefferson recommended skeptical self-restraint: "When I meet with a proposition [like the soul] beyond finite comprehension, I abandon it as I do a weight which human strength cannot lift." To Adams the limits on human understanding were "humiliating." Both of these old men expressed hope of meeting in the "hereafter" with firsthand knowledge of these "botherations."

The Didactic Enlightenment managed to sidestep this problem, like so many others, by claiming that human consciousness contained principles that went beyond natural experience: the mind had powers of "invention" and a knowledge of "essential" truths that exceeded mere observation. These powers could get out of hand; it was characteristic of the Scottish philosophy both to assert the reliability of human faculties and to minimize their independent strength. It prized a careful spirit of empirical observation and subsequent "inductive" explanation as crucial to scientific advance out of the darkness of the human past. (Simultaneous with the Scottish influence was a great veneration of Bacon as a foe of a priori theorizing. "The *Baconian* philosophy," said one popular orator, "has become synonymous with the true philosophy.") Nevertheless, this philosophy had no patience with materialistic reductions of the soul. The mind had its own capacity for free judgment of reality; it was distinct from matter. There was a principle in human consciousness that "escapes the knife of the anatomist, the tests of the chemist and the skill of the physiologist." The principle was too subtle and elusive for elaborate description, but its existence was an article of faith.

This approach to knowledge, which provided the reigning view of human nature in the religious and academic institutions of the United States, had several long-term implications. First, it clouded over technical issues about truth that Hume had raised and that once again engaged the attention of philosophers in the twentieth century. In modern accounts of the history of philosophy, nineteenth-century America appears to have included few first-rate thinkers deserving serious attention.

The Didactic Enlightenment was responsible for the view
of America as shallow, bourgeois, and unreflecting. Second, it set the terms for conflict that ultimately emerged
between science and religion. By insisting on a program
of scientific empiricism safe from any skepticism concerning the powers of mind or existence of God, it delayed,
but could not indefinitely prevent, recognition that the
methods of much scientific research challenged any exalted view of human or supernatural powers. By the 1820s
there was already alarm about the extent of research on
the brain rather than the soul; by midcentury there was
more alarm over geological research that contradicted
biblical accounts of creation. If physiology, geology, or any
other science proved inconsistent with theology, the Didactic Enlightenment was doomed to founder. Third, the
view of human consciousness, which might seem too
grandiose to researchers on the brain, was in danger of
appearing too constricted to enthusiastic democrats. We
shall see in the next chapter how many midcentury
Americans either expanded Reid's and Stewart's views of
human intuition or dismissed them as an inadequate appreciation of man's nobility.

Though assailed by some subsequent philosophers,
scientists, and champions of democracy, this version of the
Enlightenment is pivotal to understanding American culture in the century after the Revolution. If we must attend to those who grew dissatisfied with it, we must also
note that its prevalence as a religious-academic orthodoxy
explains much that was said in protest and frustration. Like
any dominant ideology, it contained compromises and
avoided problems; eventually it might seem shallow and
defective. But it avoided the anti-intellectualism of the revivals and the atheism thought to be inherent in materialistic science. It allowed preachers, educators, and orators to believe that in dispensing knowledge they were

carrying out the true work of promoting morality and progress in a new era of human freedom. And by making the problem of knowledge—how man perceives and makes use of nature—the central problem of philosophy, it cast aside the traditional theological problem of accounting for evil. Accepting the "common sense" of reality, it encouraged Americans who came under its influence to pursue happiness vigorously and to strive for self-improvement, seldom doubting that a better world would be the outcome.

This was the philosophy of an era with extraordinarily little interest in psychology. Even its critics accepted, almost tacitly, the view that there were no sinful depths to plumb in human nature. To be sure, Reid and Stewart had taught that in the hierarchy of human faculties the passions still lurked menacingly at the bottom, and Americans generally made passing reference to this "animal" element. But they did not stop long to analyze a source of difficulties that the other faculties were well equipped to control. In an age that revaluated virtue, respectability, and other ideals of behavior, an age that undercut traditional conceptions of authority and reorganized the structure of intellectual life, there was a reassuring concentration of focus on the most reliable activities of mind. The era of reorganization was endurable because it was also an era of contraction.

FOR FURTHER READING

Three outstanding works by Gordon S. Wood are indispensable to understanding this era: his compendious *The Creation of the American Republic, 1776–1787* (1969); his challenging essay on "The Democratization of Mind in the

American Revolution" in a symposium entitled *Leadership in the American Revolution* (1974); and his provocative introduction to an excellent collection of readings, *The Rising Glory of America, 1760–1820* (1971).

An influential reinterpretation of republicanism and virtue may be found in J. G. A. Pocock, *The Machiavellian Moment: Political Thought and the Atlantic Republican Tradition* (1975). For two quite different assessments of this reinterpretation, see Isaac Kramnick, "Republican Revisionism Revisited," *American Historical Review* (1982), and Daniel Walker Howe, "European Sources of Political Ideas on Jeffersonian America," *Reviews in American History* (1982).

An excellent study of the arts during the Revolution is Kenneth Silverman's *A Cultural History of the American Revolution* (1976). On the Jeffersonians and Federalists, respectively, two good studies are Linda Kerber, *Federalists in Dissent* (1970), and Lance Banning, *The Jeffersonian Persuasion* (1978).

For a broad survey of postrevolutionary American culture, see Russel Blaine Nye, *The Cultural Life of the New Nation* (1960). A more penetrating interpretation, based on studies of Charles Willson Peale, Hugh Henry Brackenridge, William Dunlap, and Noah Webster, is found in Joseph J. Ellis, *After the Revolution* (1979). Marvin Meyers, *The Jacksonian Persuasion* (1957), discusses other figures in one of the most stimulating accounts ever written of postrevolutionary political thought.

Since the bicentennial of the Revolution there have been many studies of how subject groups reinterpreted their "rights." On slaves, see Eugene D. Genovese, *From Rebellion to Revolution* (1979); on women, Mary Beth Norton, *Liberty's Daughters* (1980), and Linda Kerber, *Women of the Republic* (1980); on college students, Steven J. Novak, *The Rights of Youth* (1977); and on religious folk, Nathan O. Hatch, "The Christian Movement and the Demand for a Theology of the People," *Journal of American History* (1980).

On the meanings of revivalism, north and south, see Paul E. Johnson, *A Shopkeeper's Millennium* (1978), and Donald G. Mathews, *Religion in the Old South* (1977). On changes in the ministry, Donald M. Scott has written a valuable study: *From Office to Profession* (1978). On the lyceums, see Scott's "The Popular Lecture and the Making of a Public in Mid-Nineteenth-Century America," *Journal of American History* (1980). On the law, see Gerard W. Gawalt, *The Promise of Power* (1979). An interesting essay on reorganization in politics is Lynn L. Marshall, "The Strange Stillbirth of the Whig Party," *American Historical Review* (1967).

On fiction writing and the lives of female writers, see Mary Kelley's brilliant book, *Private Woman, Public Stage* (1984). Three excellent studies of theater and popular entertainment are David Grimsted, *Melodrama Unveiled* (1968); Robert Toll, *Blacking Up: The Minstrel Show in Nineteenth-Century America* (1974); and Neil Harris, *Humbug: The Art of P. T. Barnum* (1973).

For general commentary on the Scottish philosophy, see Morton White, *Science and Sentiment in America* (1972), and Donald H. Meyer, *The Democratic Enlightenment* (1976). On its influence among Unitarians, see Daniel Walker Howe, *The Unitarian Conscience* (1970); and among Old School Presbyterians, Theodore Dwight Bozeman, *Protestants in an Age of Science* (1977).

V

EMOTIONS AND IDEALS IN REORGANIZED AMERICA

SELF-DISSECTION

Mid-nineteenth-century American culture was a mélange of optimism and anxiety. For the individual with intellectual gifts, the era of reorganization resounded with exciting feelings of emancipation. All barriers to growth and achievement seemed to crumble. It was possible to dream of expressing one's deepest genius, of gaining fame and wealth, of furnishing leadership to the new age. At the same time, the reputed absence of barriers could enhance feelings of frustration if one's growth and attainments met with obstacles. In a culture that celebrated human potential, adult careers could seem dull and unfulfilling. One doctor was quoted as saying, "It is a misfortune to have been born when children were nothing, and to live till men were nothing."

The emancipation of the individual, moreover, conflicted with the preoccupation with social order that had been featured in every intellectual tradition. The United States had gone farther than any other nation in leveling the one church, hierarchical government, and inherited economic privilege. Americans were notoriously restless and unsettled. If God suddenly called the world to judgment, wrote an educated Argentine visitor in 1847, "He would surprise two-thirds of the population of the United States on the road like ants." Besides harboring anxieties about their individual careers, thoughtful Americans worried over the survival of good order. Conceptions of the individual soul in the mid-nineteenth century frequently glowed with optimism; discussions of social order frequently showed signs of evasion and distress.

Ralph Waldo Emerson reminded audiences of these tensions in "Historic Notes" (1880), assembled at the end of the new era. The decades after 1820 had witnessed a profound upsurge of opposition to established ways of viewing social relations. Children, once "repressed and kept in the background," were now "cosseted and pampered." Reorganization in religion and politics had meant recurrent schisms in familiar institutions and bitter charges against new ones. To someone starting out in life there was an apparent war between "intellect and affection," between the lures of the new and attachments to the old. Instead of obedience to the greater good, the "modern mind" was taught—divisively, in Emerson's view—that "the nation existed for the individual," even that "the individual is the world." One outcome of this reversal of traditional views of social order was a revolution in aesthetics: a speaker, writer, or performer sought an individuality of style reflecting personal experience and belief. The change, as Emerson recalled it, amounted to a great turning point in human psychology: "young men were born with knives in their brains, a tendency to introversion, self-dissection, anatomizing of motives." If such inward turning could be unnerving or destructive, it also might promote beneficial change. Whatever the costs to society, change was irresistible. There was keen interest in new critical methods in every field of inquiry, great receptiveness to anything novel that promised to enlarge the powers of mind.

The faculty psychology forged out of the Didactic Enlightenment prospered, not only in academic treatises, but also in casual remarks by politicians, by leaders of labor movements, by men and women in virtually every profession. It was reassuring in what might otherwise have seemed a chaotic republic to learn from a widely used textbook, Francis Wayland's *The Elements of Moral Science* (1835), that the conscience existed as "a distinct and separate faculty" to perceive the moral quality of actions just as the eyes took charge of seeing and the ears of hearing. Without this faculty, also called the moral sense, our perceptions of moral data would not "correspond" with the world outside ourselves, but fortunately we were not so imperfectly constituted. Wayland scarcely spoke of "reason," though admitting that "our intellectual powers" did help us to understand our relations to God and our fellow creatures and to form plans of action once "our moral powers" discerned our obligations. While intellect could reinforce the work of conscience, the great enemy was "strong and vehement passion." Terrible scenes of conflict, like those in Shakespearean dramas, occurred when the conscience was inadequately exercised and lacked firm control. Wayland, like numerous contemporaries, proceeded to give specific advice on methods of keeping the conscience clear, turning to matters as diverse as marital obligations, Sabbath observance, and slavery. From the simple premise that all human knowledge was acquired through the senses, he erected a generally progressive and altruistic system of social duties.

If this period had an intellectual orthodoxy, Wayland

came close to defining it. Views like his were inculcated in common schools, elaborated on in college curricula, repeated in polite circles, and brandished by reformers of the moral tone of the Republic. Though critics tagged these views "sensualism," they were free of any taint of hedonism or selfishness. They upheld an earnest, comfortable code of Christian morality that needed a minimum of external coercion. They stressed social obligation. Given the certainty that universal conscience apprehended what was proper, with a fair degree of intellectual training and control over disruptive passion, there was little reason to indulge in the hair-splitting arguments over the exact nature of virtuous action that consumed the energies of philosophers overseas. There was no need to battle over self-love and utility, pleasure and pain, or to define sects by contradictory views of human nature. Practical men could also be men of conscience, and religious leaders could point out that men and women of other denominations, however mistaken in a few doctrines, still tended to behave in the same civilized way.

As Emerson suggested, however, this comfortable outlook came to appear lifeless and imprisoning to articulate spokesmen for a rising generation. Intellectual controversy in the decades after 1820 frequently centered on new analyses of the human mind. One mark of modernity was to speak of powers in human consciousness that were not dreamed of in the orthodox philosophy.

The moral earnestness of the insurgents usually equaled that of dons like Wayland. There is a manuscript, "Of Feelings" (ca. 1850s), by Sarah Grimké, a well-known reformer from South Carolina who had settled into a career of teaching in a New Jersey community. The manuscript took the approach to human nature that was sometimes disparaged as sensual or mechanical. It examined responses of skin, eyes, ears, nose, and mouth to external objects in order to show that a sequence of events, like the workings of a watch, must take place for us to experience various feelings. From this discussion of material stimuli, she moved to feelings aroused by idealized objects and desires, particularly feelings about other sentient beings. (The example she chose concerned thoughts of someone fracturing the statue *Greek Slave* and of someone hacking apart a real woman.) "Conscience" was an insignificant term in this manuscript, which exemplified two emerging themes of nineteenth-century thought. On the one hand, the feelings furnished a promising link between physiology and ethics; on the other, the intellect held the power to create "idealities" that preceded moral judgments and stimulated moral action. In most instances, Grimké preferred an empirical test of idealities; if they "correspond" to reality, they are true. She even expressed interest in the possibility of clairvoyants testing claims about spiritualism and the afterlife. But some idealities stood for future conditions to be achieved by human action—for what ought to be—and the entire class of virtuous ideals lay beyond sensory validation: "Though no just person existed on Earth . . . I should know that all men ought so to act, that this mere idea would become a reality through their action."

It is hard to tell what prompted Grimké to write this essay, which in any case manipulated ideas of widening currency. The essay illustrates the enhanced importance of the emotions and the idealizing intellect even to those who were not philosophers by training or occupation. In some works by Wayland's academic peers similar revisions were at work. Thomas Cogswell Upham's *Elements of Mental Philosophy* (1831) asserted that both "perception" (external knowledge) and "reason" (deductive knowledge) had been overemphasized by students of human nature; the "springs of action" lay "back of the intellect

. . . in the shape of the emotions and passions." Upham
was a religious man, a teacher at Andover Seminary and
Bowdoin College; yet he expressed no alarm at this esti-
mation of human motivation. He was merely correcting
an imbalance, as he saw it, in what his generation had been
trained to believe. Thus he dissected at length the varied
activities of inner consciousness and, at even greater length,
the panoply of human affections and desires. In the end
he found reassuring evidence of human free will, an attribute he identified with self-control. The power of reflection, the capacity for remorse, the desire for community esteem—these and a dozen other motives were
sufficient to rein in even the wildest temper. "It is not uncommon," he wrote, "in almost every village and neigh-
borhood, to observe persons of naturally quick feelings,
and whose passions are obviously violent, and are prone
to foam and toss about like the waves of the sea, who
nevertheless have those passions under complete control,
even in the most trying circumstances."

Without straying too far from the terms established by
the Enlightenment, a Grimké at her writing table or an
Upham on the lecture dais could seek to understand the
emotions of the soul. Conceptions of human nature became more adventurous and eclectic when colleges engaged teachers from Europe, as when Harvard in 1831
hired Charles Follen to teach German language and literature, partly in response to student complaints about the
sterility of the curriculum. When Frederick A. Rauch of
Marshall College published *Psychology* (1841), he commenced, not with sensations on a *tabula rasa*, but with man's
"self-feeling," which distinguished him from other creatures. The universe was a system of meanings formed by
the mind of God and comprehended by signs and symbols fashioned by man's "semeiotic imagination." Rauch

dismissed the notion of faculties altogether. The mind was "a *union* . . . unfolding its life organically"; none of its activities proceeded in isolation from the others. In the wonders of each human "personality," where collective experience and individual purpose flowed together, this German-American educator located "the centre of nature, the echo of the universe."

Utterly new terminologies entered American discourse, to be adopted helter-skelter as readers found promise of making sense of present problems and future prospects. Perhaps a young man searched within himself for signs of the genius to make a reputation in the expanding audiences for literature and art. A reformer might look for some leverage to attack the materialism of a disappointing culture. A teacher might aspire to bring his lectures up to date; a minister, to lead the church to new opportunities. A young woman might seek a fulfilling vocation. All might be receptive to new ideas, sometimes fusing them with others that technical philosophers would have regarded as their opposites. Viewing the process retrospectively, Emerson and others felt that a revolution had altered public understanding of the individual.

TRANSCENDENTALISM

Of course, Emerson's "Historic Notes" did not describe all "young men"—let alone young women—growing up in America in the years after the War of 1812. Emerson was a skilled maker of legends, a popularizer of attractive ways of thinking about experiences that had not always been so coherent. Yet there is little doubt that his extensive audiences felt he was limning a historical process in which they had shared. His words also carried conviction because of his preeminence in a loosely organized movement, known as transcendentalism, of writers of great originality. Henry David Thoreau's *Walden* (1854), an account of solitary life in the woods, though only modestly successful when published, became eventually one of the touchstones of American achievement in literature—a stature it holds to this day. Emerson himself, somewhat like Thomas Jefferson, furnished inspiration to an astonishing range of Americans in every subsequent generation, from bank presidents to anarchists, all interested in self-exploration and achievement. Other participants in the transcendentalist movement included the early feminist Margaret Fuller, the great liberal preacher Theodore Parker, the earnest communitarian socialist George Ripley, and the meditative reformer Bronson Alcott—the latter best remembered, perhaps, as the prototype of Father March in Louisa May Alcott's novel *Little Women* (1868).

All of these individuals grew up amid the conflict between Unitarianism and the established Congregational churches of New England. They supported movements to bring Unitarianism closer to the yearnings of plain people in increasingly stratified eastern cities. All came to feel that the liberation offered by Unitarianism was too tepid, too aloof from the direct religious experience salient in revivalism. Despite their intellectual origins in regional sectarian controversies, all overcame this provincialism and identified their efforts with a rising spirit of liberalism that they perceived in America and the world. They were ambitious writers who sought to acquaint their countrymen with avant-garde trends in European poetry, philosophy, and biblical criticism. They were keen to dismiss the Lockean psychology which, by restricting knowledge to the senses, seemed to impoverish the mind. As Emerson explained in an essay called "The Transcendentalist" (1843), help was available from abroad:

What is popularly called Transcendentalism among us, is Idealism. . . . As thinkers, mankind have ever divided into two sects, Materialists and Idealists; the first class founding on experience, the second on consciousness; the first class beginning to think from the data of the senses, the second class perceive that the senses are not final, and say, The senses give us representations of things, but what are the things themselves they cannot tell. The materialist insists on facts, on history, on the force of circumstances and the animal wants of man; the idealist on the power of Thought and Will, on inspiration, on miracle, on individual culture. . . .

It is well known to most of my audience that the Idealism of the present day acquired the name of Transcendental from the use of that term by Immanuel Kant, of Königsberg, who replied to the skeptical philosophy of Locke, which insisted that there was nothing in the intellect which was not previously in the experience of the senses, by showing that there was a very important class of ideas or imperative forms, which did not come by experience. . . . The extraordinary profoundness and precision of that man's thinking have given vogue to his nomenclature . . . to that extent that whatever belongs to the class of intuitive thought is popularly called at the present day *Transcendental.*

Others took a less abstract approach, less concerned with dividing human beings throughout history into two categories, more concerned with the prospects for self-improvement in the modern era. If all men were born with only a *tabula rasa,* then the advantages that went with education and privilege would continue to hold sway. But inborn powers of intuition made all men and women immediately equal. Regardless of their stations in life, they possessed powers of contemplation that could enrich their souls.

The name *transcendentalism* is not completely reliable in understanding the ideas of these writers or their significance. It gained currency as a term of derision, intended to make fun of high-brow pretensions and cumbersome jargon, much as the black-faced minstrel shows ridiculed the polysyllabic hair-splitting of literati in the new age. ("Transcendentalism is dat spiritual cognoscence ob psychological irrefragibility, connected wid conscientient ademption ob incolumbient spirituality and etherialized connection.") Few Americans ever called themselves transcendentalists, though many affiliated with the forward-looking spirit that Emerson charted. Books like *Walden* or Emerson's *Nature* (1836) were too complex, furthermore, to be reduced accurately to a single tag. The group known as transcendentalists was too ephemeral and informal to have the coherent doctrine of a philosophical school or of a sustained theological movement.

But a characteristic attitude toward experience, setting goals for individual behavior, prevailed in the works of Emerson, Thoreau, Alcott, and the others, an attitude that gave their followers a sense of emancipation. *Nature* contained a startling image of the man alone in the woods, forgetful of systems of thought through which he was supposed to interpret what he perceived. In the woods a person became, in an often-quoted phrase, "a transparent eyeball," with nature circulating through him without interference by intermediaries. This was an escape from everything artificial and socially determined; it was exhilarating to feel an "occult relation" with the vegetable realm.

As "currents of Universal Being" flowed through the self, it became "part or parcel of God." No wonder orthodox critics, including the senior Unitarians, charged the American transcendentalists with mysticism and pantheism. Had *Walden* been better known, it might have been seen as a resolute experiment in living out this image—in "living without principle," as Thoreau put it, shucking traditional categories of thought and digging down to the "privatest experience." Alcott began his "Orphic Sayings" (1840) in a similar vein: "Thou art, my heart, a soul-flower, facing ever and following the motions of thy sun, opening thyself to her vivifying ray, and pleading thy affinity with the celestial orbs." His heart turned to miraculous nature, which carried intimations of divine law if not reduced to calculation or analysis. Alcott had an epigram for the transcendentalists' shared repudiation of conventional views of the well-regulated mind: "Sinners must needs reason; saints behold."

Despite the animated spirit of generational conflict—of young ministers and writers renouncing schemes of self-control favored by postrevolutionary leaders—there were important limits to transcendentalism as a movement of revolt. The movement attracted followers who were sure of their talents and expected to do well in the emerging order. Among the leaders, Emerson enjoyed great success on the lyceum circuit; Parker preached in a theater to huge congregations; and Ripley and Fuller, as well as younger transcendentalists like Thomas Wentworth Higginson, eventually established themselves as arbiters of literary taste. Their readers and disciples were often upwardly mobile young men and restless young women in search of careers appropriate to their gifts. While they thrilled to the ferment of popular culture—Alcott yearned for fame equal to that which P. T. Barnum won from entertainment and Horace Greeley from journalism—few of them revealed much sympathy for those who toiled in misery, without time to wander in the woods.* Emerson scoffed at charity to the poor. Thoreau derided laborers and farmers working hard to keep up with the expanding market economy. The Irish and French-Canadian working class remained outside the New England culture they criticized and celebrated. Alcott did take part in early antislavery societies, with Parker and Higginson joining at a later stage, and Emerson and Thoreau eventually praised the antislavery martyr John Brown. But some of the best-known transcendentalist essays belittled excessive concern for the plight of others at the expense of solitary self-exploration. In fact, transcendentalism had little to say about social reform, though it led to the creation of several utopian communities that sought to reunite intellectuals with artisans (or, as one said, "coarse people"). The movement on the whole took a dim view of sentimental meddlesomeness in contemporary problems.

Transcendentalists were dismayed by class barriers evident in the cities, and they took note of the inroads of revivalism among uneducated folk. A few transcendentalists had religious experiences akin to those prompted by revival meetings. Nevertheless, as the image of the "transparent eyeball" suggests, they virtually defined themselves as aloof from the collective emotionality of nineteenth-century evangelicalism. Though transcendentalists disparaged the "reason" as commonly understood, their stance was refined and intellectual. In the lives of some

---

*The major exception was Orestes Brownson, author of a radical article on "The Laboring Classes" (1840). Parker also wrote "Thoughts on Labor" (1841), in which he regretted the separation of the educated and well-off from an expanding class of laborers.

leaders of the movement, scholars have traced themes of repression and hurtful coldness toward others. The transcendentalists prized a rather disciplined contemplation of nature and divine law. Emerson and Parker gave fine expression to the belief in permanent truth, in ideals glistening through all great religions and coursing with universal effectiveness through the trees. Transcendentalism did not prize intense emotional experiences with other human beings. It typically avoided, moreover, the possibility that individuals would discover truths in their hearts that would differ from those of other pure searchers. The passions were almost absent from the nomenclature with which transcendentalists dissected brain and soul. It was simply taken for granted that, with "the lower passions" suppressed, the heart enjoyed access to God and nature, but the task of suppression did not seem difficult. Seldom in their public writings—not even in Fuller's *Woman in the Nineteenth Century* (1844)—is there confrontation with the possibility that anyone, at heart, possessed deeply sexual instincts or that the emancipated psyche could prove harmful. Several of the transcendentalists regarded meat-eating as a sign of sensuality, and Thoreau thought the "animal in us"—evident in sexual "cohabiting"—must be expelled if we are to follow "higher laws." The overriding goal was spiritual purification. It was a movement, as a contemporary put it, of excited brains and cool emotions.

Their inattention to emotion and disregard of the likelihood of a babel of dissent were precisely the grounds of criticism of the Emersonians by James Marsh, a graduate of Andover Seminary and president of the University of Vermont. At first, Marsh had been something of a hero to Emerson and other transcendentalists. His heavily annotated edition of Samuel Taylor Coleridge's *Aids to Reflection* (1829) had thrilled them with its distinction between "the Understanding," which conducted exact observations of the natural world, and "the Reason," redefined as an intuitive grasp of the mysteries of experience. Here really was a knife dividing mental activity into irreconcilable modes, one rational and the other imaginative; and Marsh hoped the distinction would pacify antagonism between Enlightenment traditions and religious impulses. Science and devotion had separate enterprises to carry out, that was all; a good person could give simultaneous allegiance to both. Church unity might be restored by dumping the Lockean system—by paying more attention to the "influence of feeling" and by refusing to reduce "the whole soul to the measured movements of a machine under the control of our will." Marsh was dismayed that the Emersonians took his work in the direction of greater radicalism and disparagement of orthodoxy. In his view there was no impediment to accepting the claims of ecclesiastical structure and traditional theology. The transcendentalists pretended to "no system or unity, but each utters it seems the inspiration of the moment, assuming that it all comes from the universal heart, while ten to one it comes from the stomach of the individual."

The transcendentalist movement sprang perhaps, as Emerson detailed, from a rising tendency to make the individual more important than society. Its greatest works still recall the excitement of an era of liberation. But it was not a broadly democratic movement, for all its talk of universal capacities of the soul. The "faith in man" that it held out depended on a sharply restricted outlook on personality. Its stress on originality and its renunciation of charitable feelings distinguished it from competing responses to exploitative economic arrangements and reorganized cultural institutions. It was an unusually austere effort to portray the ideal man of the new era as devoid of dangerous drives, united in a mysterious bond with nature.

ROMANTICISM

The tensions preying on Emerson's "young men with knives in their brains" were not narrowly American in origin. In the aftermath of decades of revolution and counterrevolution, European intellectuals struggled even more directly with the implications of a shattered system of political, economic, and ecclesiastical authority. The cultural tendencies of the early nineteenth century—frequently termed *romanticism*—included, on the one hand, profound explorations of human emotions and hearty celebrations of the power of heroes to unify spiritless hordes and, on the other, painful laments over being born too late for glorious deeds and mystical rumination on the harmonies of bygone eras. Wordsworth and Coleridge, Byron and Shelley, Scott and Carlyle—these great names of English literature evoke the diversity of English romanticism's investigations of human nature and history. On the Continent, too, there was a sustained shared endeavor to find new sources of social obligation based on an altered awareness of human capacities. Sometimes participants in this endeavor glorified the sentimental uprightness of ordinary people; sometimes they focused on the potency of strong emotion to drive the individual to perform unsuspected deeds. Some romantics, both of the left and of the right, pondered past examples of communities bonded in emotional assent—peasant communes, medieval principalities, or the papal church—as they recoiled from the Enlightenment's experiments with reason and planning.

American romanticism was distinguished from its European counterparts by the greater inroads the market economy made in many sectors of life in the Republic. There were no peasants to eulogize, only dim memories of hereditary rule, and little belief that the Revolution could be reversed. To be sure, some dissatisfied individuals, like the former transcendentalists Orestes Brownson and Sophia Ripley, turned to Roman Catholicism as an alternative to American shallowness and rootlessness. Some southerners alleged to see in plantation slavery the benefits of the Middle Ages as portrayed in Sir Walter Scott's novels. By and large, however, thoughtful Americans took for granted, not only the eradication of the church-state, but also the expansion of markets for all goods, including the labor of intellectuals. Their response was necessarily ambivalent. Transcendentalists, for example, derided farmers who hurried faster and faster to sell produce to men and women they would never meet; they also called for discovery of the true self that has no price. But they praised the artist with authentic wares to market, the professional who upheld high personal standards of excellence. Their visions of the isolated soul did not preclude use of the transportation system that facilitated book sales, lecture tours, and literary conventions.

In no case should the transcendentalists be given a monopoly on Americanness. Their contemporaries frequently responded to the tensions of the nineteenth century, not by twisting knives in their brains, but by thinking about the history and institutions that defined America. Some directly confronted the prospects for impulse-ridden mankind when connections to distant markets acquired significance beyond local loyalties and conflicts.

There were many expressions of the belief that man in the woods actually exhibited a breakdown of useful social sentiments. The influential French commentator Alexis de Tocqueville described the ruins of deserted homesteads as impatient Americans vanished from one half-finished venture to the next. In the forest might be found logs sprouting afresh near blackened hearthstones left behind by a family rushing off to better prospects. More typically, land was resold by a farmer who had come to regard himself as a commercial unit: "he brings land into tillage in order to sell it again, and not to farm it: he builds a farm-house on the speculation, that, as the state of the country will soon be changed by the increase of population, a good price may be obtained for it." In the resulting pattern, families lived far from one another, rather than in tidy villages. In the absence of harmonious feelings, a shallow calculation of personal advantage became the characteristic mental activity of Americans. "Nothing conceivable," wrote Tocqueville, "is so petty, so insipid, so crowded with paltry interests, in one word, so anti-poetic, as the life of man in the United States." The ruling passion, he observed, was nothing more than the love of comfort and well-being.

Tocqueville said too little about the remarkable growth of towns and cities, though he did notice the spirit of reorganization that partly offset selfish individualism in cultural life. His account is interesting, however, as a counterpoint to the attitude of Americans who toured Europe and savored its romantic literature in order to escape what they also took to be the antipoetic cast of the prevailing American temperament. This was the reason for the vogue for Scott's novels in America and the extensive readership for Washington Irving's and Henry Wadsworth Longfellow's depictions of life in English manors and Spanish castles. Life in America, complained the young Longfellow, was "prosaic to the last degree"—a difficult environment for the man of talent seeking to compose

moving works of literature. Other writers complained that
the calculating milieu impeded their efforts to give the
imagination free play.

An instructive example is a Harvard graduation address (1844) by Francis Parkman, soon to become one of
America's greatest and most popular historians. He saw
Americans tearing down the woods, draining lakes, and
damming rivers so relentlessly as to destroy all fanciful
associations with history or nature. It was a moment without charm: "the dullest plainest prose has fixed its home
in America." The national history, with its emphasis on
"cool reason," earnest deliberation, and peace-loving revolutionaries, also suppressed romantic feelings. Everywhere were signs of crass materialism. The typical American lacked "warlike ardor, preferring to watch his saw-
mill and hoe his potatoes, since these seem to him the more
rational and profitable occupations." Yet America was not
entirely lacking in sources of romantic inspiration. An imaginative child might sense in the mountains and forests
echoes of once-fearful scenes; there were beautiful crags
and lakes, now in repose, which formerly witnessed valor
and heroism. In this collegiate meditation on the contrasts between Old World and New, Parkman had located
the theme of his magnificent multivolume history of the
conflicts of French, English, and Indians in colonial
America.

As the work proceeded in succeeding decades, Parkman fulfilled the romantic goal of recapturing the emotions of bygone eras and thereby making history real. He
fed an appetite for history among nineteenth-century
readers that had two divergent sources. On the one hand,
history offered correctives to the shallow acquisitiveness
that allegedly endangered modern character. It favored
mighty conflicts of world principles set against a back-

drop of rugged grandeur, and it supplied a deliberately Shakespearean sense of the diversity of human action and passion. Parkman's La Salle, for example, was "Coriolanus-like" in his pride, vision, and feats of command; yet he collided pathetically with the duplicity of the French Jesuit regime. On the other hand, this history rested on confidence in human progress. If mid-nineteenth-century culture seemed prosaic and people seemed too preoccupied with economic gain, the age still represented an advance over the absolutism that had stifled individual enterprise and used human life immorally in the past. It was not in order to doubt human progress, but in order to appreciate it, that readers gazed on distant fields and ancient scenes.

Parkman's narratives portrayed the rugged men of the New World as superior to Europeans who crossed their paths because they were closer to nature and their feelings were farther from artificial codes of intellect. Energetic New Englanders, moreover, prevailed over a New France that was "all head." And according to these narratives, eighteenth-century England—the age of Locke—had been dull and staid, devoid of great ideas. This historical schema afforded an optimistic perspective on the prosaic America that Parkman had lamented in his college days. His great contemporaries, William Hickling Prescott and John Lothrop Motley, joined in fashioning a version of history that distanced America from the barren rationality of Europe. Their narratives condemned all "materialists" and "sensualists" who took a narrow view of human potential, thereby missing opportunities for heroic action and undervaluing the sentiments of ordinary men. These historians, who saw themselves as men of letters in close touch with an extensive reading public, upheld the importance of earnest individual endeavor, a collective awareness of destiny, and a properly enlarged view of human nature.

No historian was more influential or more philosophical than George Bancroft, who studied philology in Germany, met the English romantics, associated with the Emersonian circle, achieved power in the Democratic party, and served in James Knox Polk's cabinet. As author of a majestic *History of the United States* (1834–1874), which has been described as casting a vote for Andrew Jackson on every page, Bancroft celebrated the ascendancy of the people to political power. This history contained set pieces denouncing Locke and praising Kant; it insisted throughout on the insurgent wisdom of the common people. Inconvenient evidence was reshaped—though Bancroft believed he was rescuing the past from those who had distorted it—so that John Calvin became the fountainhead of republican liberty, the Puritans libertarians, George Washington a man of sweetness and emotion, and, astonishingly, Thomas Jefferson less of a materialist than he believed himself: "He was an idealist in his habits of thought and life, as indeed is every one who has an abiding and thorough confidence in the people."

In an essay on progress and popular judgment, Bancroft argued that no special abilities differentiated men of genius from their lesser-known contemporaries. The Platos and Luthers of history could originate no truth "which did not equally have its source in the mind of every one." Usually men of genius turned to the vernacular language to express their deepest insights. All useful revolutions in culture enjoyed the benefits of popularity. These views will seem so farfetched to modern readers, accustomed to tales of unappreciated genius and laments over the gulf separating popular culture from the highest forms of achievement, that they may doubt Bancroft's sincerity. But this was the lesson that Bancroft's democratic readers derived from their era, an image of history as "flowing on in eternal motion, with nothing fixed but the certainty of change." Though individual lives sometimes met with disappointment, "the movement of the human mind, taken collectively, is always toward something better." Unlike the churchmen of yore who treated most of humanity as fallible, unlike even the enlightened Americans of the Revolution who abhorred the mob and longed for an aristocracy of talent, Bancroft conveyed a message of universal trust. He identified his psychological assumptions in terms similar to Emerson's and Coleridge's:

> There is a *spirit in man:* not in the privileged few. . . . Reason exists within every breast. I mean not that faculty which deduces inferences from the experience of the senses, but that highest faculty, which from the infinite treasures of its own consciousness, originates truth, and assents to it by the force of intuitive evidence; that faculty which raises us beyond the control of time and space, and gives us faith in things eternal and invisible.

In some individuals judgment might be clouded by "the bias of passion"; some might see more clearly than others. But universal powers of intuition, which distinguished human beings from sense-confined animals, furnished a basis for democratic optimism.

To the modern eye, the charge that America was dull and prosaic may well seem unfounded. In literature this was the era of Herman Melville, Nathaniel Hawthorne, Walt Whitman, and Harriet Beecher Stowe as well as the transcendentalists and great historians. Great orators like Daniel Webster were admired overseas for their typically

American volcanic, true-hearted quality; this era produced Abraham Lincoln. Foreigners reported that all Americans were natural speakers, and widespread American appreciation of music and theater did not go unnoticed. In scores of colleges, new and old, professors pursued works of mind and heart. Travelers complained of the absence of the highest levels of abstract thought (how prevalent in any milieu?), and it was said that conversation in polite circles turned more rapidly than in Europe to business and gossip. To the extent that such complaints had any truth, they indicated differences between a democratic society and traditional patterns of rank and privilege. The abundance of newspapers reaching every American home—or so it seemed to European travelers—symbolized the popular literacy regarded as at odds with elite customs of the past.

When Americans made similar complaints, they were identifying the potential drawbacks of a commercialized culture: absorption in money-making and reduction of taste to the lowest common denominator. But the moans about materialism should not conceal the other side of the equation: boundless expectations. If Americans lacked the sense of history that came from exposure to castles and abbeys, their historians offered them a vision of expanding possibility and universal intellectual capacity, a vision that did not limit their dreams and achievements. Underlying both the moans and expectations, moreover, was impressive agreement on the orderliness of republican culture in spite of all its unsettling mobility. To be sure, urban mobs provided occasional exceptions to be noticed and abhorred, but it seemed clear that an essential self-restraint governed the way in which Americans moved about and dreamed. Except for certain unruly outsiders, Americans seemed rid of the lustful passions that for so many centuries had raised specters of anarchy and misrule.

THE THEOLOGY
OF THE FEELINGS

Examples could be multiplied of Americans who took an important step in their intellectual lives by rejecting Lockean psychology, often after reading Coleridge or gaining acquaintance with German thought. Generally, the Scottish commonsense psychology had given them all the assurance they needed of universal intuitions of the soul, but to repudiate Locke became a sign of recognition of a new age of consciousness. Nevertheless, it would be wrong to suppose that all Americans, or even all intellectuals, shared Emerson's individualism or Bancroft's democratic radicalism. Most academic institutions continued to honor the formulas of the Didactic Enlightenment. Two brilliant novelists, Melville and Hawthorne, can be read as dramatizing ironic and unfathomable dimensions of experience that enlightened and transcendental optimists alike neglected. Orthodox religious thinkers like James Marsh felt that proper understanding of the soul led back to time-honored doctrines rather than into a future of fragmentation and confusion.

There were three facts that no religious movement could ignore. One was the prevalence of revivalism in the culture of the United States. Some deplored it, others gave only modified approval, but few could believe that it would subside altogether. Whatever psychological constructions seminarians might give to the revivals, religious events were characterized by manipulative appeals to human emotions and deeply treasured, passionate responses. The second was the inevitability of sectarianism as denominations multiplied and divided, often as a result of revivalism, rather than finding a higher Christian unity. The third was the paradox that religion, despite this ineluctable emotionality and sectarianism, proved the greatest single support to social order. Philip Schaff, a theologian returning to Berlin to tell of his experiences as a teacher in Pennsylvania, explained that there was nothing licentious or unrestrained in the American evangelical view of freedom. Rather, the ideal American "holds his passion in check; is master of his sensual nature; obeys natural laws, not under pressure from without, but from inward impulse, cheerfully and joyfully." The problem of restraining the passions was discussed infrequently in a culture that valued the spontaneous release of the revival, but to some extent the restraint could be taken for granted as a corollary of the release. While agreeing somewhat with familiar depictions of Americans as restless and materialistic, Schaff added that they were more generous in supporting religious endeavors, more energetic in all projects of improvement, and swifter to reconcile political differences than were their European contemporaries.

Nineteenth-century revivalism did not arouse formal theoretical disputes over psychology like those of the previous century. Too much ground had been lost by the camp that believed in such traditional tenets as human inability or predestination. Even the followers of Edwards had conceded people's general ability to perfect themselves in the sight of God. For the most part the revivalists simply affirmed that procedures that worked could not fail to be godly. How else to secure the desired end of a revival than by using the emotional means that God had made available? If there was no formal psychological theory, revivalists were united in praise of the "spontaneous feelings of the human heart." Note that, in Schaff's account, the basis of order was impulsive: no irony was intended, and no contradiction in terms was foreseen. Evangelicals praised a wondrous system of "voluntarism"—a concerted, successful campaign to make the United States the most Christian nation on earth through the simple expedient of allowing each church and each individual to act "spontaneously."

The means that moved the heart might sometimes be harsh words, reminiscent of Edwards's fearful evocations of man's fate, but more often the words were soothing and sweet. Preachers praised God's and Christ's loving intentions and the softer side of human nature that was their apt recipient. A key reflection on this change was *The Theology of the Intellect and the Theology of the Feelings* (1850) by Edwards A. Park of Andover Seminary. Two styles competed for dominance over American religion, one emphasizing general statements connected by logic, the other presenting affective imagery to "the well-trained heart." These styles evoked contradictory images of God, one asserting his unforgiving judgment, the other his abundant mercy. The conflict of these styles obviously denoted a transition in the very language of Protestantism. Park tended to depict the theology of the intellect as traditional and patriarchal; the other theology, maternal in temper, was an accommodation to a democratic age. But Park declined to view the two theologies as irreconcilable. His goal was to vindicate neither one but to recognize that religion needed figurative language and emotional appeals to reach the great majority of the population. According to some critics, notably at Princeton, Park was evading intellectual responsibility and allowing intellectual truth to be submerged in popular prejudice. Certainly he was trying to reformulate a role for theologians—the traditional learned elite—in a religious climate of democratic self-expression. In saying that each style was appropriate "in its place," however, he inevitably constricted the intellect's sphere of influence, for he accorded to the feelings preeminence in sermon writing, the chief vehicle for expressing doctrine to the people, while he relegated the intellect to treatises and other specialized works. Furthermore, he acknowledged that the theology of the feelings took a deeper, longer-lasting hold than its competitor, and it was less likely to become "antiquated" by the "progress of science." Park was a formidable scholar, a great admirer of learned men in previous ages who had pursued religious truth in the dust of their studies. But he had read the signs of the times clearly enough to know that modern ministers wished a gentler—some would say, watered down—kind of training and that modern congregations craved assurance of the legitimacy of the feelings.*

Once one accepted the dominance of the feelings, it was possible to redefine the function of the churches in American culture. Horace Bushnell, Congregationalist minister in Hartford, Connecticut, was one of the most thoughtful persons to take up this challenge. As a plain country student, Bushnell had struggled in college to improve his speaking and writing abilities until he was uplifted by reading Coleridge. Thereafter he shared the excitement of Marsh and Emerson in the discovery that scientific understanding was only a limited good and that

---

*Protestant leaders made a distinction between the socially beneficial emotions and the carnal, or animal, passions. To the former they gave extravagant praise. By midcentury prominent ministers like Henry Ward Beecher were so effusive in their paeans to Christ's love and tender qualities of the human heart that church services were sometimes love feasts. Though ministers spoke less frequently of the passions, they may still have been afraid of them. Beecher in the 1830s kept a diary in which he tried to keep watch over erotic and other unwelcome "feelings feelings feelings." In 1872 he was the subject of a scandalous trial concerning charges that he had seduced a female parishioner.

the language men used allowed only approximate statements of their highest insights. To an artist, belief that perceived facts are symbols of superior levels of reality afforded challenges to new feats of verbal creativity, but to the religious thinker, in Bushnell's view, the same belief denied the prospect of ever giving intellectual validity to the tenets of Christianity. These tenets could not be proved by observation and logic; they were felt truths of human consciousness that must be *expressed* rather than demonstrated. To Bushnell, these conclusions showed the futility of theological disputation in previous generations. He was willing to endure the scorn of conservatives, like those at Princeton, who preferred the reassertion of dogma to such an "aesthetic" approach to religion. He recognized that theology's day was waning, that in the near future the seminaries would turn out men of heart.

Bushnell's best-known work, *Christian Nurture* (1847), virtually ignored doctrinal issues that delineated religious denominations. It asserted the importance of bringing up children to be men and women of "good feeling" and behavior. That revivals were central to American culture was an accepted fact, but in focusing too extremely on the conversion of young adults, assumed to be creatures of sin up to that point, revivals distracted attention from parental influence over "the plastic nature of childhood." In part the goal was church-centered: children ought to grow up feeling that they had never been un-Christian. But Bushnell emphasized larger social concerns: revivals reinforced the Americans' "hardness and rudeness," lack of "sensibility to things that do not lie in action," and want of "domesticity of character." They reflected a tendency that Bushnell repudiated—the tendency to "carry our doctrines of free will so far as to make little or nothing of organic laws; not observing that character may be, to a great extent, only the free development of exercises previously wrought in us, or extended to us, when other wills held us within their sphere."

Obviously, Bushnell stood far removed from Emerson's solitary man in the woods. Many details of his advice about effective nurture—the superiority of feeling and example over doctrine, for example, the necessity of an early acquaintance with rules, and the wisdom of preparing the child for eventual "emancipation" from the parents—have a strikingly modern ring. It is not surprising that *Christian Nurture* remained in print long after the polemical issues of its day were forgotten. Yet in some ways it showed the same shallowness remarked in the transcendentalists. It spoke of the feelings of children, but of neither passions nor instincts; it admitted little struggle for control of the will; in fact, it employed only trivial psychological terminology. While denying that human nature was naturally good, it portrayed a world in which children always responded gently to kindness, in which benevolent feelings never aroused their opposites, in which rebellion and error always succumbed to good example. It reminds us that prominent intellectual systems of this period—too late to stress original sin, too early to plumb the depths of the psyche—were poorly equipped to account for recalcitrance and evil.

Bushnell's views may usefully be compared with one other alternative to optimistic individualism. At the seminary of the German Reformed church in Mercersburg, Pennsylvania, John Williamson Nevin, brought up in America as a Presbyterian, and Philip Schaff, a Swiss educated in Germany, carried out a fruitful collaboration. Both were idealists—Nevin because of youthful reading that included Coleridge, Schaff because of the German educational milieu—but neither made his mark with speculative psychology. Rather, they were bold critics of American disrespect for the institutional church. They deplored, not only revivalism, but also the prevailing neglect of sacraments like the Lord's Supper. They were contemptuous of the isolation of private judgment from the authority of the church, and they considered the work of Calvin and Luther to have continued rather than to have broken off from the organic unity of the historical church. Their critique of individualism resembled Bushnell's, but they insisted on the bonding of human subjectivity, not in the sanctum of the family, but through deepening historical consciousness and reverence for enduring institutions. Nevin and Schaff had more kind words for Catholicism than most American Protestants could abide (their reputations have improved as a result of twentieth-century interest in ecumenism). Nevertheless, they exemplified a general tendency within religious romanticism to search for sentimental bonds of unity, to resist the fragmentation of faith, and to ground individual quests in a broader sense of identity. The woods may have been one recourse for young people with knives in their brains, but conservatives pointed them instead toward the church and history.

SOUTHERN TOWNS

The South in some respects underwent the same process of cultural reorganization as the North. But in that section there were key differences in intellectual response to change, and these require separate discussion.

By the 1850s many northerners described the slaveholding states as an archaic society, half aristocratic and half barbaric, that contrasted with the freedom and opportunity of the modern age. Southern students in northern colleges were said to lack the penetrating intellectual qualities by which men like Emerson defined the progressive impulses of their generation. Elaborate comparisons were made between the supposedly typical free laborer of the North, who attended lectures and subscribed to newspapers, and the benighted poor white of the South, who lacked any inkling of self-improvement. Some writers of the South rehearsed similar stereotypes, but with the values inverted. In their view, the leaders of southern society retained a sense of community responsibility that was vanishing in the new economic order of the North. And ordinary southerners were less prone to embrace the faddish, sometimes dangerous "isms" that newspapers and lecturers peddled.

As sectional conflict gave way to civil war, these polarities became deeply embedded in the ways in which Americans thought back on their intellectual life. The point deserves emphasis, therefore, that the South had experienced profound changes in beliefs and institutions. The repudiation of the Enlightenment was nowhere more pronounced than in the southeastern and border states. The religious skepticism and political radicalism that had found adherents among the planter intelligentsia were forgotten. Christian chaplains found a place at the University of Virginia, once a center of Jeffersonian infidelity, and a great revival occurred on campus in 1854. The Kentucky Enlightenment disappeared from view. Though southern theologians produced scores of refutations of deism, these were symbolic confrontations with a specter long since laid to rest. After a promising beginning, Unitarianism made little headway in a section where it became fashionable to observe that puritanism—the assertion of Calvinistic doctrines of divine sovereignty, predestination, and human unworthiness—survived with little modification. This observation applied especially to the Old School Presbyterians, who enjoyed great prestige in the South, but the Wesleyans and Baptists, who reorganized much of the southern populace with more inclusive views of God's grace, took equal delight in the submergence of almost every trace of Jeffersonian heresy.

Nor is it accurate to think of the white South primarily in terms of aristocrats and impoverished farmers. To be sure, some works of southern literature, like Augustus B. Longstreet's *Georgia Scenes* (1835) and William Gilmore Simms's *Wigwam and the Cabin* (1845), focused on folk life in undeveloped backwaters, sometimes in contrast to aristocratic pretension. But these works explicitly conveyed a mood of nostalgia for a world on the wane. They were signs of a national recognition that certain traditional customs were, if not passing away, increasingly marginal to the economy and to mainstream culture. Audiences for these works were similar to those for John Greenleaf Whittier's recollections of superstitions and folktales of a previous generation of northerners; they were literate townspeople conscious of a cultural transformation well under way.

Though industrialization was less evident, the South resembled the North in other indications of passage into a new economic era: improved transportation, widespread dependence on credit, and a proliferation of towns and small cities. Stories of self-made men, often going through several changes of vocation, abounded there as elsewhere. Towns everywhere in America made possible aspirations to refinement—not to the abhorred fashions of an undemocratic elite, but to solid lives of respectability. Towns had better schools; dozens of them boasted of colleges and seminaries. Their ministers were expected to be more polished and urbane and to show more civic responsibility than rustic preachers. Together with doctors and lawyers, they provided educated leadership for an informal network of associations—literary circles, libraries, thespian clubs, mechanics' associations, reform societies, and lyceums—created anew wherever towns of a few thousand persons were established. While taking it for granted that evangelical religion was essential to civilization, they gave up nothing of the commitment to progressive change that formerly inspired Jefferson and other partisans of enlightenment. Their leitmotif in fact was a kind of boosterism that could see in a modest crossroads a future Athens.

Towns of this description emerged in every state of the Old South as in the North and West. They furnished the actual basis for the age's literary fascination with man in the woods or out at sea. But an important difference in tone and emphasis could be observed in the South. The dissociated individualism ("the individual is the world") that Emerson detected at the root of intellectual life, and that other thinkers like Bushnell sought to temper, was barely present. Emerson and Thoreau never walked onto a southern lecture dais (the young Alcott did journey southward as a peddler), nor did anyone else voice praise there for unfettered self-exploration. Coleridge and Kant won the admiration of a few scholars, but not as guides to renunciation of the past. For the most part, the Scottish philosophy sufficed to give suitable recognition to human consciousness. There simply was less occasion for dramatic assertions that a new era assigned greater power to the unregulated psyche. Nevin's defense of the sacraments and the integrity of the historic church would not have sounded so defiantly out of place in a southern intellectual milieu. Self-improvement in a southern town meant temperate behavior, acquaintance with literature and art, and perhaps some knowledge of geology and natural history. Those southern writers and lecturers who did bring up the theme of the individual's role in society almost invariably stressed the organic ties essential to public order.

If intellectual life on the whole conformed to the needs and aspirations of men and women in commercial towns, a few ambitious intellectuals did pose as critics of the culture around them. Their careers paralleled romantic tendencies in the North; they also prefigured twentieth-century images of the intellectual as alienated from society. A good example is James Warley Miles, who after doing missionary work in Constantinople and Mesopotamia assumed an Anglican pastorate in Charleston. This cosmopolitan intellectual had reflected on Kant, Coleridge, and contemporary biblical criticism so creatively that his *Philosophic Theology* (1849) was immediately translated into German. But his erudition earned little respect from his parishioners and ministerial colleagues, who felt that his recognition of intuitive powers, strengthened by the growth of humanity throughout history, diminished the authority of revelation. While his religious convictions were actually quite orthodox, his style of thinking bore the taint of unwelcome liberalism. In 1850 he retreated to a professorship at the College of Charleston. Throughout his career he complained of loneliness and suspicion in the cultural environment, eventuating in ill health and declining self-confidence.

Similar complaints emanated from a circle of prominent writers—the novelist Simms, planter-politician James Henry Hammond, law professor Nathaniel Beverley Tucker, philosophy professor George Frederick Holmes, agricultural reformer Edmund Ruffin—who found in mutual friendship a substitute for cultural acclaim. Savoring romantic images of themselves as geniuses misunderstood since childhood in a crass society, they envisioned the true intellectual of their times as an outcast, a prophet without honor in a stagnating land. Their jeremiads were not entirely a literary pose: they had hard experiences— failed magazines, terminated professorships, disappointed political schemes—to support the lament that cultural reorganization had not gone far enough in the South.

Common schooling was less extensive than in other regions, and illiteracy more widespread. As a result, college teaching was often frustrating, and audiences for books, lectures, and periodicals were comparatively limited. These men thought of themselves as a circle of reformers calling vainly for greater appreciation of scientific improvements, of artistic talent, and generally of the powers of mind. Until the South manifested greater respect for the intellect, it would, in their opinion, sink ever more deeply into decline. Not only would the economy falter, but, more seriously, the morals of the people would be deficient to meet the challenges of the modern age.

In their analyses of social change, pitting the intellectual against slovenly custom and severing moral responsibility from economic calculation, these men had some northern counterparts. Out of such analyses emerged a later view of the intellectual as an independent cultural critic. This view went beyond narrow professional definitions of teachers, doctors, and lawyers. It also distinguished intellectuals as a new category from the clergy, the class of men traditionally charged with evaluating public morals. But these southern jeremiahs belonged distinctively to their time and region in their pronouncements on social order. While appealing for a new appreciation of the intellect, they were hardly champions of the emotions. They asserted, rather bluntly, that most people, particularly the uneducated, were knaves. They were, moreover, ingenious defenders of slavery and other forms of inequality. We should not mistake them for a class of disinterested men holding all practices up to criticism; by their own argument, the necessity of defending slavery was the surest demonstration of the advantages that the South might discover in supporting and honoring an intelligentsia. These intellectuals depicted themselves as being at odds with their culture; they complained of powerlessness. But their understanding of the mind was inexact and undeveloped, and they clearly upheld a vision of the intellectuals' mission as service to society's deeply entrenched interests.

MANLINESS
AND FEMININITY

In all sections the most popular form of urban entertainment, and thus the one most responsive to the mobility and reorganization of the era, was the theater. For the most part, it was not really an art form, but a species of urban entertainment that could reestablish itself wherever Americans moved. Few serious writers wrote or attended plays. Protestant ministers thundered against theaters as signs of wickedness, every bit as alarming as grogshops and brothels. Theaters did not cast aspersions in return; actors and dramatists struggled to attain respectability. There was, however, an unmistakable anti-intellectualism in most popular entertainment. It can be observed in the blackface minstrels' spoofs on grandiose wordplay and in the so-called experts' solemn professions of authenticity with which P. T. Barnum presented his humbugs to public inspection.

The theater revealed public conceptions of the mind and heart in America different from those offered in church and seminary. America's greatest tragedian was Edwin Forrest, who rose from Philadelphia's artisan class to become a great symbol of and spokesman for Jacksonian democracy. So popular was Forrest with the working classes that in 1849 a New York mob tried to suppress performances by an English rival, William Macready, who was believed to have insulted Forrest and whose style was viewed as too effete for America. When the authorities protected Macready and his partisans by firing on the mob, the toll included thirty-one dead and numerous other casualties. Forrest's much-imitated American style boasted of manly emotionality. To some extent, all dramatic styles make claims of authenticity, but it is worth noting that Forrest was one of the earliest actors to claim that he had visited insane asylums, lived in disguise among poor blacks, and taken other steps toward a scientific study of psychology. He was also known for his acrobatic skills, his brawny physique, and the volume and fury of his declamations. The emotional tone his acting elicited was almost beyond control. In addition to Shakespearean roles he preferred to play antityrannical heroes, usually in plays written to show him as a leader of peasants against a feudal hierarchy, for example, or the Incas against the conquistadores or the Wampanoag Indians against the Puritans. The suggestion is of a progression of true-hearted valor consistent with Bancroft's version of history, and Forrest's volcanic style reminds us of praise for Daniel Webster's naturalistic oratory. On the one hand, he exemplified the values of American naturalness contrasted to European artifice; on the other, he displayed a swagger that was almost as frequently criticized an element in the American temperament as its alleged workaday calculating streak.

Few could match Forrest's theatrical extravagance. Like Thoreau's private vigil at Walden Pond, his acting stands at one extreme of American romantic attitudes toward the self. More typical of the theater—and more reminiscent of the concerns of religious leaders—were the hundreds of tearjerking melodramas mounted on every American stage. Beginning early in the century with countless renditions of French potboilers, finding its way into dramas of the Revolution or the barroom, familiar to this day in summer stock takeoffs on the taste of previous generations, one problem recurred monotonously as it brought audiences to indignation, tears, and ultimate relief: a virtuous girl, desiring to wed a simple, loving suitor, was instead coerced to go off with a villain who knew a secret or held an economic advantage (the mortgage on the family farm) over her father. In this plot the organic ties of family and the impulses of the heart collided with the hard reality of cash. The staying power of audiences' fascination with such dramas of female chastity reveals a deep absorption with problems of choice and loyalty in a transformed economy.

Bushnell spoke of restoring "domesticity of character"; Park defined the theology of the feelings as essentially maternal. In much the same vein, melodramas portrayed conflict between tender womanly impulses and a world of masculine intrigue. In a brilliant interpretation of nineteenth-century literature, Ann Douglas subsumes broad tendencies like these under the rubric of the "feminization" of culture. Changes in female occupational patterns converged with technical and marketing changes in publishing to produce a vast body of writing, much of it fiction on household themes, by women who championed the softening effects of the heart on the vicissitudes of modern civilization. In Douglas's view, the sentimentalizing predilections of popular culture impoverished theology, which ought to have confronted the darkest truths of human nature, and frustrated imaginative writers, who sought to pierce through cant and convention. Her critical stance reflects the negative outlook of Old School Calvinists as well as the frustrations of men like Hawthorne who complained that their works were neglected by the vast reading public that was devouring books by "scribbling women." Without adopting that stance, we can still see the tremendous importance of these developments for the redefinition of intellectual life.

For much of Western history women had been depicted as less rational than men, as subject to lustful and hysterical impulses of the lower body unless restrained by men. Striking changes in these images gained headway in eighteenth-century America, so that females appeared less passionate and unruly than males. They were not considered intellectual equals, but their leading motives appeared to be refined, sentimental, and orderly. By the mid-nineteenth century women were associated with precisely those impulses of the heart that mattered most to the romantic sensibility. This association was metaphorical rather than philosophical; it belonged to popular superstition more than to treatises on mental science, which tended to restrict their focus to male endeavor. Nevertheless, in a far-reaching change, old views of male family governance gave way to accounts of benefits to the Republic if mothers successfully influenced the character of their sons, if wives brought husbands under their gentle moral tutelage.

There were limits to this change. No one proposed any benefits in having female civic officials. There were numerous depictions of nervous disorders—the madwoman in the attic—of intellectually gifted women (called "blue-stockings") who sought to "surpass their sex." The occupational implications were ambiguous at best. On the one hand, on market farms and in growing cities, women's work was increasingly separate from work that men went off to do. The home became a sanctuary of female influence. It was boasted that American women ordinarily enjoyed more leisure than Europeans did, were more protected and honored, were freer to exercise their sentimental sway. On the other hand, to a sharp critic like Margaret Fuller this pattern reflected fear of women and ignorance of their wishes to sharpen their intellectual gifts. Without questioning that nature intended woman to be "the tutelary genius of the home" and man the manager of "the out-of-door business of life," Fuller nonetheless pointed out that women had already "invaded" many trades and professions. In addition to sewing, factory work, sale of vegetables and flowers, and domestic service, she mentioned literature and music as fields in which women equaled men, medicine as a promising field for women, and nursing and teaching as expanding fields where they would excel. Therefore, improved education of females was an obligation of the age.

In the instance of women, the revaluation of heart and intellect reflected changes in economic life. Although it is easy enough to see, from a twentieth-century perspective, how the image of women as preeminently emotional served to justify their suppression, that image conferred certain advantages on women who wished to secure a place in a fluid economic and social system. Early Massachusetts textile mill owners, anxious to avoid their English predecessors' reputation for heartlessness, employed a work force of young women, lodged them in homelike bungalows, and published their literary endeavors. This famous experiment was short-lived, but an enduring change took place in education. Once a field for transient males, especially young ministers, teaching was professionalized and feminized during the nineteenth century. Since women were paid less than men, the result was enormous expansion of common-school education at lower cost than if men had been employed. Normal schools appeared in most states, exclusively to train women, now regarded as the fittest guardians of the impressionable hearts of children.

In one of the era's most widely read works on manners and behavior, *Treatise on Domestic Economy* (1841), as well as in numerous other books, Catharine Beecher clarified the tradeoffs affecting any new role for women in American culture. Herself a member of an astonishingly gifted family, she accepted female subservience as natural and unalterable. She took Tocqueville as authority that, where efforts were made to attain equal treatment, women were degraded and abused. In the United States a contrasting situation prevailed: women did not challenge male authority and were respected as nowhere else. Furthermore, Beecher believed that the division of labor, with each person finding his or her appropriate station, was the key to the progress of civilization. Self-control and self-sacrifice were innate tendencies in women; brought to the fore in a well-regulated society, these qualities would have a healthful republican effect. Businessmen and politicians would mirror the concern for the greatest good of others that women personified at the hearthside and in the schoolhouse. While fervently promoting the employment of women as teachers of the young, especially in the West, Beecher did not neglect the importance of improving women's intellectual capacities. The stress on self-denial and instinctive morality did not imply that women were unfit for reasoning. For Beecher as for Fuller, the issue was one of priorities in defining women's role in a century of newly opened possibilities. Yet these priorities depended on the premise that women inclined naturally to moral sentiments that men acquired by example, if at all. By profession women might become nurses or teachers, but their most becoming social role lay in voluntary service, in reform societies and church work.

Women personified a guarded, ambivalent approach to both emotions and intellect that characterized the era of reorganization. Clearly, there was no throwback to the ancient uses of reason in controlling the passions and instructing the will. Intellectual training was valuable for specific uses in an age of material progress. When women and men were educated to the utmost of their abilities, a purity of respect uplifted marriages and calmed all social discourse. The reason, as redefined in this era, was almost atrophied; logic was less important than intuition. (We shall return to this point.) At the same time, the emotions were reconceived as mild spiritual agencies. Left to themselves or, better yet, surrounded with pleasant domestic influences, feelings were tame and beneficial. This circumscription of inquiry into human psychology was an ironic consequence of an age of "self-dissection"; it was one of the sharpest differentiations between America and Europe. As Americans forgot ancient beliefs in human sinfulness, they also avoided contemporary European images of demonic genius and mass destructiveness. A restricted focus on feminine feelings may be viewed, then, as a tactic for ignoring unwelcome depths of human nature.

This process is easy to see in the Protestant revivals that were so crucial to social order. Eighteenth-century revivalism had stirred bitter controversies over base passions, echoes of which were occasionally heard in the 1820s. By the 1850s, however, revivalism took for granted a natural human passionlessness, with socially harmonious feelings awaiting the touch of Jesus' love. In the words of one hymn, composed by a woman:

Down in the human heart . . .
Feelings be buried that grace can restore:
Touched by a loving heart,
Wakened by kindness,
Chords that were broken will vibrate once more.

Women were prominent in the revival community, and their participation was no longer controversial. The release of feminine feelings pointed, not to sexual temptation or political misrule, but to the sweet harmony of refined Christian sympathy.

The same meaning may be found in the hundreds of novels and poems by women, both southern and northern, that gave the impression of a "feminized" popular culture. Orphans, outcasts, poor children, factory girls—even slaves in Harriet Beecher Stowe's fantastically popular *Uncle Tom's Cabin* (1852)—all met perils and misfortunes in a business world that could be hard and unfeeling. But in the end came reassurance that the "great world" had a "throbbing, human heart," consisting of chords of kindness that bound human beings together. Unfortunates were rescued, or tears poured forth at their deaths. Nasty figures like Simon Legree might appear, but they were not emblems of human nature, only sad, vicious wrecks testing sympathetic powers that in the end never failed. When these works addressed problems that nearly defied rational solutions, as in some novels on the degradation of factory life, they still expressed hope in "feeling one's way," in making warm human contact with the helpless and exploited.* Equality might have been an unattainable ideal, but it was possible to believe in an expanding community of feeling.

POLITE CULTURE

After looking at so many disparate writers and movements, let us turn to three questions. Who made up the audiences for these efforts? How was the intellect conceived? Was there a unified culture?

A very specific audience existed for treatises on mental philosophy. They were textbooks for college and seminary students—mostly young men from prosperous fam-

*Though in fiction this view of womanly feelings could appear evasively sentimental, in actuality it could encourage women to dedicate their lives to constructive social projects. For example, after the Civil War thousands of Yankee schoolmarms moved south and braved great hardships to live among and uplift the black freedmen.

ilies, though charitable organizations began to replenish the moral leadership of the nation by providing financial aid for poor but worthy rural sons. Authors of the treatises—men like Wayland, Upham, Rauch, Marsh, and Holmes—were likely to stress that they had made things simple and systematic. Even if they believed in the unity of the soul, they were obliged to treat mental activities one by one, thus giving the appearance of believing in separate faculties. Beyond their student audiences, they hoped their works would earn favor with an international audience of philosophers and theologians. Rauch apologized for the inexactness of the English language in discriminating between perception and sensation, and Upham confessed that in popularizing knowledge for America's aspiring students he had undoubtedly omitted information of interest to the learned community. Finally, they were attentive to the concerns of ministers and other respectable community leaders, an audience similar to that for the works of Bushnell, Park, and Schaff. Despite the varied emphases of the treatises, all these versions of psychology underscored the importance of religious conviction and sound morals. Some wrote texts on economic theory, but in general the treatises on the mind said surprisingly little about the benefits of economic progress, even less about changes in political life. Their audiences were not really indifferent to economics and politics, but there was an assumption that the moral leaders of a good community should have their minds in a different sphere. For the purposes of instruction, readers and students were held at some distance from the distracting turbulence of the times.

The audience for the transcendentalists differed in some respects. Emerson was a star of the lyceums, eventually living comfortably off proceeds from his lectures after he had given up a ministerial position that seemed uncongenial and confining. Thoreau struggled to be free of any trade. Though his needs were simpler and his success less brilliant than Emerson's, some of his discourses ("Walking," for example) repeatedly earned fees in town halls and lecture rooms. Alcott and Fuller aspired to make their name through public "conversations." These careers took cognizance of rooms filled with Americans, male and female, seeking self-improvement. Lectures in these rooms referred to the jangling realities of commerce, religious strife, and political agitation, but always as background to the urgent tasks of building a better form of civilization or attaining a more refined self-awareness. Along with the popularity of the lyceum came the expanding market for uplifting publications, organized in part around literary periodicals that promoted new directions in public taste. The magazines for which transcendentalists wrote stressed their modernity, often with overtones of a new generation's rejection of old habits and tired performances. They were addressing, not international circles of scholars, but restless though relatively comfortable Americans.

The great romantic historians took for granted an even wider literary public. Some held college posts; some lived off sales of multivolume works; Bancroft thrived in politics. But their massive labors were decidedly works of literature, not the specialized academic monographs of a much later era. Only biblical scholars foreshadowed the confined dry discourse of mid-twentieth-century universities. For all the complaints about American unimaginativeness, there were many influences—technological developments in printing, improvements in transportation and marketing, and the increasing numbers of adults thirsting for polite knowledge—that supported a literary life in history. The same influences explained the distinguished lives of successful poets like Henry Wadsworth Longfellow, the unprecedented acclaim for a singer like

Jenny Lind, or the esteem and profits flowing toward a painter like Frederic Church, who depended on a ticket-holding public rather than on the patronage of wealthy men.

Popular audiences were stratified. Parkman, Longfellow, and Church did not seek the favor of rowdies who celebrated Forrest, let alone the throngs who attended minstrel shows or read cheap newspapers. Lines were drawn between refined taste and base entertainment, just as the thoughtless mob or animalistic camp meeting differed from the spellbound audiences for Daniel Webster or the controlled revivalism of the respectable denominations. The lines were cloudy, however, in the vast readership of sentimental novels by female authors. From Susannah Rowson to Harriet Beecher Stowe, these were the authors with the largest audiences, including men as well as women, Europeans as well as Americans, and they could not be disparaged as purveyors of vulgar entertainment. They widened the cult of the heart, but in a fashion that seemed to undermine high-toned pretensions. There was stratification within this cult too. Appeals for the professional education of women nurses and teachers showed the aspirations for self-improvement of specific classes of women who would assume positions of leadership, albeit segregated ones, in advancing American morals and bringing light to the heathen world outside.

The male students who read Wayland were counterparts to the aspiring females championed by Catharine Beecher. Both were drawing a smaller circle of moral leadership within a larger polite culture, which was in turn differentiated from the supposedly less civilized world of casual laborers, frontier ruffians, and unassimilated foreigners. Intellectual refinement was an ideology by which individuals could aim to better themselves without being preoccupied with money or political power. Though hardly antagonistic to the extension of markets and democratization of politics, this ideology delineated an alternative road to eminence. It defined, at least in outline, an intellectual class that cut across economic categories and political factions, a class distinguished by proper understanding and development of the mind.

If we turn to the ways in which men and women conceived of the soul, we might conclude that, by any standard recognizable today, there was little room to be an intellectual at all. To be sure, the treatises acknowledged the uses of deductive reasoning in making logical arguments. The ministers assigned a role to intellect as one of man's God-given powers. The physician boasted of the trained knowledge that supplemented his insight and experience. There was little forthright criticism of science, though theology was sometimes repudiated as a source of obscurity and confusion. Generally, however, even educated Americans praised the intellect kept to its proper uses, with other powers ascendant in a fully developed humanity.

What was true religion? According to Rauch, whose *Psychology* offered a complex analysis of the human mind, it was "a peculiar activity of God, which announcing itself to the *heart* of man, changes it, converts it, and restores man to peace within himself, with the world, and with God." Religions that strayed into abstract speculations or worship of external nature were erroneous. What made a great poet? The answer, according to Emerson, was not superficial science, historical knowledge, or verbal skill and dexterity; literary genius flowed from energies that surpassed "conscious intellect," from simple gifts to see clearly into the meanings of nature. In less arcane explanations, literary power came from identification with common bonds of human sentiment rather than arid school-learned formulas. How to define the virtuous man? All texts agreed that it was not reason that showed him the way, but uncalculating impulses of the heart. For women the case was clearer, for their sentiments were naturally less corrupt. Legislative leaders promised that, though their heads might err, they hoped to avoid the more serious errors of the heart. The peddler or merchant who engaged solely in transactions of the head was a pitiable wretch. The reformer appealed to higher laws of consciousness, whatever reason might dictate. This was not a culture in which a person might seek praise for overriding intellect or clever logic.

The liberation of the feelings should not be exaggerated. Everywhere there was a strategic deflection of even theoretical interest in sources of behavior that might threaten public order. Certainly the passions enjoyed no fairer a reputation than in previous times. When they were discussed at all, the point was to ensure their control, now less often by the reason than by conscience or refined feelings. At the inner circle of intellectual culture there was little interest in uncontrollable feelings, driven quests, or sexual experiments—topics associated with the Werthers, Fausts, or Byrons of European romanticism. Only a few probing artists—Melville and Hawthorne among them—tried to salvage these topics from the general aversion. The intuition that found meanings in the woods, the consciousness of the past that added grandeur to ordinary scenes, the sense of enduring ideals above the flurry of sense experience, the sociable impulse that rendered help to the needy, organic feelings of connection to family and church—these were the nonintellectual components of the nineteenth-century vision of respectability. Not all the writers discussed in this chapter agreed on every point; there was notable disagreement on the values of solitary insight and collective identity. But in theories of the soul two interlocking goals were foremost: an intellect kept in place, and feelings lifted to a spiritual plane. Attention to these goals shielded the polite man or woman from the rough, acquisitive mobility for which the Republic, rightly or wrongly, was notorious.

This ideology cannot be converted into a blanket assertion concerning an "American culture" embracing all segments of the population. The image of an inner circle of respectability expanding within a larger circle of sentimental culture suggests the opposite. Experience and belief, fragmented and diverse as they were, could be comprehended by imagining concentric circles, resembling a civic equivalent to the Puritans' old notion of the supremacy of the elect within a well-ordered church. The resemblance is only vague, and important distinctions must be made. It was axiomatic that good men and women were visible in all denominations. Self-improvement was the legitimate aspiration of large numbers of men and women. In any event, there is little evidence of Americans wishing to restore a lost theocracy. But the idea of a united, progressive society, with individuals striving to find within themselves the signs of cultural refinement, promised an end to the conflicts of the past.

The relevant historical perspective was the one recounted in Emerson's "Historic Notes." The recurrent attacks on Locke and the identification of the new age with rediscovered treasures of universal human consciousness were positions taken at the end of an era of cultural schism. The irritations of enlightened men of the 1790s, when society seemed to be divided between an impotent elite and a vulgar populace, were mollified in polite culture at mid-century; few thought any longer in terms of an omnipresent insurgency against rank and privilege. The new ideology set goals for those outside circles of influence to improve their manners and give sway to their hearts. It admonished uncivil behavior among the influential, and it allowed for distinctions that would define a moral elite. Instead of regiments poised to fight each other, with the inevitable defeat of any would-be aristocracy, culture now took the form of spheres of respectability based on popular civic conceptions of the soul.

These were developments of considerable importance for definitions of a cultivated class in the late nineteenth century. What must be asked now, however, is how extensively this ideology found consent in Emerson's or Parkman's America. In the first place, no one creed or dogma was upheld in all colleges or salons. Emerson, Bancroft, Park, Nevin—virtually all prominent writers had sharp critics. Princeton was a fortress of opposition to most new ideas, and southern Presbyterians joined in defense of the Didactic Enlightenment. Almost everywhere science was taught in the Baconian fashion, as though no one had ever spoken of transcendentalism. Brownson turned to the Catholic past to reassert the primacy of reason and obedience to authority; a few southern intellectuals looked to French social science in order to get away from American prattle about intuition and transcendent laws. Phrenology, a science of determining character by observing the contours of the skull, was a great fad during the antebellum years, suggesting that not everyone was content to believe in mystical access to high-flown idealities. Spiritualism was another movement indicating widespread interest in the material basis of the soul. Because no doctrinal consensus prevailed even among intellectuals, the ideology of respectability must be defined rather loosely.

Scanning the population at large, we become more aware of the perimeters of common conviction. It is never easy to discover the historical mentalities of illiterate or

exploited peoples, but close studies of the religion and
folklore of black slaves have revealed the slaves' faith in a
collective sacred destiny "over Jordan," outside of ordinary time. This faith was, to say the least, incongruent with
the favorite images of the intellectual world examined in
this chapter. It is unlikely that Indians, Mexican-Ameri-
cans, casual laborers on canals and railroads, immigrants
in city slums, French-Canadian factory hands, or impoverished subsistence farmers in the upland South shared
much of the praise of idealism, domesticity, or the progress of mind. They existed outside the larger circles of
polite culture.

There were, however, large numbers of white Protestants at the borders of respectability. Revivals, temperance meetings, and schoolrooms served to bring them inside the circle if they would renounce sinful impulses and
unrefined customs. The reward included a new image of
themselves as literate and gentle, and it might well make
sense to the reformed to hear of self-culture, nature, and
the heart. It must be admitted that the few efforts scholars have made to unravel the intellectual history of antebellum "plain people" do not find much concern for the
internal workings of the mind. Instead, they report grand
affirmations of patriotism, pride in the collective wisdom
of the populace, and practicality of the sort once described by Tocqueville. Moreover, among articulate artisans strong loyalties to the radical side of the Enlightenment—to Tom Paine's age of reason as contrasted to
unjustifiable and widening inequality—still resounded. But
even when artisans reiterated the psychology of eighteenth-century revolution, they were likely at the same time
to voice the belief of Bancroft, Emerson, and other sages
of the new dispensation that the progress of civilization
depended on the advancement of mind. Labor move-

ments sought to create lyceums of their own and to extend the hegemony of the common school.

While recognizing that polite culture had boundaries, we should not assume that ordinary people were out of touch with abstract ideas. When so tempted, we might think of Henry Taylor, an uneducated workingman in a Massachusetts factory town who read and reread the New Testament for inspiration. He also read Emerson and some translations of Oriental poetry, though claiming that he never had much help from books. The poet John Greenleaf Whittier was impressed by Taylor's spiritual progress: "he expressed himself with remarkable precision, hesitating until the exact word presented itself. By slow degrees he reached a condition of absolute quiet—a sky of perfect serenity brooded over him; he was *in* the world but not *of* it; all outward things were illusive and unreal." Whittier was sure Taylor had attained a state of Buddhist exaltation. After hearing him speak, the poet asked whether he had read Plato. " 'No,' he had never heard of 'Mr. Plato.' I lent him a volume and he returned it soon after, saying, 'Mr. Plato had got hold of some of his ideas.' "

FOR FURTHER READING

There is no satisfactory overview of intellectual life in this period. The best starting place is Perry Miller's unfinished, posthumous work, *The Life of the Mind in America from the Revolution to the Civil War* (1965). John William Ward brilliantly probes some of the chief concerns of the period as revealed in public writing on a great political hero: *Andrew Jackson—Symbol for an Age* (1955). Rush Welter, *The Mind of America* (1975), and Lewis Saum, *The Pop-*

ular Mood of Pre–Civil War America (1980), attempt to reconstruct the ideas of ordinary people. See also Carl Bode, *The Anatomy of American Popular Culture* (1959). A valuable analytical anthology is David Brion Davis, *Antebellum American Culture* (1979).

The philosophy of transcendentalism is surveyed by Paul Boller, *American Transcendentalism, 1830–1860: An Intellectual Inquiry* (1974). For a different approach, based on the transcendentalists' responses to class differentiation in Boston, see Anne C. Rose, *Transcendentalism as a Social Movement* (1981). The most exciting approach to the transcendentalists is through their own writings. New scholarly editions are appearing of the complete works of Emerson (Harvard University Press) and Thoreau (Princeton University Press). Perry Miller, ed., *The Transcendentalists* (1950), presents a stirring interpretation of their break with Unitarianism. On the relations of James Marsh and Horace Bushnell with the transcendentalists, see Philip Gura, *The Wisdom of Words* (1981).

The best study of the romantic historians is David Levin, *History as Romantic Art* (1959). James Hastings Nichols, *Romanticism in American Theology* (1961), focuses on Philip Schaff and John Williamson Nevin. Also helpful to an understanding of romanticism are Cushing Strout, *The American Image of the Old World* (1963), and Lewis Perry, *Childhood, Marriage, and Reform: Henry Clarke Wright* (1980).

Alexis de Tocqueville is the subject of extensive and continuing commentary. James T. Schleifer's *The Making of Tocqueville's Democracy in America* (1980) is a valuable recent contribution. A thoughtful study of Tocqueville's theme is J. R. Pole's *The Pursuit of Equality in American History* (1978).

An outstanding study of southern intellectual life is E. Brooks Holifield, *The Gentleman Theologians* (1978). Drew Gilpin Faust's *A Sacred Circle: The Dilemma of the Intellectual in the Old South* (1977) is equally excellent. See also Clement Eaton, *The Civilization of the Old South* (1968), and Bertram Wyatt-Brown, *Southern Honor* (1983).

Provocative interpretations of women in intellectual life are found in Ann Douglas, *The Feminization of American Culture* (1977), and Susan Phinney Conrad, *Perish the Thought* (1976). Sensitive biographical studies include Kathryn Kish Sklar, *Catharine Beecher* (1973), and Elizabeth Alden Green, *Mary Lyon and Mount Holyoke* (1979). On women's part in revivalism, see Sandra S. Sizer, *Gospel Hymns and Social Religion* (1978).

Studies of slave culture, with important theoretical implications for all of intellectual life, are Eugene Genovese, *Roll, Jordan, Roll* (1974), and Lawrence Levine, *Black Culture and Black Consciousness* (1977).

VI

THE CULTIVATED CLASS IN THE LATE NINETEENTH CENTURY

THE IDEOLOGY
OF CULTURE

What replaced the *virtue* that leaders of the revolutionary era had praised, the virtue whose passing from public life they had lamented? The answer was slow in arriving, but by the latter half of the nineteenth century there clearly was a term that served, much as virtue had done, to designate higher ideals that must shine atop the republic. The term was *culture*.

Thomas Wentworth Higginson, formerly a transcendentalist, later editor of the prestigious *Atlantic*, defined culture in 1871:

> Culture is the training and finishing of the whole man, until he sees physical demands to be merely secondary, and pursues science and art as objects of intrinsic worth. It undoubtedly places the fine arts above the useful arts . . . and is willingly impoverished in material comforts, if it can thereby obtain nobler living. When this impulse takes the form of a reactionary distrust of the whole spirit of the age, it is unhealthy and morbid. In its healthy

form, it simply keeps alive the conviction that the life is more than meat; and so supplies that counterpoise to mere wealth which Europe vainly seeks to secure by aristocracies of birth.

Higginson, who enjoyed great influence in polite circles, echoed many old themes of republican gentlemen, particularly a rather abstemious preference for ideal goods over selfish interests. *Culture* was more aesthetic and less political than *virtue*, and despite mention of the "whole man," it had little trace of antifeminine feeling. After a century of change it was difficult even to think of any predominance of refined men in government. But the term *culture* indicated continuing faith in a hierarchy of merit that distinguished the truly "noble" person from the herd. It was sufficiently inclusive to avoid the resentments that had overturned the old republican ideology; yet it unhesitatingly distinguished the "cultivated classes" from their supposedly narrow-minded countrymen, rich or poor.

The term was not entirely new. Dr. Johnson's dictionary had related its first meaning to farming and gardening (though some examples under this category referred to cultivation of the mind), but also gave as a second meaning the general "art of improvement and melioration," with this example from the *Tatler:* "One might wear any passion out of a family by culture, as skillful gardeners blot a colour out of a tulip that hurts its beauty." Thus associations with self-control, aesthetic awareness, and social improvement clung to the term in the eighteenth century. It was by no means exclusively an American term. In nineteenth-century England it was a catchword for identifying, criticizing, and repairing defects in industrialized society. Matthew Arnold's *Culture and Anarchy* (1869), much quoted in the United States, presented culture as "the great help out of our present difficulties," as the means to reexamine and enrich dismal ways of life by "getting to know . . . the best which has been thought and said in the world." The contrast between literary visions of perfection and squalid actualities could lead to several different public stances, from lofty distaste for present-day society to earnest striving to upgrade it.

In America, culture rose to prominence, first, as a celebration of individual growth and, only second, in criticisms of society's failings. The first of these views of culture was clearly enunciated by the 1830s. Amid complaints about the unpoetic money-grubbing and sauciness of Americans, some preachers and orators lauded the endeavors of ordinary people to elevate their moral and intellectual dispositions. The Unitarian leader William Ellery Channing addressed a workingmen's association on the theme of *Self-Culture* (1838) or "the care which every man owes to himself, to the unfolding and perfecting of his nature." In a series of public lectures, *Human Culture* (1837), Ralph Waldo Emerson noted conventional uneasiness about the hostility of the age to "men of mark" and distinction. The surging impulse to self-expression need not stop with the "trivial and sordid," however. Instead of passively receiving education, "the individual declares his independence, takes his life in his own hand, and sets forth in quest of Culture." The individual learned to hear the "voice of the Eternal" in his heart instead of sinking under the practical requirements and truncated relations that a complex commercial society imposed. Both Channing and Emerson spoke of the individual's cultivation of his own inner resources; they did not regard culture as an exterior agency shaping an individual's aspirations and motives. To find the latter view of culture before the Civil War, one might have turned to promoters of home missions, including Horace Bushnell, who planned to repress the "anarchy" of the frontier and impose "a substantial and finished culture."

In Higginson's post–Civil War remarks, however, we notice a conception different from either individual growth or the imposition of good manners and literate habits. He found in culture a standpoint for criticizing America's attainments. The nation was too absorbed in material improvement and commercial gain; there was such intense "political culture" that even young children quarreled over candidates; the lyceums had deteriorated into trivial amusements; and professions had become "branches of practical activity, not intellectual pursuits." The most telling deficiency was in "literary culture." America lacked a "considerable literary class" and had "scarcely even a cultivated class." But Higginson was essentially optimistic, and culture was a concept that also pointed out positive dimensions of progress. The finest American writers—Emerson, Hawthorne, and Thoreau—were "gradually attaining a wider hold"; their fame was not limited to elite circles. Higginson distinguished between "a want of cultivated sympathy with the higher intellectual pursuits and a want of popular respect for them":

> It is this distinction which relieves the American people from the imputation of materialism. I solemnly believe that no race of practical laborers since the world began was ever so ready to feel a theoretical respect for those higher pursuits for which it could as yet spare no time. Whose photographs are for sale in shop windows? . . . statesmen, preachers, lecturers, poets—men standing low on the income lists, and high only on the scale of intangible services. . . . The community seeks wealth, but it knows how to respect its public men who are

poor through honesty, or its scholars who are poor for the sake of knowledge.

In such a milieu literature was bound to reach a full harvest eventually. In the meantime, culture provided a vantage point for measuring the gulf between material pursuits and intellectual achievement.

Culture was the key term in an ideology that honored good manners, respect for the fine arts, and acquaintance with great literature, usually with a cheerful conviction that somehow, despite the memories of Civil War, the distractions of urban and industrial change, and the incredible proliferation of literature and entertainment for the masses, great ideals were being perpetuated. Because it upheld the far-reaching importance of spiritual values amid secular change, culture may be thought of as a quasi-religious concept. It was a reminder of something more important than the pursuit of wealth. But it did not really lead to attacks on the well-to-do, many of whom subscribed to magazines like the *Atlantic*. It simply excluded from the worthy "cultivated class" the millionaire, or after the 1890s the billionaire, the man defined merely by the large fortune he had amassed. It did not suggest that most people abstain from the search for material well-being; it required only that there should be a higher dimension to their lives, a dimension defined more often by respect for literary creativity than by old-fashioned piety. Like many religions, it alternated between criticizing and justifying prevalent values among respectable people. In a way, it added up to a genteel reformulation of the jeremiad, one in which the lamentable preoccupation with material gain was offset by mounting acclaim for literary heroes.

Furthermore, this celebration of culture afforded a

pleasant sense of national unity. It took for granted, mostly without argument, the existence of national patterns of value and aspiration, which were called "Americanism." All of the writers whom Higginson mentioned were New Englanders; as he remarked without much concern, all eight of the historians whom he praised were Harvard graduates. But this regional bias, so striking to us with our modern sensitivity to American pluralism, presented no obstacle to the wish to believe in widely accepted symbols of American achievement. In time the facts would to some extent catch up with the belief, as families in many regions showed their cultivation by hanging framed photographs of revered authors, as young people played the parlor game of "Authors" with cards depicting Longfellow, Poe, and Irving side by side with Scott, Tennyson, and Dickens. Inland cities like Indianapolis, home of Booth Tarkington, came to rival Boston as centers of genteel publishing. In our time it is difficult to recall how important literary heroes were as symbols of national self-respect. Long before high schools taught citizenship, American schoolchildren learned patriotism through reciting the works of their native poets. In 1887 thousands sent greetings to John Greenleaf Whittier on his eightieth birthday.

Today we may think of this nationalistic use of literature as part of the "acculturation" of immigrants to America's cities and factories. In an effective episode in Joan Micklin Silver's film *The Immigrant Experience: The Long, Long Journey,* a gentle Polish boy named Janec, who doesn't want to be "a greenhorn," has a mortifying experience when his austere schoolmistress writes on the blackboard: "Snow-bound by John Greenleaf Whittier." She calls on Janec to begin reading, and everyone mocks his accent and stumbling delivery. What could be crueler, the film seems to ask a new generation of students, than making this boy read a beloved "parlor poet" in order to be "better than your father"? Only when he quits school to work in a slaughterhouse does Janec start on his journey to comfort, security, and self-respect. Numerous scholarly studies have shown that acculturation was usually incomplete, that preserving kinship ties remained more important than acquiring new American values. Some of these studies offer sophisticated insights into the interest of successive generations in Old World customs. These new perspectives have become available as the revered nineteenth-century authors receded from popularity and the ideology that valued culture over materialism ceased to motivate many young people.

Culture had many uses. It encouraged a degree of self-congratulation for those who appreciated fine literature. At the same time, it provided a perspective from which to comprehend social differences. In a way, this perspective resembled the traditional one that distinguished between civility and barbarism: the imagery was of *us* and *them*, lightness and darkness, ideal values and material pursuits. It could be used to intensify class differences, though the bigoted patrician castes who segregated themselves in resorts and country clubs from the 1880s on were more interested in sport and amusement than in literary culture. Generally speaking, culture was not related to the anti-Semitic, anti-Catholic, and anti-immigrant movements of the Gilded Age. It was more often a concept that established social differences as problems to be understood and ameliorated.

Culture could even provide a lens through which to view sympathetically the lives of the urban and industrial poor. From midcentury, novels like George Lippard's *New York: Its Upper Ten and Lower Million* (1854) and temperance works like Solon Robinson's *Hot Corn: Life Scenes of New York Illustrated* (1854) had emphasized lurid scenes of vice and crime in the swelling cities. This emphasis never disappeared, but it was somewhat modified in new works like Rebecca Harding Davis's *Life in the Iron Mills* (1861) and *Margaret Howth* (1861) or Elizabeth Stuart Phelps's *Hedged In* (1870) and *The Silent Partner* (1871), works of fiction that probed the barriers of "feeling" between "one class of culture" and another, between respectable men and women and despairing factory hands. In well-known works of reform like Jacob Riis's *How the Other Half Lives* (1890) the theme became more explicit. There were countless people in America's tenements for whom life did "not seem worth the living." In these tenements there was no room for any "gentle thought and aspiration above the mere wants of the body. . . . Tenement-houses have no aesthetic resources. If any are to be brought to bear on them, they must come from the outside." Riis also gave graphic accounts of hunger and disease, but the point should not be overlooked that the notion of culture was useful in explaining the distress of the cities. When Jane Addams and her associates in 1889 founded the Hull House settlement, where educated people would live in the midst of Chicago's slums, she made it clear that she was not renouncing her belief in "the blessings that we associate with a life of refinement and cultivation"; instead, she doubted that these goods could be preserved unless they were made "universal."*

---

*Riis and Addams stressed the absence of culture in working-class residences precisely because there was so much agreement on the indispensable values of exposure to culture. Others professed a belief that culture was in fact eagerly sought by all. The U.S. commissioner of labor statistics, Carroll D. Wright, wrote glowingly of a woman who sat beside him on a railway car. Her clothing and rough hands indicated that she came from the factories. "Her whole attention, however, was engaged in studying a popular magazine, and it was impossible to refrain from watching her face and learning the subject which was attracting her; she was reading an article relative to some of the great

From the vantage point of culture, similar "discoveries" were made of other "problems." It was possible to conceptualize relations between the cultivated classes and Appalachian whites, prairie farmers, Maine fishermen, Indians, and southern freedmen by contrasting one group's refinement with another's deprivation. Sometimes nothing more was intended than to furnish stories of local color for readers of popular magazines. Sometimes, as in sustained controversy over what liberation should entail for blacks, there were major disagreements. Some argued that whites owed nothing to blacks but to let them alone; others, that missionary endeavors were needed to raise blacks from cultureless racial childhood. To observe the significance of culture in comprehending social problems is not to assert that political and economic issues were always neglected. Any attempt to explain what was proposed, carried out, or overlooked in legislation during the Gilded Age solely on the basis of the ideology of culture would amount to oversimplification. Nevertheless, this ideology could profoundly limit how programs of reform were conceived, as may be seen in the black educator W. E. B. Du Bois's dissent from the racial leadership of Booker T. Washington. On the one hand, he protested Washington's lack of emphasis on political rights and his preference for industrial training over a rich classical education for talented blacks. On the other hand, Du Bois wrote el-

---

works of our best artists, and studying the engravings which accompanied it. At the cost of a dime, she was bringing into her life, at the close of her day's labour, the company of the world's great artistic geniuses." Wright was certain that in her home there must have been reproductions of art, "cheap and possibly common, but nevertheless a sure indication of the existence in her own soul, of an aspiration after something higher than the drudgery which she was compelled to follow."

oquently of the conflicted feelings evoked by being a cultural "problem." The proper goal of a black leader was "to be a co-worker in the kingdom of culture." To Du Bois this goal meant "fostering the traits and talents of the Negro, not in opposition to, but in conformity with, the greater ideals of the American Republic." To the extent that criticism of black behavior reflected sincere standards of "civilization, culture, righteousness, and progress"—rather than mockery and prejudice—the black intellectual gave his assent. Yet there remained a painfully divided consciousness: "One ever feels his twoness—an American, a Negro; two souls, two thoughts; two unreconciled strivings; two warring ideals in one dark body, whose dogged strength alone keeps it from being torn asunder."

It is tempting to dismiss culture, with its clear-cut distinction between refinement and deprivation, as a myth. The more closely historians examine post–Civil War America, the more elusive and fragmented culture actually appears. Today we sometimes like to use such terms as lower-, middle-, and upper-class culture, or somewhat differently, folk, popular, and high culture. Applied to the Gilded Age, all of these terms make a little sense. There *was* a nostalgic feeling that old "folk-ways" were dying out; the mountaineers provided favorite examples of quaint survivals of Shakespearean times. The vaudeville and minstrel shows at the center of working-class neighborhoods *were* surely different from both the "legitimate" theater syndicated to middle-class audiences across the nation and the operas and symphony orchestras supported by wealthy urban philanthropists. There *was* a popular literature, including dime novels and comic books, that transcended lower-class urban neighborhoods, and it clearly differed from the writings in middle-class mass-circulation magazines like *Ladies' Home Journal* and the *Saturday Evening Post* and, even more clearly, from the highest expressions of literary genius studied by Jane Addams and other members of the "cultivated class." But to think in terms of "levels" of culture is to imagine clearer patterns of stratification than actually existed. For example, though the planners of Chicago's grand 1893 Columbian Exposition excluded the Wild West Show, visitors enjoyed both the classical beauty of the "White City" inside the fairgrounds and the entertainment that Buffalo Bill had to offer across the street.

Furthermore, these terms ignore the influence of religion (were small-town evangelicals who despised the theater any less middle-class than people who swarmed to see *The Count of Monte Cristo* starring James O'Neill?) and of immigration (would it make sense to group the Yiddish theater with the minstrel show?). And we should not think that aspirations to culture characterized mainly the rich. The privileged elites were sometimes less interested in refinement than the middle classes were. Some complained that Yale was best known for football and exclusive clubs; a history instructor supposedly informed one young man, "if you think you came to Yale with the idea of reading you will find out your mistake very soon." The *Chautauquan,* the magazine of the highly successful program of summer education and home study for middle-class strivers, was devoted, as its subtitle proclaimed, to "the Promotion of True Culture"; it was a "high-class literary magazine adapted to the needs of practical people." Women's clubs were another link between literary culture and middle-class families.

For everyone, the term *culture* implied a sense of boundaries that defined good taste and preserved high ideals. These boundaries could be reassuring to comfortable, well-educated people, but they could seem arrogant, ironic, and troublesome as well. To the humorist Mark Twain, they were signs of smug pretension. He reversed the value system that kept him from being recognized as a great writer by ridiculing "the culture-standard": "I have never tried in even one single instance, to help cultivate the cultivated classes." He had never tried to serve "dainties and delicacies" to the "thin top crust of humanity." He had never preached to the already-converted. Similarly, the poet Walt Whitman, who once had dreamed of inspirational literature transforming the moral life of the nation, came to deplore the thin veneer of sentiment that passed for culture. With "the word Culture," he wrote in *Democratic Vistas* (1871), "we find ourselves abruptly in close quarters with the enemy." To others, the trek toward culture was a saga of degeneration. In Harold Frederic's novel *The Damnation of Theron Ware* (1896), for example, a small-town Methodist minister is transformed by his acquaintance with literature, music, science, and high-toned culture, but the results are dispiriting and disabling. In Frederic C. Howe's autobiography, *The Confessions of a Reformer* (1925), however, the journey into "a world that had confidence in literature and the power of ideas" is a liberation. Howe saw his entire life as the "unlearning" of the narrow-mindedness of his small-town Methodist upbringing; his struggles for understanding took him through a Ph.D. in economics, service in a settlement house, life among New York's literati, and years of government service. These diverse examples show that culture, though meant to be reassuring, could have the ironic effect of fragmenting any sense of coherent purpose.

Culture had no keener analyst than Jane Addams. Like Higginson and most other devotees of culture, she believed that "man's social idealism is the constructive force of progress"; and for that reason she advocated "the education of the many, that there may be greater freedom, strength, and subtilty of intercourse and hence an increase of dynamic power." In the 1870s and 1880s she had pursued her own education, emphasizing literature, in the favorite traditions of culture. By her own account, she was eventually disgusted that in "lumbering our minds with literature," her generation lost the ability to see clearly the horrors of urban slums: nothing but literary allusions came to mind, and the adage was forgotten that "conduct, and not culture, is three fourths of life." More generally, she perceived that "the first generation of college women had taken their learning too quickly" and were finding that, without meaningful activity, "the pursuit of cultivation would not in the end bring either solace or relief." Thus educated women were particularly alert to the challenge of linking intellectual life with social responsibility. The problem affected men, too. "Intellectual life requires for its expansion and manifestation the influence and assimilation of the interests and affections of others," and America had a "fast-growing number of cultivated young people who have no recognized outlet for their active faculties."

To this diagnosis of the discontent of the cultivated class she added a strong sense of the decline of virtue among residents of the slums. Hull House was founded out of a feeling that working people "live for the moment side by side, many of them without knowledge of each other, without fellowship, without local tradition or public spirit, without social organization of any kind. . . . Their ideals and resources are cramped, and the desire for higher social pleasures becomes extinct. They have no share in the traditions and social energy which make for progress." It later became fashionable in intellectual circles to disparage the "Lady Bountiful" aspects of settlement life; among the settlement workers themselves critical voices were calling for more professional social work and less condescending charity. Furthermore, modern social historians have shown that the alleged breakdown of traditions and organizations in ethnic neighborhoods was exaggerated. Still, there is no denying the appeal to the "cultured" of this program of reawakening virtue and reinvigorating intellectual life by bringing them into contact with the poor. Hull House and hundreds of other settlement houses attracted numerous young intellectuals who acknowledged that they had much to learn as well as to teach. The settlements were, in short, an important transitional institution. If we regard them, in part, as an adaptation of republican ideology to the late-nineteenth-century mystique of culture, we should also notice the early endeavor to fuse intellectual life with public responsibility in a complex society. The problem of commitment to social usefulness was explored in other ways, often by young intellectuals who had gained experience in the settlements, in the ensuing decades.

CRITIQUES OF CULTURE

The ideology of culture has never disappeared. Though the term has acquired many other meanings, even today "culture" is sometimes mentioned in a sense not too different from Higginson's or the Chautauquans'. One may hear people speak of "supporting" culture or of its supporters as "having" culture. That is, it refers to literary and artistic appreciation as a sign of national and individual enrichment, separate from and superior to technological progress and material gain. Today, however, such usage is somewhat archaic. Twain's and Whitman's contempt for the pretentiousness of "the culture standard" foreshadowed a series of twentieth-century assaults on the codifications of good taste of the Victorian era. In Higginson's mind, culture had furnished a vantage point for criticizing a spirit of shallow commercialism in society at large. To its twentieth-century assailants, culture itself was a sham, a system of mediocrity, perhaps even an indication that intellectual life had not kept pace with economic progress.

One of the earliest and most biting critiques of culture appeared in the maverick social scientist Thorstein Veblen's *The Theory of the Leisure Class* (1899). In a caustic style, blending the awkward jargon later to become typical of "sociologese" with an original comic flair, Veblen reduced "leisure class culture" to survivals of ancient rituals of class discrimination and priestcraft. Culture was really nothing more than an extravagant "cult." "Pecuniary culture," as he generally disparaged it, valued what was useless in order to differentiate its moneyed devotees from those who had to work hard for a living. Acquaintance with dead languages, vapid philosophy, and elegant literature; concern with taste, character, and ideals—all the qualities celebrated in the humanities were the trappings of "the regime of status." They were, in Veblen's view, latter-day substitutes for the folderol that delineated "reputability" and adorned gentlemen in previous ages. Though Veblen did not refer to the republican dilemmas of the late eighteenth century, in effect he dismissed culture as a system of wasteful ceremonies intended to preserve a sense of hierarchy. In this system, however, true merit was submerged, and an "efficient collective life under modern industrial circumstances" was out of the question. The emphasis on personal worth and growth was "archaic"; it amounted to a "self-centered" aversion of attention from the "matter-of-fact" necessity of "civil and industrial efficiency" in a world increasingly characterized by large-scale, impersonal organizations.

To the "leisure class culture" that rendered most intellectual discourse "futile" and obsolete, particularly in the universities, Veblen contrasted the canons of impersonal, efficient, and democratic science. Ignoring the historical links between science and genteel virtuosity, he gave credit for "the intrusion of the sciences" into intellectual life to two groups: "aberrant scions of the leisure class" who happened to be temperamentally more attuned to modern economic organization than to obscure, antiquated values; and "members of the industrious classes" who managed to find enough freedom to "turn their attention to other interests than that of finding daily sustenance." Science emerged from "without" and "below"; its impetus came from those who could not turn their backs on "modern associated life." Though science too often meant little more than inventing mechanical contrivances, its larger intellectual meaning was "the recognition of causal sequence in the practical contact of mankind with their environment" rather than ritualistic incantations and "honorific" conceptions. Though a critic of leisure-class pretensions, Veblen ironically celebrated the intellectually liberating consequences of industrial change.

In Higginson's view, which was more typical of the era, the glory of culture was its ethical distance from the march of commerce and industry. Veblen turned this distinction upside down—saying that what was closer to economic life was better—and soon a similar irony emerged in another powerful assault on the ideology of culture, the essay "The Genteel Tradition in American Philosophy" (1911) by the Harvard philosopher George Santayana. He, too, was highly idiosyncratic, as different from Veblen as both were from Americans in the mainstream of culture, but the term "genteel tradition" so perfectly expressed disillusionment with received notions of good taste that it entered critical language irreversibly. Santayana also associated intellectual vitality with contemporary economic changes and disparaged cherished ideals as trappings of superficial comfort:

> The truth is that one-half of the American mind, that not occupied intensely in practical affairs, has remained, I will not say high-and-dry, but slightly becalmed; it has floated gently in the backwater, while, alongside, in invention and industry and social organization the other half of the mind was leaping down a sort of Niagara Rapids. This division may be found symbolized in American architecture: a neat reproduction of the colonial mansion—with some modern comforts introduced surreptitiously—stands beside the sky-scraper. The American Will inhabits the sky-scraper; the American Intellect inhabits the colonial mansion. The one is the sphere of the American man; the other, at least predominantly, of the American woman. The one is all aggressive enterprise; the other is all genteel tradition.

The link between the "genteel tradition" and the "American woman" may remind us of Ann Douglas's critique of the "feminization" of American culture (discussed in the previous chapter). Indeed, Santayana could write rather caustically of the American educational system in which "the teachers, even for the older boys, are chiefly unmarried women, sensitive, faithful, and feeble; their influence helps to establish that separation which is so characteristic of America between things intellectual, which remain wrapped in a feminine veil and, as it were, under glass, and the rough passions of life."* At the same time, Santayana was one of the first to attribute the genteel tradition to the collapse of Calvinism. He did not, like Veblen, stress the persistence of religious thinking. "The sense of sin [had] totally evaporated," and "Good-will became the great American virtue." Only a few great writers, like Hawthorne, dismissed the fancies of culture, and even they were too often "in danger of being morbid, or tinkling, or self-indulgent."

Twentieth-century rebellions against Victorian culture will receive more attention in the next chapter. But in Veblen's work, which grew in influence in succeeding decades, we find the assertion that the humanities are elitist, unscientific, and irrelevant to modern problems. And in Santayana we may already observe the assumption—so important in modern intellectual life, at least until recently—that criticism of the American literary past provides a way of understanding religion, sex roles, economic behavior—in a word, American civilization. Though

---

*Protests against late-nineteenth-century culture often focused on ladylike dominion over taste. Consider E. E. Cummings's "A High-Toned Christian Woman" (1923):

> The Cambridge ladies who live in furnished souls
> are unbeautiful and have comfortable minds
> . . . .
> they believe in Christ and Longfellow, both dead

Since modern feminists, for very different reasons, often share this hostility toward what is now called "the cult of true womanhood," they have generally failed to raise some obvious questions about its antifeminine biases. This is a good illustration of how hard it is to gain a historical perspective on nineteenth-century "culture." Veblen, too, though sympathetic to women as workers, disparaged women's culture and education as a form of conspicuous consumption.

he criticized what "the culture-standard" upheld, in a sense
Santayana agreed that one could assess the "mentality" of
Americans by examining their writers. If the problem of
commitment provides continuity from the late nineteenth
century to modern intellectual life, these beliefs in the importance of science and literature were other prominent
signposts to the direction of change.

UNIVERSITIES

While "culture" infused a vague but widely honored ideology, the most remarkable specific institutional change in
intellectual life during the post–Civil War decades—indeed, during all of American history—was the emergence
of the university. A French traveler at midcentury, cited
approvingly by Higginson, reported that "for . . . the academic class—or class devoted to pure literature—there is
as yet no place in America. Such a class must as yet conceal itself . . . beneath the politician's garb, or the clergyman's cravat." Higginson added that the diffuse new
careers in journalism and reform emerging in the era of
reorganization offered little freedom for sustained intellectual activity. This situation was transformed by the
emergence of a network of universities, although it still
might have been questioned whether the academic
profession was devoted to "pure literature."

The transformation followed no single blueprint. While
most of the old religiously oriented colleges and seminaries endured in increasing isolation and obscurity, a few
raised new funds, discarded the traditional lockstep curriculum, created new departments and specialized schools,
and attracted larger faculties and student bodies. Harvard, for example, adopted the elective system in 1869,
permitting greater specialization for both students and
teachers, established a graduate department in 1872, and

added business to the other "intellectual professions," like law and medicine, for which it offered specialized instruction. Prominent new universities were named after wealthy donors, frequently men of little personal education, who got them started: Cornell in 1868, Vanderbilt in 1873, Johns Hopkins in 1876, Stanford in 1885, Clark in 1889. Some originated with a special mission that influenced older schools: Cornell was adamantly nonsectarian and nonelitist; Hopkins featured advanced seminars for graduate fellows; Clark emphasized the sciences. The University of Chicago, founded in 1892 with pecuniary support from John D. Rockefeller, was pervasively Baptist; it emphasized both its nonelitism and its strong commitment to graduate education. In addition, some of the most important universities were state-financed. California, Nebraska, Wisconsin, Michigan, Illinois, and Indiana all became centers of both undergraduate and graduate education. Though run as public schools, most had clear nonsectarian Protestant commitments. All were coeducational. Some had schools of agriculture in keeping with the terms of the Morrill Land Grant Act of 1862, and other forms of vocational education followed naturally.

Diverse in their local histories, all these universities had a tendency to view success in terms of numbers. To a few critics, this tendency reflected the typical reliance on businessmen as trustees (a reliance equally apparent in churches, museums, and other institutions of the Gilded Age); to Santayana, this tendency revealed the "moral materialism" of Americans with their "singular preoccupation with quantity." Just as Americans boasted of the number of homes illuminated by electricity from Niagara Falls or the number of miles of asphalt in Buffalo, "the President of Harvard College, seeing me [Santayana] once by chance soon after the beginning of a term, inquired how my classes were getting on; and when I replied that

I thought they were getting on well, that my men seemed to be keen and intelligent, he stopped me as if I was about to waste his time; 'I meant,' said he, 'I meant *what is the number* of students in your classes.' " In truth, President Charles W. Eliot, though an urbane man who prided himself on his devotion to "educational ideals," was preoccupied with numerical growth: "I find that I am not content unless Harvard grows each year, in spite of the size which it has attained." The head of the University of Nebraska disclosed his "entire political creed" as this goal: "a thousand students . . . in 1895; 2,000 in 1900." In any case the national figures were formidable: there were 52,000 undergraduates in this country in 1870; by 1890 there were 157,000; the figure rose to 238,000 in 1900 and to 598,000 in 1920. Only a fraction went on to graduate study—5,700 in 1900—and the college-going portion of the overall population remained under 5 percent throughout the nineteenth century. Nevertheless, the rise of the university was a topic of mounting interest in books and periodicals. Compared with previous eras, there now existed thousands of positions associated with "intellectual life," as the term was increasingly used, providing a reasonable if not princely income, and blending a vague sense of public service with some occasion (now considered work instead of leisure) for independent thought and reflection.

The preoccupation with numbers and opportunity served in different ways to modify the customs of German universities that were widely praised as models. Requirements for the Ph.D. degree were strengthened so that it signified the ability to conduct specialized research of an advanced kind. In Germany the doctorate was a fairly accessible general degree held by many other graduates besides those few who went on to teach in universities. In America, too, after it was introduced in the 1860s, it was awarded freely, even on an honorary basis, but by the turn of the century it had become a standardized degree distinguishing its scholarly recipients from the generality of the cultivated classes. William James disparaged the "Ph.D. octopus" that suffocated university life, and others complained of the narrowness of many professors, but the degree proved essential to legitimating credentials in rapidly expanding institutions. If Ph.D.'s were common in Germany, professorships were scarce. In America, without much discussion, a great many teachers in a proliferating number of departments—certainly not just the chairmen—were entitled professor. (Even today, an American "professor" may be treated in Europe as though he possesses a rare distinction that he is unaware of.) In other words, even while the Ph.D. marked off the academic specialist from other professionals, there was considerable opportunity to aspire to the highest vocational titles within the universities.

In many discussions of the new institution there were obvious echoes of the old republican concern with "virtue." The university, according to Eliot, stood for "plain living against luxury." These echoes could have either elitist or democratic overtones. On the one hand, it was possible to picture the degree bearer, secluded from the materialistic world and earnestly pursuing knowledge, as a member of a disinterested aristocracy of merit. Though professors did not come primarily from wealthy backgrounds, the university was one place where the term *gentlemanly* was used frequently and favorably. The university was called "a civilized commonwealth." Its leading citizens might speak of themselves as "a fraternity of the educated" and aspire to great influence in society. In his 1902 inaugural address as president of Princeton, Woodrow Wilson explained that the university was "not for the majority who carry forward the common labor of the world" but for "the minority who plan, who conceive, who superintend, who mediate between group and group and must see the wide stage as a whole. Democratic nations must be served in this wise no less than those whose leaders are chosen by birth and privilege." On the other hand, it was possible to take heart in the extension of university education to hordes of first-generation students. Perhaps they would overcome the vulgarizing effects of democracy and extend disinterested idealism more broadly throughout society. At the "people's college," Cornell, President Andrew Dixon White cherished the vision of his graduates taking over and ennobling the political offices, newspaper editorships, and other seats of power and influence in America.

Eloquent professors of English, philosophy, history, and the classics furnished some of the era's most ardent defenses of "culture." Amid all the disturbing signs of economic and social change, the university seemed well equipped to preserve acquaintance with the noblest expressions of human intellect and artistic creativity. It might ensure the persistence of ideals. The "true aim of culture," according to one colorful Cornell professor, was "to induce soul states or conditions, soul attitudes, to attune the inward forces to the idealized forms of nature and of human life produced by art, and not to make the head a cockloft for storing away the trumpery of barren knowledge." In an age that fostered crass outlooks, education might stimulate the development of the entire human personality. While some defenders of culture depicted a highly spiritualized character, others were more in favor of critical intellect. An emancipated intelligence gave a person needed perspective on the shortcomings of society and the bad choices it proposed. There were also distinctions between views of culture that stressed its conservative implications—its fixity and stability—and others that appealed glowingly to the progressive realization of ideals. In intellectual history, the study of philosophy, and appreciative reading of great literature, the student learned, as a Michigan professor wrote in 1889, that "the past has never been destroyed, but has found a higher being in each new present." At many universities, lecturers who promoted an inspiring, cosmopolitan view of culture were highly popular campus figures and valued emissaries to the world outside.

But they could also seem bitter and embattled. The defenders of culture were hugely successful in remodeling the old-style college curriculum with its narrow emphasis on the Didactic Enlightenment. By supporting the elective system, they did away with texts like Wayland's and eliminated unimaginative drills in mathematics and ancient languages. They succeeded in placing before thousands of students novels, poems, philosophical works, and great histories to an extent that would once have seemed unimaginable. Yet they were uncomfortable with the businesslike organizations of universities, and they grumbled that most undergraduates were loafers and philistines, more interested in banjo tunes, football, and college slang than in Dante or Shakespeare. They often frankly admitted that the intellectual life of the universities, despite the ideals of service that presidents voiced so attractively, had minimal influence in the world outside. Even within the university gates, they eventually realized that the elective system had fragmenting consequences that augured poorly for the vitality of ideals in a well-rounded citizenry. Students of engineering or agriculture were beyond their reach, and science increasingly seemed split off from philosophical inquiry or artistic appreciation. The defenders of culture sometimes disparaged those great devices of specialization, the Ph.D. and the dissertation, as enfeebling enemies of rich and genteel discourse.

Though the term "two cultures" was introduced by the British scientist-novelist C. P. Snow only in 1959, in fact the post–Civil War university witnessed a segregation of science from liberal arts that would have astonished Cotton Mather or Thomas Jefferson and that has remained a prominent feature of intellectual life ever since. While university presidents spoke of educating the whole man and some efforts were made to make undergraduate education coherent, the professors were divided into separate departments with considerable autonomy in developing their course offerings. Furthermore, national organizations emerged in their separate fields, with their own meetings, scholarly journals, and specialized literature—organizations of increasing importance in defining standards that affected a professor's methods of inquiry, reputation, and mobility. The American Chemical Society was founded in 1876, for example, the Modern Language Association in 1883, the American Historical Association in 1884, and the American Physical Society in 1899. While the founders often believed that all these professions could be pursued as sciences, it was hard not to speak in terms of two broad orientations. The president of Johns Hopkins, Daniel Coit Gilman, put the best face on these patterns in 1903:

> While the old line between the sciences and the humanities may be invisible as the equator, it has an existence as real. On the one side are cognitions which may be submitted to demonstrative proof; which do not depend upon opinion, preference, or authority; which are true everywhere and all the time; while on the other side are cognitions which depend upon our spiritual natures, our aesthetic preferences, our intellectual traditions, our religious faith. Earth and man, nature and the

supernatural, letters and science, the humanities and the realities, are the current terms of contrast between the two groups and there are no signs that these distinctions will ever vanish.

But even this polite distinction was subject to further confusion. The American Economic Association was founded in 1885, the American Sociological Society in 1905, and by World War I it was common to refer to a tripartite division that included the social sciences. The study of man, in other words, could be appropriated by those who sought "fact" and "demonstrative proof." Only undergraduates were asked, halfheartedly, to believe that all these approaches to knowledge somehow meshed. Specialization had delineated quite separate paths to intellectual careers.

If "culture" emboldened defenders of the humanities, especially as central to the teaching function of the university, the allure of the sciences emanated from research. Even the "productive" historian or classicist was likely to honor this term. Once referring simply to inquiry, the word *research* now denoted the technical pursuit of knowledge within professional disciplines. To support useful contributions (which had the side effect of adding luster to a university's reputation), sabbatical leaves were introduced, teaching loads were reduced, a few full-time research positions were created, and graduate training was directed to the aim of producing the definitive monograph on a small subject—with the faith that the ultimate result would be the drawing of an ever larger area of human experience or natural phenomena into the realm of verified knowledge. Within the university, the narrowness of research topics did not prevent talk of "pure" science untouched by materialistic concerns. Models of purity included the much admired German universities and,

most of all, the sweeping revision of scientific understanding that had followed Charles Darwin's *Origin of Species* (1859). Minute research could subdue the changing
universe to the control of theory.

The dispassionate researcher could be contrasted to the
man who hid "behind the fortress of 'liberal culture,' " ignoring the thrust of new discoveries and doubting the value
of technological improvements. Increasingly, research was
tied to claims of utility, not only in the universities, where
presidents and leading professors had to concern themselves with public relations, but even more strongly in the
research institutes pioneered by Thomas Alva Edison at
Menlo Park and imitated by leading business firms. And
for the hundreds of scientists and social investigators employed by government agencies and for those supported
by private philanthropies such as the Russell Sage Foundation or the Carnegie Corporation, there was less need
to discuss the quality of "intellectual life" than there was
in the university. The call to concentrate on the social
benefits of research was irresistible.

Thus the tremendous development of the university
as a haven for intellectual endeavor was accompanied by
an awareness of cleavages that only genial presidents could
downplay. Besides the internal cleavages between students and professors and, within the faculty, between humanists and scientists (both groups remaining aloof from
vocational instructors), important quandaries arose from
the universities' separation from what was usually called
"real life." Did education give young men and women
anything to fit them for the world besides college ties and
business contacts? Could university research compete with
practical-minded alternatives in the world outside: where
were the Edisons and Luther Burbanks of academia? The
university brought together a large intellectual class—a
professoriate—but the links between teaching, research,

and creative thought were ambiguous. Some of the most penetrating thinkers of the period—like the philosopher Charles Sanders Peirce, who is greatly admired today—could not keep a position in academia and lived in marginal obscurity. The novelist William Dean Howells was urged by a Harvard friend not to accept an academic position: it would stifle his imagination. In the 1890s several social scientists, whose criticisms of existing institutions offended donors and injured public relations, were harried out of university positions.

The term *intellectual* appeared for the first time in the 1890s to define an alumnus or alumna of a university as a critical thinker who was not trapped by the prejudices and conventions of society at large.* Since then, the idea of the freedom of thought of the university intellectual has had recurrent appeal. Yet it has sometimes jarred with the prejudices and conventions of the university itself as a utilitarian institution within society. Two other beliefs of the 1890s have also persisted. The first is the belief that most "bright young men" go into science. The second belief is that, of the remainder, those who can write engagingly enough to reach a public may find careers outside the university. Throughout the twentieth century, many creative and influential writers have tended to scorn the timidity and pedantry of academic discourse. Their scorn may seem unjustified if we consider only the best thinkers

*It appeared in an essay by William James, "The Social Value of the College-Bred," which accorded intellectuals an importance corresponding to that of "the aristocracy in older countries." Everywhere else selfishness and manipulable passion prevailed; "we stand for ideal interests solely." James adopted the term from France, where it had been used in derision of writers who had protested against anti-Semitism in the notorious Dreyfus trial. Richard Hofstadter discusses the original radical meaning of the term in *Anti-Intellectualism in American Life* (1963).

who worked under university auspices, and it may have receded in the post-1950s expansion of academia. Well before that, the research capacities of American universities were envied abroad. Nevertheless, for an understanding of intellectual life in America, it is important to see the universities not only as having provided the occupational basis for thousands of intellectual careers, but also as having raised, in the view of many of the most ambitious and restless, conventions of sterile discourse to be avoided. The first decision facing a would-be intellectual between 1900 and 1945 concerned whether to pursue a career inside or outside the professoriate.

RELIGION AND THE CULTURE OF INQUIRY

One striking feature of both the ideology of culture and the institution of the university was their complacency regarding the once vexatious questions of theology. Neither was antireligious; both took it for granted that the best American ideals were vaguely Protestant. But the specific religious content of those ideals seemed less important than the confidence that somehow, despite the contrasts among economic classes and ethnic groups, despite vast changes in industrial organization and steady advances in human knowledge, there remained, as a scientist-president of the University of Wisconsin put it, "a dimly-seen something towards which we stretch forward our hands." There were few religious skeptics, even among university scientists. Yet professors who liked to discuss Christian faith in their classes gave up the practice, not because it was inappropriate, but because students were indifferent.

This complacency may seem surprising because we are often told that the late nineteenth century witnessed a battle over the implications of science and Darwinism.

Probably no subject in the history of American intellectual life has been more widely misunderstood than the reception of Darwin's theory of evolution. To be sure, one die-hard Princeton theologian, Charles Hodge, wrote *What Is Darwinism?* (1874) and gave the answer, "It is Atheism." To Hodge it was intolerable to think that the Creator had "abandoned the universe to itself to be controlled by chance and necessity, without any purpose on his part as to the result, or any intervention or guidance." Moreover, some other evangelical Protestants, mainly those outside the circles of polite culture and academic learning, expressed similar criticisms in the 1860s and early 1870s. And from the other side, a few often-cited (but little read) champions of science began to distort history by maintaining that Christianity had generally impeded the advance of learning. John William Draper, professor of chemistry at the College of the City of New York, offered a *History of the Conflict between Religion and Science* (1874), and Cornell's President White followed with *The Warfare of Science with Theology* (1895).

The significance of each of these three points has often been exaggerated. First, Hodge was an exception to the general reaction of orthodox Protestant theologians. Summarizing recent studies of the ease with which Hodge's colleagues received evolutionary theory, David A. Hollinger has given this reformulation: "What is Darwinism? It is Calvinism!" The president of Princeton, James Mc-Cosh, loyal to both Calvinism and the Didactic Enlightenment, argued forcefully that it would be disastrous to oppose the findings of science; it was far better to reconcile these findings with overriding faith in God's ultimate purposes. "Natural selection" was God's chosen means to effect the biological changes that Darwin observed; other dimensions of human experience, such as the maintenance of "high ideas and sentiments," remained unaffected by the theory. Kept in its proper place, "the principle of natural selection" was, according to the immensely popular lecturer John Fiske in *Through Nature to God* (1899), "intensively Calvinistic; it elects the one and damns the ninety and nine." In short, Darwinism described a hard cruel world, with invisible purposes beyond human agency, that would have comforted the Puritans. Fiske, like McCosh, glorified the progressive sentiments of love and idealism that characterized the family as a sphere of moral relations and softened the random workings of natural process.

Second, to imagine a huge "fundamentalist" counterattack on Darwinism in the Gilded Age is to read backwards from the 1920s and 1970s. Historians who dredge up examples of popular anti-evolutionism ignore the unmistakable triumph of Darwin's views among those who cared about such matters and the unconcern of most others. By 1885 one of the most popular American ministers, Henry Ward Beecher, declared the controversy "past and closed." Evolutionism had simply been absorbed into a spirit of confidence in the progress of culture and morality.

Third, what should we make of texts like Draper's and White's? Whatever the long-run implications of the metaphor of "warfare" between science and religion, few prominent scientists, churchmen, or educators of the period predicted that science was likely to overturn religion. Those few who did speak of "warfare" were usually not really antireligious; they were simply defending a broad-minded religious viewpoint, one that was comfortable with secular progress. As Hollinger has concluded, "most of the period's discourse about 'warfare' . . . aimed to prove that there was no such warfare." If there was a religious movement that had difficulty in accommodating Darwin's vision of change occurring through brutal accident, it was the genial progressive mainstream, with its emphasis on God's love and humanity's increasing perfection. There was a wholesale effort, not to refute evolution, but to imbue it with sentiment and purpose. Rather than mutability and waste, evolution exhibited godly lawfulness, a process in which history was fulfilled. According to Fiske, society revealed "the evolution of the most exalted spiritual qualities which characterize Humanity."

There was undeniably ample evidence of doubt and anxiety in the spiritual lives of many Gilded Age intellectuals. Popular evangelicalism had long taught Americans to think of faith as the outcome of a crisis in which the calculations of the head conflicted with the outpouring feelings of the heart. Many early-nineteenth-century intellectuals had recounted scenes of searing internal conflict in their early professional lives. In part, the metaphor of warfare between science and religion was a generalized Victorian restatement of this familiar struggle. The increasing professionalization of science suggested that the head was following its own course successfully, but religious faith involved more groping and less assurance of where the world was heading. The point was not that science was atheistic but that religion was, more than ever, an inward experience of the heart. By the 1880s, many Americans were apt to reflect, like the great English Victorian poets Tennyson and Arnold, that they were living in an age when certainty of faith was receding and spiritual crisis had reached an acute form.*

---

*Tennyson's often quoted *In Memoriam* is a poem of doubt.

> *Behold, we know not anything;*
> *I can but trust that good shall fall*
> *At last—far off—at last, to all.*

Change was a dramatic and inexorable element of life—not merely the career transitions that carried individuals from small towns and agrarian backgrounds to big cities and impressive universities, but enormous social changes as seen in large-scale corporations and frightening social conflicts. It was possible to imagine dreadful episodes of class warfare and apocalypse, made familiar in a number of best-selling novels, ruining dearly achieved prosperity and respectability. It was more typical of the "educated classes," however, to feel that the religious uniformity of the past was shattered and that the lines of future social integration could be only dimly perceived. In America, with its numerous denominations, and with new ones like Christian Science and Spiritualism being added all the time, this feeling came easily. It is fair to say that evolution was widely accepted because, in the diverse adulterated versions popularized by men like McCosh, Beecher, and Fiske, it shored up faith in progress, even if the ultimate ends were unknowable.

We may distinguish three broad strategies for responding to "modern" crisis. First, although there were almost no atheists, there were highly publicized advocates of "ag-

---

Arnold's *Dover Beach* has a beautiful stanza on receding faith:

> *The Sea of Faith*
> *Was once, too, at the full, and round earth's shore*
> *Lay like the folds of a bright girdle furled.*
> *But now I only hear*
> *Its melancholy, long, withdrawing roar,*
> *Retreating, to the breath*
> *Of the night-wind, down the vast edges drear*
> *And naked shingles of the world.*

nosticism." This new term was introduced by British scientists to distinguish the unknowable realm of theology and metaphysics from the hard facts of nature that science was continually subjecting to human knowledge. In America, Robert Ingersoll ("the great infidel") won a public following with his militant assaults on the pretensions of religion, which he was driving "from the realm of reason . . . to the darkness of conjecture." Faith had no foundation in fact; the obligatory stance of any honest person was doubt. There were a few small experiments in creating new religions based on nothing more than cosmopolitan ideals of decent behavior. The Ethical Culture Society, founded in 1876, had considerable appeal to intellectuals, Jewish and Christian alike, in eastern cities. Yet it seems clear that the primary significance of agnosticism was as a bogeyman to be deplored by preachers trying to mobilize the faithful in an era of unsettling change.

Second, by far the most common strategy was to institutionalize doubt as part of the Protestant diagnosis of the era. "Doubt is mostly a modern thing," said one minister after another, in order to define the social context in which the intellectual of the new age searched for faith. There was quicksand everywhere; the faith of the fathers had to be reformulated as historical certainty eroded. It had to be recast in terms of feelings and ideals. Whatever science revealed about the universe, no matter how complicated society might appear, there was an irreducible consciousness of "absolute dependence," wrote the Congregationalist liberal Newman Smyth in *The Religious Feeling* (1877). In an age that questions everything, wrote John Fiske in *The Idea of God as Affected by Modern Knowledge* (1886), many have concluded that faith is a "mere superstition," but so deep was the religious impulse that it was "not likely that any one of them has ever really succeeded in ridding himself" of faith. Once this feeling was acknowledged, the next step was to accept culture itself as infused with God's unfolding purpose. "The line often drawn between the sacred and secular," wrote Theodore Munger in *The Freedom of Faith* (1883), was unknown in Scripture. While science and society might appear to be beyond religion's control, there was a bland confidence that God was "immanent" in the direction of cultural progress. This outlook could be given formal philosophical statement in a system of all-transcending idealism. It had "Christian Socialist" proponents who foresaw a gradually achieved Christian commonwealth that would mollify the workings of the competitive marketplace. But it also prevailed as an optimistic attitude of implicit faith.

The third strategy had only a few practitioners in the late nineteenth century, but it has looked most impressive in retrospect. Exemplified by the philosophers Chauncey Wright, Charles Sanders Peirce, William James, and John Dewey, it proposed what Hollinger has called "the culture of inquiry." It began by accepting a Darwinian account of a universe of chance and accident, an unmoored universe that gave good cause for doubt and uncertainty, and it proceeded to look for appropriate methods of lifelong questing. It is hard to define these four thinkers by what they had in common, except to say that all placed greater emphasis on the methods of science than on any temporarily acclaimed version of truth. It is easier to define them by noting how they differed from both the agnostic few who would accept as real only the discoveries of natural science and from the complacent majority who hailed the timeless verities of culture or the certainty of moral progress. Though a small circle of New Englanders, they were to have expanding influence after 1900—not in peddling a specific New England codification of truth, but in promoting "pragmatic" attitudes toward human inquiry.

In this circle, the impact of Darwin does seem profound, though not, as might be expected, as a critique of religion. What was more important was the undermining of the Scottish commonsense philosophy, with its suspicion of theory and its glorification of plain Baconian observation. None of the four was a thinker easily summarized; their views changed, and they disagreed with one another. But all were confronting, in a profound way, the limited certainty of human knowledge. They took up the question, suppressed in the Didactic Enlightenment, of what perspective we have to establish truth if even the human mind is a product of natural history. Other questions arose from the confusing array of cultural signs—the language—through which ideas of truth are communicated; others, from the unavoidable role of human imagination in contriving hypothetical accounts of the universe and from the inescapable importance of prejudice and human need in holding various ideas at one time or another to be true. There was an underlying realization that humanity's assurances were relative to time and place. Neither the dogmatic certainty of the "tough-minded" scientist about what constituted reality nor the progressive idealism of the "tender-minded" advocates of religion and culture—to use James's famous distinction between two kinds of temperaments—had any sure footing in a universe of variation and chance. Many of their writings examined the functions of words in a particular situation—an endeavor that gives them a certain appeal to linguists of the 1980s. Yet they insisted that words without implied actions were meaningless.

Though Wright, the least influential, could be bitterly skeptical about human pretensions, for the most part these men were no iconoclasts. Peirce wrote one essay, admittedly for a popular audience, that made an argument for the existence of God not too different from other extensions of inescapable feelings of absolute dependence.

James, the most popular before 1900, offered well-known justifications for religious belief: *The Will to Believe* (1897) and *The Varieties of Religious Experience* (1902). Both critics and admirers sometimes understood him to say that there was no limit to believing just about anything. Certainly he felt that belief in God could be justified by human needs, and he was notoriously open-minded about Spiritualism and other modern cults. (In Santayana's faint praise, James was "friend and helper of those groping, nervous, half-educated, spiritually disinherited, emotionally hungry individuals of which America is full.") It is unclear just how far he meant to extend the limits of justifiable belief. He preferred "piecemeal" change over any absolutism. While not rejecting Spiritualism out of hand, for example, he certainly proposed to put its claims to the test of scientific method. On the whole, James's purpose seems to have been to combat those agnostics who placed a misguided confidence in the fixity of truth and the objectivity of human perception. The mind that decided what was true was itself part of the changing process. Thus in the enduring struggle to make the best of the universe, there was no reason to shrink from the most ennobling and creative beliefs available at a given moment in time. Science was important, but so was faith.

Dewey went further toward forsaking his religious upbringing (though he always respected the feeling of communal reunification to which the highest forms of art and religion gave expression). It is to Dewey that we owe the most trenchant and dramatic account of *The Impact of Darwin on Philosophy* (1910), and by "philosophy" he meant the general world view of great numbers of people. Though not as oversimplified as the books that depicted warfare between verifiable science and credulous religion, his work did portray religion as a "seething vat of emotions," inhospitable to intellectual progress. But he also saw the mainstream of Western science and moral philosophy as dependent on the notion of the species, particularly *homo sapiens,* as a "fixed form and final cause." No one spoke any longer, as medieval thinkers had, of faculties and essences; everyone laughed at the old account of opium putting people to sleep because "it had a dormitive faculty." But modern explanations—"that knowledge of the plant that yields the poppy consists in referring the peculiarities of an individual to a type, to a universal form"— were no better. They showed a preference for "the changeless, the final, and the transcendent" over "the pathless wastes of generation and transformation." What was at stake went beyond accuracy in explanation. The old view of nature conveyed "the idea of purpose," that all living organisms grew toward fulfillment of their ideal nature. Even when physics and chemistry had ceased to analyze final causes in the nonorganic world, the study of life was still believed to show such intricacies of design that the notion of a purposeful universe was confirmed. This belief became untenable, however, when Darwin showed that the intricacies of adaptations were due, not to "a prior intelligent causal force," but to "constant variation and the elimination of those varieties which are harmful in the struggle for existence that is brought about by excessive reproduction."

What remained? Dewey rejected the accommodating theologies that hailed God as superintendent of the processes of variation and adaptation. There was too much variation in useless directions, too much left to accident and futile struggle, to sustain this cheerful outlook. What remained was to cling fast to the scientific method exemplified by Galileo and other adventurous minds. Now that humanity had to accept "the principle of transition" in human affairs, it was necessary to behave scientifically in politics and morals. The result would be a greater liberation from centuries of fatalism and irresponsibility. It was up to mankind to identify social problems and to invent ways of solving them. It was time to discard useless habits of philosophers and to develop a new program concentrating on specific, changing conditions of human life.

In *Pragmatism* (1907) James popularized a name for the "ism" that Wright and Peirce had set in motion and that he and Dewey were elaborating. Since the great influence of pragmatism came in later decades (though James died in 1910, Dewey was a luminous presence in intellectual life until his death in 1952), we shall return to the movement's meaning to less prominent men and women. What should be mentioned here is that, in James's exciting formulation of pragmatism, problems of faith and social unity were uppermost. Because he described theories as nothing more than "instruments" and truth as nothing more than "the practical consequences of acting on a belief," James's pragmatism could be made to sound hardheaded and irreverent. Because he said that pragmatism could approve religion if that was "what is better for us," he could be made to sound like an uncritical champion of the mushiest religiosity. In fact, however, he compares his own religion with that for which the Puritans had died: the acceptance of "a drastic universe from which the element of 'seriousness' is not to be expelled." He was "willing to take the universe to be really dangerous and adventurous, without therefore backing out and crying 'no play.' " Despite all the talk of conflict between science and received traditions, it was explicitly the complacent, diluted theology of the nineteenth century that pragmatists repudiated.

James's writings were neither addressed to nor centrally concerned with the working classes. Yet in *Pragmatism* he launched his attack on "the airy and shallow optimism of current religious philosophy" by quoting at length

from a pamphlet by a revolutionary anarchist. After re-
counting deaths by suicide and starvation in the tenements, this pamphlet blasted philosophers who prattled
sweetly of the perfection of God's world. Tragic facts refused to be glossed over, and the rationalizations of philosophy would soon be destroyed. It may have amused
James to shock his genteel audiences by quoting a class
enemy in order to show the superiority of pragmatism. He
offered no program of revolution; he showed less interest
in the settlement houses than Dewey and other contemporaries; and few, if any, of his illustrations of piecemeal
problem-solving referred to life in the slums. Nevertheless, his version of pragmatism repeatedly raised images
of social solidarity. To give but one famous example of a
pragmatic test of faith, he spoke of the consequences of
believing in the trustworthiness of others:

> A social organism of any sort whatever, large or
> small, is what it is because each member proceeds
> to his own duty with a trust that the other mem-
> bers will simultaneously do theirs. . . . A govern-
> ment, an army, a commercial system, a ship, a col-
> lege, an athletic team, all exist on this condition,
> without which not only is nothing achieved, but
> nothing is even attempted. A whole train of pas-
> sengers (individually brave enough) will be looted
> by a few highwaymen, simply because the latter can
> count on one another, while each passenger fears
> that if he makes a movement of resistance, he will
> be shot before any one else backs him up. If we
> believed that the whole car-full would rise at once
> with us, we should each severally rise, and train-
> robbing would never even be attempted. There are,
> then, cases where a fact cannot come at all unless
> a preliminary faith exists in its coming. *And where*

faith in a fact can help create the fact, that would be an insane logic which should say that faith running ahead of scientific evidence is the "lowest form of immorality" into which a thinking being can fall. Yet such is the logic by which our scientific absolutists pretend to regulate our lives!

An important dimension of pragmatism was the vision of a reintegrated society in which disturbing conflicts would disappear. Religion was so important to James, in the end, not just for individual peace of mind, but also for the reunification of industrial society. However awkwardly and tentatively he may have offered this vision, the goal of social reconstruction was destined to be an abiding feature of the appeal of pragmatism.

THE INTELLECT
UNMOORED

If we ask who was an intellectual in this period, we find that the answers are clearer than they were in the first half of the nineteenth century. Fewer persons were struggling to get a hold on an amorphous, shifting intellectual vocation; more persons had a clear relation to well-defined institutions of national scope. There were still throwbacks to the earlier era: some small-town lawyers or ministers and college teachers, for example, went through lives quite like those of their own counterparts of an earlier day. But they probably were less confident of their significance as an intelligentsia. For the intellectually ambitious, the local and rural were in eclipse. The era has been described as "the nadir" of the small college, as a time when "no eminent lawyer ever reads a book." And we have noted the excitement of discovery with which a man like Frederic Howe left behind the values of his birthplace and jour-

neyed through the university, the settlement house, and
big-city literary circles. In each of these departures, he
enjoyed the comradeship of a small circle of intellectuals,
but always with the commitment to doing important work
in a new national cause.

We have observed two interlocking developments of
great importance: the glorification of culture as a reser-
voir of intelligent idealism at the top of society; and the
emergence of the university as an institution through which
ambitious young people passed and in whose confines a
specialized "intellectual life" found nourishment. In society at large, a few carried on the Emersonian life of a free-
lance public moralist. We may think of Fiske's endless addresses on the social meanings of evolution, of Theodore
Roosevelt's highly successful *The Winning of the West* (1889),
or of the popular lecturer Josiah Strong's *Our Country*
(1886), which expressed both alarm at social breakdown
in the cities and in the West and overriding confidence in
the expansion of the remarkable Protestant civilization of
America. But even those who worked for more bureaucratic and professional institutions like the university could
make a name for themselves by responding to public concern over the character and destiny of the nation. Thus
the historian Frederick Jackson Turner, who had made a
life journey somewhat like Howe's, won enduring fame
both inside and outside his field of specialization when he
delivered a lecture during the Columbian Exposition on
"The Significance of the Frontier in American History"
(1893), a lecture confirming the general sense that a long
era had come to an end and new challenges awaited
American inventiveness. The numerous specialists who
neither sought nor gained such fame found satisfaction
in knowing that leaders of their professions appealed to a
wide audience. Only in retrospect would it be clear that
specialization and public edification might pull in oppo-

site directions, creating a division between academic discourse and the broader influence of men of letters.

We have noted strains and fissures in respectable culture that would assume greater importance after World War I: the ambiguous relation between high culture and popular taste; assaults on the pretensions of gentility in the name of civic efficiency or literary creativity; the polarization of science and the humanities; the dormancy of evangelical criticism of evolutionary science; and early assertions of "pragmatic" approaches to social problems. To these might be added a profound uncertainty as to whether the fulfillment of America's institutions depended on individual striving or collective endeavor. To emphasize the divisions that foreshadowed future intellectual movements, however, is to ignore the complacency and resistance to change that the most probing late-nineteenth-century thinkers concluded was a prominent trait of human intellect. "Old ideas give way very slowly," said John Dewey. "They are habits, predispositions, deeply engrained attitudes of aversion and preference." In attributing great liberating consequences to Darwin, he was offering a prediction rather than describing actual change. In matters of belief, said William James, "we are all extreme conservatives." Faced with a new experience, we seek the solution that requires "a minimum of disturbance" to our old "stock of opinions." Pragmatism did not seek total repudiation of "old truths"; it sought a gradual adjustment that would maintain a sense of harmony and equilibrium between past and present. Dewey and James well understood the vague optimism about culture and progress that most of their intellectual contemporaries cherished.

Nevertheless, there were profound alterations in thinking about the intellect itself. For one thing, the mind had become a subject of research. In the universities, and to a lesser extent in small colleges, the old course on mental philosophy, usually taught by the president and employing a textbook like Wayland's, passed away. In its place came new departments of psychology, often boasting professors versed in German methods of laboratory research. The lines between professional specialties were still permeable: both James and Dewey began as psychologists and moved back into philosophy, where their colleagues discussed codes of language or overarching ideals. But there was little talk of the mental "faculties" any longer, little confidence that human beings possessed means of perception that mirrored the realities of nature, few references to a reason giving authoritative judgment over perceptions, and slight faith in a moral sense pointing the way toward conscientious behavior. Gone also was the transcendentalists' celebration of man's glorious universal intuition.

There was no unanimity concerning what replaced common sense, reason, conscience, and intuition. Though researchers in "physiological psychology" flourished in universities, no single account of mental functioning controlled research and teaching. Some scientists did sections of the brain or sought to understand the nervous system. Some adopted imagery from physics and spoke of pent-up or expended energy. Some recorded aspects of mental behavior—for example, attention spans or retention of information—that could be analyzed statistically. Some classified the genetic stages of human development (in this period G. Stanley Hall of Clark popularized the term "adolescence"). Some sought to describe the interplay between biological instincts and the persistent ideals of culture and religion. Some concentrated on clinical observation of particular cases of abnormal behavior and psychosis. Some, influenced by Darwin, discussed mental behavior in terms of adaptations to environment. In this chorus of discordant voices there was one leitmotif. Though not always clear in the origins of psychological scholarship, it was identified retrospectively in Edna Heidbreder's useful survey of *Seven Psychologies* (1933) as "the gradual modification of the notion of rational man":

> . . . when experimental studies of thinking were undertaken, the evidence pointed almost at once to a conception of thought as an activity far less severely rational than it had seemed [from the Greeks to the Enlightenment]. Perhaps the most telling experiments . . . are those which, adapting the methods of animal psychology to the examination of human thought, have repeatedly revealed the large amount of "typically animal" trial and error in human thinking under these conditions, and have repeatedly emphasized similarities rather than differences between human and animal performances. From the opposite standpoint . . . study of apes has also indicated the continuity of human with animal intelligence. And not only have the intellectual processes themselves been conceived as less rational than they seemed; such as they are and whatever they are, they have come to be viewed as far less decisive than they were formerly thought to be in determining human conduct. . . . There is a notable agreement among psychologists that the rational and cognitive sides of human nature have been enormously overemphasized in the past.
>   . . . The human beings psychology now studies . . . are creatures in whom emotion and impulse are powerful factors in determining conduct and

in whom reason seems less decisive than was long supposed. They are creatures, too, who seem not to be put together according to any very obvious mosaic plan of construction, whether of conscious elements or of motor reactions.

In the psychologists' view of mankind, there were many problems. What was the relation between the emotions (the old "heart") and physiology? In William James's influential view, the emotions were shadowy expressions of "the feelings" that arose when the organism was stimulated by various experiences ("we feel sorry because we cry"). This distinction was useful to "behaviorists" who sought to modify the physical experience of the organism, but it did not deter James himself from praising independent exertions of "the will" to gain control over feeling. Similarly, what was the relation between the individual's consciousness and the social environment? Those who placed greatest emphasis on the human organism often questioned the adequacy of genteel civilization to human emotional needs. When George M. Beard, for example, turned from the study of electricity to the subject of *American Nervousness* (1881), he warned that society, while wide open to intellectual expression, nevertheless required emotions to be "repressed." The consequence of "constant inhibition" was self-exhaustion. But any psychologist interested in "higher mental functions" and adaptations to environment might take a more positive view of the reciprocity between mind and society. In a few decades, some psychologists would be interested in how a corporation or society could manipulate the loyalties of its people—and even in the practical applications of psychology to advertising. The essential point, however, is that the didactic account of the faculties, which had formerly been the foundation for learning about self, nature, and society, had given way to vexing problems for research and experiment.

The psychologists may not be taken to represent all groups of intellectuals. Their greatest influence came later. Even in the universities, they were sometimes regarded as ungentlemanly assailants of religion and culture. To study people and animals in a laboratory or to focus on irrationality could seem like "dirty," morbid work rather than prestigious science. Nevertheless, departments were not so specialized that the interests of psychologists had no counterparts in other fields. Veblen was one of many social scientists who criticized atavistic and dysfunctional aspects of culture, who portrayed beliefs as "lagging" behind social evolution and "psychic factors" infiltrating even such rational structures as the law. Even in a humanistic field like history, eager young researchers gave up the romantic focus on great heroes and abiding ideals and sought a more objective view of selfish and group purposes in the evolution of institutions.

In some of the more popular forms of philosophical idealism, "rational man" may not have fared so badly. That is, ministers and lecturers who taught that the universe exemplified a rational, orderly form in the mind of God sometimes encouraged listeners to believe in a power in their consciousness capable of apprehending that higher reality. The purpose of life, in this view, might consist in perfecting human nature by rising to a higher degree of insight. Reason itself, however, was seldom invoked.

Harvard's Josiah Royce, the most celebrated and compelling university idealist, also eschewed the term *"reason."* It is striking, indeed, how completely Royce accepted the psychologists' view that in "the stream of consciousness" efforts to sort out intellect, will, and emotions were illusory. He also embraced the Darwinian view of thought processes as adjustments to the environment, with shared intellectual life consisting in large part of "memories, or hints, or fragments, of former adjustments." And to demolish the Scottish sense of the empirical self perceiving the natural world, he turned to studies of child development which proved that the self was meaningless without "social experience." The appeal of Royce's philosophy—for he is an unfortunately neglected American writer—lay in his efforts to provide an understanding of human life that went beyond "the little drama that is acted within the momentary limits of a finite consciousness." In this endeavor he rejected the familiar argument that there was a design in the universe that individuals could observe with awe. Instead, he worked from psychological aspects of fleeting experience—memory, making plans, intimacy and repulsion, shifting images of self, and creation of "idealizations"—to a moving statement of the impossibility of knowing "in time . . . that complete expression of my will, which in God, and for God, my whole life at once possesses." While for Royce the thrust of philosophy was toward consciousness of God as eternal and absolute, for our purposes he stands as a seeker of truth in a community of shifting and imperfectly understood experience. The universe *was* rational, but "since now we see through a glass darkly, you cannot expect at present to experience your human selfhood in any one consistent and final expression."

The ideology of culture occasionally sought to restore "rational man." But it did so only as expatiated by curmudgeons and misfits, by men gritting their teeth at what was more typically proclaimed in the name of culture. Disgruntled professors fought to retain classical languages so that students would learn ancient values like balance and temperance. E. L. Godkin of the *Nation* criticized the "mental and moral chaos" resulting from too much superficial education. True culture could not be popularized; it belonged to an elite who had learned mental discipline. But the bitterness of such protests reminds us that, in the main, culture—or "pseudo-culture" as Godkin called it—appealed to sentimental taste rather than rigorous intellectual striving. In the ideology of culture, commendable human traits were a concern for growth and health, the susceptibility to be moved by great literature, uncalculating devotion to the progress of great principles, and resistance to the temporary expedients of reason.

This is not the first period of American intellectual life in which we have noticed a degradation of reason. Despite Heidbreder's useful summary of turn-of-the-century psychology, it seems clear that previous generations had toppled Plato's charioteer and erected in its place the heart, the common sense, or intuition. But always there had remained some image of a hierarchy of faculties to keep lustful and antisocial passions under control. Perhaps such a hierarchy survived implicitly in culture and idealism (though Higginson saw "Passion, a hand straying freely through all the chords, and thrilling all with magic," as the source of living art). In any event, there now existed a professional subcommunity of analysts of human nature—the psychologists, plus some social scientists and philosophers—who cast down even the surrogate charioteers, who routinely viewed human beings as organisms adrift in a universe of changing and uncertain vectors. To some, life appeared highly dramaturgical, a set of flimsy conventions. To others, even sexual drives had an energetic force that could not constructively be repressed. (G. Stanley Hall compared Royce's idealistic "vagaries" to masturbation and insisted he knew of "cases" where the two went together.) How far this drifting biological view of human nature would win public acceptance was unknown, but it certainly posed difficult problems of "adjustment" for twentieth-century conceptions of the intellect.

In the short run, it was surprising that this view did not prove more unsettling. "Nothing seems more striking in comparative terms," concludes John Higham in a searching analysis of American culture of the 1890s, "than the relative absence in the United States of the radical subjectivity that was entering European thought." The hold of culture, the sense of social obligation, and the comforts of professional life were too strong for many intellectuals to venture into radical experiments in art or philosophy that did not communicate earnestly, even cheerfully, with the public. Any reader of Carl E. Schorske's *Fin-de-Siècle Vienna* (1980) will be impressed anew by the complacent perimeters of intellectual life in fin-de-siècle America, by the paucity of pronouncements that a coherent culture had fragmented and that it was pointless to try any longer to make sense in public. Schorske presents creative minds toying with shards of fractured meaning, exploring interior voids, assailing privileged systems of disquisition. A period of extraordinary creativity was also, in Europe, a period of incoherence and disenchantment. What was different in America that kept even the most adventurous minds on a safer course?

Higham suggests that the United States was a large country with a social order sufficiently fluid for intellectuals to take advantage of opportunities to extend their experience and influence. "For Americans the external world retained a promise of ultimate goodness and harmony," and both genteel celebrants of culture and pragmatic analysts of social problems were likely to deplore the "morbidity" and "egoism" of Europe. Though some worried about the closing of the frontier, most felt that American society offered adequate "elbow room" for intellectual careers. We should not forget the security and "reputability" that the mass literary markets and established universities extended to those seeking careers in a nation that appeared to be consolidating a century of advance toward international preeminence. Many of Schorske's key figures in Austrian history—Sigmund Freud, in particular—felt frustrated and imprisoned by institutions closed to them as a tolerant, progressive order seemed to be crumbling. They experienced crises of professional rejection in a context of political disintegration, mass hostility to culture, and bigotry. Since history and social order were no longer repositories of confidence, creative minds turned inward. How different was the outlook of middle-class Americans who left small towns and entered circles of "respectable opinion," who felt it was possible to "democratize culture," and who were experiencing—despite the undermining of eternal verities—increasing public confidence in the progressive use of expert intelligence.

The point is hard to document, but it seems doubtful that intellect was losing ground despite the newly current views of human psychology. The key battles had been fought and forgotten in previous eras. In Emerson's generation, theologians had worried about views of science degenerating into "fragments of atoms, floating hither and thither, without centre of attraction or bond of unity"; critics of the transcendentalists had been concerned over the submergence of authority in a sea of private judgments; orators had hymned the advantages of ceaseless change; and young intellectuals in the South had linked their reputations to the defense of slavery while their northern counterparts had warred against the monstrous sin that corrupted polite institutions. These conflicts over subjectivity and power lay in the past, and society now seemed calmer and more secure. Few intellectuals, even among the settlement workers, allied themselves with labor protest. Instead they defined themselves in a series of new intellectual subcommunities. Thousands of professors, scientists, engineers, and writers—many of them first-generation intellectuals—knew themselves to be men and women of training and intellect. "The college-bred," as James called them, were healthy critics and constructive functionaries in society. They were responsible citizens, the technicians of a brightly unfolding future. The uncertainties of the age of reorganization lay in the past; they knew nothing of the anti-intellectualism and disillusionment of subsequent decades. (Schorske finds an analogue to fin-de-siècle Vienna in post–World War II America.) Unmoored as the concept of intellect may have been, the turn of the century may well have been the high water mark of confidence and reputation among intellectuals in America.

FOR FURTHER READING

Alan Trachtenberg's *The Incorporation of America* (1982) is an interesting brief survey of American culture during the Gilded Age. Another useful survey is Howard Mumford Jones's *The Age of Energy* (1971). A wide range of documents can be found in Neil Harris, ed., *The Land of Contrasts* (1970); Henry Nash Smith, ed., *Popular Culture and Industrialism* (1967); and Perry Miller, ed., *American Thought: Civil War to World War I* (1954).

For sensitive interpretations of change in intellectual life, see two essays by John Higham: *From Boundlessness to Consolidation* (1969), and "The Reorientation of American Culture in the 1890's," in *Writing American History* (1970). See also Larzer Ziff, *The American 1890s* (1966).

Two useful studies of genteel culture are Stow Persons, *The Decline of American Gentility* (1973), and John Tomsich, *A Genteel Endeavor* (1971). A good starting point for analyzing Victorianism is the special issue on "Victorian Culture in America," *American Quarterly* (1975). See also William G. McLoughlin, *The Meaning of Henry Ward Beecher* (1970). Indispensable on the English background are Walter E. Houghton, *The Victorian Frame of Mind* (1957), and Raymond Williams, *Culture and Society* (1958).

The best book on the universities is Laurence R. Veysey's *The Emergence of the American University* (1965). There are many good studies of individual universities, of their presidents, and of leading scholars. On more general topics, recommended works are Dorothy Ross, "Socialism and American Liberalism: Academic Social Thought in the 1880s," *Perspectives in American History* (1978); Thomas L. Haskell, *The Emergence of Professional Science* (1977); and Burton Bledstein, *The Culture of Professionalism* (1976). There are several valuable essays on specialized intellectual life in Alexandra Oleson and John Voss, eds., *The Organization of Knowledge in Modern America* (1979).

On doubt and anxiety in religious thought, see Paul A. Carter, *The Spiritual Crisis of the Gilded Age* (1971). The most reliable guide to religious responses to Darwinism is James R. Moore, *The Post-Darwinian Controversies* (1979). On other dimensions of religion, see Henry F. May, *The Protestant Churches and Industrial America* (1949), and William R. Hutchinson, *The Modernist Impulse in American Protestantism* (1976).

The most accessible historical approach to the pragmatists is through the biographical essays in Paul K. Conkin, *Puritans & Pragmatists* (1968). Bruce Kuklick's *The Rise of American Philosophy* (1977) focuses on the intellectual context at Harvard, and David Hollinger takes a broader historical view in "The Problem of Pragmatism in American History," *Journal of American History* (1980). For two different perspectives on early psychology, see Dorothy Ross, *G. Stanley Hall* (1972), and Nathan G. Hale, Jr., *Freud and the Americans* (1971). A probing interpretation of the psychological strains of industrialization as they surfaced in cultural life is T. Jackson Lears, *No Place of Grace* (1981).

VII

MODERNITY
AND
SERVICE

CULTURAL RELATIVISM

In the years between World War I and World War II, years
that included a decade of widely celebrated prosperity and
another of unrelenting depression, the ideology of culture crumbled. Nothing seemed plainer to intellectuals than
the dependence of great systems of faith and reason on
hidden motives and irrational fetishes and prejudices.
During this period the iconoclastic journalist H. L.
Mencken launched regular attacks on the cruel hypocri-
sies of Puritanism; and widely read historians like Vernon
Louis Parrington, Charles A. Beard, and Mary Beard exposed the manipulation of democratic ideals by commercial interests. In a famous critique of the Enlightenment,
Carl L. Becker in 1932 spoke of "magic words" through
which a historical age conceals its guiding assumptions,
words that scarcely need definition but convey tacit views
of "the way things work" or "the way things ought to be."
Even the Age of Reason had been saturated with unex-
amined prejudices; history in general was characterized not
by intellectual progress but by a succession of "climates of
opinion."

[319]

INTELLECTUAL LIFE IN AMERICA

To notice that such suspicion of hidden assumptions flourished in the particular climate of the interwar era is not to discredit it as an aid to historical inquiry. Certainly it is valid to regard some of the key terms of late-nineteenth-century Victorian gentility as "magic words." In fact, it was partly in reaction to an era when so many customs and beliefs had been upheld as "verities" that suspicion became such an attractive intellectual posture. As we have seen, no word had been imbued with vaguer and more potent magic than "culture," the defining quality of an educated and idealistic stratum in a society concerned about class division and materialistic habits. It is of particular significance, therefore, that the genteel term *culture* was extensively reexamined after World War I.

This reexamination proceeded with greatest clarity in the new discipline of anthropology, particularly in the publications and Columbia University seminars of Franz Boas. Born and educated in Germany, Boas was committed to the tradition of close observation of scientific data; yet he was also philosophically troubled that the meanings of data shifted in accordance with the viewpoints of different observers. Instead of impeding inquiry, this problem became the focus of the new science to which Boas furnished pioneering and influential leadership. The meaning of a material or spiritual fact—a blanket, a musical instrument, or a religious tale—existed only in terms of the cultural whole of which it was a part. By spending fifteen months in 1883–1884 among the Eskimos and succeeding years among other tribes of the Pacific Northwest, Boas found confirmation for his belief that "the idea of a 'cultured' individual is merely relative" to the system of meanings in which that individual grew up and lived.

Boas took exception to an evolutionary view of human history derived from the old schema of civility and savagery and given new force by supposedly Darwinian accounts of biological "progress." The evolutionary view detected one recurrent pattern of development in which human races moved from primitive to higher forms of civilization. This view, Boas wrote, ignored "the relative value of all forms of culture," took our own period as "the ultimate goal of human evolution," and deprived us of "the benefits to be gained from the teachings of other cultures." The point was not that the so-called primitive cultures were fixed and unchanging; their ways of life reflected complex responses to historical experiences that fit no preconceived pattern. And they could not be ranked, or even understood, according to intellectual systems drawn from the history of Europe and the United States.

Furthermore, Boas believed that in the culture of any given people, those elements that Europeans and Americans tended to rate as "higher"—political rites and religious beliefs—were really secondary responses to deeper human needs that had to be satisfied in the midst of drift and change. All cultures had a physiological and psychological basis that required the anthropologist to be alert to everyday life and common emotions rather than to ideals and formalities. Boas tended to be skeptical of the possibility of discovering scientific laws about any level of experience: "not only our ability and knowledge but also the manner and ways of our feeling and thinking [are] the result of our upbringing as individuals and our history as a people." This skepticism led to criticism of Boasian anthropology in the second half of the twentieth century, when "structuralists" in various fields were once again emboldened to seek fundamental likenesses in human culture. But for Boas and his followers the most exciting prospect was to see the diversity of human responses to experience. They sought to divest themselves of preconceptions and to immerse themselves in fieldwork among "peoples whose perspectives and development have almost nothing in common with our own."

Boas was a scholarly specialist who, for most of his life, had little to say on topical issues. His intellectual concerns sprang from philosophical problems that had arisen in Western science and from the extraordinary observations he made among Eskimos and Kwakiutls, far away from American public life. Yet he repeatedly hinted that the anthropological conception of culture liberated us from the prejudice that "our" civilization was absolutely superior to others. Even "emotional reactions which we feel as natural are in reality culturally determined," and anthropology "opens to us the possibility of judging our own culture objectively." Although he offered such hints as early as the 1880s, this German scholar was scarcely mentioned in the prevailing late-Victorian discussion of culture. After World War I, however, his students showed a remarkable flair for publicizing the idea of "cultural relativism" in literary magazines and best-selling books.

In 1919 Edward Sapir distinguished "genuine" from "spurious" cultures in the *Dial*, a new magazine whose editorial board included John Dewey and Thorstein Veblen, a magazine explicitly dedicated to the task of "reconstructing" society after World War I. Indian societies, Sapir explained, encouraged both group cohesion and the spiritual fulfillment of individuals—qualities sadly lacking, as the war had shown, in the supposedly advanced civilizations. In *Coming of Age in Samoa* (1928) and *Growing Up in New Guinea* (1930), Margaret Mead taught a large readership that there was nothing natural or inevitable in the tensions and frustrations of adolescence in repressive industrial societies; some of the supposedly primitive cultures treated this stage of life much more successfully. In an article in the *Century* magazine (1929) and in her book,

Patterns of Culture (1934), Ruth Benedict used the Indians of the Southwest to contrast cooperative and competitive modes of human intercourse. The influence of Boas's students extended beyond a year or two; their works stood as essential texts of American higher education for at least three decades. More than any other group, they were responsible for demolishing Victorian certainties about culture.

Within the social sciences, particularly sociology, the reconceptualization of culture had lasting consequences. Charles Horton Cooley in *Social Process* (1922) dismissed the Victorian view as "a decoration or a refuge or a mystical superiority"; a true culture was nothing less than "growth to fuller membership in the human organism." To see culture as "relative" suggested the possibility of a detached vantage point from which the trained observer could detect the conflicts and shortcomings of American adjustments to modern conditions. Sometimes social scientists tried to suspend their own values and to be as neutral as fieldworkers in the midst of an Indian tribe, but there was a decided temptation to take the stance of a cultural critic. In their two studies of *Middletown* (1929, 1937) in times of prosperity and depression, works that remained essential educational texts for decades, Robert S. Lynd and Helen M. Lynd uncovered patterns of unhappiness and unfulfillment in the "culture" of midwesterners, whom they regarded as typical of American life in general. And in *Knowledge for What?* (1939) Robert S. Lynd faulted other social scientists who refrained from cultural criticism and thus neglected their responsibility to point the way toward reconstruction. But even for scholars who were less certain what our culture was and what was wrong with it, the term *culture* was central to analyzing the demands of society and the basic needs of individuals. In *Culture* (1952), an inventory of varying definitions of the term, A. L. Kroeber and Clyde Kluckholn came across so many scores of meanings that there was nothing to do but list them. Victorian confidence in a single uplifting form of culture had long since been shattered.

The redefinition of culture began to create an aura of subdued crisis in humanistic fields. Instructors in Western Civilization courses or lecturers on touchstones of literary appreciation might be regarded as guardians of a discredited tradition. This is not to deny that humanities instruction expanded (Robert S. Lynd charged that university presidents promoted the liberal arts in order to distract attention from the more controversial, critical work of social scientists). But an unmistakable defensiveness surrounded efforts to foster awareness of the classics of Western culture in a milieu where culture itself appeared to be a highly relative concept. Some widely read historians, like Becker, adopted a witty attitude toward fluctuations in the "climate of opinion" from one era to the next; others sought to develop a "New History" relevant to solving modern problems and building a better civilization. Even those professors of literature who clung to Victorian notions of "the best which has been thought and said" were hard put to show the relevance of their teachings to contemporary literature. In the world outside their departments lurked too many men of letters who despised the tradition of Howells and Longfellow, who scorned the comforts of genteel taste, and who championed the new and modern.

REBELS AND EXILES

Incisive as the writings of Sapir, Mead, and Benedict were, it is hard to imagine them gaining much public notice without a general shift in perspective that occurred among professional writers and their audiences. After all, Boas had addressed the relativity of culture for decades without much public fanfare. His students wrote English more attractively than he did, but his own reputation rose along with theirs in a post–World War I milieu in which youthful experiments and yearnings for reconstruction gave a new tone to literary circles.

Perhaps it is misleading to say "post–World War I." The rebels of 1919 were aware of experimental writers who preceded them—particularly Theodore Dreiser, Edward Arlington Robinson, Edgar Lee Masters, Carl Sandburg, and others who had bucked the genteel tradition. There were statements of comradeship with Walt Whitman. And Lewis Mumford's *Herman Melville* (1929) culminated a campaign to rescue a major author from the oblivion into which he had fallen in the canons of polite taste.

In addition, as the historian Henry May has argued persuasively, most signs of rebellion were evident in the years immediately preceding the war. In poetry, T. S. Eliot, Ezra Pound, William Carlos Williams, and others were already experimenting with free forms of verse that struck genteel critics as defying all respected ideals and regularities. Indeed, Louis Untermeyer attributed Eliot's "Love Song of J. Alfred Prufrock" (1915) to "the muse of a psychopathic ward drinking the stale dregs of revolt." In art, the photographer Alfred Stieglitz had opened his own New York art gallery where he exhibited the works of Matisse, Cézanne, and other radical European painters, as an alternative to stuffy showcases for the rich. The Armory Show of 1913 appalled older critics with its display of cubist and other nonrepresentational works; but it was a financial success. In drama, by 1916 Eugene O'Neill had joined forces with the Provincetown Players, and a new era seemed at hand. The New York offices of new magazines were havens for men and women who embraced an exciting new identification: they were the "young intellec-

tuals" or the "new intelligentsia." The *Masses* (founded
1911), a "REVOLUTIONARY" magazine with "NO RE-
SPECT FOR THE RESPECTABLE," published works by
Max Eastman, John Reed, Floyd Dell, and other literary
socialists. The *New Republic* (1914) gave a forum to young
analysts of society like Walter Lippmann, who was turning to the authority of the psychoanalyst Sigmund Freud
in order to attack the barren political rationalism of the
past. *Seven Arts* (1916) featured Van Wyck Brooks, Randolph Bourne, and Waldo Frank, among other aspirants
for an American renaissance that would overturn the sterile
genteel tradition; its contributors included John Dos Passos and Robert Frost. Just to mention these few names is
to observe how many of the liberating voices of the interwar decades were already calling for a new order in the
arts and society. Greenwich Village in New York, where
many of them lived, became a jazzy national symbol for
political radicalism, free love, and literary experiment.*

In the opinion of some, the charm and creativity of
Village life in the postwar years fell victim to urban
congestion and the transient fashions of revolt. Yet the
memoirs of intellectuals who reshaped literary culture indicate that their work made greatest headway after 1919.
To be sure, the dream of reconstruction died rather
abruptly. Lewis Mumford recalls in *Sketches from Life* (1982)
that New York "never wore a brighter look" than in 1919.
Recording his share of bright hopes and romantic adventures in the city literary scene, he writes:

> The term Reconstruction has become unintelligi-
> ble now, in the sense it was used in 1919. . . . Re-
> construction here carried the hopeful notion that

---

*Warren Beatty's film *Reds* (1981) vividly reconstructs Greenwich Village life in this era.

the war had given each country such a jolt that
every institution, shaken off its ancient base, would
be searchingly re-examined and reshaped on a
more humane pattern—as if the invisible structure
of men's minds were as accessible and as open to
reorganization as shell-pocked fields or broken-
down bridges. It now seems strange to think that
. . . Reconstruction . . . could for even a short
while have seemed so full of promise.

In New York State a Reconstruction Commission in which
intellectuals joined hands with bankers, businessmen, and
other professionals labored to advise Governor Alfred E.
Smith in the 1920s. Yet the general feeling was, as Mumford puts it, that these "bright dreams faded out," submerged beneath "the deepest slough of 'normalcy,' as that
blandly corrupt nonentity, Warren Harding, who became
our postwar President, called it." But the dreams came to
life again during Franklin Roosevelt's New Deal, "sometimes, as with public housing, on a scale and with a swift-
ness that surprised even those of us who believed in them."

It tells us much about the wide-ranging interests of
interwar men of letters that Mumford wrote on both Melville and public housing. It was typical of the experience
of many of these intellectuals that they felt their interests
to be out of phase with political realities in the 1920s,
coming to fruition only during the depression decade.

The belief that talented writers were at odds with
American society during the 1920s gave rise to the image
of a "lost generation."* In *Exile's Return* (1934) Malcolm

---

*The phrase comes from a remark of the expatriate poet Gertrude Stein:
"You are all a lost generation." Ernest Hemingway took it as an epi-
graph for *The Sun Also Rises* (1926), a novel that popularized images
of the wanderings of Americans in France and Spain.

Cowley discounted many of his friends' self-dramatizations, but he still traced an epic of tremendous importance for understanding the transformed beliefs of "the American educated classes." His own journey from western Pennsylvania paralleled those of many other young writers from middle America. At college they had been "deracinated": exposed to an academic "culture" that was little more than a "veneer," that had no relation to the outside world, they lost "our own culture, such as it was, . . . receiving nothing real in exchange." Scores of them went to Europe, serving as truck and ambulance drivers during the war or wandering as expatriates in the 1920s. Among the results was "a spectatorial attitude," a feeling that America "wasn't our country any longer." Their suspicion of old moralities and Victorian sentiments was personified by Hemingway's hero in *A Farewell to Arms* (1929), who said: "I was always embarrassed by the words *sacred, glorious,* and *sacrifice,* and the expression *in vain.*"

Some replaced visions of old homesteads with images of exotic places that somehow promised an alternative to America. In *Axel's Castle* (1931), one of the earliest and most important analyses of "modern" literature, Edmund Wilson discussed two options that seemed open to the artist—to concoct unreal worlds of symbolism or "to find the good life in some country where modern manufacturing methods and modern democratic institutions do not present any problems to the artist because they haven't yet arrived." But these escapes were ephemeral and unsatisfying, no better than the drinking binges and suicides that Cowley and other chroniclers of the 1920s recounted. Ultimately, the epic ended in "return," in an ambivalent endeavor to make a literary life in America, which was, for all its failings, native ground. Writers returned with reverent attitudes toward art that distanced them from "the masses," but they returned to work in popular publishing houses and advertising firms. It is not hard to understand the attraction, in this literary milieu, of the anthropologists' claims that all cultures are relative and that some of them give young people more genuine help in growing up.

In the epic that Cowley sketched may be seen two paradoxical consequences. First, a pattern of deracination and alienation became a leading complaint about the life of an intellectual in America. In fact, alienation and marginality became badges of creativity and independence— an ironic reversal of older conceptions of the public responsibilities of the cultivated classes. Second, there was an unanticipated discovery that industrial America had room, and even prestige, to offer the alienated. There were literary jobs that made it possible to construct comfortable, semirural lives in Connecticut, New Jersey, and Pennsylvania; even Hollywood had its own rewards and snares. The public implications of private revolt were more insidious. The self-dramatized rebellions of Greenwich Village types really took place on a public stage; they strengthened the connections between popular culture and consumerism. After all, self-denying "culture"—as Higginson had defined it, for example—had been opposed to materialism; youth revolt could signal a new concern for personal satisfaction. In one of his most ironic passages, Cowley pointed out how the rebels turned into a "vanguard of new styles of buying and spending":

> Thus, *self-expression* and *paganism* encouraged a demand for all sorts of products—modern furniture, beach pajamas, cosmetics, colored bathrooms with toilet paper to match. *Living for the moment* meant buying an automobile, radio or house, using it now and paying for it tomorrow. *Female equality* was capable of doubling the consumption

of products—cigarettes, for example—that had formerly been used by men alone. . . . The exiles of art were also trade missionaries: involuntarily they increased the foreign demand for fountain pens, silk stockings, grapefruit and portable type-writers. They drew after them an invading army of tourists, thus swelling the profits of steamship lines and travel agencies. Everything fitted into the business picture.

Cowley was careful to add that Greenwich Village did not by itself alter consumer habits and that business had not deliberately plotted "to render the nation extravagant, pleasure worshipping and reckless of tomorrow." But he was conscious of the capacities of a new economy to ab-sorb gestures of creative eccentricity and defiance—ca-pacities that may remind some readers of the fate of the "youth culture" of the 1960s.

COSMOPOLITANISM
AND THE PEOPLE

Writers who came to maturity in the 1920s have re-hearsed in their memoirs the curious interplay between individual quest and cultural change. If Mumford re-minds us of dreams of reconstruction and Cowley of the paradoxes of alienation and consumerism, these were simply facets of the work of an interwar generation of men and women of letters who refashioned intellectual life in America. We are discussing perhaps fifty persons of sig-nificant literary accomplishment and several hundred more who worked for magazines and publishing houses, mostly in New York, and who offered books, articles, and poems of their own. Their positions often depended on the centralization of cultural institutions. Acutely aware of the distances they had traveled from small towns and ethnic neighborhoods, most of them sought to measure American attainments by standards they considered modern and cosmopolitan. If they embraced anthropological insights and hoped for greater communal solidarity and self-expression, this was only a tactical stance along the way to an artistic renaissance in America. With few exceptions, they retained an old-fashioned concern for a literary achievement that would ennoble a materially advancing civilization—not by politeness but by striking originality. There were enormous contradictions in the search. They were keenly interested in the state of popular culture: would great art uplift it or defy it? And they were uncertain what to make of America's folk backgrounds: would great art reveal idiosyncratic creativity, or would it spring from the rhythms of American speech and humor?

As with so many other movements, the defining preoccupations of these intellectuals are most easily defined in negative terms. They were "modernists" because they repudiated the Victorian world view that we have called the ideology of culture. Often they echoed Santayana's complaints about the discrepancy between pretentious idealism and the vital realities of social life. Van Wyck Brooks assailed the lifeless "highbrow" and "lowbrow" cultures in his essay, "America's Coming-of-Age" (1915); Randolph Bourne attacked unquestioned prejudices in "This Older Generation" (1920); Lewis Mumford accused American culture of "blankness" and "boredom" in *The Golden Day* (1926); and Cowley borrowed Santayana's terminology to characterize the new aspirations of American literature in *After the Genteel Tradition* (1937). Cowley took particular note of the Nobel Prize acceptance speech (1930) by Sinclair Lewis, the first American to win the prize, with its bitter remarks on "the divorce in America of intellectual life from all authentic standards of importance and reality."

But where could authentic standards be found? Modernism took for granted the impossibility of permanent, consensual answers to this question. Modernism was frequently associated with a frank critical attitude toward actual life and, just as frequently, with a heightened interest in artistic forms and symbols. It attended to spontaneous expressions of the people as opposed to "genteel" or commercialized formulas, but also, just as frequently, it acclaimed radically experimental works that left most people unmoved. It featured attacks on morality, probing looks at sexual and other "animal" instincts, and an atheistical attitude toward universal flux; yet some modernists, like T. S. Eliot, became political and religious conservatives, and many were impressed with the powers of intellect to impose order on experience. Modernism was an international style of repudiating nineteenth-century regularities and verities. In America, it seldom reached the rebellious, incomprehensible "dadaistic" depths characteristic of some European movements, because of two recurring and overlapping preoccupations: the wish to justify American attainments in the highest cosmopolitan terms, and the wish to discover valuable sources of feeling in American life.

This group of intellectuals took pride in their openness and cosmopolitanism. Men and women who were more conscious than previous intellectuals of their marginality to the rest of society, they were unable, for the most part, to conceive themselves as a natural aristocracy or a guiding cultivated class. At best, they were critics of society or fugitives on a lonely journey. Unprotected as a group by class prerogatives, they were relatively free of special distinctions of race, gender, and social class among themselves. All of them looked with disdain on the standard fare of ladies' culture in the past and present, but among serious writers there was little difference in the standards of judgment applied to females as opposed to males. Marianne Moore, Edna St. Vincent Millay, Willa Cather, and Lillian Hellman escaped the pejorative sphere of the nineteenth-century "scribbling women." In this respect, the world of free-lance letters had a more attractive record, by late-twentieth-century standards, than did political, religious, or academic institutions where discrimination by gender remained common practice. Part of the lure of modernism was a new experimental attitude toward sexual equality.

The record with regard to blacks was not so bright, mainly because society as a whole was less resistant to women's rights (as evident in the constitutional amendment favoring women's suffrage) than to equal rights for blacks. An example may help to recall the color line: when O'Neill in *Emperor Jones* (1921) wrote a major role for a black actor, instead of a white in comic blackface, he had to go to Macy's to find an actor, Charles Gilpin, who worked there as an elevator operator. When Gilpin's performance won awards, the New York Drama League threatened to bar him from their annual dinner until protests from other winners broke the barrier down. Nevertheless, the modernist movement provided a matrix of encouragement for the black literary movement known as the Harlem Renaissance, and the free-verse experiments of black poets Langston Hughes and Countee Cullen earned critical praise that would once have been unthinkable. A few black writers, like Jean Toomer, mingled easily among Greenwich Village literati. At the same time, condescension and literary fashion grated against the sensibilities of talented young blacks who wished to be known, first and foremost, as writers rather than as voices out of Harlem. There is justice in the ironic title of David Levering Lewis's book, *When Harlem Was in Vogue* (1981). In the 1930s, as intellectual groups became more political—particularly within the Communist party—contact between blacks and whites became more frequent and egalitarian. But there is still testimony that some blacks resented exploitation by intellectual comrades and patrons. Even so, compared with the organization of intellectual life in previous eras, the new spirit of openness was striking.

Ethnic and cultural diversity was a new, exhilarating quality of the world of letters, especially in New York. The most extraordinary change in intellectual life was the suspension of belief in a unitary culture that required either the "Americanization" or the exclusion of foreigners. As early as 1916, Bourne had welcomed reports of "vigorous nationalistic and cultural movements" among immigrants; perhaps America would transcend the "parochialism" of the ideology of culture. The schools and settlements would have to give these movements a place in shaping a new "trans-national" civilization. The Anglo-Saxon college student who made friends with foreign-born young men and women had already discovered new perspectives. His friends were "oblivious to the repressions of that tight little society in which he so provincially grew up. He has a pleasurable sense of liberation from the stale and familiar attitudes of those whose ingrowing culture has scarcely created anything vital for his America of to-day." The next step, as Bourne foresaw it, would be for the student's broadened perspectives to become characteristic of American life in general. Such hopes did not gain much respect in society at large for twenty years, but they provided one of the strongest internal attractions of the emerging urban literary life. While Cowley's *Exile's Return* retraced the epic of southerners and midwesterners who came to New York via Europe, it should be added that they joined forces there with Jews who, after migrating to America, were expanding their own knowledge of world culture.

This pattern was already evident before World War I. German Jews nearly dominated the editorial boards of the *New Republic* and *Seven Arts;* one of them welcomed Van Wyck Brooks's and Bourne's affiliation with the latter magazine because it relieved "the onus of being non-Anglo-Saxon." Another praised the *Liberator,* a 1920 successor to the *Masses,* as a model of "that ideal society which we all wanted," a society without racial barriers and merging the great insights of all traditions. Outside the little magazines, the New York scene was also illuminated by the presence of Jewish intellectuals born in Eastern Europe, of whom Morris Cohen was the most celebrated. As professor of philosophy at City College of New York, Cohen had a domineering teaching style and a faith in permanent values somewhat in conflict with the modernist outlook; but his undisputed eminence at a municipal college symbolizing the openness of intellectual life in America made him a revered figure in the self-consciously cosmopolitan milieu. By the 1930s a new generation of Jewish intellectuals—like Alfred Kazin, Lionel Trilling, and the brilliant circle who founded *Partisan Review* (1934)—could take for granted an exciting subculture generally committed to modernism in art and left-liberal views in politics. What little remained of the expectation that Protestants educated at Ivy League colleges should dominate a gentlemanly world of literature was even further shattered by the diaspora of Jews and liberals from fascist Europe. Expatriation began to run in a new direction: instead of Americans taking off to Europe, Europeans were finding refuge here. The "cosmopolitan culture" of America became a matter of intense, frequently articulated pride.

The rise of this circle of city intellectuals was not greeted with acclaim throughout the nation. Long-standing resentments of eastern domination were, at worst, mingled with new strains of anti-Semitism and antiradicalism. Serious signs of discontent appeared in a series of important works on the abiding sectional differences and the distinctive geographical cultures of America. Frederick Jackson Turner turned from the frontier to *The Significance of Sections in American History* (1932), and Bernard De Voto praised the richness and vitality of *Mark Twain's America* (1932). In a seminal scholarly work, Walter Prescott Webb of Texas discussed the transforming effect on civilization of *The Great Plains* (1931); more polemically, he assailed eastern monetary and cultural domination in *Divided We Stand* (1937). The academic study of American history fell within the purview of the Mississippi Valley Historical Association, which had little room for women, blacks, or Jews, for modernism or cosmopolitanism.

Yet in one section, the South, modernism received as sharp an expression as in New York. It has long been something of a puzzle that a section often considered economically and culturally backward—"the nation's number one economic problem," according to the Franklin Roosevelt administration, and a horrid land of lynchings and labor violence in the minds of northern intellectuals—should have fostered many of the most accomplished writers and critics of the modernist movement in America, among them, Allen Tate, John Crowe Ransom, Cleanth Brooks, William Faulkner, and Robert Penn Warren. Furthermore, nowhere else were the Boasian and Freudian doctrines of culture and psychology turned so relentlessly to regional self-criticism as in the sociological works of Howard Odum and his associates at the University of North Carolina. Surely the South had none of the cosmopolitan advantages of Proust's and Joyce's Paris; it had little of the ethnic and cultural diversity found in New York. But most of the southern literati had wandered outside the region: Faulkner had been a Royal Air Force flier in World War I, and Tate had loved Greenwich Village before recoiling from its bewildering freedom. Moreover, all were well read in cosmopolitan literature, and most found intense intellectual comradeship in places like Chapel Hill, Nashville, and New Orleans. Though their major works appeared through New York houses, they cherished their own little magazines, the *Fugitive, Sewanee Review, Southern Review,* and *Social Forces.* We should be wary of the image, which Faulkner in particular enjoyed presenting to outsiders, of solitary geniuses in a climate of primitivism and decadence. Though they wrote much of loneliness and tragedy, they were not really on their own as they wrote for an international audience. Nevertheless, it was by returning from cosmopolitan circles and writing on southern themes that most of them discovered their place in modernist literature.

The solution to the puzzle, as Daniel Joseph Singal recently pointed out, lies in recognizing the tenacity of Victorian culture in the South. There was an atmosphere of "evasive idealism," to use the words of the transitional novelist Ellen Glasgow, in which the conventions of respectability blended with myths of cavalier gentility and visions of an industrialized future. While writers in New York appreciated the openness of America, even while they complained of deracination and struggled for self-expression, the southerners felt burdened by a sense of historical hypocrisy and unacknowledged evil.

The burden could be shifted in different ways. In the famous symposium *I'll Take My Stand* (1930), Tate, Ransom, and ten colleagues sought to recover a simple agrarian civilization superior to the industrial model promoted from the Northeast. No one can reduce Faulkner's fictional world to capsulized meanings, but Singal emphasizes its modernist endeavor to observe, from many angles of vision, the complexities of achieving a human sense of identity amid a history mingling great evil with moments of honor. And some of the sociologists gazed almost exclusively at the brutal underside of southern gentility. What is most impressive, however, is the regularity with which southern writers—Tate, Ransom, and Warren, most notably—turned from regional issues to the disturbing loss of faith that followed the shattering of Victorian culture. On the one hand, they searched for a fulfilling cause and an enduring tradition. On the other, they promoted literary theories that were far removed from the old faith in progress, theories of "New Criticism" that detached the work of art from its historical contexts, giving no answers to perennial questions beyond the tension between intellect and emotion crystalized in the symbols and form of a single text. Nothing was possible except internal snatches of meaning in a culture without verities; a searing self-knowledge replaced confidence in the uplifting progress of history. One of the great ironies of the post-Victorian literary world was the absorption of the antiparochial culture of New York in the profound uncertainties of Tate's "Ode to the Confederate Dead" or Faulkner's novels of Yoknapatawpha County.

When Cowley's exiles returned to America, they often looked to folk experience for sources of authentic American art. If we compare them with Higginson and late-

nineteenth-century men of letters, we notice a similar interest in artistic standards upheld in European capitals and
a similar stress on the nationally redeeming possibilities of
literature. While Higginson and other custodians of culture had adopted a "progressive" view of great literature
civilizing the simple preoccupations of the folk, however,
many intellectuals of the 1920s and 1930s directed their
curiosity toward the uninstructed genius of ordinary people. Among the people might be found a lode of myths
and songs, dreams and tales, much nobler than the out-
put of Tin Pan Alley, Madison Avenue, and Hollywood.

The most telling instance of the new attitude toward
the folk appeared in the career of Constance Rourke.
Brought up in Grand Rapids, Michigan, Rourke went east
for her education, made a tour of Europe, returned to
teach at Vassar, and then went back to Grand Rapids,
where she lived as a free-lance writer and wrote a series
of books on folk culture, of which the best remembered
is *American Humor* (1931). Anxious to get past the intellectuals' habitual disparagement of the sterility of "lowbrow"
culture, she redirected attention to the spontaneous fun
and myth-making traditions of common Americans. Aware
of English scholarship on the folk-religious origins of the
"high" art form of Greek drama, she came close to reiter-
ating George Bancroft's faith that all significant creations
in the upper reaches of culture had their roots in the re-
sourcefulness of the people. Though she was sometimes
criticized by contemporaries for turning her back on
modern art and lavishing praise on minstrel shows and
yankee peddlers (and more recently by academic folklorists for mixing commercialized popular culture together
with authentic folk sources), her influence was considerable. Even Van Wyck Brooks, the sternest critic of America's lack of a "usable past," admitted that she deepened
his appreciation of America's heritage. Perhaps if intellec-

tuals moved closer to the people, they would see something more than materialism and pretension.

Rourke's move back to Grand Rapids in 1916 was a prophetic gesture heralding countless other endeavors to narrow the gap between intellectual status and folk vitality. In this context we may think of white patronage of the Harlem Renaissance, the intellectuals' interest in jazz, prize-winning plays about black life such as Paul Green's *In Abraham's Bosom* (1927) and Marc Connelly's *Green Pastures* (1930), and collections of black folklore by southern scholars such as Edward C. L. Adams's *Congaree Sketches* (1927), Guy B. Johnson's *John Henry* (1929), and Howard Odum's "Black Ulysses" trilogy—*Rainbow Round My Shoulder* (1928), *Wings on My Feet* (1929), and *Cold Blue Moon* (1931). To this list may be added the most powerful opera in the American repertory, George Gershwin and DuBose Heyward's *Porgy and Bess* (1935). But the list does not stop with works about black life; the score of the great "modern" dancer Martha Graham's best-known work, *Appalachian Spring* (1944), used an old Shaker melody to hold together a sequence of folk rites. There were commercially successful efforts to distract the public's mind in distressing times by recalling the simple emotions of country life. One interesting example was the novel *State Fair* (1932) by an Iowa-born journalist, Phil Stong, who had first gained public notice by befriending the Italian anarchists Nicola Sacco and Bartolomeo Vanzetti and recording their death-cell conversation. The novel was turned into a musical in 1945. Similarly, Lynn Riggs's "folk-play" *Green Grow the Lilacs* (1931) became the musical comedy *Oklahoma* (1943). By that time the white Okies had been treated in less sentimental fashion in John Steinbeck's novel *The Grapes of Wrath* (1939), turned into a movie by John Ford and a "folk" song by Woody Guthrie.

Some of these examples suggest an accommodation

between folk themes and modern forms of art and entertainment. Others indicate a new reliance on the camera,
recording devices, and technological improvements. In the
1930s government programs, particularly the Federal
Writers Project, with the combined purposes of employing artists and transcribing rural life, intensified the intellectuals' campaign to record and photograph the folk. One
result was a compilation of the memories of ex-slaves, given
book form as *Lay My Burden Down* (1947). The director of
that project was a Boston Jew, Benjamin Botkin, educated at Harvard and the University of Nebraska, a teacher
in Oklahoma, founder of the journal *Folk-Say* (1929), head
of the Library of Congress's folklore division, and a writer
whose subjects included folklore and folk song in virtually every region of the United States. It was not the
government, but *Fortune* magazine, that dispatched the
writer James Agee and photographer Walker Evans in
1936 to observe the lives of tenant farmers in the Deep
South; their *Let Us Now Praise Famous Men* (1941) blended
still-haunting images of the tenants' homes and faces with
Agee's stream-of-consciousness reflections on the meanings of their lives. Besides the government-sponsored
programs, magazine reports, and sociological surveys, we
may notice the National Folk Festival at St. Louis, organized by Constance Rourke, among others, in 1934. One
historian has given the name "documentary imagination"
to the intellectual fashion of trying to get directly to the
texture of "the common man's life." Here was an acceptable way out of the evasive sentimentality and condescending idealism of previous generations. Communist
party influence among intellectuals in the late 1930s meant
a further transfer of artistic loyalty from the products of
social elites to those supposedly truer to the aspirations of
the people. It called for proletarian novels and plays about
strikes instead of the genteel tradition. It replaced the

music of the great masters with the folk songs of Pete Seeger and Woody Guthrie, spirituals sung by Paul Robeson, prison songs by Leadbelly, and musicals on folk subjects like Earl Robinson's *Ballad for Americans* (1939). The latter instance of newly created "folk" music touched off so much popular interest that it was even played at the 1940 Republican National Convention.

The appeal of the Communist party to some intellectuals depended on many themes addressed in this chapter. The party offered a modern ideology of scientific reconstruction; it was a haven for alienated intellectuals who sought cosmopolitan contacts among whites and blacks, among former Protestants and Jews. It developed a "popular front" strategy that made commercialized culture less threatening because it was infused with redeeming folk motifs. It joined New York and Oklahoma with "vanguard" thinkers in European capitals. It repudiated "chauvinism" of race, class, and gender and assailed the polite codes of conduct of the Victorian era. Perhaps most important, it offered a sense of belonging to a "cause" that overcame the separation of intellect and faith, the uncertainty about the sources of truth and direction of history, that seemed to so many modernists the vexing malady of the twentieth century. In the 1950s, the Communist pasts of intellectuals were often taken as signs of "un-Americanism," but the appeal of the party in the 1930s was largely an expression of American faith in an era when faith otherwise seemed parochial or unattainable.

Of course, there is no way of studying the motives of all who supported the party or voted for its candidates. There has been too much punishment, distortion, and dissembling. But these motives were clearly related to a search for authority and responsibility that went well beyond Communist circles. Both Tate and Ransom, as we have noted, analyzed the decline of religion in taking their stand with the agrarian South. Ransom had been enraptured by the idea of young writers "manifesting themselves in the capacity of a Cause; about which they have Convictions." His excitement was comparable to that of the deracinated Cowley in Europe telling a friend that it was time "to write some political manifestoes. . . . I am eaten with the desire to do something significant and indiscreet." Besides these gestures on the part of lonely writers, there was extensive discussion in polite circles of Joseph Wood Krutch's *The Modern Temper* (1929), a bleak analysis of the unraveling effects of science, of a world of "unresolvable discord" from which there was no escape. How was it possible for an educated person to find roots and carry out tasks of practical importance in a culture that lacked the coherence of the Eskimos and in an intellectual milieu devoid of certainty? It may suffice here, in order to identify the Communist party as a leading example of the quest for commitment and coherence, to recall that ex-communists later savored the quasi-religious image given the movement in a famous symposium of apostates, *The God that Failed* (1949). Even those with a lingering nostalgia for the movement—as some of the voices recorded in Vivian Gornick's *The Romance of American Communism* (1977)—speak of communism's passionate release from loneliness, its promise of integrating the individual into a meaningful social "whole." One of them compares Marxism to Luther's revolution; to listen to another, writes Gornick, "is to feel oneself in the presence of a true religious struggling for visionary life in a rigid, frightened church."

Looking back over the diverse writers of the interwar period, we may regard them as architects of legendary ways of viewing the decades of the 1920s and 1930s. They have influenced Americans ever since to think of the 1920s as an era of intellectual alienation, youthful immorality, and political aridity and, in contrast, to think of the 1930s as an era of intellectual influence, popular radicalism, and successful political leadership. In many ways these characterizations are legends, neither completely true nor completely false; they are undergoing scholarly reconsideration today. Certainly not all young people of the 1920s were irreligious, wore flapper costumes, or drank bootleg liquor; and Herbert Hoover's leadership as secretary of commerce and president now has scholarly admirers. By the same token, patient anxiety now seems to have been more typical of the citizenry during the depression than outwardly expressed anger, and the vacillating programs of Franklin Roosevelt have many critics. Whatever historians may come to agree about the people and political leaders during these decades, the legends remain significant for what they tell us about the intellectuals' struggles to redefine their relation to politics and society. The contrasting images of isolation and commitment highlight the intellectuals' sense of themselves as a distinct group cut off from the traditional social order and seeking new positions of strategic influence. For a deeper comprehension of this search, we must turn from those who took a new view of culture from the vantage point of non-Western tribes or modernist experiments. We must examine those who sought roles as pragmatic problem solvers.

USEFUL INTELLECTUALS

A large and growing class of intellectuals saw themselves, not as marginal to society, but as uniquely useful. They beheld in themselves the potential to guide America to new levels of harmony and prosperity. Most of them were graduates, with advanced degrees, of the expanding universities. They were engineers, attorneys, scientists, and social scientists employed by universities, government

agencies, research institutes, business firms, and even settlement houses. (By 1911 Jane Addams was already com-
menting on the change from the old settlement workers
who said that "we must do something about the social disorder," to younger ones who said, "We want to investigate something.") They shared a common belief in the social benefits of professional expertise. Because of their deep
respect for the intellectual leadership of John Dewey we
may refer to them collectively, even though few were philosophers, as "pragmatist" intellectuals. Another useful
name was coined by the historian Richard Kirkendall, who
called them "service intellectuals."*

These intellectuals, comfortable in the employ of
business and government, may appear polar opposites to
the alienated modernists and radicals; and in important
respects that is true. Though both were exploring new careers in a complex society, the free-lance writer might feel
like a perpetually maladjusted fugitive, while the expert
might slip into the role of bureaucrat. But there were
points of contact too. Both groups shared a repudiation
of the old ideology of culture, a fascination with reconstruction, and an awareness of approaching a new era.
They honored common heroes, preeminently Dewey. To
the service intellectuals he was the apostle of intelligence
applied to social problems; to the modernists he was the
guide to a permissive spirit of self-expression in schools
and society. Some of the free lances worked as publi-
cists—that is, as popularizers of expert knowledge. And
some, with whatever private feelings of alienation, earned
incomes from centralized publishing houses or even from
the public relations departments of corporations. Never-

---

*Kirkendall's term *service* nicely blends the overtones of wartime intelligence, whose significance we shall see shortly, with older religious ideas
of selfless vocation.

theless, the pragmatist intellectuals had fewer self-centered preoccupations with exile and alienation. They geared their efforts to attain, not the bohemian freedom of Greenwich Village, but the satisfactions of social utility.

Since the mid-nineteenth century there had been calls to substitute trained professionals for well-intentioned amateurs in order to handle social tasks such as sanitation, civil service reform, or charity. Some notable reformers had achieved good effects by mastering large amounts of information, much of it statistical, on issues ranging from slavery and prostitution to mental health and conservation. A good example was Carroll Wright, who was commissioner of the Massachusetts Bureau of Statistics of Labor, went on to become the first U.S. commissioner of labor statistics in 1885, and later was named president of Clark. Wright epitomized the belief that properly organized information would help impartial citizens find solutions for social distress and economic conflicts. His goal was to distinguish the "public interest" from the rancor of the parties in conflict, a goal to be carried out by the expert investigator as an altruistic vocation. Journalists like Jacob Riis, in a less systematic way and with a less detached tone, had voiced a similar goal. "Facts, facts piled up to the point of dry certitude, was what the American people then needed and wanted," recalled the muckraker Ray Stannard Baker. By 1909, when the Russell Sage Foundation subsidized a major survey of wages, working hours, houses, schools, health, and dozens of other topics in Pittsburgh, a basic pattern of using social research in the aid of social reform, supported by private wealth and directed at a nonpartisan citizenry, was well established.

Intensifying this pattern was the emergence of universities with engineering, agriculture, and social science departments committed to the ideal of utility. One of the most admired qualities of German higher education was its close relation to the bureaus of government. College presidents like Woodrow Wilson, as we have seen, spoke of the requirement, even in democratic republics, of an educated class to direct public affairs. Many college spokesmen believed that in a nation where elected officials were too often corrupt there was a pressing need for well-trained, nonpartisan leaders comparable to Old World aristocrats. Both Theodore Roosevelt and William Howard Taft as presidents of the United States convened study groups on special topics like conservation. Professors and college graduates served on commissions, regulatory agencies, and scientific and technical bureaus. These experiences and similar ones at state and city levels fostered hope in further collaboration between experts, philanthropists, and government as a nonpartisan entity. They gave a special meaning to James's and Dewey's appeals to the use of scientific intelligence to confront social problems.*

World War I decisively altered intellectuals' attitudes toward power. While Cowley, Hemingway, and Faulkner went to the Western Front, hundreds of college men congregated in Washington and other centers of government. Academicians served in military intelligence, con-

---

*When Frederic Howe, a dedicated service intellectual, was working toward the Ph.D. at Johns Hopkins, one of his teachers was the distinguished English observer of American government, James Bryce. Howe was inspired by Bryce's statement that "America, with no leisure class devoted to statecraft, was to be saved by the scholar." Howe's teachers also included Woodrow Wilson, who had a similar vision. But when Wilson later campaigned to be president of the United States, he bowed to public suspicions of intellectual management: "What I fear is a government of experts. . . . What are we for if we are to be scientifically taken care of by a small number of gentlemen who are the only men who understand the job." Nevertheless, as wartime president Wilson greatly enlarged the national role of experts.

ducted research on weapons development, and administered psychological tests to soldiers. To a previously unimaginable extent, the federal government abandoned laissez-faire precepts and assumed responsibility for directing the economy and managing society. The War Industries Board, the War Trade Board, the Capital Issues Board, and the War Finances Board mobilized, licensed, regulated, and financed economic activity. The Railroad Administration unified and supervised the nation's transportation system and their work force; the Food Administration regulated the production and consumption of food; and the Fuel Administration took command over energy. The War Labor Board in its effort to prevent work stoppages compelled employers to recognize unions; and the War Department seized Smith & Wesson and Western Union in order to enforce employees' right to join unions. The Committee on Public Information enlisted scholars and journalists to spread a patriotic interpretation of war issues throughout the nation. The Emergency Fleet Corporation and U.S. Housing Corporation provided residences for workers, while the U.S. Shipping Board hired and trained architects for what amounted to a large-scale experiment in planned public housing. Scores of intellectuals, particularly historians, assisted in preparing for peace negotiations, some of them attending the president at Versailles. Others joined agencies that marshaled public and private support for relief and reconstruction in war-ravaged Europe.

The unforgettable result was a massive demonstration of the capacity of government, in a concerted, nonpartisan response to crisis, to extend its functions of planning and control. So many intellectuals were employed that the Cosmos Club in Washington, according to one magazine article, resembled "a faculty club of all the universities." Throughout the war, the article continued, professors "fought, and they managed affairs, thus refuting the ancient libellous assumption that they constituted an absent-minded third sex." Then the academics were demobilized, and as another article put it, the Cosmos Club fell under "the dark cloud of peace."

Wartime experience strengthened a conviction, built up over many decades, that intellectuals had a special nonpartisan role to play in service of an expanded national government. It had been noticed during the Civil War that experts and professionals found useful assignments that had been denied them in Jacksonian politics. In the widely read utopian novel *Looking Backward* (1888), Edward Bellamy had pictured a nationalistic society mobilized as in warfare, but for publicly beneficial projects instead of for slaughter. One of William James's most popular essays, "The Moral Equivalent of War" (1911), offered a similar vision of carrying the martial spirit into laudable peacetime endeavors. In *The Promise of American Life* (1909), the founder of the *New Republic*, Herbert Croly, used the military term *reconstruction*—so fashionable after the war—to describe a crusading program of nationalism and reform. World War I accentuated the opportunities for experts and technicians in a state of mobilization. John Dewey wrote several essays on "the social possibilities of war." Thorstein Veblen, who worked for the Food Administration, saw models for far-reaching social change. A prominent economist, Wesley C. Mitchell, predicted that after the armistice countries would continue to use "the same sort of centralized directing . . . for the new purpose of reconstructing their own life at home." The war had demonstrated the advantages of reform brought about through "intelligent experimenting and detailed planning" rather than through "agitation or class warfare."

Another economist, Rexford Tugwell, who was to become a major figure in the New Deal, called the war "an industrial engineer's Utopia."

After the war, the excitement of intellectual service died down, and few academics retained government positions of control and management. Nevertheless, it would be wrong to suppose, as a few commentators have done, that intellectuals disappeared from government. Thousands continued to work, mainly in technical and advisory roles, at every level of government. At the federal level, programs in agriculture, law, and economics persistently needed experts, and Secretary Herbert Hoover regarded his Commerce Department as a continuing center for the collaboration of scholars, businessmen, and private philanthropists that had flourished during wartime. In a decade when it was often said that society had grown too complex to do without technical expertise, professors and their protégés also found many new positions in the research, personnel, and public relations divisions of large firms. Whether such positions were permanent or consultative, they were surrounded by an aura of beneficial service in an era of expanding prosperity. The mounting belief that scholarship benefited society may also be seen in increased foundation support for social science. In 1921, for example, $181,500 was given for research and graduate education by one hundred leading foundations; in 1927, the figure was close to $8 million.

Hoover, whose programs as wartime relief administrator and secretary of commerce made him a guiding light to progressive social scientists, sought as president to realize the fullest advantages of social research and systematic planning. He launched major commissions enlisting some of the ablest economists, sociologists, and political scientists in the universities, and he envisioned a reorganization of the executive branch in which reforms could be coordinated outside the contamination of the electoral and legislative processes. The stock market crash, a terrible drought, and surging unemployment cast a pall on these efforts at fact-finding and administrative reform. Hoover retained the late-nineteenth-century conviction that, once the facts were surveyed, men of intelligence and objectivity would agree on social measures. Little direct state intervention in economy or society would be necessary. In the context of the depression, this faith seemed futile, and Hoover's standing among intellectuals plummeted. The myth emerged that only in the New Deal did intellectuals return to federal service.

Hoover's successor, Franklin Roosevelt, continued several of the intellectuals' programs, particularly in agriculture, that were already in place in Washington. In addition, building on Alfred E. Smith's and his own experiences as New York governors, he relied on the much discussed "brains trust" of intellectual advisers who helped the president formulate policies outside the give and take of congressional politics. To the small circle of trusted consultants—Tugwell, Raymond Moley, Felix Frankfurter, Adolph A. Berle, Jr.—were added flocks of other intellectuals in every corner of government, including the multitude of agencies like the Agricultural Adjustment Administration (AAA) and the Tennessee Valley Authority (TVA) thrust forward in response to the depression. Newspapers and magazines were filled with articles on "professors in politics," as had not been true since World War I. There were critics: the disillusioned Al Smith said they should put on raccoon coats and do their planning in Moscow. But the government's resort to intellectuals had public relations benefits: the idea spread that businessmen and politicians had failed to counter the nation's crisis and now, as in war, it was time to call on experts who knew how to interpret data and devise solutions. "Only

thoroughgoing experts," it was said, "can do the work."*
Even without considering public relations, there was no
doubt that the wealth of new agencies needed social scientists, attorneys, economic specialists, and policy advisers
(as well as college presidents, like TVA's Arthur E. Morgan and Harcourt A. Morgan, who were experienced ad-
ministrators). The reliance on university intellectuals
throughout the federal bureaucracy became even more
important during World War II, and despite election-year
rhetoric about reducing the size of government, it has
never since abated.

SUBCURRENTS
OF ANXIETY

The story of the interwar years has sometimes been told
as an epic victory in intellectual life. So it must seem to
those who believe that intellectuals should be less abstract
and arcane than they are, closer to power and real life.
To be sure, the brains trust was controversial; some cried
that too much responsibility accrued to men who never
faced an electorate or met a payroll. But major victories

---

*Commentators on the brains trust sometimes recalled the old repub-
lican belief in the need for a natural aristocracy who could surmount
mundane political considerations. In an article entitled "Don't Shoot
the Professors" (1934), Jonathan Mitchell commented that professors
were the closest American substitute for the landowning classes from
which Britain and Prussia had recruited a disinterested civil service.
The scientific ideal and scholarly temperaments elevated professors
above the temptations to which the rest of the population were subject.
In 1938 Lindsay Rogers, a Columbia professor who had served Alfred
E. Smith in New York, commented: "Because the federal government
has an insufficient number of expert civil servants comparable to those
in Great Britain's administrative class, every national crisis sees a descent of professors on Washington."

surely went to those who believed that America had for too long neglected its brainpower, that scholarly training had a direct bearing on public affairs, and that an administration listening to experts was better able to mobilize all the resources of a great nation. The Hoover administration had respected these beliefs in a modest way, but the New Deal went further to cultivate an atmosphere of excitement and social experimentation. There was less emphasis on the sober certitudes of fact-finding, greater emphasis on trying things out and evaluating the results.* When the New Deal also began to hire writers and artists to write state histories, to present plays, and to document folk life, there were additional changes in emphasis, suggesting on the one hand that the government had a special care for intellectual life and, on the other, that writers and artists had special bonds with the people.

If we examine the story from the viewpoint of the intellectuals, we see that the feeling of triumph was mixed with strains of doubt and self-criticism. For some, social service meant positions as functionaries with little need to worry about overall objectives; for many thoughtful persons, however, new public responsibilities spotlighted the inability of modern intellectuals to fix ultimate principles. The subcurrents of anxiety that flowed through the 1920s and 1930s may be expressed through these questions: Could social science actually provide secure guidance to policymakers? And were the citizenry and their representatives capable of understanding the complexities of public affairs? On these points the concerns of pragmatist in-

---

*This "hit-or-miss" approach, a source of great excitement at the time, now has many scholarly critics. The historian Barry Karl says that "the New Deal used social scientists as though they were astrologers, playing their programs for daily action without regard for the mysteries of the system."

tellectuals paralleled those of other exiles from the confidence of Victorian culture.

The first subcurrent surfaced in *Seven Arts* in 1917 when Randolph Bourne criticized Dewey and his wartime followers. Bourne spoke of "having come to a sudden, short stop at the end of an intellectual era." True to the revolutionary sentiments of many prewar radicals, he was appalled by the enthusiastic enlistment of intellectuals in the war effort and by Dewey's attempts to relate the war to progressive purposes. Bourne had shared his contemporaries' rejoicing in pragmatism as a liberating philosophy, but now he concluded: "The war has revealed a younger intelligentsia, trained up in the pragmatic dispensation, immensely ready for the executive ordering of events, pitifully unprepared for the intellectual interpretation or idealistic focusing of ends." This was a shock: in giving up on Victorian culture, young radicals had thought they were repudiating hypocrisy and shallowness, not idealistic goals and criticism of the state. "To those of us who have taken Dewey's philosophy almost as our American religion, it never occurred that values could be subordinated to technique." Dewey of course had never been indifferent to values, but Bourne detected an "unhappy ambiguity in his doctrine as to just how values were created." With intellectuals glorying in government service, it seemed clear that the new orientation had diverted their attention from the quality of life in American civilization. Pragmatism helped to accommodate them to careers of technical service, but at the sacrifice of utopian goals and critical detachment.

Bourne's dissent had little influence on the immediate situation. After his death in the terrible 1918 epidemic of influenza, other thinkers, worried about the drift of intellectual life, repeated the charge that pragmatism, when "pushed to extremes," as one of them put it, "becomes a justification for almost anything."* Bourne became a symbol of courage and foresight. His views reappeared, with approval, in one of the ablest reconsiderations of the loss of guiding values, written shortly after World War II, Morton White's *Social Thought in America* (1949). Because of a subsequent tendency to celebrate Bourne as a solitary hero, we are likely to forget the subdued, but persistent, dilemma that perplexed social science throughout the 1920s and 1930s. Research funds were growing, positions of influence were proliferating inside and outside the universities, and the reputation of social scientists for objective rendering of data was enviable. Yet the possibility of constructing an orderly "philosophy of life," one that could indicate what should be done with expanding human knowledge, seemed ever more remote.

There were several reasons for this frustration. For one thing, in an era when philosophy of science held wide interest, fields like physics and mathematics, which formerly epitomized the discovery of natural laws, now seemed beset with their own uncertainties. Euclidian geometry was shown to depend, in part, on human assumptions, which could be varied—as in the instance of Albert Einstein's theory of relativity—in order to comprehend previously neglected aspects of reality. The philosopher

---

*There were attempts to believe that science provided a "higher" authority, but these attempts generally focused on the *methods* of science and failed to establish absolute social objectives. This observation applies, for example, to Dewey's most persistent philosophical critic, Morris Cohen, many of whose comments on the naive optimism of the pragmatists resemble Bourne's. But few philosophers in recent decades have been impressed by Cohen's defenses of such concepts as scientific reason and natural law. Even those thinkers who attached themselves, overtly or secretly, to the doctrines of communism too often found themselves in the position of defending the shifting policies of the Soviet state.

Kurt Gödel demonstrated that the truth of a mathematical theory could not be verified without referring back to its own premises; and the same circularity was bound to prevail in other fields. Quantum physicists discussed the inevitable effects of observation itself on the matter being observed; to learn one thing, as the problem was popularized in Werner Heisenberg's "uncertainty principle," the scientist was bound to distort others. The language systems in which findings were expressed exacted their own ambiguities: several prominent schools of philosophy sought to reduce the gap between semantics and actual references to the concrete world. According to the fashionable *Philosophy of "As If"* (English translation, 1924) of Hans Vlaihinger, there was no escape from acts of faith in which the would-be objective observer accepted provisional assumptions about the nature of the world that were essentially fictions. According to Ernst Cassirer's more profound work, *Philosophy of Symbolic Forms* (1929), all of human culture was made up of symbols. Science, despite its astonishing achievements in mastering the natural world, was in some ways as metaphorical as poetry. Since the authority of social science depended heavily on the prestige of science, its practitioners could not ignore the inroads of relativism. Action and judgment were unavoidable aspects of human life, but ultimate principles were unknowable.

Within social science itself there were competing theories that undermined belief in fixed laws and principles. Within economics, for example, tremendous gains derived from applying models of economic behavior that postulated rational patterns of buying and selling things, but some economists claimed that this approach arbitrarily ignored modern psychology's findings about irrational human motivation, and others complained that it sidestepped the central social-scientific issue of the effects of institutions on individual behavior. Within psychology, to take another example, there was intense popular and learned interest in the work of Freud and his followers in the psychoanalytic movement, work that stressed the twisted path between unconscious motivation and actual human behavior. Yet American social scientists were also enormously influenced by the work of John Watson, B. F. Skinner, and the behaviorists, who opted to avoid inexact references to unseen drives and memories and to study instead only overt behavior stimulated by visibly controllable forces. Similar choices existed in other fields, with diminishing likelihood that any one theory could be used to disprove another. Social science was not a coherent movement, but a set of alternative approaches to knowledge. While the individual scholar might feel that his choice was the best one, there was abundant awareness of the arbitrary, even irrational, nature of initial choices. Devotion to a great teacher, curiosity about one facet of human life, the social rewards for one style of research—these and other factors could influence the researcher's starting point. Social science generalists meanwhile found themselves picking and choosing among different sets of assumptions as they turned from one topic to the next.

The utility of social science was so widely hailed that the crisis was not profound or disabling. A common observation regarding social scientists, in fact, was that they were willing to concentrate on small patches of human experience without asking fundamental questions. For every Margaret Mead or Ruth Benedict pronouncing on public issues, scores of anthropologists accumulated data on tiny, remote cultures simply because that was what anthropologists did. Historians were so particularistic and untheoretical that the relation of their scholarship to science was frequently disputed. Even in sociology, which supposedly took in the entirety of society, many were comfortable surveying one topic in detail while leaving thorny questions to the masters in the field. In the 1920s, some of those masters believed their fields were relevant to the creation of a new era of increased control over human affairs, but others stated quite explicitly that social science offered no ultimate authority to suggest which social policies were wisest. The question of values dangled outside the sphere of scientific knowledge. The researchers on President Hoover's Commission on Recent Social Trends explained that each of them had an "individual scale of values" but that as a group they had not strayed from objective fact. While in the 1930s some considered the social scientists' objectivity to be an abdication of judgment, Walter Lippmann summarized the views of many service intellectuals when he wrote: "The power of the expert depends on separating himself from those who make the decisions, upon not caring, in his expert self, what decision is made." When the greatest gains of the new era—prosperity and harmonious personnel management—were dashed by depression and strikes, the critical inability of the scholars to fix values and unite on policy took on graver dimensions. Only World War II, when there was once again abundant service to perform in a fully mobilized nation, restored the technicians' confidence in their utility—and gave a new relevance to Bourne's earlier dissent.

The second source of anxiety—the relation between objective knowledge and a democratic citizenry—may also be traced back to World War I. The Committee on Public Information (CPI) had been astonishingly successful in bombarding the public with propaganda, oversimplifying the war aims of the Allies, and linking doubt and criticism with treason. The repression of German-Americans during the war and the "Red Scare" afterward raised, in a menacing way, the issue of the government's power to squash dissent and mislead its citizens. From the 1920s on, the term *propaganda* recurred throughout discussions of civic life: even the American Revolution and the Constitution were reexamined to show how small groups had wielded control over the public at large. Often such studies were quite cynical in their attitude toward the use of rhetoric to accomplish covert purposes. This trend in scholarly circles was accompanied by two others in the popular press: the waning of progressive faith in marshaling facts to enlighten an impartial citizenry, and the undeniable power of advertising to create consumer demand.

Edward L. Bernays—a nephew of Freud, a former member of the CPI, and the man usually called the founder of public relations—wrote *Crystallizing Public Opinion* (1923), a book that sought to give experts in opinion guidance the stature of respectable professionals. These new men and women were to be superior to the ballyhoo artists and confidence men of the past; they were technically proficient in exploiting public sentiments for their clients' benefit. In a world where truth was an archaic concept and crowd psychology was inescapable fact, society needed experts who could promote the interests of America's corporations. In the 1920s political candidates began to add public relations branches to their campaign staffs. Even the social scientists in the executive branches of government were obliged to consider *how* to bring their findings before the public.

The most thoughtful analyst of these trends was Walter Lippmann. Before the war, in *Drift and Mastery* (1914), he had addressed the problems of democratic government in an age of transition when international affairs and technical knowledge were assuming vast importance. "Science," he had written, "is the culture under which people can live forward in the midst of complexity, and treat life not as something given but as something to be shaped." Lippmann had worked for the great muckraker Lincoln Steffens and for a socialist city administration in Schenectady, New York. He had advised Theodore Roosevelt on labor problems and served in a military propaganda office in Europe. Though he had not reacted to the war with Bourne's bitterness, his comments on the competence of the public became intensely disillusioned.

In *Public Opinion* (1922), Lippmann concluded that the CPI was only an extreme case of the public's tendency to think in stereotypes, value-laden preconceptions that were easily exploited by those with the most control over sources of information. It was foolish, he argued, to ignore this fact by praising the mythical "impartial" citizen who delegated authority to elected representatives. The Jeffersonian faith that truth would prevail in a fair contest was unfounded; the reformers' faith in amassing facts was doomed to failure. It was no longer possible to believe in the efficacy of common sense or the human heart. A theory of the modern democratic state needed to examine the creation of group symbols and codifications of "the facts." It required new attention to the socializing influences of parents, teachers, and national leaders. Lippmann did not disparage the place of technical knowledge within government itself: to the contrary, he envisioned "intelligence bureaus" organizing information for decision-makers in every agency. But the public was incapable of understanding all the complicated data relevant to determining and implementing policy—an observation that Lippmann extended further in *The Phantom Public* (1925). The critical issue in a democracy was civil order, not the rule of the people. Yet Lippmann went on to a distinguished career as a political commentator, informing the public in broad and reflective terms on the nation's editorial pages.

Lippmann's reflections pointed out another dimension of the "documentary imagination" of the interwar years. Many young men and women who went into the field with note pad, camera, or recording machine had goals beyond transcribing what they saw and heard. They wished to devise for the public new images of problems outside its experience. Consider the mission of a young filmmaker, John Grierson, who spent the years 1924 to 1927 studying the movies and other media on a Rockefeller research fellowship in social science. According to a friend and associate:

> Men like Walter Lippmann were saying . . . that the older expectations of democratic education were impossible, since they appeared to require that the ordinary citizen should know every detail of public affairs as they developed from moment to moment. With Lippmann, Grierson agreed that the view of education which assumed that stuffing the citizen with facts would enable him to act intelligently according to his interest, was untenable in a complex society. . . . [Instead of] the indiscriminate transmission of facts, Grierson [proposed] the possibility of a selective *dramatization* of facts in terms of their human consequence. Interpretation through the dramatic media could give individuals "a common pattern of thought and feeling" with which they could usefully approach the complex issues of modern living. The power to tap the springs of action had slipped away from the schools and churches and come to reside in the popular media, the movies, the press, the new instrument

of radio, and all the forms of advertising and propaganda. Grierson proposed to study the dramatic
and emotional techniques by which these media had
been able to command the sentiments and loyalties of the people where many of the instruments
of education and religion had failed.

Grierson attracted the attention of Charles Chaplin, Erich
von Stroheim, and others in Hollywood who "were also
concerned to reason out the problem of putting the emotional power of the film at the service of mature thinking." Grierson did most of his creative documentary film-
making outside the United States, but his views were a
thoughtful example of a growing interest in the propagandistic uses of drama in awakening public consciousness. They provide a link to films such as John Ford's
Grapes of Wrath (1940), made in Hollywood, and Pare
Lorentz's *The River* (1938), a presentation of the conditions, land, and people along the Mississippi made for the
Farm Security Administration, as well as numerous other
examples of "documenting" social problems, in print or
on stage, in order to crystallize public opinion. It was not
unusual for the creators of these works to compare their
techniques with those of advertising, with the difference
that they were supposed to benefit the people rather than
vested interests. One derivation from concerns like
Lippmann's was a selective "realism," in which the "committed" artist sought an educational use of media to shape
and manipulate public opinion.

We may regard Lippmann as a disillusioned radical,
impressed by modern science and psychology, and trying
to preserve progressive policies in a complex and contradictory form of government. Documentary "realists" acted
in keeping with these aspects of his thought. But we may
also regard him as a modern "publicist," sensitive to the

latest trends in academic research, as an influential middleman interpreting to a literate public the conclusions of political scientists who were undermining traditional republican theory and the conclusions of sociologists who were increasingly fascinated by the techniques of social control.

In political science, as in most other departments of knowledge, there was rising commitment to study actual behavior instead of abstract categories. The field was considered an empirical science concentrating on group conflict and pressure groups rather than "higher laws" or the theories of ancient thinkers; it was too objective to recommend specific policies, its focus resting instead on the institutions, processes, and psychological patterns that destroyed utopian expectations. In *Propaganda Techniques in the World War* (1927), Harold D. Lasswell stated baldly assumptions that were also evident in many other works. "Familiarity with the ruling public" had bred "contempt" on the part of politicians who had discovered that traditional republican ideals were delusions. Political rhetoric still paid lip service to those ideals, but in actuality politicians would continue to "inform, cajole, bamboozle and seduce in the name of the public good." Charles E. Merriam's *Political Power* (1934) stressed the ability of elite groups to dominate masses of human beings "as if by some magnetic attraction or aversion."

Political scientists were exposing the same gap between the technical complexity of government and the irrationality of the public that disturbed Lippmann. Meanwhile, many sociologists were minimizing the distinctions between savage and civilized life and between democratic and authoritarian forms of government, distinctions that had been central to an American ideology of individualism. The striking discovery of the 1920s was that all societies were obliged, in one fashion or another, to control their members. Thus, the proper subjects for research were the varied means by which governments carried out that end. E. A. Ross's *Social Control* (1901), one of the earliest analyses of society's need to abridge individual freedom, was reissued in the 1920s and sold more copies than when it first appeared.* Ross predicted that as society increased in complexity there would be greater inequality; the classes growing in power included not only employers and managers but also "the learned castes and professions" who acquired so much more knowledge than ordinary citizens. To postwar social researchers, determined to observe behavior rather than rhetoric, it seemed clear that many institutions with ostensibly high-minded purposes—family and church, Boy Scouts and school—actually functioned to check the individual and strengthen the social order. Of the 229 chapters in a well-known college text, Kimball Young's *Source Book for Social Psychology* (1927), for example, at least one-third dealt with social control. Some of the headings are instructive: "Early Social Conditioning"; "Public Opinion as Formulated by the Few"; "Prophylactics against Mob Mind"; and "Propaganda and Social Control."

To understand the uses of the concept of social control, we may notice two preoccupations of social scientists

---

*Since social control had many conservative champions, it may seem ironic that Ross was a radical who was fired from Stanford in 1900. His approval of labor unions and criticism of corporations earned him the enmity of Mrs. Leland Stanford. During World War I he was embroiled in trouble again when he returned from overseas and made a public speech that some citizens found deficient in "open and aggressive patriotism." Ross apologized that, having been out of the country, he was unaware of the need to make a "vigorous statement" of his loyalty. Ross's position seems less ironic, however, if we regard him as a progressive who saw labor unions as quelling social conflict and unregulated corporations as foes of social control.

working outside the college classroom. First, there was a frank endeavor to structure the new institution of the high school so that it would turn out well-adjusted members of society. Second, there was intense interest in the sociology of the work place: instead of smoldering conflict, factories could become scenes of efficiency and contentment. All such discussions assumed that the results would be beneficial to the social order as a whole as well as to employers and the members of the "learned castes and professions" whose services they hired.

The international depression and the rise of European dictatorships accentuated American uncertainties over the fixing of goals and the competence of the public. In the end, they gave a heightened urgency to the issues of the viability of democratic government and the relation of intellectuals to power—so much so that the prevailing attitudes of the 1920s toward propaganda and social control now seem astonishingly cynical. But this change occurred only after considerable intellectual discourse concerning the possible superiority of communism and fascism.

Although Hitler never had more than a handful of admirers among American intellectuals, Lenin and the early Soviet leaders were frequently applauded for their experiments in social change. It was not necessary to join the Communist party in order to take such a view: a good number who called themselves pragmatists saw in the Soviet Union the inevitable direction of twentieth-century government. One of Dewey's ablest followers, Sidney Hook, explained repeatedly in the early 1930s the similarities between pragmatism and Marxism. Only the mounting evidence of rule by a minority party, suppressing all other factions and murdering its critics, dampened such enthusiasm. Eventually many of the pragmatists who had praised the Soviet Union, including Hook, became vehement anticommunists. In an interesting reversal of judgment, Stalin's Russia came to epitomize an undemocratic absolutism, opposed to the open-minded philosophy of pragmatism and making the worst conceivable use of the propagandistic power of the state and the slaughterous potential of modern technology.

Because it promised to save capitalism and prevent the rise of Bolshevism, and because it was free of textual dogmas like Marx's works, Mussolini's fascism was, if anything, even more appealing to intellectuals of the late 1920s and early 1930s. In fact, the Italian leader shrewdly pretended that William James's writings had greatly influenced him—a claim that enhanced his attraction to Americans. One of James's most eminent students, Horace Kallen, appealed for patience while the Italian experiment had "the freest opportunity . . . of demonstrating whether it be an exploitation of men by a special interest or a fruitful endeavor after the good life." Unfortunately, when Kallen met Mussolini, he found that Il Duce knew almost nothing about James. Nevertheless, the fascist "experiment" seemed to combine the spiritual regeneration of the people with the planned coordination of private interests: it was the triumph of objective realism over doctrinaire theory. A serious undercurrent of fascination with Mussolini lingered among pragmatist intellectuals until the mid-1930s, when Italy's invasion of Ethiopia, imitation of Hitler's anti-Semitism, and support for Franco's overthrow of the Spanish republic dashed his reputation in America. From that time on, the new word *totalitarianism* gained increasing fashion with Hook, Kallen, and many others to summarize the insight that there was something valuable in American democracy, for all its frustrations, that communist and Nazi dictatorships lacked. When Russia and Germany signed a pact in August 1939, and both attacked Poland in the following month, the insight seemed confirmed. As World War II mobilized intellectuals in new positions of service, as previously noted, the crisis of preserving democracy from foreign menace submerged whatever remained of the feeling that the knowledge of experts clashed with the vagaries of public opinion.

The most revered intellectual in America during these years was Dewey. His name was invoked, almost ritualistically, by those who championed "mastery" over "drift," objective investigation over obscuring dogma. So many foolish things were said in his name that historians are obliged to point out that he was not always responsible for what his followers said and did. His own educational theories, for example, were more complex statements of the problem of training lively intellects than some of his disciples' incantations of "free expression" and "group adjustment" would indicate. He himself never tolerated the militaristic excesses of Mussolini. He headed a committee that exposed the atrocities of the Moscow trials. Though he is sometimes criticized today for the seemingly aimless experimenting of the New Deal, he actually kept his distance from the Roosevelt administration and offered his own criticisms of its absence of guiding purposes. His political loyalties lay closer to the ideal of democratic planning upheld by the Socialist party—one movement that nearly disappeared in the age of Hitler and Stalin.

Dewey's prestige derived, not from his involvement in victorious movements, but from his unflinching, sustained effort, despite the cynicism and desperation around him, to maintain a democratic faith in an age of complexity and change. Others turned to oversimplified versions of pragmatism or to alternative authorities like Marxism, Catholicism, or the sociology of social control. But if Dewey saw any contradiction between efficiency and democracy, he unhesitatingly affirmed them both, never doubting the necessity of social control, never questioning the value of individual participation in society. Today his philosophical reputation has waned—he was too inconsistent—and historians are more interested in some of the extreme and foolish applications of his ideas than in what he himself wrote. But he may yet be recognized as a major American example of the ability of a gifted thinker to be involved fully in his time and yet to transcend its limitations.

It is possible, then, to regard Dewey as a creative individual who became a symbol of liberation and integrity to a long generation of intellectuals. He was an inspiring hero in an era that looked eagerly for signs that the individual could surmount pressures to conformity and resist the confusion caused by the disintegration of traditional verities. To thousands of readers, his long life personified the hopes for scientific method and human control over the natural and cultural environment. His works, like those of Edwards, Emerson, and a few other American thinkers, repay close attention by the reader who compares his carefully balanced insights with the cults that derived from them. Even his greatest admirers, such as Joseph Ratner, compiler of his *Intelligence in the Modern World* (1939), recognized his involvement in an "essentially discordant, unintegrated" period of history and acknowledged that his work inevitably reflected some of its "multifarious splits" and shortcomings. Still, his adamant faith in democratic use of the methods of human intelligence enabled him to leap across the dogmatic positions at which others stopped.

Yet Dewey did not wish to be read as a solitary, exceptional thinker with a problematical relation to the preoccupations of his era. In *A Common Faith* (1934), perhaps his most accessible work, he repudiated the notion of "knowledge as an accomplishment of a lonely mind." He believed in the "communal origin" of knowledge as deeply as Constance Rourke believed in the folk sources of myth and humor. He went on to call for a new religion concerned with "the community of causes and consequences in which we, together with those not born, are enmeshed." The day when religion consisted of the rites and superstitions of a self-contained tribe was long since past; the subsequent habit of using religion to divide humanity into the elect and the damned had impeded the progress of democracy; and atheism and agnosticism had presented incomplete pictures of individual life, nature, and human relations.

> The ideal ends to which we attach our faith . . . assume concrete form in our understanding of our relations to one another and the values contained in these relations. We who now live are parts of a humanity that extends into the remote past, a humanity that has interacted with nature. The things in civilization we most prize are not of ourselves. They exist by grace of the doings and sufferings of the continuous human community in which we are a link. Ours is the responsibility of conserving, transmitting, rectifying and expanding the heritage of values we have received that those who come after us may receive it more solid and secure, more widely accessible and more generously shared than we have received it. Here are all the elements for a religious faith that shall not be confined to sect, class, or race. Such a faith has always been implicitly the common faith of mankind. It remains to make it explicit and militant.

This faith in a common heritage almost suggests a yearning for renewal of the idea of a universal culture— a yearning that would be much in evidence in the 1940s and 1950s. The thinker whom Bourne attacked so bitterly during World War I lived to personify, in many minds, a universal democratic outlook which was, despite its imperfections, worth fighting for at home and worth promoting abroad.

DISSOCIATED INTELLIGENCE

By the 1920s and 1930s the noun *intellectual* had a secure place in the American vocabulary. It did not necessarily exclude doctors, lawyers, ministers, and other members of the traditional educated classes, but it referred primarily to three groups who were by education and profession distinct from the rest of the population: free-lance men and women of letters, college professors, and experts who served business and government. An issue on which observers might part company was the degree of critical independence that ought to characterize intellectual status. To those who believed that the intellectual classes should furnish moral reflection and guidance in perilous times, the free lance might seem too dependent on publisher and marketplace, the college professor too isolated from public concerns, and the service intellectual too enmeshed in bureaucracy. To those who admired intellectual commitment in the service of society, however, critical detachment was an archaic luxury. Images of intellectual life in the era wavered between alienation and commitment, powerlessness and institutional service.

The prominent issue of relating the intellectuals to the public and to power should not obscure the deeply unsettling problem of the nature of intellect itself. Sharply discordant views were expressed on this problem, and to some observers the absence of an integrated conception of human thought and feeling was a sign of the malaise that wracked modern life.

T. S. Eliot, the avant-garde poet who shocked many admirers by converting to Anglo-Catholicism, described this lack of integration in terms that became a catchphrase among serious writers. A "dissociation of sensibility" had unsettled the English mind in the seventeenth century, and from it "we have never recovered." Subsequent waves of literary taste had never healed the divorce between thought and emotion. The problem was not that human beings had previously been ignorant of their separate capacities for thinking and feeling; clearly, Eliot knew that the terminology of the faculties reached back to the Greeks. The problem was that thought and emotion ceased to be co-ordinated activities, and human utterances became dried up or sentimental, in either case dissevered from the full complexity of experience. Eliot was writing about poetry, but his comments were part of a modernist lament at the shattering of the synthesis offered by the medieval church. We may observe that this lament severely oversimplified the history of both medieval and modern thought. Nevertheless, the diagnosis struck home to twentieth-century intellectuals who believed that in the aftermath of genteel culture it was difficult to come to terms with emotion. Both Tate and Ransom, for example, agreed that "dissociation of sensibility" underlay the woes of modern civilization. Both argued that scientific reason had undercut religious faith; both sought to fix their convictions by returning to a simple agricultural situation. Both earned their greatest influence, however, in academic settings where they promoted an approach to literature, the "New Criticism," discovering in poetic texts the integration of intellect and emotion that society in general failed to permit.

The disorderly human urges—lust and destructiveness—were discussed as they had seldom been in the nineteenth century. Although Freud's writings made little headway in departments of psychology, terms like *id, libido, eros,* and *subconscious* became commonplace in public conversation. The prevalent nontechnical use of terms like *paranoid, neurotic,* and *complex* suggested common acceptance of irrational components in all of life. This acceptance could be remarkably unfearful. There is no reason to suppose that purchasers of Sears, Roebuck self-help manuals entitled *Ten Thousand Dreams Interpreted* or *Sex Problems Solved* believed that they had disabilities requiring strenuous therapy. More likely, they believed that their Victorian forebears had been hypocrites, that it was unhealthy to inhibit deep feelings, and that everyone deserved to be happy. Even works whose influence was more restricted to intellectual circles, like Karen Horney's *The Neurotic Personality of Our Time* (1937), fractured the once clear boundary between sanity and insanity; feelings of emotional isolation and low self-esteem were widespread, but not irremediable, phenomena. With much justice, the historian Warren Susman has called the 1930s "the age of Alfred Adler," the psychoanalyst whose concepts of the inferiority complex and individual adjustment were very fashionable among intellectuals. Dale Carnegie's *How to Win Friends and Influence People* (1936) provided glimpses of widespread American anxiety to be popular and to fit in well with others.

Obviously, there could be a big difference between releasing sexual inhibitions and conforming well to social institutions. The reception of Freudian theories in America included many naive and distorted notions of how easily psychic issues could be identified and resolved, how easily an individual could work out the appropriate management and expression of desires. In the 1940s, Lionel Trilling and others dissatisfied with the shallowness of American conceptions of thought and culture rediscovered Freud as the great explorer of the mind struggling for mastery over itself, as the champion of the ego trying to still the conflict and thus to comprehend reality. But theirs was emphatically not the popular Freud of the 1920s and 1930s. If intellectuals experienced a "dissociation of sensibility" in those decades, it was partly because prevailing stereotypes of human drives and needs distracted attention from the goal of intellectual mastery. It did not matter whether people were "letting everything go," as conservatives said in the 1920s, or were resolutely "holding back" their feelings, as radical critics rejoined. Neither of these popular, contradictory descriptions of American character had much to say about the place of intellect in an integrated sensibility.

In university social science departments a different orthodoxy dominated: behaviorism. Unseen forces were altogether disregarded in favor of measurable regularities of stimulus and response. It was not always clear that this preference conveyed any larger view of society and the universe: it made psychology a "realistic" field, in that its practitioners observed the actions of human beings in the same way they observed those of mice. But it could be expanded to the belief that human nature was as completely malleable as the materials that engineers bent and shaped. While this belief could sometimes be disturbing, as in some analyses of public opinion, it could also lend comforting confidence to discussions of social control in a business civilization.

Famous studies of the effectiveness of various person-

nel policies among Western Electric workers at the Hawthorne Works in Cicero, Illinois, disclosed what is still called
the Hawthorne effect: workers' productivity increased in
response to all experimental stimuli. It did not matter, for
example, whether lighting was increased or decreased.
What mattered was improved morale resulting from the
experiments' creation of small groups. These findings
prompted numerous other studies of group adjustment as
the key to happiness and efficiency in modern institutions. Happiness, adjustment, psychic rewards—these are
different goals from intellectual growth. Not only was the
sensibility divided; its intellectual side was slipping out of
sight.

The term *reason* was largely missing from intellectual
discourse, and *intellect* was seldom mentioned. But even
behaviorists believed in the uses of intelligence. Dewey,
Lippmann, and virtually every social researcher who aspired to public influence favored the term *intelligence*, with
its strong links to the wartime reliance on expertise as the
basis for decision-making. Business, government, and academic departments shared in this way in using the language of war to define the usefulness of intellectuals. Individuals had different "quotients" of intelligence, but the
general implication was that it was not the genius, creativity, or flair of the thinker that was most important; what
mattered was to have the right kind of training to use the
right methods in the right position in a properly organized institution. The individual's "scale of values" was
immaterial; with the right training he would hold his biases
in check. In a sense, then, producers of intelligence were
interchangeable. In place of the old idea of the hierarchy
of the intellect, it was now more appropriate to speak of
a broad stratum of researchers and technicians. Service
intellectuals seldom paused to consider the nature of mind;

they simply knew what to do.* Intelligence was a form of dispassionate endeavor to which moral quandaries and unconscious gratifications were irrelevant. In this view of the public responsibilities of intellect, much more than in religion or English poetry, the idea of a "dissociation of sensibility" seems thoroughly apt.

In conclusion, it is appropriate to turn back to Dewey, who ardently sought an integrated understanding of self, nature, and society. In "The Unity of the Human Being" (1937), he urged a convention of doctors to pay more attention to the " 'higher,' intellectual and moral" relations of the individual with other human beings. To the ancient motto, "A sound mind in a sound body," he added a new one, "A sound human being in a sound human environment." The "whole business" of "any profession" was "the construction of a proper human environment that will serve, by its very existence, to produce sound and whole human beings, who in turn will maintain a sound and healthy human environment." This advice may have caught Dewey at one of his most circular and least cogent moments, but it indicates the difficulty of bridging the gap between intelligence and ethics. In *A Common Faith* he treated the difficulty as a religious one. It would be unfortunate, wrote Dewey, to discard with supernatural theology the imaginative "idealizations" by which people dedicated themselves to high purposes. Intelligence and

---

*This statement may seem overdrawn, but I wish to emphasize a distinction from older views of intellectual activity. Of course, many service intellectuals had liberal educations; in fact, such an education helped to distance them from the public and give them the aura of a disinterested civil service.

emotion were not opposed to each other: "There is such a thing as passionate intelligence. . . . One of the few experiments in the attachment of emotions to ends that mankind has not tried is that of devotion, so intense as to be religious, to intelligence as a force in social action." Though intense emotion could destroy institutions, it could also have, as part of a new "unification" of human purpose, profoundly beneficial consequences.

If we contrast the modernist poets' search for unity inside the confines of a text with Dewey's groping efforts to coordinate intelligence with emotion and imagination, we see tremendous disparity in conceptions of intellectual life in this era. While some intellectuals felt increasingly marginal to society and divided in their own consciousness, Dewey had faith that, "whether or no we are, save in some metaphorical sense, all brothers, we are at least all in the same boat traversing the same turbulent ocean."

FOR FURTHER
READING

Intellectual life in the 1920s has been somewhat neglected, except for the field of literature, to which a splendid guide is Frederick Hoffman's *The Twenties* (1955). For a general study of intellectuals in the 1930s, see Richard H. Pells, *Radical Visions and American Dreams* (1973). Warren I. Susman has been an astute and influential commentator on both decades of intellectual history; his works include " 'Personality' and the Making of Twentieth-Century Culture," in John Higham and Paul K. Conkin, eds., *New Directions in American Intellectual History* (1979); "Piety, Profits, and Play: the 1920s," in A. Quint and Milton Cantor, eds., *Men, Women, and Issues in American History* (1975); "The Thirties," in Stanley Coben and

Lorman Ratner, eds., *The Development of American Culture* (1970); and a collection of documents entitled *Culture and Commitment, 1929–1945* (1973).

A difficult but rewarding book on Boas and the rise of anthropology is George W. Stocking's *Race, Culture, and Evolution* (1968). For the cultural debate over the American "folk," see Richard M. Dorson, *American Folklore and the Historian* (1971), and Joan Shelley Rubin, *Constance Rourke and American Culture* (1980). Many twentieth-century views of art and culture are interpreted in Charles Alexander, *Here the Country Lies* (1980).

The classic study of the pre–World War I revolts against Victorian ideology is Henry F. May's *The End of American Innocence* (1959). See also Leslie Fishbein, *Rebels in Bohemia* (1982). The best historical study of modernism focuses on the South: Daniel Joseph Singal, *The War Within* (1982). William Stott's *Documentary Expression and Thirties America* (1973) is a helpful book. There are also numerous memoirs as well as useful biographies such as William L. O'Neill, *The Last Romantic: A Life of Max Eastman* (1978), James Hoopes, *Van Wyck Brooks* (1977), and Ronald Steel, *Walter Lippmann and the American Century* (1980).

On the radical intellectuals, see Daniel Aaron, *Writers on the Left* (1961), James B. Gilbert, *Writers and Partisans* (1968), and Frank Warren, *Liberals and Communism* (1966). For the concentration of many writers on the goal of cosmopolitanism, see David A. Hollinger, "Ethnic Diversity, Cosmopolitanism, and the Emergence of the American Liberal Intelligentsia," *American Quarterly* (1975). Black intellectuals are given contrasting interpretations in Nathan I. Huggins, *Harlem Renaissance* (1971) and David L. Lewis, *When Harlem Was in Vogue* (1981).

Trenchant articles on the pragmatist intellectuals include William E. Leuchtenberg, "The New Deal and the Analogue of War," in John Braeman et al., *Change and*

Continuity in Twentieth-Century America (1964); John P. Diggins, "Flirtation with Fascism: American Pragmatic Liberals and Mussolini's Italy," *American Historical Review* (1966); Barry D. Karl, "Presidential Planning and Social Science Research: Mr. Hoover's Experts," *Perspectives in American History* (1969); and Richard S. Kirkendall, "Franklin D. Roosevelt and the Service Intellectual," *Mississippi Valley Historical Review* (1962). All four authors have written important books on related topics.

On the vexing problem of ethics and political theory, see Edward A. Purcell, Jr., *The Crisis of Democratic Theory* (1973), and R. Alan Lawson, *The Failure of Independent Liberalism* (1971). A more general survey of social thought may be found in Robert Crunden, *From Self to Society* (1972). This chapter does not delve into one field where nineteenth-century "higher laws" gave way to new attitudes toward expert information and where the resulting absence of fixed principles made intellectuals keenly aware of "drift" in decision-making—the courts. A useful survey is John W. Johnson, *American Legal Culture, 1908–1940* (1981).

VIII

THE DISCONNECTION OF INTELLECTUAL LIFE

RENEWAL AND
ORTHODOXY

The history of intellectual life since World War II has consisted in part of postscripts to the 1920s and 1930s. Until quite recently, most of the leading figures in both literary culture and academic fields have been men and women whose work commenced in those decades. Memoirs of that era appear almost annually—most recently those of Lewis Mumford and Malcolm Cowley as well as posthumously published diaries of Edmund Wilson—all of them supplying bridges between the intellectual milieu of the cold war decades and the themes of prosperity and depression, alienation and commitment, cosmopolitanism and modernism, that preoccupied the interwar literary generation. Works by Eliot, Hemingway, Faulkner, and Warren have taken their places as canonical texts of American literature, admired throughout the world and setting the standard against which new generations of writers are measured. Cults have surrounded the great 1930s filmmaker Orson Welles and the influential stage director John Houseman. New films like *The Way We Were*

(1973) and *Reds* (1981) exploit the public sense that the 1920s and 1930s still hold important meanings.

University intellectuals publish few memoirs and diaries; they are less inclined to make of their personal sagas the substance of intellectual life. But the concerns of the physicists whose collaboration led to the atomic bomb, of historians and anthropologists who grappled with the relativity of cultures, and of sociologists and political scientists who concentrated on behaviorism, public opinion, and social control have remained central to academic discourse. Recent studies of Howard Odum, Charles Merriam, Franz Boas, and Lionel Trilling treat them, not as relics of a distant past, but as formulators of continuing dilemmas in scholarly practice. Moreover, the mutual dependence between government and educated professionals has grown ever stronger. The Eisenhower administration claimed to employ more professors than the Franklin Roosevelt administration did; the Kennedy administration conspicuously imitated the New Deal's reliance on intellectuals; and each subsequent president has brought in his own cadre of experts and consultants. State and local governments have found they needed planners and technicians in ever increasing numbers, while universities have adjusted course offerings and research commitments to serve the needs of institutions in both the public and the private sector. Throughout this chapter, we shall observe how intellectuals took their bearings in recent decades from memories and legends of what public life and private manners were like in the 1920s and 1930s.

It would be foolish to say that nothing new has happened. Randolph Bourne died of influenza; today, genetic science is on the verge—or so many people think— of developing weapons against far more mysterious diseases. The study of women has toppled assumptions about history that had prevailed for centuries. Sexual mores have changed so profoundly that what once was condemned as degrading now appears normal. Schools that a century ago gave up Greek and Latin for French and German now face the elimination of all language instruction while they dream of placing every student at a computer terminal. Discussions of diplomacy and warfare address a peril unknown in previous eras: nuclear annihilation.

No one denies that the content and context of intellectual life have changed. Pragmatism, for example, commands little attention; Dewey's reputation lies in eclipse, his works out of print and unread. Professors worry about the gulf between their interests and those of their students, who anxiously look for jobs. Students are hazy about the 1950s and 1960s, let alone the decades of prosperity and depression. Some critics complain that the men and women of letters are vanishing, victims of the proliferation of specialized knowledge and the consumer habits of a media-oriented public. A host of new terms are coined to suggest the passing of an old era, replaced by something with no better name than "postindustrialism." Ideology is dead; the future shocks people's senses; pseudo-events benumb them; and those searching for commitment are left with awkward labels like "new left," "neo-orthodox," "post-Protestant," "postliberal," "neoconservative," "new federalist," "new populist," or even "new ethnic." One writer sees a worldwide emergence of "protean man" moving rapidly through many affiliations—the nth degree of deracination. Others are impressed anew with the compulsion to fit into large-scale organizations.

Each of these worries and celebrations has been especially fashionable at particular moments. The terms here conflated may have had a big play for only a year or two. But if we view the past three decades as a unit, we are struck by the persistent anticipation that the vectors of the 1920s and 1930s have at last spent themselves—that we are on our own. Perhaps Americans are vaulting into the future; perhaps they can skip back over the errors of previous decades and recover something lost.

Religion has seemed at times on the verge of disappearing from intellectual life. If we turn back to the experience of modernist and pragmatist intellectuals between the world wars, the irrelevance of Christianity and Judaism to their endeavors strikes us as remarkable. They had broken from the nineteenth-century pattern of intellectual leaders speaking from within an evangelical faith. When they thought about religion at all, it was as something remote. Although Prohibition endured throughout the 1920s as the "Great Crusade" of rural Protestantism against modern iniquity, intellectuals generally paid it little heed. They were caught by surprise when several states passed laws against teaching the theory of evolution in public schools. They thought that controversy over Darwinism had long since subsided; then suddenly anti-evolutionism emerged as a repudiation of all the evils of urban intellectual life. The conflict drew national attention in the famous 1925 "monkey trial" of the schoolteacher John T. Scopes in Dayton, Tennessee. Though Scopes lost the trial, the intellectuals succeeded, to their own satisfaction, in turning his antagonists into laughingstocks. The popular religion of America was, more than ever, *outside* the circles of literature and science: it was belittled by H. L. Mencken and Sinclair Lewis; it was left behind in the small towns from which the exiles had departed. Those who tried to find commitment in a Christian faith, the Eliots and Tates, usually chose Episcopalianism or Catholicism, and they did so as a deliberate gesture of stepping outside the realm of their intellectual confreres. They understood that the prevailing temper of intellectual life was cosmopolitan and irreligious.

In regarding religion as alien to their endeavors, intellectuals failed to perceive dynamic events within American Protestantism. They ignored new movements concerned with personal holiness and the millennial dispensation that united American sects with missions around the world. They were largely unaware of doctrinal movements within evangelical seminaries that challenged symbolic interpretations of the Bible and questioned the "social gospel" of charitable works to please a loving God. Under the new banner of "fundamentalism," theologians deplored the dilution of Christian teachings and raised one issue as the test of true Christian faith: belief in the literal truth of the Bible.* Men of letters could ridicule Scopes's prosecutors, but having cut themselves off from the religious strivings of most Americans, they were in no position to assist liberal or reform-minded ministers and seminarians in the contest to define the twentieth-century meanings of Christianity. They were hardly aware of the battle. Thus, those who continued to advocate reformist, modernist viewpoints within the churches lacked the backing of the educated classes that they had once been able to take for granted. The distance between intellec-

---

*Though the origins of the term are disputed, "fundamentalism" was related to the twelve volumes entitled *The Fundamentals* (1910–1913), edited by Ainzi C. Dixon, Louis Meyer, and Reuben A. Torrey, and distributed by the millions among seminarians, ministers, and laymen. In general, it is fair to say that, while many intellectuals like to picture fundamentalists as hypocrites on the model of Sinclair Lewis's fictional Elmer Gantry, in these and other works the case for biblical inerrancy was argued carefully and with deep conviction. The intellectuals' disparagement, therefore, could only have enhanced the volumes' appeal to an audience concerned about the issues they raised.

tual life and religion widened, not only because of the intellectuals' indifference, but also because of the strengthened conviction among Protestants that scriptural truth was, after all, at odds with science.

By the mid-1930s there were signs of renewed interest among intellectuals, if not in fundamentalism, at least in traditional Christianity. Feeling that they were faced with a poor choice between relativism and the absolutism of European dictatorships, some men and women sought in religion a way of justifying moral commitments in a confusing world. The change may be seen, for example, by contrasting two books by an economist at Ohio Wesleyan University, Gilbert H. Barnes. In 1926 he had collaborated on a textbook celebrating the open-mindedness and objectivity of social science. Human nature was "infinitely plastic," and there was no difficulty in bringing about a "fundamentally different social order" through applied intelligence. A few years later in *The Anti-Slavery Impulse* (1933) he proudly hailed the influence of revivalists, not scientists, in launching a majestic social reform. It was religious zeal, not skepticism, that emboldened those who labored heroically to build the kingdom of God on earth. Even Walter Lippmann, convinced that "the acids of modernity" and the "secular image of man" had dissolved social restraints and prepared the way for fascism and communism, considered a conversion to Catholicism.

In the 1940s and 1950s, some of those who articulated a new interest in religion were extremely influential in literary and scholarly circles—among them, Paul Tillich, Reinhold Niebuhr, Will Herberg, and Perry Miller. Though they hardly constituted a school or movement, together they gave to religious inquiry an intellectual respectability that it had lacked for years. Though they differed in many ways, none of them envisioned a return to "fundamentals." All regarded religion as a search to understand the individual's condition in the baffling modern world; and in elaborating on this condition they favored words that permeated much intellectual discourse of the 1950s—words like "irony," "tragedy," "complexity," and "ambiguity." They joined in the insight that the church had for too long been affiliated with the secular world view of the middle classes and thus had fostered overly optimistic views of human nature and historical progress. Their works dealt in subtle ways with the ancient religious paradox of being *in* the world but not *of* it: the individual inevitably faces crises of moral choice within society, but it is erroneous to identify religion with human culture.

Their work tried to escape the narrowly American focus of religious discourse. They and their associates translated and interpreted the previously neglected writings of theologians in Continental Europe—preeminently Martin Buber, Albert Schweitzer, and Karl Barth—who had repudiated the takeover of religion by science, secular institutions, and progressive culture. Religious profundity began with a conviction that God was "other" than the world, not readily available through historical experience. The long legacy of the Enlightenment's belief that the meaning of life was contained within human time and human society was declared bankrupt. An obscure nineteenth-century Danish critic of the Enlightenment, Sören Kierkegaard, became one of the most widely discussed writers of the American 1950s. His depiction of individual moments of agony and "leaps to faith" amid the "absurdity" of life in historical time seemed to have prophesied the painful predicament of the human spirit in the modern age. "Existentialism" became a code name for the view that the human being is condemned to make awesome choices and fashion an individual sense of wholeness and identity without certain knowledge of any absolute source of meaning in history or culture. This terminology became fashionable—popularized in mass-circulation magazines and wielded earnestly in college bull sessions—because it gave even the person who could not take the leap to conversion a perspective on the shattered faiths of bygone generations, faiths whose hollow optimism had been exploded by depression and holocaust. Not only did it point out the failings of churches reduced to social institutions in the secular world; as most Americans used the terminology, it also distanced the individual from pseudo-religions like science and communism.

The careers of the four men we have mentioned exemplify the converging, yet varied, new interest in religion. Paul Tillich was one of those European theologians whose works, in translation, caught hold in the United States. Then in 1934 he moved to New York's Union Theological Seminary as part of the great exodus of luminous thinkers from fascist Europe. While his contributions to the history of religious doctrines were important in their own right, his most important influence on intellectual life was simply that he traversed the gulf between secular cosmopolitanism and religious inquiry. His respect for a Judeo-Christian heritage stemming from both testaments of the Bible seemed less sectarian and exclusive than the familiar American Protestantism. His definition of God as "the Unconditional," with which the divided, time-bound individual hungered to make contact, was congenial to those who were dissatisfied with secular relativism and who believed that everyone had a religion, even if it could not be articulated in terms of existing denominations. His castigations of "spurious" faith within socially shaped religions echoed the intellectuals' aspersions on the pretensions of culture. Tillich's admiration of expressionist art and literature, which disassembled conventional forms in order to convey the puzzles of existence, and his abiding social radicalism made it impossible for New York intellectuals to dismiss him as a sectarian theologian outside their realm of conversation. He was one of many refugees who made American intellectual life seem less narrow than it had been before.

Reinhold Niebuhr, born in Missouri and educated at the seminary of the German Evangelical church, had been a "social gospel" minister for thirteen years in Detroit before coming to Union in 1928. Even then, he remained for some time a Marxist before finding his role as the single most influential exponent of what was called neo-orthodoxy. As a religious writer, particularly in *Moral Man and Immoral Society* (1932) and *The Nature and Destiny of Man* (1943), he renounced virtually all of the liberal divergences from the Reformed (or Calvinist) view of man as an inevitable sinner. He likewise chided revivalists for their shallowly optimistic emphasis on religious experience and their belief that grace may be easily and permanently attained. Sin, however unintended, was unavoidable in human communities; and human beings, despite their strivings for ultimate meaning, could never fully transcend those communities. In spite of this bleak portrait of human ethical pretensions, Niebuhr never forgot his original driving concern for social justice. *Moral Man,* for example, included a sensitive appraisal of Mohandas Gandhi's struggles to merge "truth-force" with political responsibility. Much of Niebuhr's appeal was to ministers and laymen who sought a more "realistic" world view without forsaking the quest to improve human society.

By the 1950s, however, Niebuhr had come to see the Soviet Union as a horrid illustration of the menace of human societies that had relinquished the orthodox view of the value of individual souls and the sinfulness of collective life. American democracy, in contrast, exhibited redeeming elements of "modesty" and "humility." Thus in

The Irony of American History (1952), *Nations and Empires* (1959), and numerous polemical articles, he ardently defended the world leadership of the United States despite the admitted burdens of arrogance in its industrialism and imperialism. Contradictions and imperfections were inevitable within human society, but there was no avoiding "the actual urgencies of history" brought forward in the struggles between godless despotism and "the moral treasures of a free civilization." Communism, devoid of any religious warning against "the element of pretension in all human achievements," had produced the most "monstrous" atrocities in all of history. In America, in contrast, religious critics were free to challenge complacency. The drifting pragmatic realism in America became, in Niebuhr's view, the nation's greatest virtue. Anticommunism became, in a sense, the one political absolute for a group of prominent postwar liberals to whom Niebuhr appeared the most profound theologian of modern America; among them were the historian Arthur Schlesinger, Jr., the labor leader Walter Reuther, the diplomat George F. Kennan, and many others. More recently, Niebuhr has been criticized for the unrealistic character of his stereotypes of both the Soviet Union and United States—for forgetting his original insight into the mixture of good and evil in human collectivities. It is, to use his term, ironic that this rich and rewarding religious thinker is best remembered for his role in formulating a political position in the troubled postwar world. Neo-orthodoxy was shaped and weakened by its social and political moment, just as had been the religious movements that it criticized.

Herberg was a second-generation American Jew brought up as an atheist. He was the author of a Ph.D dissertation in philosophy of science, a scholar keenly interested in Freud, and an intelligent critic of modern literature—in short, a shining example of New York cosmopolitanism. He was also a communist, one of the best read and most intellectually adept figures in the party in the late 1920s. He offered notable revisions of communism's antiquated views of science in the age of Einstein and searching criticisms of party dogmas on literature, labor unions, and race—the sort of internal criticisms the party lacked after he and other nimble minds were driven out. His expulsion, which came in 1929 when Soviet leaders preferred a faction other than his own (the majority) for American leadership, led to a tense confrontation with Stalin at a Comintern meeting in Moscow. For the rest of the 1930s and early 1940s he continued in various "communist opposition" movements dissenting from Soviet dogma that American capitalism was soon bound to collapse. At first this position called for the kind of polycentrist communism, adaptive to national circumstances, that in recent decades has been championed by Yugoslavian and Italian communists. In time, however, the admission that American institutions possessed enough strength and flexibility to weather depression, war, and internal turmoil paved the way to increasingly conservative politics. By the mid-1950s Herberg was on the editorial board of the right-wing *National Review*. In the historian John Diggins's phrase, he was part of "Stalin's gift to the American right."

Herberg's writings on religion made him a figure of national significance. In *Judaism and Modern Man* (1951), he helped to popularize existentialism while explaining his own conversion to Judeo-Christian religiosity. Viewing both communism and liberalism as secular gods that had failed, critical of psychoanalysis and other therapies that substituted adjustment and selfish preoccupation for genuine human insight, he rejected both the Marxist critique of religion as an opiate and the contemporary association of religion with "peace of mind." Instead of "positive thinking," he explored a universal religious need expressed through terms like *crisis, risk, urgency, venture, decision, absurdity, insecurity, peril, homelessness of spirit, a search for commitment with fear and trembling*—all the key words of neo-orthodoxy. Every page of this compelling book revealed, he said, his enormous debt to Niebuhr.

In the early 1950s, many believed that a national revival of religion was imminent, and church and synagogue attendance attested to a "turn to religion." In *Protestant-Catholic-Jew* (1955) Herberg evaluated the current religious situation by returning to the old Protestant idea that the visible church is inevitably, at least in some measure, false. Although converts poured into the churches and President Eisenhower addressed the American Legion on the theme of "Back to God," American religious institutions were shallow, unsearching, conventional. Americans pictured God, wrote Herberg, as "a great cosmic public utility" capable of charging up their lives but not of transforming them. The Judeo-Christian sects, more and more indistinguishable from one another, were in danger of being homogenized into a genial "civic religion" that left political leaders as insulated from criticism of their pretensions as were communist dictators. Indeed, this development seemed nearly irresistible, since the real impetus to increasing religious affiliation was social, not spiritual. Religion provided a sense of belonging in a society that frowned on nonconformity; this was especially important to third-generation immigrants whose parents had struggled to be Americanized by giving up traditions. Though this impetus was powerful and understandable, and though churches and synagogues were admirable social institutions, there was no denying the paucity of authentic religious stirrings in a vast middle-class society. Herberg's anticommunism matched Niebuhr's in intensity, but his critique of religion was less focused on the illusions of the 1920s and 1930s, when he had wandered as a nonbeliever, and more aggressive toward the fashions of the 1950s. While neo-orthodoxy has faded from prominence, his discussions of civic religion and ethnic identity continue to engage scholars, even those who lack his own religious yearning.

Perry Miller was mentioned in the early chapters of this book as a scholarly authority on American religious history. He belongs in this chapter as a historical figure in his own right, one who indicates how the religious interests of Tillich, Niebuhr, or Herberg could reach a man who was probably an atheist. He described his fascination with American history as a kind of exile's return after World War I. Seeking adventure in Africa (he had also toured with a troupe of actors), he watched oil drums, the products of American capitalism, being unloaded on the Congo and decided to go back to the university in order to discover "the innermost propulsion of the United States." It has puzzled many readers of his distinguished books (see For Further Reading, Chapters I, II, III, V) that, having begun at a scene of economic imperialism, he devoted much of his life to expounding the theological vision of colonial Puritans. This was not a hot topic in the 1920s when history aspired to be scientific; his professors warned him against throwing his career away. Furthermore, though he was friendly with left-wing intellectuals like Lillian Hellman, there is scarcely a passage of "social commitment" in his writings. (He wrote sympathetically of some advocates of self-expression and youth revolt, but he never failed to understand the rationale for social control.) While some of his Harvard colleagues, who seldom discussed theology in their works, retained genteel affiliations with Episcopalianism and Unitarianism, he as an atheist mastered Calvin's *Institutes of Religion* and the Reformed theology of John Cotton and Jonathan Edwards. Finally, while he spoke of generalities like the New England or American "mind," he cherished religious thinkers whose systems had a recondite dimension that was inaccessible to most of their countrymen. Those ironies embedded in his work have bedeviled his reputation: at first admired among those who were recovering an interest in religion, more recently he has been dismissed as too religious, too eastern, and too elitist.

Miller wrote so little of his own views of religion that he defies interpretation in terms of any personal life quest. He was historically important, however, because he proved to thousands of readers, who had accepted the view of puritanism taught by Mencken and other debunkers, the subtlety and complexity of the lost language of the Reformation. Just as Niebuhr identified his stance with "orthodoxy" and Eliot traced the "dissociation of sensibility" to the English civil wars, Miller went back to the seventeenth century to find a great intellectual and spiritual synthesis that had been in transformation ever since. Change had many sources: among them, the hidden paradoxes of the system itself; the strangeness of experience in the new land; the institutionalization of the church; and confrontation with modern scientific habits of thought. The latter two at least resemble the themes of overtly religious thinkers among Miller's contemporaries. He alluded frequently to the diminished authenticity of religious crisis as the church became a social institution. And he hinted darkly that even the Puritans had flailed bravely, but futilely, against the forces of drift and uncertainty awaiting the modern "mind." (In fact, one recurrent criticism of his work has been its substitution of the existentialists' God for the Puritans'.) In his passionate *Jonathan Edwards* he quoted Kierkegaard in the process of turning the Northampton revivalist into a surprisingly modern intellectual, one who anticipated the conundrums of Einsteinian physics and the limits of social science. He even reminded readers—in a passage some took as autobiographical—of an "atheism more profoundly conscious of God than [Edwards's antagonists] could experience. . . . A vision of beauty for which the existence or nonexistence of matter is but a verbal quibble, a beauty which, being seen, puts the creature beyond all anxiety concerning his own annihilation."

It is hard to say what Miller learned about the oil drums, but perhaps the "innermost propulsion" of America arose out of a desperate effort to hold on to shards of religious meaning while forgoing none of the conventions of scientific intelligence—an effort that left Miller himself as neither a theologian nor a social thinker, but as a historian of transformations ennobled by moments of solitary intellectual courage. In any case, the one era about which he never wrote with analytical brilliance was his own. He is likely to be seen in retrospect as a disappointed seeker whose principal influence, ironically, was on specialized scholarship. Herberg applied to his own generation the Protestant insight that a faith bounded by historical development was not authentically religious. For Miller there was only history.

The new interest in religion among intellectuals led, as we have seen, to many private ironies. The gap between intellectual life and popular evangelicalism remained unbridged. A general history of religion in modern American society would have to proceed from the holiness crusades of the 1920s to the much touted revival of the 1950s and then on to the astonishing success of Billy Graham, Oral Roberts, and a host of other evangelists in fusing elements of the old-time camp meeting with the media of radio and television. Media evangelists renewed the

fundamentalist claim that genuine American values consisted of nothing more than literal faith in the Bible. To
many intellectuals, the derisive attitude of Mencken and
Sinclair Lewis appeared newly appropriate. Mid-twentieth-century revivalists directed their performances at
stimulating waves of conversions that readers of Tillich or
Kierkegaard must regard as spurious, while the new fundamentalists, for their part, deplored the philosophical
glosses on the Bible from which the neo-orthodox defined the human condition. While prominent political liberals found inspiration in Niebuhr's works, the more important connection between religion and politics was
probably that which the Nixon and Reagan administrations encouraged between their conservative programs and
the radio and television ministry. Nixon invited Graham
regularly to the White House and fell on his knees in the
rose garden to find the wisdom to bomb Hanoi. Reagan,
who found, according to journalists, that the fundamentalists' concerns with sexual morality and school prayer
could bring together a constituency that might divide over
other economic issues, promised a convention of Christian broadcasters that he would proclaim 1983 "the Year
of the Bible."

Some twentieth-century holiness religions, like the Je-
hovah's Witnesses, are explicitly antipolitical; others,
gaining visible support from President Jimmy Carter,
profess the abiding interest of Christianity in the poor and
dispossessed. Nevertheless, in the 1970s the national
media and politics highlighted the emergence of a
"born-again" assault on intellectuals as threats to American
values. Intellectuals were labeled "secular humanists,"
corrupting the church, the school, and the family and
weakening America's resistance to socialism. The teaching of evolution resurfaced as a symbolic issue testing society's allegiance to *either* the intellectuals *or* the Bible. Those

who believed that the issue was decided in the 1920s, if not the 1870s, and that advances in the field of genetics had deepened the explanatory value of evolutionary theory responded with disbelief. They seldom denied, however, that *secular humanism* was a fairly accurate term for the continuing strain of pragmatist social thought in intellectual life. The idea that the Bible should be the basis of thinking about the natural world never invaded intellectual life; it lurked in the outer worlds of politics and public education. And in the controversy, it became clear that the neo-orthodox rapprochement between intellectuals and religionists was a thing of the past. Many writers and professors were churchgoers, but they were less likely in the 1980s to use terms like *irony, sin,* and *God* in their scholarly and public utterances than they had been in the 1950s.

It was not only Niebuhr, Miller, et al., whose significance had receded. American intellectuals were deeply impressed by Martin Luther King's leadership of the black civil rights movement of the 1960s and by the revitalization of Catholicism under Pope John XXIII. The Baptist preacher, the Italian pope, and the movements that they mobilized seriously conflicted with the antireligious prejudices of the interwar years. They raised visions of social regeneration quite different from the private yearnings of a Tate or Lippmann, and their radicalism separated them from cold war neo-orthodoxy. In America, they challenged the narrowly confined cosmopolitanism of the intellectuals to make sense of social movements much more broadly based than the Harlem Renaissance or the Communist party. The new movements among blacks and Catholics could not be as lightly dismissed as could rural evangelicalism, if only because in some ways they appealed to intellectuals for support and understanding.

King was a learned man who had written a doctoral

dissertation at Boston University on Paul Tillich and who collaborated effectively with white liberal ministers and seminarians. He had wrestled with Niebuhr's discussions of sin and society; he had read thoughtfully both Marx and Gandhi; and like few other public figures, he brought philosophical and theological conceptions to the fore in moments of social conflict. In *Stride toward Freedom* (1958) he spoke of learning from Hegel that "growth comes through struggle"; and he told a television talk show host shortly before his murder that he had no fear of death because unmerited suffering is redemptive. At the same time, he was a Baptist minister who spoke powerfully of the emotions of southern blacks. He had an extraordinary knack for blending the language of theological schools with that of black people in prophecies of historical change. His 1963 Lincoln Memorial speech (moving from "I have a dream" to the words of the spiritual, "Free at last, Free at last, Great God a-mighty, We are free at last") and his last sermon ("I've been to the mountaintop. . . . I've seen the promised land") were public events that struck no one as conventional episodes in civic religion. These were among the most dramatic moments of rising insistence that American society could no longer ignore the realm of moral values, that it must find in religion the strength of conviction to realize new standards of justice.

King repeated this theme throughout many confrontations with segregationists and in hundreds of speeches to religious and campus gatherings. "In the final analysis the problem of race is not a political, but a moral issue," he declared. Religion, false to its "prophetic mission," had permitted the human soul to be deprived of its "man-ness," had failed to combat "secular forces" dividing and oppressing mankind. In a sense, segregation was like communism. He even quoted the ex-communist Whittaker Chambers that "at the heart of the crisis of our times" lay the perception that Christian faith "has lost its power to move anyone to die for it." While King's impact on liberal ministers and seminarians was profound, however, his general intellectual influence was short-lived. His religious defiance of the status quo was not what Herberg and conservatives who had found God had contemplated. (In 1964 Herberg presented an angry theological criticism of civil disobedience to segregation laws; it was only when the state commanded idolatry, in violation of the First Commandment, that the religious person was entitled to resist.) Secular liberals and radicals, meanwhile, accepted Christian nonviolence only as "tactical" means of coordinating southern blacks and embarrassing the power structure. Black militants rejected it as too accommodating, too ineffectual, too bourgeois. By the 1970s there was almost no trace of King's Christian existentialism and Gandhian nonviolence in intellectual discourse.

In *Protestant-Catholic-Jew* Herberg called attention to the remarkable transformation of American Catholicism from "a conglomerate of foreign churches" to one of the "equilegitimate" expressions of the common religion. In the process, like other denominations, it had tacitly abandoned claims to being the one true faith and (showing a flexibility that the Comintern lacked) accommodated itself to American social reality. It supervised a wide variety of benevolent and educational institutions; its social outlook was "conservative" and "realistic"; and the spreading "preoccupation with intellectual life" in the midst of a church whose membership had once been overwhelmingly lower class was impressive. There can be little doubt that Herberg was right about the integration of Catholics into middle-class society and politics. But the place of Catholics and their institutions in intellectual life deserves a few comments.

Catholic colleges and universities were little affected

by the pragmatist, relativist strain of social thought discussed in the preceding chapter. In the late 1930s, however, when the absence of fixed principles became a much discussed problem in intellectual circles, Catholics joined the fray as they seldom had before. Catholic University, Fordham, and Georgetown furnished criticisms of Dewey and defenses of "unchanging fundamentals" to join those emanating from other institutions. At a time when the president of the University of Chicago, Robert Maynard Hutchins, was calling for a return to the medieval unities of Thomas Aquinas, a Catholic writer was addressing the central concerns of many intellectuals when he compared pragmatism to "the theme song of Hitler's storm troopers." Another wrote that "the modern secularized American hates and fears the original American culture [based on enduring values] and that the modern Catholic finds himself in sympathy with it." The milieu of the late 1930s, in short, made it easier than ever before for Catholics to enter the general discourse of scholars and men of letters without forsaking denominational loyalties. From the 1940s on, the cosmopolitan ideal that called for Catholics, Protestants, and Jews to overcome their parochial past gave way to a nonsectarian ideal with greater respect for religious identities. Anticommunism heightened the importance of articulating values shared by Americans of all religious and political "persuasions."

The "turn toward religion" of the 1950s similarly had the effect of broadening intellectual life while segmenting it into different religious subcommunities. Catholics were more likely than before to be published in literary periodicals and learned journals besides those affiliated with their church. Intellectual life became less exclusively secular. Nevertheless, many writers continued to believe that Catholicism was itself "totalitarian" and that its criticisms of pragmatist relativism issued from bad faith. A simplistic attack on Catholic antidemocratic attitudes, Paul Blanshard's *American Freedom and Catholic Power* (1949), sold widely. Senator Joseph McCarthy's anti-intellectualism deepened suspicions that Catholicism was inimical to free inquiry.

When John XXIII began his reign, a new spirit of openness became evident in the international church. American bishops participated in the Second Vatican Council (1962–1965), which abandoned the Latin mass and other signs of Catholic distinctiveness. Instead of championing what was left of the medieval synthesis, the church now seemed an arena of change where world peace, the rights of women, and the sufferings of the Third World's millions had eloquent champions. Secular liberals who admired King also admired John. While the anti–Vietnam War activities of radical priests Daniel and Philip Berrigan offended many conservative Catholics, it was no longer possible for anyone to regard Catholicism in its entirety as a bastion of reactionary views. One distinguished Catholic priest, President Theodore Hesburgh of Notre Dame, became the best-known white advocate of racial equality; another, Richard Drinan, became a prominent liberal congressman—until a later pope required his withdrawal from politics. By the 1980s Catholic bishops were the vanguard of the "nuclear freeze" movement. Yet the Catholic church remained too diverse to be united in one attitude toward society and politics. A prominent group of conservative Catholic intellectuals, of whom the best known is William F. Buckley, found in traditional faith the strength to oppose "the hideousness of a science-centered age" with its impoverished view of the human spirit and its dogmatic recourse to the bureaucratic state. Some Catholics have been allied with fundamentalists in efforts to link controversies over abortion and birth control with the insidious workings of "secular humanism."

It seems unlikely that anyone in the last quarter of the twentieth century could articulate a single Catholic position in intellectual life, as some of Dewey's critics thought possible in the late 1930s, and equally unlikely that anyone could attack Catholicism, in terms like Paul Blanshard's, as alien to the American spirit of free inquiry. When the hierarchy in Rome took measures in the late 1970s to suppress modernist doctrines in theology and scriptural interpretation, as taught by Hans Küng and other "heretics," there was a reminder that Catholic teachings were not open to unregulated drift. How this reminder affected American Catholic intellectuals is not yet clear, but to the extent that this ecclesiastical controversy was noticed in intellectual discourse in general, it merely paralleled bitter disputes over the inerrancy of the Bible among Lutherans, Southern Baptists, and other American denominations. That is to say, it merely strengthened an awareness that the tolerant accommodation of the 1950s and 1960s between intellectual and religious inquiry was under attack. To be sure, there was less of the intellectuals' obligatory hostility to religion, but within religious institutions there was abundant dislike of intellectual independence. And critical independence remained the source of much of the esteem that intellectuals retained in America.

By the ninth decade of the twentieth century there was little expectation of a common faith that could bond intellectuals with the people. Dewey's vision of a shared humanitarianism was as dead as the evangelical mainstream of the nineteenth century. There was renewed interest in Mormonism and in smaller cults and sects that had previously been ignored in the endeavor to define "American" religion. Intellectuals might be privately religious, as they had not been before World War II, and almost annually best-selling books—such as those on "the death of

God" and "Christian atheism" in the late 1960s—revealed continuing public interest in religious ethics. But even those scholars who specialized in religious studies were apt to deride what one called "the bandwagon era of theological thinking." It had proved easier to study the sociology or history of religion in the paths marked by Herberg and Miller than to propound a convincing orthodoxy, one that was not subject to fads and was not ignored in other fields of intellectual inquiry, one that would hold interest for more than a few months. Some looked backward and attributed the confusion of religion to the fragmentation of the Reformation or the this-worldly focus of the Enlightenment. Others thought the world had entered a peculiar "post-modern" stage in which it was impossible to give religious questions public coherence. As for intellectuals, whatever their role in society might be, they were not keepers of the faith.

ANTICOMMUNISM

After forty or fifty years the most intense intellectual disputes normally recede from memory. There were few recriminations over the Great Awakening in the 1780s or over transcendentalism in the 1880s. But old battles over the intellectuals' involvement with the Communist party in the 1930s are still refought in the 1980s.

Memoirs appear from some who opposed Stalinism and others who embraced it. The trial of Alger Hiss, a fair-haired boy in the New Deal whose life was ruined by the disclosures of Whittaker Chambers and the opportunism of Congressman Richard Nixon, works its way through the courts and controversial books, leading some to hope for the symbolic vindication of their class, convincing others of the still unexpiated guilt of the intellectuals. The unresolved puzzle of the atomic physicist J. Robert Oppenheimer's relations to communist espionage fill hours of televised docudrama. Michael Straight, former publisher of the *New Republic*, reveals that he passed government information to a Soviet agent. A feud erupts between Lillian Hellman and Mary McCarthy: McCarthy calls Hellman a liar for playing down her Stalinist sympathies in a book on the anticommunist activities of the 1950s, *Scoundrel Time* (1977); they exchange heated words in the New York press; others take sides; Hellman initiates a slander suit. Their confrontation inspires Norman Mailer to publish an open letter seeking reconciliation between two writers whom he admires. After the repression of the Polish Solidarity movement, Susan Sontag startles a New York rally with her charge that the intellectuals have for decades refused to face the fact that communism and fascism are identical; and the *Nation* devotes an entire issue to the aftershocks. A new book, William O'Neill's *A Better World* (1983), details the disloyalty and dishonesty of Stalinist intellectuals that gave McCarthyism the appearance of legitimacy. A young reviewer in the *New York Times* counters that the Stalinists did no harm; another young writer replies that by perpetuating lies and defending totalitarianism they did more than any right-wing movement could "to destroy the possibility of building a genuine and serious Socialist movement." Perhaps these are the last gasps of an old conflict, but the persistence of pain and anger over so many decades is remarkable.

The number of intellectuals who joined the party is easy to exaggerate. There were groups of communists in places where intellectuals congregated—college campuses, urban apartments, Hollywood studios, New Deal bureaus—but always in small numbers, and usually with a persistent feeling of engagement in a movement extrinsic to intellectual life. It was too full of "grime and stink and sweat," as one convert admitted, too full of pretentious posturing, too much in love with ugly language, too closed-minded and dogmatic, and too faction-ridden to appeal to men and women who took pride in their aesthetic sensibilities and critical independence. In the early 1930s, when many writers felt that the world was collapsing and that the Soviet Union reflected the workers' state of the future, the party spurned intellectual members. After 1935, when the party eagerly sought to embrace artists and writers in a vaguely defined "popular front" supporting Roosevelt from the left, most intellectuals were already wary of Stalin's extermination of his Russian opponents, the abrupt shifts in party line, and signs of Soviet expansionism. Some settled into the role of "fellow travelers," keeping a little distance from the party's maneuvers, but glorying in the bonds between intellectuals and the people that both the party and the New Deal wished to create. By 1940 Soviet policies had smashed most of these illusions, though they sometimes reappeared during World War II. Those who did join and remain in the party frequently describe the period as one of intense intellectual and emotional discomfort, almost as a penance. Intellectuals who valued intellectual consistency were more likely to support the Trotskyist and other "left opposition" movements, vilified by the communists, while others, including the influential *Partisan Review* circle, held fast to the cosmopolitan standards of artistic modernism, taking the Stalinist abasement of literary taste as singularly damning evidence of the "totalitarian" stifling of human creativity.

The blunt fact is that by far the greatest number of intellectuals throughout the 1930s were never sufficiently attracted to the Communist party to be members, fellow travelers, or left-wing rivals. They were too involved in other obligations of life in times of depression and, after that, of war. Despite the much publicized popular front youth movements on college campuses, for example, less than .5 percent of students participated in their activities. Of this small number, perhaps twenty thousand students, only a tinier percentage represented the somewhat hidden remnants of communists. What accounts, then, for the disproportionate emotional significance of Stalinism in intellectual discourse down to the present? A short answer would be: the cold war. A more satisfactory answer must separate two overlapping, but ultimately very different, versions of anticommunism within the United States: the subtle and often prescient response of intellectuals who had passed through or near Marxism while analyzing what was new and challenging in postwar society; and rampant McCarthyism that denounced almost all intellectuals as "soft" on communism or at least "creeping socialism."

The first version had several variations. It included Niebuhr and liberal writers like Granville Hicks and Max Lerner, who saw in the gullibility of American communists and the tyranny of the Soviet Union counterimages that justified the continuation of pragmatic social programs as sponsored by the "progressive" wing of the Democratic party. It included lifelong exponents of democratic radicalism like Irving Howe, Mary McCarthy, Dwight Macdonald, Paul Goodman, and Lewis Mumford—a diverse group that might have joined in the complaint, as the drama critic Eric Bentley put it, that the "Russian disaster" was "the greatest historical tragedy of the past hundred years, because . . . it represented the desolating disappointment of the great hope of our era: the hope of Socialist humanitarianism." It included notable scholars in art and literature, who turned their backs on the "dreary" politics of the 1930s (in Lionel Trilling's phrase) and devoted their lives to explicating what was finest in Western culture. It included social theorists like Herberg, the sociologist Daniel Bell, the philosophers

Sidney Hook and Lewis Feuer, and the historian Daniel Boorstin, who turned their dialectical skills, honed in the factional disputes of the 1930s, to extensive appraisals of how postwar society actually worked. Throughout the 1950s and 1960s most of these theorists took anticommunist liberal positions close to Niebuhr's; in the 1970s some joined Irving Kristol as "neo-conservative" analysts of business enterprise. Finally, it included ex-communists who became vehement "men of the right" (as Whittaker Chambers called himself). Joining Herberg and Chambers on the *National Review* were literary critic Max Eastman, sociologist James Burnham, political theorist Frank Meyer, and novelist John Dos Passos.

Although the anticommunism, often passionate, of these writers was sometimes raised to disparage their ideas, they ranked among the most influential and incisive thinkers of the third quarter of the twentieth century. No other group, however defined, was more formidable. The elusive American renaissance has been sought in many eras of our history, but seldom noticed are the extraordinary achievements, particularly in social theory and literary criticism, of those intellectuals who openly repudiated Stalinism from close experience.*

---

*Bell's survey is relevant: "Our intellectual nestors"—he mentions Trilling, Hook, Edmund Wilson, Niebuhr, Dos Passos, Lerner, and others—"were in their late twenties and thirties when they made their mark as a new generation. . . . They were intense, hortatory, naive, simplistic, and passionate, but, after the Moscow Trials and the Soviet-Nazi pact, disenchanted and reflective; and from them and their experiences we have inherited the key terms which dominate discourse today [1957]: irony, paradox, ambiguity, and complexity." Bell went on to say that "few figures" could "match the stature and work" of Dewey, Beard, Holmes, Veblen, Brandeis, and other giants of "the first political generations of the century." But the new leaders were less optimistic, more inclined to find "wisdom in pessimism, evil, tragedy, and despair."

A few examples must suffice. To Herberg's and Niebuhr's writings it would be appropriate to add Burnham's
The Managerial Revolution (1941), arguing that both Marxist and capitalist theory failed to account for the emergence of huge institutions run by "production executives,
administrative engineers, supervisory technicians, plant
coordinators, government bureau heads and commission-
ers." This book predicted adjustments in individual careers, economic and social institutions, and political power
that have since become the staples of sociological description of the "post-industrial era." Bell's *The End of Ideology*
(1960) discovered a new era imposing on intellectuals the
task of presenting visions of a worthwhile future without
the distorted views they had cherished of the American
worker, the economy, or world politics.* Boorstin's three-
volume *The Americans* (1958, 1969, 1973) applied insights
similar to Herberg's and Bell's, describing an America
whose fundamental conditions precluded any need for
systematic economic or political thinking. Bell's and Boorstin's views have been attacked, usually by optimists on the
left who believed that moralistic individualism or social
conflict still had room to transform America or who objected that Bell and Boorstin seemed to celebrate con-
formities that they should deplore. But *The End of Ideology*
and *The Americans* remained readable and provocative when
their critics' works passed out of print. Macdonald's at-

---

*Since the term *ideology* can be used in many ways, it should be noted
that Bell used it to refer to a passionate belief in the power of ideas to
revolutionize society. The term is also sometimes used to include the
mixture of ideas and beliefs that justify a society's composition and
purposes at a given time. Generally in this book, except when referring to Bell, the term is used in this second sense, as when we spoke
of the "ideology of culture" or, later in this chapter, when we discuss
"the end of ideology" as itself an element in postwar ideology.

tacks on "mid-cult" writing and art in *Against the American Grain* (1962) did not shrink from deploring. His contempt for ersatz popular culture began in *Partisan Review*'s battles against the popular front; during World War II his own little magazine *Politics* expressed moral outrage at the depersonalizing effects of total war. Later, as a writer in *Esquire* and the *New Yorker*, he launched for a wider audience what has become an agonizing, unending discussion of the survival of high culture in a media-ridden society. Trilling also found his voice in *Partisan Review*, seeking to escape both the crudeness of Stalinist attitudes toward art and the asocial, ahistorical stance of the New Criticism. His *The Liberal Imagination* (1953), reassuming Matthew Arnold's burden of distinguishing the claims of culture and the self-controlled intellect in a middle-class society, made him the most admired literary critic in postwar America.

McCarthyism is a term derived from Senator Joseph McCarthy's public speeches and congressional investigations of the 1950s, charging that communist spies had infiltrated the government (especially the State Department and the army) and universities (especially Harvard) and that their superiors connived to hide them. The term is usually extended to cover investigations by the House Un-American Activities Committee, particularly in the motion picture industry, as well as trials under the Smith Act of officers of the Communist party. There were also FBI investigations, state inquests, and internal purges and blacklists that cost some persons their jobs, particularly in universities, labor unions, and the entertainment industry. In the background were the "atom secrets" trial of Julius and Ethel Rosenberg and the perjury trial, also involving espionage, of Alger Hiss. The realization that Russia, too, had atomic weapons added to public fright at revelations of scientist-spies. The Korean War intensified revulsion at communist agents who supposedly shaped Far Eastern policy and thereby "lost China," as Hiss was accused of doing, along with the obscure Johns Hopkins professor Owen Lattimore whom McCarthy wildly called "the top Russian espionage agent" in the United States. The press, movies, and television fanned up a public mood that at times approached hysteria.

For the intellectuals, more was at stake than anticommunism. McCarthyism emerged after nearly all had recoiled from the party; those few who remained were soon sent reeling by Nikita Khrushchev's revelations of Stalin's crimes and by the Soviet occupation of Hungary. What bothered the intellectuals was *anti-intellectualism*—a newly fashionable term referring to the abuse that McCarthy, with great political success, poured on them as a privileged class ("It has not been the less fortunate or members of minority groups who have been selling this Nation out, but rather those who have had all the benefits that the wealthiest nation on earth has had to offer—the finest homes, the finest college education, the finest jobs in Government. . . . The bright young men who are born with silver spoons in their mouths are the ones who have been worst"). McCarthy's supporters in journalism derided "eggheads," "twisted-thinking intellectuals," Phi Beta Kappas who lacked common sense. Those who felt under attack lumped McCarthyism together with the 1952 electoral defeat of Adlai Stevenson—the presidential candidate most admired by intellectuals in the twentieth century—and the vast popularity of Dwight D. Eisenhower, whose presidential candidacy had been opposed by Trilling and other Columbia professors who knew him as a university president. The fact that McCarthy had no respect for Eisenhower, that the *National Review* read Eisenhower out of the conservative movement, and that the John Birch Society eventually accused him of being a communist agent did little to mitigate the feeling that these times were like the 1920s, only worse, with a fumbling president, a new Red Scare, raging anti-intellectualism, and deeper causes for alienation than ever before.

Two sets of considerations complicated the intellectuals' reactions to McCarthyism. First, it was clear that innocent persons—that is, persons who had never been communists or fellow travelers, or if they had been, had not the remotest contact with espionage or governmental policy—were hurt. Some were unemployed, at least in their fields of competence, for many years, a few for the rest of their lives. There were some suicides and jail sentences, many broken marriages. It was possible, therefore, to attack McCarthyism in the name of civil liberties, fair play, and common decency, to describe its victims with pathos, to uphold the values of free inquiry as essential to democracy, and never to examine communism at all. Both McCarthy and the Un-American Activities Committee were so irresponsible and undiscriminating that they would have seemed farcical if they had not done so much harm. In the early 1950s, the most common intellectual reactions were equally sweeping in their defenses of all McCarthyism's targets. Intellectual life was at stake, and it was convenient to believe that Hiss and the Rosenbergs must be nothing more than innocent liberal and Jewish victims of unscrupulous know-nothings.

The second set of considerations emerged more slowly: some communists had been spies. Moreover, the party had been so given to tactics of secrecy and so bound to instructions from Moscow that it scarcely honored the ideal of free inquiry. Communists had behaved unscrupulously themselves in their treatment of other human beings. And the party had led many intellectuals, who were prompt to see Hitler's atrocities, to deny Stalin's. What to make of these considerations was a problem that many intellectuals had difficulty in resolving. Early suggestions that the universities should review the competence of communists on their faculties without congressional intrusion raised their own dangers of persecution. Sidney Hook's "Heresy, Yes—Conspiracy, No!," published in the *New York Times Magazine* (1951), struck many readers as assuming a priori the guilt of all communists. Two books by accomplished literary men who rebuked McCarthy but also criticized the united front of intellectuals were widely resented and condemned: Leslie Fiedler's *An End to Innocence* (1955) and Peter Viereck's *The Shame and Glory of the Intellectuals* (1953). Both held that the Constitution protected even foolish speech but that spies ought to be punished without a murmur of liberal protest—a distinction that seemed novel and threatening in the 1950s. Fiedler took a scathing view of sentimental, uncritical attitudes that liberals carried over from the Moscow purges to the Hiss and Rosenberg cases, attitudes that prevented the emergence of responsible social criticism in America. Viereck was no less scathing toward the chic "anti-anticommunism" that was the liberals' disgrace, a substitution of unthinking postures for true intellectual independence. "It is not necessary," wrote Fiedler, "that we liberals be self-flagellants." But it was time for confession and self-examination: a confession that good intentions could lead to "deceit and abuse of power" and a self-examination that could transform "a liberalism of innocence" into one of "responsibility."

These were maverick positions at the height of McCarthyism, but they gained wider plausibility in subsequent decades. For one thing, the fact that some communists were Soviet agents became nearly irrefutable. Though Hiss and the Rosenbergs have unflinching defenders, some scholars, using newly declassified documents, have reconstructed cases against them that have gained widespread and respectful attention. About other cases, which never were *causes célèbres*, there is little controversy. Even Oppenheimer, while protesting his own loyalty, alleged that a friend asked him to pass information to the Soviet Union. The cases of British double agents, who were college comrades of Michael Straight, furnished the basis for John Le Carré's best-selling novels with their bitter themes of betrayal and disillusionment. McCarthy's and Nixon's behavior had not come to appear more laudable, but criticism of intellectual innocence in an often perfidious world no longer seemed perverse or daring.*

It was always possible, of course, to call allegations of espionage a "hoax" if one believed the Soviet Union incapable of evil. A larger reason for changing reflections on McCarthyism was deepening disenchantment even among those who had once been most uncritical. Khrushchev's revelations and the Soviet Union's suppression of revolt in Hungary did their part. The great novelist Alexander Solzhenitsyn deeply moved cosmopolitan, liberal intellectuals; and the mounting evidence of Soviet anti-Semitism helped to dissolve whatever confusion lingered on. There were changes in America, too: the party's decision to purge the popular front leadership and go underground; the death or retirement of those who could be hurt by franker treatment of the past. When the Polish

---

*By the mid-1960s it had been disclosed that liberal anticommunist groups (including *Encounter* magazine in which Fiedler first published his essay on the Rosenbergs) had been covertly subsidized by the CIA. As the historian Christopher Lasch turned the tables on those who savaged other liberals for damning Hitler while condoning Stalin: "the anti-Communist liberals cannot claim to have defended cultural freedom in the United States with the same consistency and vigor with which they defended it in Russia." Both sides had been "had"; both had applied double standards.

Solidarity movement rose against communist dictatorship in the 1980s, Russia had no remaining intellectual defenders. It had once been inadmissible in many circles to say that the intellectuals had been vulnerable to McCarthyism because some had defended the crimes of Stalin; now it was virtually a cliché. In a sedate confession in *The Dream of the Golden Mountains* (1980) Malcolm Cowley, who had once used the *New Republic* to belittle charges about the Moscow purges, reflected: "What the fellow travelers did not realize at the time is that they were accepting responsibility for decisions which they had no share in making and which might be changed overnight by a cablegram from Moscow. Neither did they realize that, as a result of their deep concern for human values, they were acting under instructions from a party that consistently disregarded human values for the greater good of the movement, or that the greater good might be confused with some momentary advantage to be gained in a factional or personal struggle for power."

The greatest irony was that the captivation of some liberal intellectuals by the Soviet Union had coincided with its vilest atrocities under Stalin; disenchantment coincided with what was widely regarded as a "thaw." In the late 1950s and early 1960s it was possible, even fashionable, to observe that the U.S.S.R. and the United States were becoming, as Burnham had predicted, increasingly alike. If this was not exactly complimentary to either nation, it was a starting point for making one's terms with American society and politics. The emerging theory of American institutions was that they were large and less than democratic—certainly the Jeffersonian vision that every man's voice counted equally was outmoded—but in crucial respects they were responsive to various organized constituencies. Most important, the corporations, labor federations, farm blocs, denominations, bureaucratic agencies, and other entities balanced one another in a state of mutual cooperation and vigilance that could be described as "pluralism." There was some sadness in the loss of innocence that this theory acknowledged, but the cheerful fact was that America was not dominated by any extreme faction that could sacrifice the good of others to its ends. The intellectuals' maturing account of the rise and fall of McCarthy contributed to the spread of this view of America.

Most of the anticommunist intellectuals had been appalled by McCarthyism, which had threatened venerable institutions like Harvard and cherished positions in government service. Most anticommunists were not anxious to take Fiedler's position that intellectuals as a class were somehow implicated in Hiss's guilt. Without detailing all the steps anticommunists took in defending themselves against McCarthyism, while cutting themselves off from its most luckless victims, what deserves our attention is their concurrence in an explanation for McCarthy's ascendance and downfall. A series of works—from Bell's anthology of essays, *The New American Right* (1955), to Seymour Martin Lipset's *Political Man* (1960)—ascribed support for the witch-hunt to the "paranoid" legacy of agrarian radicalism and to "status anxieties" among the "new rich" and ethnic groups eager for feelings of "belonging." Whether these ascriptions have any factual validity has sometimes been questioned, especially by scholars who admire the populist tradition, but the account has had continuing appeal to scholars interested in demonstrating that the political system was sound at its center. McCarthyism appeared to be an aberrant instance of excessive power falling briefly to an extremist manipulator of the anxieties of marginal and transitional groups. This demagogue was struck down, moreover, by responsible "centrist" figures in the Republican party and other mainstream institutions. Thus the lessons of McCarthyism, according to this account, were the danger of popular radicalism and the advantages of a pluralistic system that organized the discontented into "interest groups." McCarthyism took place, in sum, *outside* a complex industrial system that required a class of experts and managers. The anticommunists who favored this account did not refute McCarthy's abuse of intellectuals as a privileged class; instead, they renounced the dream of the 1930s that intellectuals should have close bonds with the people.

McCarthyism was profoundly important, beyond the individual lives that it threw off course, because it forced reorientations of intellectual life. For some intellectuals, it quickened a sense of betrayal and expiation, a loss of confidence, a feeling that their class had wandered without guiding values through times of peril and deceit. It led to an unmistakable withdrawal from social criticism that has lasted several decades, a willingness to do one's work— writing book reviews, teaching classes, filing reports, composing scripts—without any illusion of historical significance. For other intellectuals, it encouraged castigation of the people as alien to and resentful of intellectual enterprise. This group regarded intellectuals as central to the institutions that really counted: they were analysts of critical trends and educators of technically competent youth, responsible for breakthroughs in technology and improvements in managerial style. Survey research indicated by the 1960s that intellectuals enjoyed considerable public prestige; the gloom of the anti-intellectual nightmare of the 1950s had subsided. With it had disappeared the ideal of Hull House and John Dewey—the ideal, remembered only for the illusions of the popular front, of proximity to the public and sympathy with its values.

There was much evidence of an "end of ideology," in Bell's sense, an acceptance of large institutions of the mixed economy and political pluralism, a disbelief in the likelihood or desirability of mass action, and a distrust of prescriptions for wholesale change. The analysis of status and anxiety became a stock in trade of social science, without further reference to McCarthyism. For better or worse, the claim was made repeatedly that concern about one's place in "the organization"—how one fit in and what one's prospects were for rising—was endemic in modern society. This key was used to explain the formulas of popular culture, the vogues of popular sociology, psychology, and religion, and many other features of what John Kenneth Galbraith called *The Affluent Society* (1958) or *The New Industrial State* (1967). The "inner-directed" man of the past had given way to the "other-directed" creature of the present, according to David Riesman's *The Lonely Crowd* (1950) and William H. Whyte's *The Organization Man* (1956). This discovery has been restated in one study after another for thirty years. Usually these studies have focused on nonintellectual groups, but one of their implicit themes has been the obsolescence of any hope of mobilizing intellect and emotion to perfect society.

COUNTERCULTURE

While expounding on "the end of ideology" in the 1950s, Daniel Bell commented on the "underlying restlessness" of younger intellectuals who felt they were born too late to experience the excitement of the 1930s, who "flailed" against "the culture," who longed for "a cause to believe in," sometimes with "a deep, desperate, almost pathetic anger." Their elders at least had illusions to regret, but they were living flat lives in "the fat fifties." Thus they cultivated an interest in Zen Buddhism, beatnik poetry, and other fringe movements. If social analysts could predict the future, Bell might have pointed forward to the intellectual radicalism of the 1960s. Instead, he emphasized the impossibility of faith in "apocalyptic" change. He said of his generation that "this may well have been the *last* radical generation for a time," a speculation that in a few short years sounded ridiculous.

At the end of the next decade, Philip Slater in *The Pursuit of Loneliness* (1970) thought he could discern "two cultures" virtually at war:

> The old culture, when forced to choose, tends to give preference to property rights over personal rights, technological requirements over human needs, competition over cooperation, violence over sexuality, concentration over distribution, the producer over the consumer, means over ends, secrecy over openness, social forms over personal expression, striving over gratification, Oedipal love over communal love, and so on. The new counterculture tends to reverse all of these priorities.

The conflict appeared so intense and serious that Slater wrote apocalyptically "that old-culture moderates or liberals will be given the choice, during the next decade or so, between participating in some way in the new culture and living in a fascist regime. The middle is dropping out and choices must be made. . . . If the old culture is not rejected then its adherents must be prepared to accept a bloodbath such as has not been seen in the United States since the Civil War, for genocidal weapons will be on one side and unarmed masses on the other." This rhetoric was not unusual when Slater wrote, but in a few years commentators would be observing how much the 1970s resembled the 1950s (and 1920s), especially among young people who cared mostly about their own careers and personal pleasure, not about communal renovation.

Both these forecasts, so soon unfulfilled, illustrate the fragmentation and packaging of time that began with legends of the 1920s and 1930s and became characteristic of modern intellectual life. If ideology died, the cause may not have been that intellectuals lost faith in the possibility of change; it may be that they discovered that change is ceaseless in modern society but not deep or enduring. They may have become inured, that is, to decennial shifts in fashion.

Consider the career of Paul Goodman, a writer for *Partisan Review* and *Politics* in the 1940s who became a guru of the "new left" in the 1960s. In the decade between, he wrote his thoughts in notebooks, as he explained when they were later published, because "I had no one else to write for or talk to." His "bright schemes" were "evidently not wanted by anybody"; there were no political revolts among the young to encourage him; he "suffered from bleak hours of nothing to do or plan during lonely walks along the river." He despaired of getting his works published: *Growing Up Absurd* (1960) was rejected by a dozen publishers before becoming one of the celebrated works of social criticism in the new decade. By the time he published his notebooks in *Five Years* (1966), he was "too busy" to keep them up. He was "embarked, at 50, in the odd but grateful episode of being a Student Leader." He was flying to round after round of conferences on social planning. Publishers and magazines, including *Playboy* and the *New York Times Magazine,* sought his commentary, and he spoke regularly on college campuses. He published at least eight more books before his death in 1972, with others appearing posthumously. But by the 1980s the "crazy young allies," for whom and to whom he spoke powerfully, no longer abounded, and the cycle of neglect and fame that his life dramatized moved into a new phase. Among a new generation of students his eclipse was probably almost as complete as in the 1950s. Whatever aesthetic, philosophical, or informational value his works may retain in a wide variety of fields—poetry, fiction, gestalt therapy, city planning, linguistics, education—took second place to the coming and going of an extensive youthful cult.

When survivors speak of "the sixties," they have in mind many different events and images: the Peace Corps; the civil rights movement and subsequent demands for "black power"; the resistance to the war in Vietnam; the rise of rock music and the huge "happening" at Woodstock, New York; new artistic styles from "mod" to "pop" to "camp"; new styles in dress and length of hair; experimental courses; angry campus disruptions; firebombed libraries and the shootings at Kent State; street battles during the 1968 Democratic convention in Chicago; hippies, yippies, and flower children; unrelenting media coverage of the young; the violent aftermath of the Symbionese Liberation Army and the Westchester County Brinks robbery. "The sixties" also included airports full of soldiers, the assassinations of John F. Kennedy, Robert L. Kennedy, and Martin Luther King, and riots in many inner cities. "The sixties" are sometimes remembered as a quaintly silly Age of Aquarius, a time when football players painted flowers on their helmets, or as a tragic time when bright youngsters ruined their lives, a time of drugs, sanitaria, and suicide. But for many campus intellectuals the decade remains an unforgettable interlude between the "silent generation" of the 1950s and the "me generation" of the 1970s. There exists a tendency to romanticize the decade as a time when campus life was keen and earnest, when social change was brightly imminent. There are students today who lament that they were born too late.

Many writers who were cast into prominence in the 1960s took it as their role to deny the end of ideology and to forecast changes of momentous consequence. Slater's vision of Armageddon followed naturally Norman Mailer's best-selling reportage in *The Armies of the Night* (1968) and *Miami and the Siege of Chicago* (1968). It should not be forgotten that the well-known "activist" Tom Hayden published a manifesto, *The Trial* (1970), envisioning a network of insurrectionary "liberated zones" carrying on a battle against police and government; and his was one of the more solemn and tactically cautious ventures in the genre. Other commentators were concerned less with military confrontation and more with religious renewal. Goodman, in *New Reformation* (1970) and other works, taught college students to compare their rebellion to Luther's. A Yale law professor, Charles Reich, discovered that two previous stages of human consciousness had given way to a new one, "Consciousness III," which replaced small-town and corporate preoccupations with the discovery that "the individual self is the only true reality." His *The Greening of America* (1970) briefly set the terms for older people's polite conversation about the young. A more thoughtful historical interpretation, Theodore Roszak's *The Making of a Counter Culture* (1969) saw in youth movements a healthy openness to mysticism and magic—to all human "non-intellective" capacities—that contrasted with the old left's uncritical respect for science. "The primary project of our counter culture," Roszak wrote, "is to proclaim a new heaven and a new earth so vast, so marvelous that the inordinate claims of technical expertise must of necessity withdraw to a subordinate and marginal status in the lives of men." Recalling the exhilaration that "budding intellectuals" felt when cult figures like Goodman, Mailer, Norman O. Brown, Herbert Marcuse, Timothy Leary, and (in a new phase) Leslie Fiedler addressed them—some spoke of sex, some of Zen, or psychoanalysis, or religion, or literature, or drugs—the cultural his-

torian Morris Dickstein speaks of "the startling conjunc-
tion" they made "between the world of ideas and a new
mode of experience, a new consciousness."

Dickstein goes on to notice how these messages have
already lost their power:

> . . . the sixties are long over. So much of what these
> men advocated has either been obscenely, obsti-
> nately frustrated, or, worse still, has come to pass,
> with the mixed results we have come to expect in
> all human affairs. Commune life, the death of the
> family, open marriage, the politics of confronta-
> tion, educational reform, participatory democracy,
> mind-changing chemicals—all these promises have
> been simultaneously fulfilled and undermined. In
> some respects our society will never be the same;
> in other ways it never really changed.

In the 1960s the promise of cultural regeneration seemed
authentic enough for some "budding intellectuals" to "drop
out" altogether. But even at the time there were debunk-
ing criticisms of the counterculture, and these have grown
formidable in postmortems on the decade. The first dismissed the would-be reformation as a conflict of generations, no less destructive because it could be explained
psychologically; the second dismissed it as a contrivance
of the mass media and Madison Avenue, and thus not very
dangerous at all.

The first criticism surged throughout the long, learned,
and angry *The Conflict of Generations* (1969) by Lewis Feuer,
a professor at the University of California who had no use
for Goodman and other panderers to childish fantasy.
Feuer's was only the most extreme (in length, learning, and
anger) of numerous analyses of "the generation gap," often
written by veterans of the old left, taking a withering look

at all the harmful follies of the. past. In laying bare the "Oedipal" roots of political protest—the resentful emotions that undermined altruistic idealism—the campus revolts did as much as any other events of the cold war era to put an end to ideology.

For an example of the second criticism, we may take Tom Wolfe's *Radical Chic* (1970), a sarcastic account of the composer Leonard Bernstein's fund-raising party for the Black Panthers. Wolfe's experiment in the "new journalism" popularized the view of radicalism as fashionably foolish (he found New York's 1960s "the wildest, looniest time since the 1920's"). But the criticism was made more seriously by radicals themselves. Marcuse found in his own rise to celebrity status confirmation of "my philosophy, which is in this society everything can be co-opted, everything can be digested." And Roszak, after noting how fashion designers, feature editors, and advertising men were parading messages about "today's rebellious youth," worried that the counterculture might not "survive these twin perils: on the one hand, the weakness of its cultural rapport with the disadvantaged; on the other, its vulnerability to exploitation as an amusing side show of the swinging society." Ideology ended for some of his contemporaries in the sad realization that their fears were right; they were "co-opted."

Ideology expired twice, then, in the decades after World War II, first in the crumbling "dream of the golden mountains" of those who were young in the 1930s, and second in the unrealized "non-intellective" reformation of those who were young in the 1960s. One fact of intellectual life in the 1970s and 1980s was the awareness among these two groups of writers and scholars that their careers had been episodic, floating in and out of political phases. Yet there was no way of predicting the consequences of the opposing lessons: that youth periodically revolts against the old order; and that the media in a mass society have the power to exaggerate and deflate changes in cultural styles.

EQUALITY
AND ELITISM

Just as the overwhelming majority of intellectuals and students were not Marxists in the 1930s, most were not radicals or hippies in the 1960s. "The movement," as left-wing intellectuals and students called themselves, customarily exaggerated its political power and underestimated the importance of its impact on uncommitted students. It was always eager to "take to the streets," or to drop out, and it expressed constant dismay at the lives of privilege and responsibility awaiting university-trained young people. Protests against student draft deferments were the first sign of this dismay; bitter assaults on the "multiversity" as an arm of the "military-industrial complex" (a phrase actually originated by Eisenhower) came later. Yet the fact remains that it was in the universities and among the most highly educated Americans that "the sixties" had their most profound and lasting consequences.

Some of these consequences were paradoxical. As part of the assault on "the establishment," for example, there was extensive criticism of the uses of knowledge to train experts and managers for government and "corporate" institutions. This criticism was particularly ferocious in controversies over campus recruitment visits by a chemical company that made napalm for bombing Vietnam and over Defense Department–sponsored research by university professors. At the same time, however, there were criticisms of "rigid" university requirements and "irrelevant" or "elitist" courses. Many colleges and universities dismantled their systems of mandatory courses and made room for new "relevant" ones on subjects that interested students, like comic books, science fiction, or the music of Bob Dylan. Similarly, grading standards were relaxed, sometimes with the rationale that students would pursue subjects for their intrinsic merits rather than "just to get a grade." By the 1970s some promoters of these reforms were distressed by the results: increasing numbers of pre-professional students anxiously preparing for positions in the corporations, students who had no time for optional liberal arts courses and who resented grades lower than an "A" that might keep them out of a professional graduate program. The reforms of the 1960s facilitated a transition from the old ideal of the service intellectual to a narrower and more personally ambitious conception of graduate education, from the old notion of a quasi-aristocracy characterized by critical independence to more self-centered career orientations.*

Some concerns of the 1960s became institutionalized in intellectual life—that is, they went beyond being matters of protest and agitation and were incorporated into the legal forms and organizational structures that controlled the behavior of intellectuals. This appears to have happened with the concept of ecology. In the training of

---

*It was sometimes observed that rebellious students in the 1960s, especially the children of college-educated parents, felt they could get a job regardless of their campus behavior. By criticizing the professional aspects of education, they overlooked the importance of expanding universities, particularly the state institutions, to large populations of first-generation students. And in the recessive economy of the 1970s, with no war to absorb surplus young people, students knew they could not automatically gain admission to graduate programs or positions in firms. In any case, Roszak and other fervent champions of the counterculture could not have been surprised at how things worked out. They had predicted that, if the new consciousness failed to take hold, the next generation would be on the way to technological despotism.

young professionals after the 1960s, for example, more formal attention was likely to be paid to the human and natural environment than had been in previous decades. In some ways this concern may even have replaced the old notion of Christian service. The law, furthermore, required enough attention to the "environmental impact" of business projects and government policies to furnish considerable employment for scientists, historians, folklorists, archaeologists, anthropologists, and especially lawyers. Beyond these formal changes, the term *ecology* had a lasting meaning among educated professionals that many of the anti-authoritarian slogans of the 1960s ("Power to the people," "Don't trust anyone over thirty") never acquired.

A better example is the concept of "equal opportunity." A majestic work of collaborative social science, Gunnar Myrdal's *The American Dilemma: The Negro Problem and Modern Democracy* (1944), had singled out "equality of opportunity" as central among the beliefs that united Americans, though it was violated by the nation's laws and customs. Myrdal's predictions of post–World War II changes in the status of blacks, regarded as too optimistic when offered, were borne out by events. But by the mid-1960s it was apparent that the civil rights movement was moving beyond demands to end Jim Crow laws. The issue arose of de facto inequality, not just the patterns of segregation enforced by law, but the practical consequences of a history of racial oppression. The issue became urgent when blacks appeared to advocate positive remedies in the admissions, hiring, and promotions policies of colleges, contractors, and government agencies. Some of these institutions took voluntary steps to increase black representation in the 1960s, and in the next decade government and the courts established legal pressures to accelerate the process. Since these steps sometimes implied reverse discrimination against whites competing for the same position, they could be viewed as infringements of the principle of equal opportunity. There were also complaints that they were ineffective in helping blacks, especially in the educated professions. Few issues have divided intellectuals with greater bitterness. The journalist Theodore White, reflecting on twenty-five years of American politics in *America in Search of Itself* (1982), summarized among the discontents that had led to the election of Ronald Reagan: "the division of Americans by race and national origin into groups, each entitled to special privileges." Equality, in White's view, had created "a monster whose shadow hangs over all American politics today." But equality retained a standing in law, unthinkable at the end of World War II, that defined some of the terms of intellectual life. Furthermore, the subjects of slavery and racial oppression in the New World began in the 1960s, as never before, to command the attention of some of the most intelligent and productive investigators in history, sociology, psychology, and economics. The changes they introduced in the content of intellectual discourse might prove more significant than those in institutional contexts.

American Dilemma had observed, in a seldom discussed appendix, "a parallel between the position of, and feeling toward, women and Negroes" in a society with lingering "atavistic" attitudes of paternalism. In the early 1960s, however, female equality was not a prominent concern of "the movement." (The subject scarcely arose in early collections of new left writings, and Goodman's *Growing Up Absurd* assumed, without criticism, that women had such worthy experiences in motherhood that they were spared the frustrations of males in the work place.) By the middle of the decade, female radicals were attacking male comrades for treating them as inferiors, dependents, and sex objects; soon thereafter, they were issuing manifestos against "sexism," a new word coined to parallel "racism," suggesting a pattern of de facto oppression and exploitation that must be rooted out. As with racial equality, there had been forerunners: Betty Friedan's *The Feminine Mystique* (1963) was a landmark of modern feminism. But it was not until the end of the decade that "consciousness-raising" groups brought women's grievances to the fore in intellectual circles and media attention made sexual discrimination a national issue.

Because the historical experiences of women were in some ways dissimilar to those of blacks—women as a class were less deprived, less disenfranchised, less poorly educated, less excluded from national media—women were able to take greater advantage of new requirements of equality. There were some charges that women had, in fact, blunted the drive for black equality. Moreover, leaders in fields that had traditionally been part of women's sphere—preeminently elementary school teaching—complained that with so many new opportunities open to talented women, their fields were suffering a decline in quality. Feminists pointed out that gains in women's rights and status were often exaggerated; much institutional discrimination persisted. The failure of the signal feminist issue of the 1970s, the Equal Rights Amendment to the Constitution, was due to many causes, but surely it indicated limits to public acceptance of equality between the sexes. Nevertheless, there was no doubt that in some academic fields and professions, as well as political discourse, the 1960s launched an era of greatly increased participation by women. Not only was there a new legal context of "affirmative action," but there also emerged a lively, urgent scholarship and popular literature written from a feminist perspective. The appearance of *Signs* (first published, 1975), an impressive journal of feminist scholarship on women, with a long list of editors and contributors, might therefore be taken as a second milestone in modern intellectual feminism.

We have previously commented that the 1960s submerged the old ideal of the service intellectual. Another notion of the interwar years also showed signs of vanishing: cosmopolitanism. Here too there was a paradox: early participants in "the movement" frequently viewed themselves as exemplars of a new world that would transcend parochial differences of religion, ethnicity, and gender. Their endeavors somewhat resembled Randolph Bourne's 1916 appeal for a "trans-national America," as they pieced together fragments of disparate religions and philosophies in fashioning a new ideology of freedom in which blacks and whites, men and women, would strive for new levels of consciousness. For some individuals this striving has not ceased: some feminists believe, for example, that the pursuit of equality will liberate men from sex roles that have limited their intellectual and emotional growth. But by the late 1960s there was an unmistakable tendency to disparage the cosmopolitan ideal as an illusion that deprived women, blacks, white ethnics, Indians, homosexuals, and other minorities of opportunities for a satisfactory intellectual identity. In the intellectual pluralism of ensuing years, differences in background regained so much importance that one might almost speak of re-racination.

Many sources of this change stemmed from outside intellectual life. Advocates of black power made "white liberal" a term of reproach, often with overtones of anti-Semitism. The warfare between Israel and the Arab bloc gave Zionism greater respectability than it had ever previously possessed among Jewish intellectuals. White ethnics, reacting angrily to black gains in civil rights and urban politics, sought to raise their own images of group solidarity and to disclose patterns of WASP (white Anglo-

Saxon Protestant) discrimination against the descendants of European Catholics. Refinements in public-opinion polling made the predilections of ethnic groups—as well as women and, in some cities, homosexuals—a new element in political campaigning and journalistic coverage of public issues. The change was soon reflected in the institutional contexts of intellectual life: as the liberal arts "core" curriculum disintegrated, universities added new programs in Afro-American studies, Jewish studies, ethnic studies, Native American studies, and Chicano-Riqueño studies, frequently with bitter controversy over the fitness of those who were not born into a particular subculture to teach a newly defined constituency. As affirmative action programs focused attention on the distribution of power and prestige among groups defined by race and gender, in addition to the supposedly neutral application of standards of merit and ability, candidates for positions and financial grants were asked whether they belonged to various "minorities"—a request that once would have seemed appalling evidence of discrimination. Furthermore, the change was reflected in the intellectual concerns of writers and scholars—for example, in the statistical discovery of the persistent dominance of ethnoreligious factors over ideological programs in the history of voting behavior or in the substitution of ethnic and sexual identity for older notions of character.

Modernist intellectuals since the 1910s had disparaged the values and preoccupations of the middle classes (the "booboisie," Mencken called them). But in lampooning the "culture" of the Victorians, they generally cherished their own aspirations for creating an authentically "high" culture. The wish to discriminate between spurious and genuine culture had lingered in *Partisan Review*'s attacks on the popular front and in Macdonald's derision of "mid-cult" in the 1950s. Even in that decade, however, some expressed concern that "high" art, music, and literature had become too esoteric and detached—a dead end in a mass society. Meanwhile, discontented writers complained that America's most prestigious intellectuals were too comfortably dependent on the privileged classes. In 1953, for example, the poet Delmore Schwartz charged Lionel Trilling, an honored figure because of his searching appraisals of the liberal conscience, with caring too much about "the ideas and attitudes and interests of the educated class." (The charge was accurate enough; the fact that it was offered in criticism was a harbinger of things to come.) By the late 1960s spokesmen for the young were decrying the "elitism" of the culture into which they had to be "indoctrinated" if they wished to rise in society. One critic spoke of Trilling's "implicit snobbishness" and "mandarin exclusiveness"; others said that it was time to turn the tables and let the elders learn from the young.

The issue of "elitism" could be raised crudely: Why were Plato, Beethoven, and Picasso more deserving of study than the Beatles or the black convict Eldridge Cleaver? Two professors of English announced that "high culture propagates the values of those who rule." Some feminists dismissed Western philosophy as "irrelevant" to them. A historian ridiculed his profession's concentration on "Great White Men." But there were forceful critiques of the blindness of conventional "culture" to patterns of segmentation and exploitation in the economy and society; of the fatuity of placing a few figures from a few eras (Periclean Athens, Elizabethan England, the Enlightenment, Transcendentalism) on pedestals to stand for the timeless concerns of "Western man"; of the ignorance that resulted from overlooking "nonliterary" sources and "nonelite" cultures; of the impotence of an intellectual ideal divorced from popular concerns; and of the alienation experienced by first-generation college students whose education had no connection with their backgrounds or future jobs.

None of these arguments was entirely new. But they all converged to damage seriously, perhaps to destroy, the conception of intellectual life as a network of prestigious vocations, informed by acquaintance with a single culture, with peculiar responsibilities for leadership. It had long been commonplace to observe that America offered abundant opportunities for "intelligent" leaders but that the people were generally apathetic. Such observations had been made brilliantly in Myrdal's *American Dilemma,* which praised "the Pullman class" (not the porters but the travelers; today we would say the airport class) for their cosmopolitanism, their willingness to take risks and make sacrifices, and their feelings of responsibility for the nation as a whole. This class of business and professional men had been "fairly open to talent from below and . . . contained a disproportionate amount of the nation's brains and courage." Most important, "its members have been willing and prepared to take the leadership made so easy for them by the inertia of the masses." Thus, Myrdal concluded, American society was notable for the initiative of its enterprising leaders, but it also had a great weakness: the "passivity" and "inertia" of the masses. Similar observations were made in the 1960s by those radicals who sought to organize communities of the poor. Indeed, there was heated debate over whether poverty was a dispiriting "culture" in its own right, and one argument for expanding educational opportunities was to lift greater numbers into the dynamic, cosmopolitan class. But the attack of "elitism" tended to view this argument with suspicion: neither the privileges of the establishment nor the pretensions of "high" culture had any justification.

Brilliant new scholarship undermined belief in the

"inertia" of the masses by demonstrating the existence of articulate leaders and vital cultural systems among all kinds of laboring folk and "ordinary" people, from slaves to prairie farmers, from women's circles to ethnic factory hands. The values of an immigrant family who struggled to stay together were every bit as legitimate as those of the rootless, ambitious "Pullman class." These demonstrations raised serious new questions about how the most educated classes maintained their power, questions of lively concern to historians and social scientists. But they undermined the cosmopolitan ideal, and it was unclear how they could lead to a new educational "core," free of elitism, that might unify intellectual life and endow professions with some ideal of learning that went beyond technical training. In the universities, particularly in the humanities, it was not uncommon by the mid-1970s to hear professors speak of "crisis."

OBJECTIVE DISCIPLINE

All roads led to the university. This institution had been ingeniously set up in the late nineteenth century so that it not only furnished higher education to increasing numbers of young men and women but also carried out research of considerable importance to other social institutions. It brought together dissenters and bohemians with pragmatists and those who wished to serve important functions in the existing society. It upheld the traditions of Western culture while supporting specialized science. Not in itself a center of wealth and power, it employed faculty and educated students whose services were valuable to prosperous, powerful institutions. In some ways an ivory tower, it built up ancillary relationships with independent laboratories, foundations, professional societies, corporations, and every level of government. Combining such diverse energies, it proved in one century to have a magnetic, consolidating hold on intellectual life.

The university was certainly not a monolithic institution. Varying greatly in size, funding, and mission, universities changed by emulating one another, and yet they preserved their distinctiveness. They were sufficiently decentralized that professors gave keenest interest to affairs in their own departments. Yet they were sufficiently alike that students and professors could transfer from one to another at important stages in their careers. America had no single center of intellectual activity, but despite all this diversity and mobility, universities were able to sustain a policy of common, exclusive legitimacy. In 1810 Moses Stuart left a pastorate to come to Andover Seminary and teach biblical literature, a subject in which he had little preparation. At that time, such an appointment was not unusual, and Stuart taught himself so successfully that he became one of America's most distinguished scholars. It is unlikely that any Ph.D.-granting university at the end of the century would have hired him, and his chances of mastering a specialized discipline would have been remote.

The universities replaced the churches as centers of intellectual life. This did not mean that churches diminished in number, nor did it necessarily mean that ministers became less well educated. It did not imply that churches in general were opposed to the growth of universities or that universities in general conceived themselves as antireligious. But the clergy became less prominent as an intellectual class, less important in the advancement of learning and production of knowledge, than the rising, secularly defined professoriate. The point is evident in the relative numbers of ministers and professors as revealed in U.S. census statistics.

The Disconnection of Intellectual Life

Year	Clergymen	Professors
1900	118,000	7,000
1930	149,000	62,000
1940	141,000	77,000
1950	171,000	127,000
1960	202,000	179,000

After 1960 the census used different classifications, so figures are not strictly comparable. But in 1979 it reported
282,000 ministers serving parishes and 461,000 university
teachers (a figure that does not include others classified
professionally as scientists or social scientists). Moreover,
ministers had no function in the transmission of intellectual knowledge and values to compare with the training
of Ph.D.'s. In 1900 the number of Ph.D.'s awarded was
382; by 1930 it had risen to 2,299; by 1950 to 6,633; by
1960 to 9,829; and by 1970 to 29,866. Ministers remained
a large prestigious group, often counted among the educated professions, but intellectual life was increasingly
dominated by professors whose Ph.D.'s certified their
competence in specialized scholarship.

Gentlemanly amateur traditions nearly vanished in the
nineteenth century, and most of the intellectual professions depended on the universities for training and leadership. The same was true of government employees,
though in all professions those who taught and those who
practiced "in the field" might well hold unflattering stereotypes of one another. In some professional schools
professors were likely to be supplemented by "veterans"*

---

*In coining this term in *The Community of Scholars* (1962), Paul Goodman proposed that veterans would bring a greater sense of reality to
the universities and, at the same time, contribute to humanizing the
professions. They might help to create a "philosophy of medicine" or

who knew the field from a practical angle. But the university rewarded productive research most of all, and those without the Ph.D. were likely to be regarded as second-class citizens.

The principal exception to the university's twentieth-century dominance over intellectual life was the free-lance world of letters centered in New York. This was the world where Frederic Howe felt he got a second education among the Greenwich Village literati and where Dwight Macdonald encountered two of the three important "educational institutions" in his life, *Partisan Review* and the Trotskyist movement. (The other was Phillips Exeter Academy. Significantly, he omitted his alma mater, Yale.) For several decades New York was a center of manifestos, little magazines, animated talk of literature and revolution. Men of letters disliked the sterility, as they saw it, of the universities. Mencken was most extreme, but Lewis Mumford wrote sweetly of "Mannahatta, my university," and congratulated himself on qualities in his work "that I could not have achieved by climbing the academic ladder step by step." What made possible this alternative intellectual life was the expanded literate public and the system of small publishing houses that offered writers fees for reviews, monetary advances for bright ideas, and editorial and copywriting jobs to see them through hard times.

In recent years it has been widely reported that the free-lance intellectual is dead—or has joined the university. The introduction to a recent issue of *Daedalus* magazine (1983) regretted that the man of letters "has disap-

---

a "social theory of engineering." But he recognized the second-class status, and he puzzled over the problem of moving the universities closer to society without aggravating their dependence on corporations and the military.

peared, leaving a large cultural void that no other figure or institution seems to fill." Literary criticism had become the province of university dons, who did not "imagine one of their principal obligations to be the enlightenment of an uninstructed anonymous public." Some contributors to *Daedalus* felt that literary criticism had become "incomprehensible to laymen," thus worsening the effects on literacy of the advent of television and, soon to follow, the computer. The literary historian Daniel Aaron saw evidence that society still included many intelligent readers, dissatisfied with both arcane "serious" writing and "trashy" best-sellers, but without the guidance once supplied by the Edmund Wilsons, Lewis Mumfords, and Malcolm Cowleys they were lost in the literary marketplace. Besides serving as middlemen between avant-garde artists and the public, the men of letters had also discussed the cultural implications of science, history, and religion; they had reported on foreign travels and assessed American manners and morals. Without them, public discourse was stratified and impoverished.

It was unclear how the man of letters (the term arose before there was much self-consciousness about "genderized" language) died. Aaron emphasized the demise of financially shaky magazines during the depression of the 1930s. He also suggested that politics had crowded out other interests in the 1930s and that men of letters turned to "personal concerns" after World War II. We might add the mergers and corporate takeovers that eliminated independent publishers, magazines, and booksellers and replaced them with diversified, multinational communications firms keeping a close watch on costs and profits. It also seems relevant to add the diminished self-confidence that attended the repetitive ends of ideology in the 1950s and 1970s. But all of these explanations ignore the positive, consolidating power of the universities luring intellectuals to positions of prestige and security within their walls. After the 1960s most of the essayists in the surviving journals of intellectual life—*New York Review of Books,* for example, or *Commentary*—had academic affiliations.

Daniel Bell once offered a simple distinction "between the intellectual and the scholar. . . . The scholar has a bounded field of knowledge, a tradition, and seeks to find his place in it, adding to the accumulated, tested knowledge of the past as to a mosaic. . . . The intellectual begins with *his* experience, *his* individual perceptions of the world, *his* privileges and deprivations, and judges the world by these sensibilities." In the postwar world the scholar's position appeared more realistic and attractive than the intellectual's, and past knowledge became less germane to scholarly endeavor than the "recent literature" of a specialized field, literature that might extend back no farther than a few years and make no reference to traditional categories of the good, the true, and the beautiful. The boundaries between scholarly "contributions" and public discourse became, in many instances, impassable.

There were periodic complaints that scholars had gone too far in abdicating the traditional responsibilities of intellectuals and abandoning high-minded discussion of the human condition and the good society. Such complaints were commonly made by opponents of the Vietnam War, most eloquently by the distinguished linguist Noam Chomsky. In *American Power and the New Mandarins* (1967), he reproached the self-serving "pseudo-scientific posing" of scholars who, in the name of "the end of ideology," drew up a new program of "value-free" expertise, in which they enjoyed prestige and comfort: "Anyone can be a moral individual, concerned with human rights and problems; but only a college professor, a trained expert, can solve technical problems by 'sophisticated' methods. Ergo, it is only problems of the latter sort that are real." Thus there was an element of self-aggrandizement in their prescriptions for Third World peoples and American society. Chomsky repeatedly praised Bourne's heroic criticism of Dewey and the pragmatists of World War I, and his own book deserves equal rank as an incisive dissent from prevailing tendencies in intellectual life.* Nevertheless, since many opponents of the war had nothing but scorn for "elitism" in higher education, the force of this analysis of value-free expertise was diffused and muted.

Other critics, after the Vietnam War, pointed out modes of abdication that had little to do with sharing in political power. Scholars might have few illusions of political influence and still recognize the personal gratification and professional rewards that flowed from specialization. Discussions of ethics, history, political and aesthetic ideals had led to inconclusive talk of irony and ambiguity. It was more personally satisfying to address narrow questions that had answers, at least as they were defined within the perimeter of one discipline. Academic disciplines, furthermore, looked askance on popularizers who "rehashed" ancient questions, while they supported the advancement of researchers who made concrete findings relevant to a well-bounded discourse. Usually, these findings were determined by the availability of "hard" information subject to quantitative investigation. There was no denying the "substantive" progress made in newly "sophisticated" fields. Yet there were complaints that psychology had turned away

---

*Chomsky's hard-hitting attacks on individual scholars did nothing to limit their subsequent influence. For example, he singled out for criticism an article by Ithiel de Sola Pool on "The Necessity for Social Scientists Doing Research for Government" (1966), but Professor Pool was a leader in the increasingly influential fields of applied social science and policy studies in the 1970s. He had harsh words for Zbigniew Brzezinski's "America in the Technetronic Age" (1968), but Brzezinski went on to become President Carter's national security adviser.

from issues raised by Aristotle, Locke, or Freud; that English had ceased to instruct the common reader in literary appreciation; that political science had forsaken the high road of political theory; that economics had substituted a hypothetical calculus for the study of institutions; that anthropology was more concerned with abstract models than actual cultures; that sociology had lost touch with history; and that history had lost its will to offer syntheses of the progress of humankind. In most fields these complaints smacked of the discontent of old guard scholars whose fields had passed them by (although the recession of the 1970s and 1980s aroused wider sensitivity, sometimes rather opportunistic, to popular contempt for overspecialized and unreadable scholarship). In philosophy, which had lost its traditional standing as the keystone of scholarly inquiry, there was noticeably wide interest in Richard Rorty's *Philosophy and the Mirror of Nature* (1979), a book seeking to redefine this discipline in relation to the time-honored "conversation of the West."

For the most part, complaints about the narrowness of academic disciplines command our attention, not because they succeeded in restoring respect for high culture, but because they highlighted the rampant segmentation of the universities. The centripetal pressures of specialization separated scholars from most common discourse, except for comparisons of methods and desultory conversations about academic politics. Chomsky had called the professors "mandarins," but few of them had the role in government that the term implied. Others spoke of the "intelligentsia," but few retained the sense of obligatory dissent and criticism implicit in that term. It was probably most accurate to speak of "academic specialists" confined in their present-minded disciplines. Yet there was no doubt of the universities' prominence as major social enterprises. The research they supported was essential to business, medicine, communications, transportation, welfare, law—to numerous activities in what came to be called the public sector and the private sector. They imparted fundamental language and mathematical skills (some said not well enough), as well as technical and professional training, to many thousands of young people who moved into positions of responsibility in a complex social system. They were flexible enough to furnish places for alienated and cultivated thinkers, even those who resisted dominant trends, without sacrificing the indispensable purposes of technical research and training.

The universities nourished an ideology that was different from the nineteenth-century glorification of cultural ideals and also from the 1930s and 1960s radicals' belief in the need for a drastic overhaul of society. It was an ideology that accepted the importance of a succession of short-run problems—both in society and in the internal discourse of scholarly subcommunities—problems that required limited, expert solutions. The "end of ideology" was, as Chomsky claimed, itself an ideology. When this ideology was challenged in the 1960s, one of the nation's keenest analysts of the social position of intellectuals, Edward Shils of the University of Chicago, identified the prevailing strategy: neutralize and accommodate the dissenters, but recognize that "the stability of the larger society depends . . . on the maintenance, within the culture and the institutional system of the intellectuals, of the predominance of that element which accepts an objective discipline and the integration of academic institutions into the central institutional system of American society." Shils's technically complicated language mirrored his view of the relations between intellectuals and society.

This strategy had unmistakable appeal in the midst of

affluence that seemed to afford unlimited means of support, both for the accommodation of mavericks and for
the maintenance of objectivity. For the universities, the
period from the 1940s to the mid-1970s witnessed steady
expansion in the number and size of institutions, in the
munificence of their budgets, in the elaborateness of research technology, and in the variety and amount of
funding for individual scholars. Intellectual life came to
depend on an expansive economy, and in the succeeding
period of "stagflation" there were bound to be some dis-
tressful reappraisals. No one called for return to the
idealized culture of the Victorians; there was not enough
agreement on what an educated person ought to know.
No one knew if the crisis was temporary, but the signs of
reappraisal were unmistakable.

In *Daedalus* (1978) the president of Johns Hopkins,
Steven Muller, offered a convincing historical perspective. World War II had inaugurated thirty years of "mobilization" in which the universities had accepted the rewards of close partnership with government—lavish
funding, hosts of students, a strong sense of social importance—without considering its costs, including "exaggeration . . . of the virtues of applied research." Now universities were awakening to their dependence on
government in a time of shrinking funds and entangling
regulations. What had sustained the partnership was the
"pragmatic" outlook of the New Deal, which had suggested that all problems could be solved "without the need
for theory or philosophy," without considering "the in-
tractability of historic and human conditions." Academic
disciplines had hardened this outlook by cutting free from
values and emphasizing their "objective and carefully
measured" contributions. As a result, universities faced the
awesome difficulty of rebuilding consensus on what a hu-

man being needed to know. "Basic research and pure scholarship" must be reinvigorated, while professional and vocational education returned to a subsidiary station in institutions whose paramount obligation was to transmit values. These were not simply inheritances from the past: in a "new humanism," individuals must understand the technologies on which they daily depend and must gain adequate knowledge of global realities from which no one is insulated. It was time to "shake off nostalgia for a recent past in which too much was taken for granted, and to regain self-confidence."

This reappraisal was unusually optimistic, but even Muller did not minimize the difficulties of discovering "an internal consensus of values" and a new commitment to purpose in a fragmented community of scholars, surrounded by a pluralistic and anti-elitist world. Many scholars might assent to Muller's view that "the inner core of values of the modern university is . . . founded upon reason and its rigorous application." But if pressed to define reason in relation to the individual and society, could they reach agreement?

HARD TIMES

In the intellectual life of the postwar era, there was no consensus on the respective merits of reason, the emotions, and the will. The terms survived from earlier centuries, with fragments of meaning attached to them, and political thinkers deployed them in various efforts to construct a coherent outlook on the relations between humanity, society, and nature. Because of their concern for philosophical consistency and respect for tradition, conservatives probably gave the greatest attention to classical and medieval conceptions of human nature. Thus one writer, Russell Kirk, averred that conservatism credited emotion with more importance than reason-worshipping liberalism. According to another conservative, Frank Meyer, however, "conservatism is not antirational": it simply insists on the use of reason within "the civilizational tradition." And other conservatives blandly accepted a world of competing interest groups. Liberals and radicals occasionally championed emotional self-expression or debated the power and limits of reason, but their arguments were usually keyed to the political affairs of the moment. Rather than dissecting the autonomous capacities of the individual, they were apt to speak vaguely of human "needs" that were being frustrated or fulfilled.

The single time when ancient questions of human nature threatened to regain prominence was the interlude of the 1960s, when many young people (and the sages they admired) expressed a desire to expand consciousness and to escape the repressiveness of scientific reason and technological complexity. The celebration of "non-intellective" human capacities often led to a kind of quietism; it was the faith of communes and dropouts. But because it arose simultaneously with violent confrontations on campuses, including some destruction of research facilities and much abusive treatment of professors, it prompted a "counterreformation" in which the powers of reason and respect for authority received impassioned defenses. Parallels with the cultural controversies of the Great Awakening had the ring of relevance, both to students and to their teachers. But this episode produced no new Edwards or Chauncy, and it would be hard to show that it arrayed any enduring cohorts of emotion and reason. At most, as we have seen, it promoted the theory that the conflict of generations, particularly in a media-dominated society, was bound to excite sporadic revolts against intellectual authority. In the 1970s public discourse shifted to the needs of the elderly and to another subject that fascinated intellectuals—the midlife crisis.

In the wake of the 1960s, some analysts viewed society at large as catering to immaturity and antirationality. Explanations varied: the lack of intrinsically rewarding work; the coddling of children in their most self-absorbed stages; the snares of advertising obsolescent goods; the sexual revolution and the decline of genuine intimacy; the collapse of faith in common purposes or higher laws. Taken together, such analyses suggested that the counterculture of the 1960s had succeeded in portraying American society as self-centered, alienating, and unfulfilling even though it failed to establish any conviction that alternatives were viable. It was hard to know what to make of contradictory evidence in popular culture. Did the extraordinarily popular film *Star Wars* (1977) with its mystical evocation of "the Force"—"trust your feelings," whispers the old knight to the novice—suggest a yearning for "a cause to believe in," even an oversoul? What should be made of computer games with their romantic scenarios set in the Middle Ages or the valiant future? Technological culture offered no shortage of fantasies.

Wherever these fantasies might lead, a number of writers in the 1970s agreed on the epidemic dimensions of American "narcissism." The other-directed had been reduced, it seemed, to exposed, insecure selves, lacking any hope of finding intellectual strength or social purpose. For the aesthetic, moral, and political systems of the past the American was substituting a desperate concern for how he or she felt. This analysis was summarized and broadened in a vigorous work of cultural criticism, *The Culture of Narcissism* (1979) by Christopher Lasch of the University of Rochester. Starting with reports from psychoanalysts that the typical "repressed" patient of the past was giving way to a new type of shallow, impulse-ridden character, Lasch moved to other signs of what he called a "dying" way of life, particularly among the educated middle classes. "Having no hope of improving their lives in any of the ways that matter, people have convinced themselves that what matters is psychic self-improvement: getting in touch with their feelings, eating health food, taking lessons in ballet or belly dancing, immersing themselves in the wisdom of the East, jogging, learning how to 're-late,' overcoming the 'fear of pleasure.' " Ranging learnedly through a broad array of topics in both popular and avant-garde culture, Lasch indicated that the functions of the man of letters were still vital in some corners of the universities.

Some of Lasch's arguments echoed complaints about public opinion and spurious mass culture in the 1920s; they built upon themes in Riesman's discovery of the *Lonely Crowd* or Goodman's sympathy with the drifting young in *Growing Up Absurd.* The loss of intrinsic satisfactions and enduring values had become a traditional theme of American conservative and radical writers since the "Love Song of J. Alfred Prufrock" and *Middletown,* a theme that was often expressed by treating cultural patterns as diseases. Lasch's discovery that "strategies of narcissistic survival" actually reproduced "the worst features of the collapsing civilization" may even remind us of Cowley's comments on the Greenwich Village idea and the spread of consumerism. If Lasch's diagnosis was unusual in its comprehensiveness and incisiveness, it also appeared at a moment when many outside intellectual circles were unusually receptive to what it had to say. A popular song by Judy Collins bemoaned a "hard time for lovers" when everyone was saying, "I got to be *me.*" President Carter was so taken with Lasch's book that some commentators thought it unseemly for a political leader to lean so heavily on *this* kind of intellectual. After retreating to Camp David to meditate on his failures and those of the American people, Carter made a famous televised speech on "the erosion of confidence in the future," on the tendency to "worship self-indulgence and consumption," and on the discovery that "piling up material goods cannot fill the emptiness of lives." It was time to turn away from "a mistaken idea of freedom" as "the right to grasp some advantage over others."

Perhaps Carter meant to increase hope of improving lives in ways that really mattered. Otherwise, his appeal for collective psychic self-improvement might have substantiated Lasch's analysis of cultural malady. In any case, Ronald Reagan targeted this speech as damning evidence of Carter's infidelity to the people. There was nothing wrong with them; the trouble was their leadership. After the 1980 elections, popular and political interest in the concept of narcissism abated, though cultural critics still were likely to offer similar depictions of the effects of America on personality.

Perhaps that was the nub of the problem in the latest era of intellectual life: the important social issues centered on personality rather than on mind. Within the boundaries of most scholarly fields, the intellect still seemed a serious matter. The shocks of the late nineteenth and early twentieth centuries had long since been absorbed. Relativism no longer disturbed social scientists as it had in the 1920s, and human irrationality no longer was the unsettling lesson of psychology. Science could be "objective" without eternal verities, and cognitive psychology was less fearful of human thinking processes. There was abundant faith in the scholar's powers of reasoning and observation even as scientists approached breakthroughs in understanding the chemistry and physiology of thought processes.* But in the new dispensation there was less connection than ever before between the intellectual and the public. Unlike the Puritan preacher before his congregation, the disinterested gentleman amid the republican electorate, or the Victorian in the genteel tradition, the scholar in the last quarter of the twentieth century stood apart in a realm of specialized discourse. The results of research could be applied, perhaps even popularized, but was there a connecting notion of intellect to unite the scholar with his countrymen? That issue was posed in Muller's and other reappraisals of the universities and in laments on the demise of the man of letters. The resolution was unpredictable, and the grounds for optimism, in an age of narcissism, only dimly visible.

FOR FURTHER
READING

For this period there are fewer secondary texts, and the best guides are often the interpretative works mentioned

---

*There was even a new version of the faculty psychology, though not so called, one in which the left hemisphere of the brain figured as the house of masculine, discursive, logical thought; the right, as the home of feminine art and sensitivity. In Plato's terminology, the left should be the charioteer of the orderly personality, but in Julian Jaynes's speculative *The Origin of Consciousness in the Breakdown of the Bicameral Mind* (1976) the right is the hemisphere through which the gods spoke to prehistoric human beings. The dissociation of sensibility was, then, a fact of ancient history, not an indictment of modern culture. "We are now," wrote Jaynes, "in a position where we can look back and see the history of mankind on this planet in its proper values for the first time and understand some of the chief features of the last three millennia as vestiges of a previous mentality."

in the chapter. See, for example, those by Will Herberg, Reinhold Niebuhr, Daniel Bell, David Riesman, Lionel Trilling, Christopher Lasch, Theodore Roszak, Paul Goodman, Noam Chomsky, and Edward Shils. Two general histories give some attention to intellectual life: William E. Leuchtenburg, *A Troubled Feast* (1973); and James B. Gilbert, *Another Chance* (1981).

Sydney E. Ahlstrom's *A Religious History of the American People* (1972) is particularly helpful on twentieth-century movements. The best study of fundamentalism is George Marsden's *Fundamentalism and American Culture* (1980). Cushing Strout's *The New Heavens and the New Earth* (1974) is a thoughtful interpretation of "civil religion."

On cold war liberalism, see Robert Booth Fowler, *Believing Skeptics* (1978). On the transit from Marxism to conservatism, see John P. Diggins, *Up from Communism* (1975). On Daniel Bell and others who are called neo-conservatives, see Peter Steinfels, *The Neo-Conservatives* (1979). A handy anthology is William F. Buckley, ed., *American Conservative Thought in the Twentieth Century* (1970).

The best book on the 1960s, particularly its literature, is Morris Dickstein's *Gates of Eden* (1977). See also Christopher Lasch, *The Agony of the American Left* (1969), and, from a more conservative perspective, Ronald Berman, *America in the Sixties* (1968). Robert Wuthnow's *The Consciousness Reformation* (1979) studies its subject in one locality—Berkeley, California.

Conceived during the McCarthy era and published in the 1960s, Richard Hofstadter's *Anti-Intellectualism in American Life* (1963) is a brilliant synthesis of many themes in American intellectual life. Another provocative interpretation of intellectual history from the vantage point of the 1960s is Christopher Lasch's *The New Radicalism in America: The Intellectual as a Social Type* (1965).

AFTERWORD

A friend who read this book prior to publication told me that the last chapter ought to be entitled "An Obituary for Intellectual Life." I had not intended to write a dirge, but I see my friend's point. Viewed from the 1980s, recent intellectual life appears to have been filled with forsaken hopes and frustrated missions. Dreams of the golden mountains—to use Malcolm Cowley's phrase once more—often came to sad ends. This was true of communists and fellow travelers who lived through McCarthyism, while losing their illusions concerning the American people and the Soviet state. But it was equally true of others who envisioned a religious renewal in the 1950s or who celebrated a consciousness revolution in the 1960s. Ideals of service and cosmopolitanism disintegrated. Promoters of high culture fell under attack as elitists. If men and women of letters were a vanishing species, what sources existed for artistic experiment and critical independence? It was hard to believe in an American renaissance. The pragmatic approach to problem-solving might have provided an alternative to these crumbling ideals and programs. As increasing numbers of men and women devoted their energies to specialized professions requiring long and careful training, there might have been widespread belief in the social benefits of applied intelligence. But during the administrations of Jimmy Carter and Ronald Reagan, it was frequently observed that many problems are unsolvable. Articulate university spokesmen worried that an era of close partnership between government and academia was passing away: there was not enough money to sustain it, and academics had lost self-confidence. A gloomy picture was made even darker by the trenchant analyses at the start of the 1980s of American narcissism. The counterpart to a diminishing belief in social progress was a desperate self-absorption.

If my friend is right, perhaps it is appropriate that readers will see this book for the first time in that year long dreaded by those who fear a future of technological oppression and mindless gratification: 1984. But I do not think the omens are all so unpropitious. If we could survey the opinions of current practitioners in many fields of intellectual inquiry, from nuclear physics to social history, and from genetics to linguistics, they would probably report on exciting recent advances in knowledge and challenging problems for research. For many of them, the future of intellectual life might look as exciting as it did to any Americans in previous generations. Furthermore, in spite of criticisms made of affirmative action and antidiscriminatory regulations, there is unquestionably greater equality of access to higher education and professional positions than ever before in American history. Intellectual life is less exclusively the prerogative of males from the privileged classes than at any previous time. One may hope that this record will improve and that, as it does, some of the cruder hostilities to "high" culture will lose their popularity. When we review the rapid changes that have occurred over short periods of time in the recent past, such hopes do not seem impossible.

Nevertheless, I cannot conclude with rosy predictions. The truth is that, when this book was being written, the foundations of intellectual life were shakier than at many other times in the past. For every field that felt it was advancing, another felt on the defensive. Even though equality of opportunity was being institutionalized, slowly and imperfectly, there was no widely held, optimistic faith, comparable to those we have observed in previous eras, to ally intellectual life with visions of progress. Still, there is no reason to write an obituary. We have previously discussed too many jeremiads on the fragmentation of Puritanism, the assaults on reason, the collapse of virtue, the degradation of equality, and the pretensions of culture to believe that intellectual life must come to an end just because some cherished ideals have fallen apart. We cannot be certain how intellectual life will be reconceptualized or how institutions that affect writers, researchers, artists, teachers, and professionals will change. It is altogether possible that this book has neglected events that will seem by the year 2000 to have laid the basis for important new departures in the relations between American intellectuals and the peoples and institutions of the world. Having seen how foolish predictions made in 1960 seemed in 1970 or those made in 1970 seemed in 1980, I will refrain from making predictions to be reviewed in later years.

I do think, of course, that a sense of the past will help us to make sense of the changes we must live through. It is helpful to know how far we have come out of hierarchical conceptions of civility and virtuosity and how difficult it has been in previous eras to make sense of the responsibilities of intellectuals in a democratic society. Our problems are not identical to those that engaged intellectuals in previous eras; we feel out of touch with some of their solutions, and others we deplore. But once we have tried to understand John Winthrop and Cotton Mather,

Jonathan Edwards and Thomas Jefferson, Ralph Waldo
Emerson and W. E. B. Du Bois, Jane Addams and Walter
Lippmann, and many others discussed in these pages, we
are less likely to feel that current problems are unique and
insurmountable. Though it is currently unfashionable to
peruse history for inspiration, every student of history
knows of expressions of intellectual courage in the past
which, understood in context, help us to face our own hard
times. I hope this book will lead readers to make similar
discoveries. Perhaps some will feel emboldened, with William James, "to take the universe to be really dangerous
and adventurous, without therefore backing out and crying
'no play.' "

INDEX

ABOUT THE AUTHOR

Lewis Perry was born in Somerville, Massachusetts. He majored in English literature at Oberlin College and had graduate training in theater and industrial and labor relations before he received his Ph.D. in history from Cornell University. He has received grants and fellowships from the American Council of Learned Societies, the National Endowment for the Humanities, and the John Simon Guggenheim Foundation.

Perry is now professor of history at Indiana University and since 1978 has been the editor of the *Journal of American History*. Before going to Indiana, he taught for twelve years at the State University of New York at Buffalo. He has written two previous books, *Radical Abolitionism* and *Childhood, Marriage, and Reform*.